# The Neurobiology
## of Learning and Memory
### SECOND EDITION

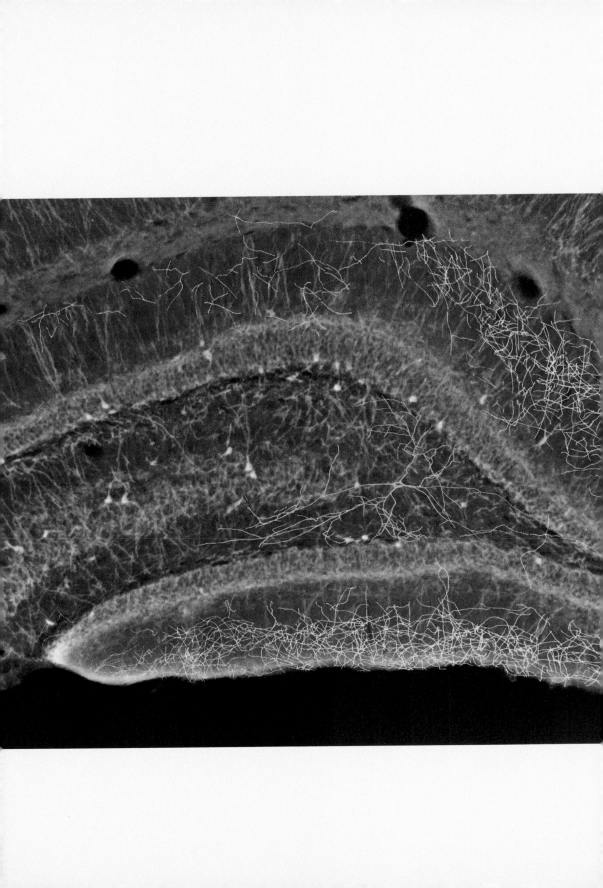

# The Neurobiology of Learning and Memory

## SECOND EDITION

### JERRY W. RUDY
University of Colorado, Boulder

 Sinauer Associates, Inc. Publishers
Sunderland, Massachusetts 01375

Oxford University Press is a department of the University of Oxford. It furthers the University's objective of excellence in research, scholarship, and education by publishing worldwide. Oxford is a registered trade mark of Oxford University Press in the UK and certain other countries.

Published in the United States of America by Oxford University Press
198 Madison Avenue, New York, NY 10016, United States of America

© 2018 Oxford University Press

Sinauer Associates is an imprint of Oxford University Press.

For titles covered by Section 112 of the US Higher Education Opportunity Act, please visit www.oup.com/us/he for the latest information about pricing and alternate formats.

Address editorial correspondence to:
Sinauer Associates
23 Plumtree Road
Sunderland, MA 01375 U.S.A.
publish@sinauer.com

Address orders, sales, license, permissions, and translation inquiries to:
Oxford University Press U.S.A.
2001 Evans Road
Cary, NC 27513 U.S.A.
Orders: 1-800-445-9714

Library of Congress Cataloging-in-Publication Data
Rudy, Jerry W., 1942-
    The neurobiology of learning and memory / Jerry W. Rudy, University of Colorado, Boulder.—Second edition.
        pages cm
    Includes index.
    ISBN 978-1-60535-230-5 (hardcover)
    1. Memory—Textbooks. 2. Learning—Textbooks. 3. Neurobiology—Textbooks.
    I. Title.
    QP406.R83 2013
    612.8—dc23
                                                                2013042526


9 8 7 6 5 4 3

Printed in the United States of America

# Preface

The scientific study of learning and memory, originally the domain of psychologists, now is shared by scientists trained in a variety of disciplines that include biochemistry, cellular–molecular biology, electrophysiology, neuroanatomy, and neuropsychology. The work of hundreds of scientists from these diverse fields has produced an explosion of knowledge about the neurobiological basis of learning and memory that almost defies comprehension. As was the case for the First Edition of this book, this revision represents my attempt to integrate some of what we have learned from this interdisciplinary approach into a coherent framework that can be understood by students who have a rudimentary background in psychology and neuroscience, as well as by the wider scientific community.

During the seven years separating the two books, the field has continued to explode with new methods, findings, and ideas. Thus, the challenge of how to compress an enormous and diverse field into a manageable end product was even greater for the revision than for the original book. Fortunately, the general organization of the First Edition provided a framework for achieving my goal of introducing students to the field without getting lost in too many details. Nevertheless, my major challenge was trying to decide what to include, and I am sure that not all will agree with my choices.

Thus, this book is organized into three major sections and written to tell three large, interrelated, and fascinating stories. This organization results in telling the tale from the bottom up: it progresses from neurons, synapses, and molecules that provide the synaptic basis of memories, to the neural systems that capture the rich content of our experience. Although the organization remains the same, new chapters have been added to each section, chapters have been reorganized, and the level of detail has been increased.

The first chapter provides a brief conceptual and historical overview of the field. Part 1, *Synaptic Basis of Memories,* introduces the idea that synapses modified by experience provide the basis for memory storage. It describes the long-term potentiation methodology used to study how synapses are modified and the concepts needed to understand the organization of synapses. The eight chapters in Part 1 are organized around the idea that the synaptic changes that support long-term potentiation evolve in four overlapping stages referred to as generation, stabilization, consolidation, and maintenance. The goal of each chapter is to reveal that each stage depends on unique molecular processes and to describe what they are.

The six chapters in Part 2, *Molecules and Memories*, build on this foundation to show how molecules and cellular processes that have been identified from studies of synaptic plasticity also participate in the making of memories. These chapters discuss some of the basic conceptual issues researchers face in trying to relate memory to synaptic molecules and describe some of the behavioral and neurobiological methods that are used. The chapters describing the processes involved in memory formation and consolidation have been extensively modified to provide a more detailed account of the molecular events that are engaged to ensure that established memories endure. Both the chapters on memory modulation (Chapter 13) and the fate of retrieved memories (Chapter 14) have been extensively modified to provide a more in-depth account of the relevant processes.

The five chapters in Part 3, *Neural Systems and Memory*, are organized around the multiple memory systems view—that different neural systems have evolved to store the content contained in our experiences. This part of the book features three chapters on the hippocampus (Chapters 15 to 17). The first of these begins with the story of Henry Molaison (H.M.) to establish the historical foundation linking the medial temporal hippocampal system to episodic memory, while the next develops the relationship between the neural system that supports episodic memory and the indexing theory of how this is accomplished. The third of these chapters discusses issues that relate this system to semantic memory, Ribot's Law (that memories become resistant to disruption as they age), and systems consolidation. The next two chapters finish Part 3. Chapter 18 describes the cortico-striatal system and its relationship to what are called behavioral actions and habits, and the final chapter describes the neural systems involved in the acquisition of emotional memories and provides an update of current research on how these memories can be suppressed or removed.

In writing this book, I wanted to provide a broad context in which to introduce the key concepts and facts that are central to a particular topic. I made no attempt to be comprehensive in the material I covered. Instead, I tried to maintain a level of description and discussion that was sufficient to ensure a basic understanding of the relevant principles and processes, without reaching a level of detail that would be tedious. If this approach proves successful, then I will have provided the reader with a foundation to continue an in-depth exploration of this field, while presenting some of the remarkable achievements of many wonderful researchers who have made this field one of the great scientific adventures of our time.

## Acknowledgments

I am most grateful to the many scientists who have helped to create the field this book represents, and I regret that I didn't have the space to represent more of their great accomplishments. This revision also benefited greatly from interactions with the many undergraduates who were enrolled in my course over the past five years. Their questions and discussions motivated me to write the Second Edition. I thank Professor Ryan Bachtell for serving as a sounding board for some of the new material and his thoughtful input.

I thank Sydney Carroll, Editor, for her encouragement to undertake this project and Sinauer Associates for supporting a Second Edition of this book. The preparation of this book benefited greatly from the staff at Sinauer Associates. I would like to thank Chelsea Holabird for steering the book through the production process, and Chris Small, Janice Holabird, and Elizabeth Morales for their talented design ideas, book layout, and artwork.

Once again my wife, Julia A. Rudy, assumed major editorial responsibility for the final product. Without Julie's involvement, I cannot imagine how this project would have been completed. Her editorial skills and commitment to excellence are directly responsible for the book's organizational clarity and readability.

## About the Author

Jerry W. Rudy

Jerry W. Rudy is College Professor of Distinction in the Department of Psychology and Neuroscience at the University of Colorado, Boulder. He received his Ph.D. in psychology from the University of Virginia in 1970, and joined the CU Boulder faculty in 1980. The author of over 150 peer-reviewed research papers and book chapters, Dr. Rudy has served on the editorial boards of the *Journal of Experimental Psychology: Animal Behavior Processes*, *Psychobiology*, *Developmental Psychobiology* (Editor in Chief), *Behavioral Neuroscience*, *Neuroscience & Biobehavioral Reviews*, *Learning and Memory*, and *Neurobiology of Learning and Memory* (Associate Editor). He also served on the governing board and as President of the International Society for Developmental Psychobiology. He has received grant support from the National Science Foundation, the National Institute of Mental Health, and the National Institute of Health. Professor Rudy's research interests center on learning and memory processes. His research focused primarily on understanding the complementary contributions the hippocampus and neocortex make to learning and memory and the influence immune products have on memory. He is currently the director of the undergraduate neuroscience program at the University of Colorado, Boulder.

# Table of Contents

# PART 3
## Neural Systems and Memory 285

## 15 Memory Systems and the Hippocampus 287

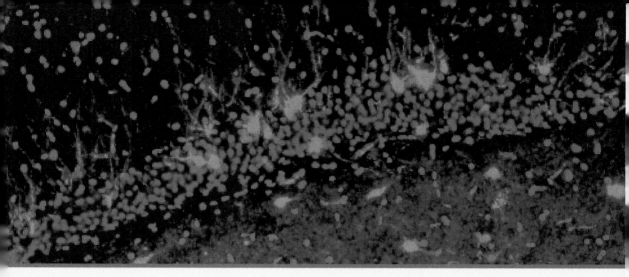

# 1 Introduction: Fundamental Concepts and Historical Foundations

Our uniqueness as human beings derives in large part from evolutionary adaptations that permit experience to modify connections linking networks of neurons in the brain. Information conveyed into the brain by our sensory channels can leave a lasting impression on neural circuits. These networks not only can be modified, the information contained in the modifications can be preserved and later retrieved to influence our behavior. Our individual experiences act on these networks to make us who we are. We have the ability to learn a vast array of skills: we can become musicians, athletes, artisans, skilled craftsmen, or cooks. Experience tunes our emotions to our environments. We acquire food preferences and aversions. Incredibly, without intention, we also lay down an autobiographical record of the events, times, and places in which our experiences occur. We are connected with our past and can talk about it. We learn and we remember.

Historically, the study of learning and memory has been the domain of philosophers and psychologists who have defined the relevant phenomena and many of the important variables that influence them. Only recently have brain scientists seriously weighed in on this topic. Armed with sophisticated methods to measure and manipulate brain processes and conceptual frameworks to guide their application, neurobiologists have now made enormous inroads into the mystery of how experience modifies the brain.

Consequently, an important field now exists called the **neurobiology of learning and memory**. Scientists working in this field want to know how the brain stores and retrieves information about our experiences. The goal of this book is to present an account of some of the major accomplishments of this field and to provide a background that will facilitate the understanding of many of the issues and central assumptions that drive research in this field.

## Learning and Memory Are Theoretical Concepts

The terms "learning" and "memory" are often used as if they are directly observable entities, but they are not. *Learning and memory are theoretical concepts used to explain the fact that experience influences behavior* (Figure 1.1). A familiar example will suffice to make the point.

You have an exam tomorrow. So, over the next few hours you closet yourself with your books and class notes. You take the test and answer the questions to the best of your knowledge. Later you receive your grade, 90%. Assuming that your grade would have been 50% if you had not studied, then a reasonable person (the professor) would assume that you learned and remembered the information needed to pass the test. The key phrase here is "would assume." Learning and memory were never directly observed. The only directly observable events in this example are that (a) you spent time with your notes and books, and (b) you took the test and performed well. That you learned and remembered is inferred from your test performance and the professor's knowledge that you studied.

**Learning and memory are theoretical concepts**

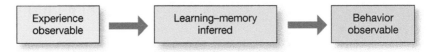

**Figure 1.1**
Learning and memory are unobservable, inferred processes used to explain the fact that our past experience influences our behavior.

Larry Squire (1987) provided a useful definition of the terms learning and memory: "Learning is the process of acquiring new information, while memory refers to the persistence of learning in a state that can be revealed at a later time" (p. 3). Other, more restrictive definitions have been proposed. They usually also stipulate what learning and memory are not. For example, a restricted definition would appropriately exclude fatigue, maturation, and injury that might result from or be associated with experience.

Although learning and memory are theoretical concepts, neurobiologists are motivated by the belief that they have a physical basis in the brain. A slight modification of Squire's definition provides a useful definition of the field: the goal of neurobiologists working in this field is to understand how the brain acquires, stores, and maintains representations of experience in a state that permits the information contained in the representation to be retrieved and influence behavior.

## Psychological and Neurobiological Approaches

The study of learning and memory is the domain of both psychology and neurobiology. It is useful to point out some fundamental differences between the two approaches.

### Psychological Approach

The general goal of psychology is to (a) derive a set of empirical principles that describe how variation in experience influences behavior, and (b) provide a theoretical account that can explain the observed facts. The study of memory became a science when Hermann Ebbinghaus developed the first methods for assessing the acquisition and retention of a controlled experience. He recognized that to study "pure memory" required a methodology that could separate what the subject already has learned from what the subject is now being asked to remember (Ebbinghaus, 1913). To do this, he invented what are called **nonsense syllables**. A nonsense syllable consists of a vowel placed between two consonants, such as *nuh*, *vag*, or *boc*. These syllables were designed to be meaningless so they would have to be learned without the benefit of prior knowledge. Thus, for example, *dog*, *cat*, or *cup* would be excluded. Ebbinghaus made up hundreds of nonsense syllables and used them to produce lists that were to be learned and remembered. Among the task variables he manipulated were factors such as the number of times a given list was presented during the memorization phase and the interval between the learning and the test phase.

Hermann Ebbinghaus

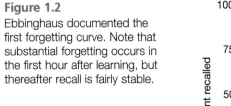

**Figure 1.2**
Ebbinghaus documented the first forgetting curve. Note that substantial forgetting occurs in the first hour after learning, but thereafter recall is fairly stable.

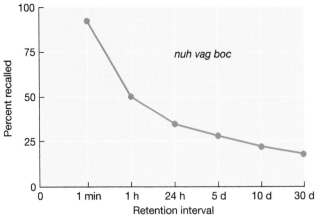

Ebbinghaus worked alone and was the only subject of his experiments. He found that his test performance increased the more he practiced a given list. He also documented the fact that retention performance was better when he spaced the repetition of a given list than when the list was repeated without inserting a break between the learning trials. He also documented the first "forgetting curve." As is illustrated in Figure 1.2, retention was excellent when the test was given shortly after the learning trial, but it fell off dramatically within the first hour. Remarkably, the curve stabilized thereafter.

Empirical principles such as those produced by Ebbinghaus's experiments led to theoretical questions about the underlying structure of the memory (Figure 1.3). Consider Ebbinghaus's forgetting curve. One could imagine that

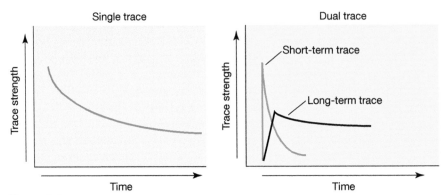

**Figure 1.3**
The single-trace theory explains Ebbinghaus's forgetting curve by assuming that the strength of a single memory trace declines monotonically as a function of time between learning and the retention test. The dual-trace theory explains that the forgetting curve results from two memory traces whose strength decays at different rates.

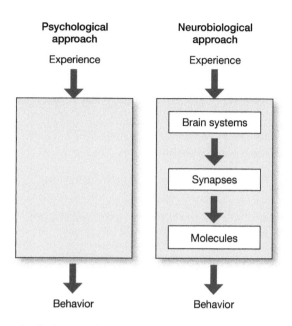

| Psychological approach | Neurobiological approach |
|---|---|
| Experience | Experience |
| | Brain systems |
| | Synapses |
| | Molecules |
| Behavior | Behavior |

**Figure 1.4**
Psychologists study only the relationship between experience and behavior. Neurobiologists study how experience influences memory-dependent behavior by its influences on brain systems, synapses, and molecules.

this behavioral function is a direct reflection of the property of a single memory trace, the strength of which declines monotonically as a function of the retention interval. In essence, the behavioral function directly represents the decay properties of the memory trace. Another theorist looking at the same data might be struck by the fact that although the rate of forgetting is initially rapid there is very little change after the first hour. This theorist might propose that the forgetting curve is a product of two memory traces with different decay rates: a short-term memory trace that decays relatively rapidly and a long-term memory trace that has a much slower decay rate. Note in both cases hypotheses are put forth that point to properties—memory strength and memory traces with different decay rates—that defy direct observation.

A fundamental feature of the traditional psychological approach is that a single methodology is used to collect the data and to test theory. Psychologists do not directly manipulate or measure brain function. They vary only the nature of experience and measure only behavior (Figure 1.4). Thus the psychological approach can be described as operating at a single level of analysis. Psychological research has identified critical phenomena and concepts that provide the starting point for neurobiological investigation.

## Neurobiological Approach

Psychologists study only the relationship between experience and behavior. Neurobiologists study how experience influences memory-dependent behavior by its influences on brain systems, synapses, and molecules.

The goal of neurobiology is to relate the basic facts of learning and memory to events happening in the brain. If, in the above example, the dual-trace theory was established as valid by psychological experiments, the neurobiologist would want to know what are the properties of the brain that support two different memory traces. This goal requires a multi-level approach. In addition to using the behavioral methods of psychology that reveal how task variables such as trial spacing and repetition influence learning and retention, the neurobiological approach requires methods for:

- determining the regions of the brain that make up the brain system supporting the memory;

- determining how synapses that are potential storage mechanisms are altered by experience; and

- manipulating and measuring molecules in neurons that ultimately support the memory.

Thus, the neurobiological approach is an interdisciplinary, multi-level approach. It combines the behavioral methods of psychology with the methods of anatomy, electrophysiology, pharmacology, biochemistry, and genetics. Because the methodologies of each discipline are complex and require specialized training to learn, different scientists often combine their individual skills to attack the problem.

## Historical Influences: The Golden Age

The full-scale application of neurobiological methods to the study of learning and memory is a relatively new development. However, many of the important phenomena, concepts, insights, and methods that drive the field emerged over 100 years ago. Thirty-seven years ago, in his comprehensive review of the psychobiology of memory, Paul Rozin (1976) described the last decade of the nineteenth century as the Golden Age of Memory because many of the basic phenomena and ideas emerged during that period.

Théodule Ribot

### Phenomena and Ideas

It was at the beginning of that decade that the French psychologist Théodule Ribot published his classic *Diseases of Memory* (1890). He was motivated by the belief that the study of brain pathology could provide insights into the normal organization of memory. His studies of many clinical cases led him to believe that the dissolution of memory accompanying pathology or injury followed an orderly

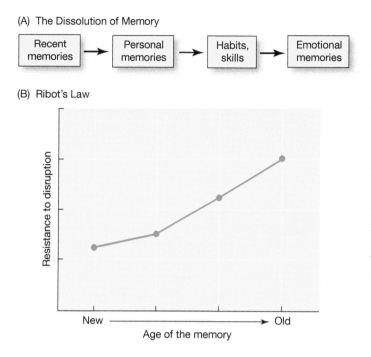

(A) The Dissolution of Memory

Recent memories → Personal memories → Habits, skills → Emotional memories

(B) Ribot's Law

Resistance to disruption

New ──────────→ Old

Age of the memory

**Figure 1.5**
(A) Ribot believed that after a brain pathology or injury the dissolution of memory followed an orderly temporal progression. Recent memories are the first to be lost, followed by autobiographical or personal memories that also have a temporal gradient. He believed that habits and emotional memories were the most resistant to dissolution. (B) Ribot proposed that older memories are more resistant to disruption by traumatic events than newer memories. This hypothesis is called Ribot's Law.

temporal progression. He proposed that recent memories are the first to be lost, followed by autobiographical or personal memories that also have a temporal gradient (Figure 1.5). He believed that habits and emotional memories were the most resistant to dissolution. Ribot's insight anticipated the modern development of the multiple system perspective that is discussed in Chapter 15. This is because his insight implies that there are different categories of memory and they are supported by different neural systems.

The idea that there is a temporal progression to memory loss—that old memories are more resistant to disruption than new ones—is often referred to as Ribot's Law (see Figure 1.5). This generalization begs the question, *what is it about old memories that makes them resistant to disruption*? This question, which remains at the center of contemporary research and is the source of both excitement and controversy, is more fully discussed in Chapter 17.

It was also during this period that Sergei Korsakoff (1897) described the amnesic syndrome that now bears his name. Patients with this syndrome display what would now be called a severe, **anterograde amnesia**. They are not able to remember events experienced after the onset of the syndrome. However, early in the disease, memories established before the onset of the syndrome are generally preserved. Thus, they initially display very little **retrograde amnesia**.

Sergei Korsakoff

Korsakoff believed that the primary defect was an inability to form new memories. His interpretation of the deficit included two ideas. One idea was that the pathology impaired the physiological processes needed to establish and retain the memory. Today one might say that the mechanisms of memory storage or consolidation are impaired. The second idea was that the pathology in some way weakened the associative network that contained the memory or, in modern terms, produced a retrieval deficit, that is, the core memory trace is established but cannot be accessed. Korsakoff believed both factors contributed to the syndrome. Whether memory impairment is the result of a storage or retrieval failure can still be the source of heated debate in the contemporary literature.

One can only marvel at the insights contained in William James's *Principles of Psychology* (1890). An often noted contribution was his conception of memory as a sequence of processes initiated by an experience that begins with a briefly lasting sensation he called **after images**, then to the stage he called **primary memory**, and to the final stage he called **secondary memory** or **memory proper** (Figure 1.6).

Primary memory was viewed as the persisting representation of the experience that forms part of a stream of consciousness. Secondary memory contained the vast record of experiences that had receded from the stream of consciousness but could be later retrieved or recollected: "It is brought back, fished up, so to speak, from a reservoir in which, with countless other objects, it lay buried and lost from view" (James, 1890, p. 646). An object in primary

William James

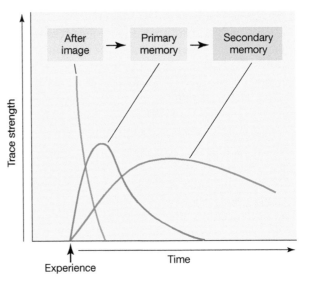

**Figure 1.6**
William James proposed that memories emerge in stages. The after image is supported by a short-lasting trace, then replaced by the primary memory trace. Secondary memory is viewed as the reservoir of enduring memory traces.

memory is not brought back: it was never lost. Thus, we have the roots of the modern distinction between short-term memory and long-term memory that remain central to modern investigations of the neurobiological bases of memory.

James devoted an entire chapter to the brain. However, the absence of any relevant information precluded an attempt to directly relate memory phenomena to any specific regions of the brain or mechanisms. Nevertheless, he strongly believed that the retention of experience was not a mysterious mental property but that "it was a purely physical phenomenon, a morphological feature . . ." (p. 655). He even provided a connectionist model of the memory trace to bolster his belief. In at least two places he used the term **plasticity** to describe the property of the brain that allows it to be modified by experience. For example, in his discussion of memory he wrote, "What happens in the nerve-tissue is but an example of that plasticity or of semi-inertness, yielding to change . . ." (p. 655). Thus, modern developments would come as no surprise to him.

## *The Neuron Doctrine and Synaptic Plasticity*

During this era, the foundation for modern neuroscience—the neuron doctrine—emerged (see Shepard, 1991). Camillo Golgi had developed a method (now called the Golgi Stain) that allowed what came to be called neurons to be visualized. However, there was debate about how these elements were organized to support brain function.

A prominent idea that was backed by Golgi was called reticulum (network) theory. According to this theory the nervous system represented an exception to cell theory—the idea that the fundamental element in the structure of living bodies is a cell. Instead, nerve tissue was organized into a continuous network rather than discrete independent units. Golgi believed that the branches from the cell body we now call dendrites were in contact with blood vessels and functioned only to provide nutrients to the cell. The business end of the nerve cells was carried out by what are now called axons, which he believed were continuous (fused) with each other and formed the reticulum or network (Figure 1.7). A significant problem with this view is that it prohibits the formulation of a principle for how transmission between nerve cells could occur.

Many individuals contributed to the dismissal of reticulum theory (Shepard, 1991); however, the great Spanish neuroanatomist Santiago Ramón y Cajal is generally acknowledged as the most important opponent of reticulum theory and father of the **neuron doctrine**—the idea that the brain is made up of discrete cells called nerve cells or neurons that are the elemental signal units of the brain

Santiago Ramón y Cajal

**Figure 1.7**
(A) Camillo Golgi. (B) Golgi developed a method (now called the Golgi Stain) that allowed what are now called neurons to be visualized. Based on his observations, he believed in the reticulum or network theory of the organization of nerve tissue.

(A)

(B)

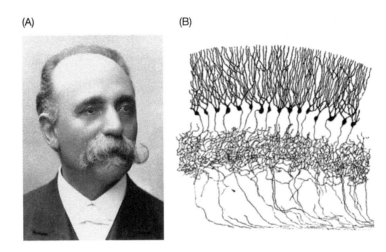

(Ramón y Cajal, 1894–1904). (See Box 1.1 for a list of key elements of the neuron doctrine.) He refined Golgi's method to increase its reliability and, based on his anatomical descriptions, forcefully argued that neurons are not fused but are contiguous (for example, Ramón y Cajal's 1894 Croonian lecture, partially reproduced in English in Shepard, 1991). This conclusion led to the now accepted view that neurons are truly independent, genetically derived units that are composed of (a) the cell body or soma, (b) dendrites, and (c) a single axon. With this conceptual breakthrough Ramón y Cajal also was able to figure out the brain's basic wiring diagram—axons could travel short or long distances but they always terminated at specific locations among fields of dendrites. Axon endings were contiguous with dendrites but not continuous (fused) with them. Sir Charles Sherrington (1906) subsequently named

---

### BOX 1.1 Elements of the Neuron Doctrine

- The neuron is an anatomical unit—the fundamental structural and functional unit of the nervous system.
- The neuron is composed of three parts: cell body, dendrites, and axons.
- Neurons are discrete cells, which are not continuous with other cells.
- The points of connection between neurons are called synapses.
- The neuron is a physiological unit. Electrical activity flows through the neuron in one direction (from dendrites to the axon, via the cell body).
- The neuron is the developmental–genetic unit of the nervous system.

this axon-dendritic junction—the point of contiguity between axons and dendrites—the **synapse**. The functional significance of this anatomical arrangement was recognized by Ramón y Cajal in what is called the Law of Dynamic Polarization, the idea that a neuron receives signals (nerve impulses) at its dendrites and transmits them via the soma, then along the axon in one direction—away from the cell body.

At the very heart of contemporary investigations of the mechanisms of memory storage is the **synaptic plasticity hypothesis**, which posits that "the strength of synaptic connections—the ease with which an action potential in one cell excites (or inhibits) its target cell—is not fixed but is plastic and modifiable" (Squire and Kandel, 1999, p. 35). However, this hypothesis was not initially universally embraced. In the 1890s there was a heated debate as to whether neurons maintained a fixed structure throughout the lifetime of an individual (see DeFelipe, 2006). Further testimony to Ramón y Cajal's brilliance was his position on this issue and his willingness to speculate from his anatomical descriptions that the points of contiguity between axons and dendrites (synapses) provide opportunities for modification by experience. In his theory of cerebral gymnastics he even proposed a model of how this could happen (see DeFelipe, 2006). Thus, Ramón y Cajal is also acknowledged for the development of one of the field's most important ideas.

## Behavioral Methods

The Golden Age documented important clinical phenomena that provided initial insights into memory organization and produced ideas that remain fundamental to contemporary investigations. Remarkably, this period also produced some of the essential behavioral methods that in one form or another continue to be used to study how the brain supports learning and memory. Ebbinghaus's contribution already has been discussed. His work provided the basis for the scientific study of human memory.

Neurobiologists want to understand how the brain supports learning and memory. Studies of normal people and patients with brain damage can identify interesting phenomena that can provide some insight into the organization of memory. However, there are obvious major ethical concerns that constrain the direct manipulation of the human brain. Thus, to directly manipulate and measure brain events, neurobiologists have relied extensively on methods that allow the study of learning and memory with nonhuman animals. During the Golden Age, Ivan Pavlov and Edward L. Thorndike developed methodologies that remain essential to contemporary researchers who study the learning and memory processes of animals.

Pavlov (1927) began his career shift from studying digestive physiology to investigating the integrative activity of the brain. In doing so, he developed

**Figure 1.8**
Pavlov in his laboratory.

the fundamental paradigm for studying associative learning and memory in animals (Figure 1.8). The essence of this methodology, called classical or Pavlovian conditioning, is that a neutral stimulus such as the ringing of a bell (called the conditioned stimulus or CS) was paired with a biologically significant event such as food (called the unconditioned stimulus or US). The US caused the dog to salivate; this response is called the unconditioned response or UR. As a consequence of the several pairings of the bell (CS) and food (US), simply ringing the bell caused the dog to salivate. The response to the CS is called the conditioned response or CR. The ability of the CS to evoke the CR is believed to be the result of the brain associating the occurrence of the CS and US (Figure 1.9). Today no one uses dogs or measures the salivary response to study learning and memory in nonverbal animals. However,

**Figure 1.9**
In the Pavlovian conditioning method, two events called the CS and US are presented together. Subsequently, the CS evokes the response called the CR. Psychologists assume that the CS evokes the CR because the CS gets associated with the US. Psychologists and neurobiologists continue to use this method to study associative learning in animals.

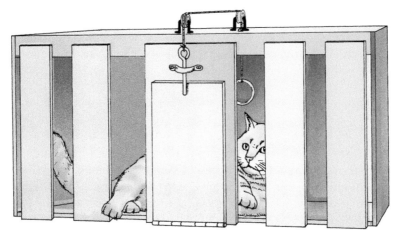

**Figure 1.10**
Edward L. Thorndike invented the methodology for studying what is now called instrumental learning or Thorndikian conditioning. Cats, dogs, and chickens were placed into his puzzle box and had to learn how to manipulate levers to escape.

many neurobiologists still use variations of the Pavlovian conditioning methodology to study learning and memory in other nonhuman animals.

It was also during the Golden Age that Thorndike (1898) published his dissertation on animal intelligence in which he provided a methodology that permitted an objective investigation of how animals learned the consequences of their action. He invented what is referred to as Thorndike's puzzle box (Figure 1.10). An animal such as a cat or chicken would be placed in a wooden crate and to escape it had to learn to depress a lever to open an escape door. Thorndike's experiments provided the foundation for study of what is now called **instrumental learning** or Thorndikian conditioning. Variations of his methods continue to be extensively employed to reveal the systems of the brain involved in how animals learn to adapt their behavior based on the consequences of their actions.

Edward L. Thorndike

## Core Themes

Scientists from a wide range of disciplines have been intrigued by questions about how the brain supports learning and memory. Their efforts have generated an enormous literature that even seasoned researchers find overwhelming. No single book can begin to do justice to the current state of knowledge.

However, it may be possible to provide a road map for appreciating some of the major accomplishments of this field and provide a foundation for future study. To achieve this more modest goal, this book is organized around three large themes that represent much of the field: synaptic plasticity, molecules and memory, and memory systems.

## Synaptic Plasticity

Contemporary neuroscientists believe that the synapse is the fundamental unit of memory storage. For synapses to support memory they have to be plastic or modifiable. The last 30 years have yielded remarkable insights into the molecular processes that are engaged to support changes in the strength of synapses. Thus, the goal of a major portion of this book is to present many of the important findings and ideas that have been generated by this field.

## Molecules and Memory

Memories result from behavioral experiences. The past 30 years also have witnessed the development of many useful behavioral procedures for studying memory formation in nonverbal animals. Armed with these behavioral methods, researchers have been emboldened to determine if memories are a product of some of the same cellular–molecular events that alter the strength of synaptic connections. Bringing ideas from the study of synaptic plasticity to the study of memory formation is one of the most dynamic and exciting adventures in brain–behavioral sciences. Thus, a section of this book describes how memory researchers have been able to use what has been learned from studies of synaptic plasticity to begin to uncover the molecular basis of memory.

## Memory Systems

The content of our experience matters to the brain. One of the important achievements of the modern era has been the realization that the brain has evolved neural systems that are specialized to capture and store the varied content generated by our experiences. This idea is generally represented by the term multiple memory systems. For example, different systems have been identified that enable us to keep track of the episodes that make up our personal history and to record emotionally charged events to protect us from danger. These stand apart from other brain systems that enable us to learn the consequences of our actions and acquire the routine and not so routine skills and habits that enable us to interact successfully with our environment.

The last section of this book provides an introduction to some of the important developments in this domain.

## Summary

In this chapter a number of fundamental concepts were described that provide a background needed to go forward. Some of the historical foundation for the field was also presented. Many of the core phenomena, concepts, and behavioral methods that are central to the neurobiology of learning and memory emerged in what Rozin called the Golden Age of Memory, the last decade of the nineteenth century. These ideas are intimately linked to individuals (Ebbinghaus, James, Korsakoff, Pavlov, Ramón y Cajal, Ribot, and Thorndike) who have provided a context from which the central themes that guide contemporary research emerged.

## References

DeFelipe, J. (2006). Brain plasticity and mental processes: Cajal again. *Nature Reviews Neuroscience, 7,* 811–817.

Ebbinghaus, H. (1913). *Uber das Gedachtnis: Untersuchungen zur Experimentellen Psychologie.* Leipzig: Dunke and Humboldt. Trans. by H. A. Ruger and C. E. Byssennine as *Memory: a contribution to experimental psychology.* New York: Dover.

James, W. (1890). *Principles of psychology.* New York: Holt.

Korsakoff, S. S. (1897). Disturbance of psychic function in alcoholic paralysis and its relation to the disturbance of the psychic sphere in multiple neuritis of nonalchoholic origins. *Vesin. Psychiatrii 4:* fascicle 2.

Pavlov, I. P. (1927). *Conditioned reflexes.* London: Oxford University Press.

Ramón y Cajal, S. (1894–1904). Textura del sistema nervioso del hombre y de los vertebrados. Trans. by N. Swanson and L. W. Swanson as *New ideas on the structure of the nervous system in man and vertebrates.* Cambridge, MA: MIT Press, 1990.

Ramón y Cajal, S. (1894). The Croonian lecture: la fine structure des centres nerveux. *Proceedings of the Royal Society of London, 55,* 444–468 (in French).

Ribot, T. (1890). *Diseases of memory.* New York: Appleton and Company.

Rozin, P. (1976). The psychobiology of memory. In M. R. Rosenzweig and E. L. Bennett (Eds.), *Neural mechanisms of learning and memory* (pp. 3–46). Cambridge, MA: The MIT Press.

Shepherd, G. M. (1991). *Foundations of the neuron doctrine.* New York: Oxford University Press.

Sherrington, C. S. (1906). *The integrative action of the nervous system*. New York: Charles Scribner's Sons.

Squire, L. R. (1987). *Memory and brain*. New York: Oxford University Press.

Squire, L. R. and Kandel, E. R. (1999). *Memory from mind to molecules*. New York: W. J. Freeman and Company.

Thorndike, E. L. (1898). Animal intelligence: an experimental study of the associative processes in animals. *Psychological Review, Monograph Supplement 2, no. 8.*

# PART 1
## Synaptic Basis of Memories

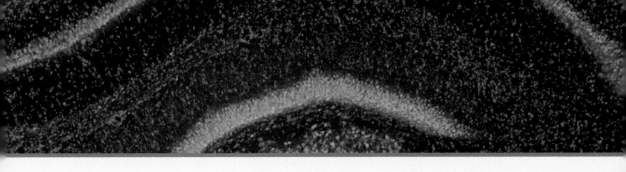

# 2 Mechanisms of Synaptic Plasticity: Introduction

What properties of the brain allow it to acquire and maintain information generated by our experiences? Conventional wisdom is that memories are stored in large networks of interconnected neurons and that experience leaves its impact by modifying the connections between those neurons (Teyler, 1999). Thus, neurobiologists are motivated by the belief that the information content of our various experiences persists in a retrievable form because the synapses (points of contact between neurons) can be modified by experience. The strength of an existing connection can be increased or decreased by experience. As noted in the previous chapter, this synaptic property is known as plasticity. This was Ramón y Cajal's (1894–1904) big idea, that synapses are plastic.

It is unlikely that a single synapse is the fundamental unit of memory, but many neurobiologists believe that changes in synaptic strength among groups of neurons can represent experience. This belief has attracted a large number of scientists to the study of synaptic plasticity and generated an enormous and complex literature. The work of these scientists has yielded some important clues about how the brain acquires and stores memories.

The goals of this chapter and several that follow are (1) to present some of the fundamental concepts and methodologies needed to understand how synapses are modified and (2) to highlight some of the important findings that provide the clues to how synapses might store memories. Insights into the mechanisms of synaptic plasticity come from studies of neurons completely isolated from the organism. Such artificial preparations have proven to be invaluable to understanding how synapses are modified. However, keep in mind that any clues derived from the study of synaptic plasticity must be tested in behavioral experiments before a claim can be made that a synaptic mechanism supports a memory. Specifically, it must be demonstrated that this mechanism operates in an intact animal to support the effect an experience has on a behavior that depends on learning and memory.

## Two Approaches to Studying Synapses that Support Memory

In an ideal world one would like to study how experience actually modifies the synapses that support a memory. This turns out to be a daunting task because it requires locating that **memory trace** (also called the **engram**) and its natural sensory inputs.

Karl Lashley (1950) is generally credited with mounting the first serious attempt to locate the memory trace. His attempt was unsuccessful and discouraging. Workable approaches to this problem, however, began to emerge in the late 1960s. One of these, sometimes called the **simple system approach**, emerged from a deliberated strategy, while another emerged from a discovery called **long-term potentiation** (**LTP**) in a region of the brain called the hippocampus. These approaches are described below.

### *Simple System: The Gill Withdrawal Reflex*

Biologists believe that the answer to a big question often can be found by reducing the problem to its most elementary form. If you believe that a memory trace is created when experience modifies some synaptic connections, then you need an animal with the simplest nervous system that can support a modifiable behavior. In this case you would be willing to sacrifice the complexities of the human brain and the richness of the memories it can support to gain other important advantages. Specifically, with the right animal it might be possible to locate the neural circuit that supports the memory and study the synaptic connections in this circuit that are modified by experience.

In the late 1960s, Eric Kandel (1976) followed this strategy to initiate a research program that focused on an invertebrate named *Aplysia Californica*, a large sea slug. This animal has several important properties.

Eric Kandel

- It has a behavior called the gill withdrawal reflex that can be modified by experience.

- It has a relatively simple brain, located in its abdomen, called the abdominal ganglion, which has far fewer neurons than any vertebrate brain.

- The cell bodies of these neurons are very large, almost visible with no magnification.

- The location of individual neurons is consistent from one animal to another.

The gill of the sea slug is the principle organ for extracting oxygen. The **gill withdrawal reflex** is a defensive behavior the animal displays when its skin is stimulated. See Figure 2.1A for an illustration of the gill in its normal state and when a tactile stimulus is applied to its siphon. Note that the gill contracts when the siphon is touched. This simple behavior can be modified by experience. If the siphon is tapped every few seconds, the amplitude of the response decreases. This change in behavior is called **habituation**: *the magnitude of the response decreases with repeated stimulation*. After the response has diminished, if there is a significant pause between taps, the response to the next tap will increase. This is called **spontaneous recovery**: *with the passage of time between stimulus presentations the response to that stimulus can recover*.

The phenomenon of habituation coupled with spontaneous recovery is referred to as **short-term habituation**. If the experiment is repeated over several days, the amount of spontaneous recovery greatly diminishes. This is called **long-term habituation**. The gill withdrawal reflex also can become more responsive by strongly stimulating (shocking) the animal's tail. Thus, a strong stimulus to the tail greatly enhances the gill withdrawal response to the relatively weak stimulus applied to the siphon (Figure 2.1B). This is called **sensitization**.

The set of phenomena just described is not unique to sea slugs. Reflexive responses elicited in other animals, including people, also habituate, show spontaneous recovery, and can be sensitized by strong stimulation. So, although habituation is a simple behavioral adaptation, it is quite general. Behavioral habituation clearly meets the definition of learning and memory. In some way, information contained in the tap persists in a form that can influence behavior.

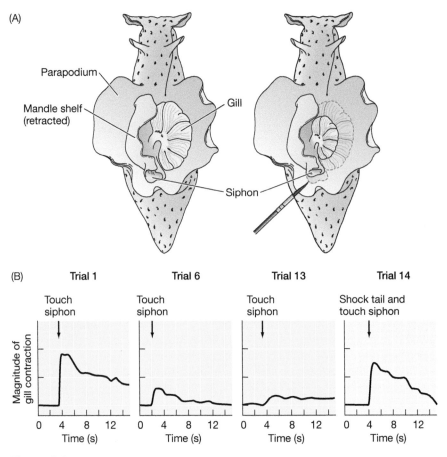

**Figure 2.1**
(A) An illustration of the gill of *Aplysia Californica* in a relaxed state (left) and its withdrawal when the siphon is touched (right). (B) The gill withdrawal reflex habituates. Note that on Trial 1 a touch to the siphon produces vigorous withdrawal but that by trial 13 the same stimulus fails to elicit a response. Sensitization is illustrated on trial 14 where a strong shock applied to the tail restores the response.

Figure 2.2 illustrates the *Aplysia* abdominal ganglion structure and the locations of the large cell bodies of its neurons. Remarkably, the abdominal ganglion can be isolated from the body of the animal while still connected to the sensory neurons that respond to the siphon taps and to the motor neurons that, when activated, cause the gill to retract. This feature makes it possible to identify the exact connections that participate in the gill withdrawal reflex, that is, to map out the circuit of neurons that support the behavior. Once the part of the neural circuit that is modified by repeated taps is discovered

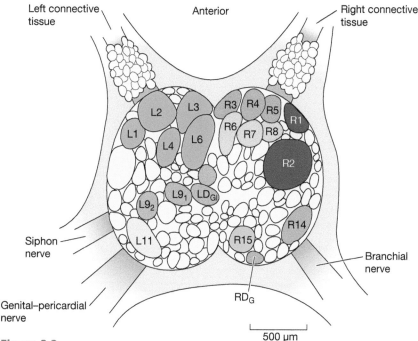

**Figure 2.2**

The abdominal ganglion of *Aplysia Californica*. The cell bodies are large and identifiable from one animal to another.

(Figure 2.3), one is then in a position to study synaptic mechanisms that allow experience (repeated taps) to modify the gill withdrawal behavior.

Kandel and his colleagues were able to locate the site of the memory trace—the set of synapses connecting sensory neurons from the siphon to the motor neurons that controlled the gill withdrawal reflex. The part of the circuit that was modified was the synapse. Repeated tapping caused changes that weakened the strength of the synapses connecting the sensory and motor neurons.

The story of just what happens when the gill withdrawal reflex habituates is about discovering synaptic mechanisms that participate in this change. Much of this has been described in Kandel's papers, including one based on his Nobel Prize address (2001). The goal of this discussion, however, is only to introduce the logic behind the simple system approach. By trading complexity for simplicity, researchers who have employed the simple system approach have made important contributions to the understanding of how experience modifies synapses and have provided important clues to how memories are made.

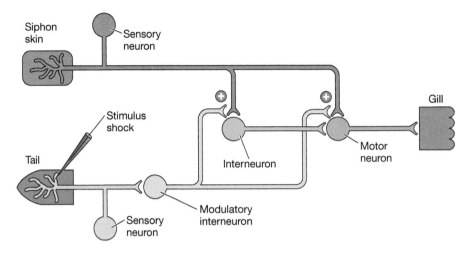

**Figure 2.3**
A diagram of the neural circuit that supports the gill withdrawal reflex and sensitization. Stimulation of the siphon activates a sensory neuron that synapses onto an interneuron and a motor neuron, which produces the contraction of the gill. Habituation occurs because repeated taps to the siphon weaken the synaptic connections between the sensory and motor neurons. Note that the circuit activated by tail shock connects to the sensory neuron. Stimulating the tail enhances the size of the gill withdrawal reflex elicited by the siphon.

## Long-Term Potentiation in the Hippocampus

No one would seriously imagine that the information contained in the modified sensory–motor synapses of a sea slug remotely resembles that which is contained in the modified synapses that would let you recall where you went to lunch yesterday and who was with you. This kind of information requires memory traces that are far more complex and integrated. Yet, it is becoming increasingly likely that specific circuits that contain such complex traces can be identified in mammalian brains. However, there is good reason to believe that a structure in the brain called the **hippocampus** contains modifiable synapses that can maintain this kind of information (see Chapters 15 and 16). Moreover, the anatomical organization of the hippocampus is well known.

Indeed, the hippocampus has a very interesting anatomical organization—a so-called trisynaptic circuit—that attracted neurophysiologists who were interested in studying neuron-to-neuron communication. This circuit is shown in outline form in Figure 2.4. The three components of the circuit are:

1. Neurons in the entorhinal cortex connect to a region in the hippocampus called the **dentate gyrus** by what is called the **perforant path**.

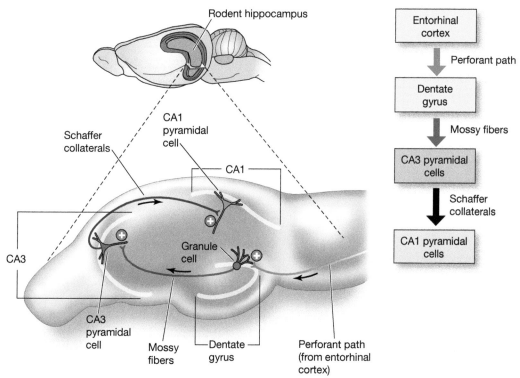

**Figure 2.4**
The hippocampus has a very interesting anatomical organization. This schematic representation of the rodent hippocampus shows the direction of the flow of information.

2. Neurons in the dentate gyrus connect to the **CA3** region by what are called **mossy fibers**.

3. Neurons in CA3 connect to neurons in the **CA1** region by what are called **Schaffer collateral fibers**.

Although it is not possible to study specific neuron-to-neuron connections in the intact hippocampus, the organization of the hippocampus makes it possible to study connections between neurons in one region or subfield with neurons in another subfield. The specific methods are described in a later section. The basic strategy is simple: you stimulate a set of fibers known to synapse onto neurons in a particular subfield and record what happens in that region when the impulse arrives. If the fibers connect to cells near the recording electrode, you will detect a response in those neurons.

Working in Per Andersen's laboratory, Timothy Bliss and Terje Lomo (1973) took advantage of the anatomy of the hippocampus in a living rabbit to determine if it was possible to modify the strength of synapses. They

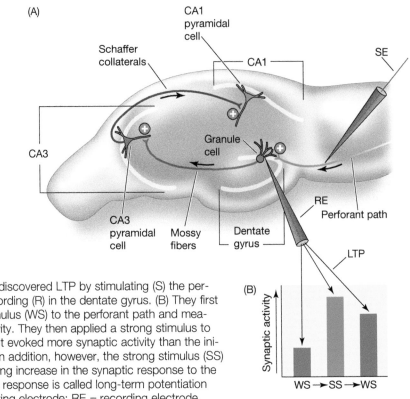

(A)

**Figure 2.5**
(A) Bliss and Lomo discovered LTP by stimulating (S) the perforant path and recording (R) in the dentate gyrus. (B) They first applied a weak stimulus (WS) to the perforant path and measured synaptic activity. They then applied a strong stimulus to the perforant path. It evoked more synaptic activity than the initial weak stimulus. In addition, however, the strong stimulus (SS) produced an enduring increase in the synaptic response to the WS. This enhanced response is called long-term potentiation (LTP). SE = stimulating electrode; RE = recording electrode.

Timothy Bliss

stimulated the fibers in the perforant path and recorded synaptic activity that occurred in the dentate gyrus (Figure 2.5). Their experiment was simple:

1. They established that a weak stimulus applied to the perforant path would evoke some synaptic activity in the dentate gyrus.

2. They next delivered a stronger stimulus to the same perforant path fibers, which evoked a bigger synaptic response.

3. They then repeatedly presented the weak stimulus and found that it now evoked a bigger response.

Thus, the strong stimulus potentiated the response to the weak stimulus. The potentiated response lasted a relatively long time (several hours). This phenomenon is called long-term potentiation (LTP). As noted, neurobiologists believe that experience is stored in the brain because it modifies the strength of synapses connecting networks of neurons. Thus, Bliss and Lomo's discovery of LTP was greeted with great enthusiasm because it provided a way to study how synaptic strength can be modified by experience. Hundreds of researchers have dedicated their scientific careers to the study of LTP as a model system for discovering the synaptic mechanisms that produce lasting changes in synaptic strength. The work of these scientists has greatly increased our understanding of these mechanisms and identified a number of important molecules and processes that are likely to be involved in making memories. To appreciate their discoveries, it is necessary to have a detailed understanding of the methodology used to study LTP and its conceptual basis.

Terje Lomo

## The Conceptual Basis and Methodology of LTP

Although Bliss and Lomo discovered LTP in the hippocampus of a living rabbit, the most widely employed basic procedure for studying LTP centers on what is called an **in vitro preparation** (Figure 2.6A,B). It requires dissecting a very thin slice of tissue from the hippocampus and placing it into a special chamber that contains a cocktail of chemicals in a solution that will keep the slice of tissue functional for several hours. A stimulating electrode is then positioned to deliver electrical current to a chosen set of fibers and a recording electrode is placed in the region where these fibers terminate.

Bliss and Lomo (1973) stimulated the fibers in the perforant path and recorded the synaptic response in the dentate gyrus. Many researchers choose instead to stimulate the Schaffer collateral fibers and record the response of the pyramidal cells in the CA1 subfield (Figure 2.6C). The recording electrode is placed in the extracellular space among a population of pyramidal cells in CA1. It records the extracellular **excitatory postsynaptic potential** (**EPSP**) in a particular area and is referred to as the **field potential** (also called the **field EPSP** or **fEPSP**). The field potential is a critical concept because it is what is measured in an LTP experiment.

(A)

(B)

(C)

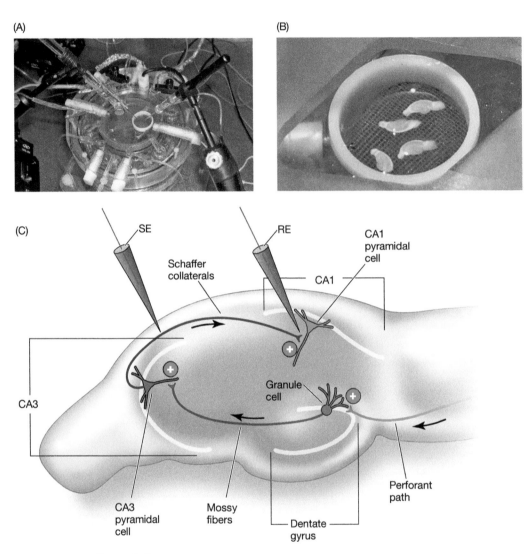

SE

RE

Schaffer
collaterals

CA1

CA1
pyramidal
cell

Granule
cell

CA3

CA3
pyramidal
cell

Mossy
fibers

Dentate
gyrus

Perforant
path

**Figure 2.6**
LTP can be studied in tissue slices taken from the hippocampus. This is called an in
vitro preparation. (A) The recording apparatus consists of a large chamber that is filled
with fluid needed to keep the slice viable, a small chamber that holds the slice being
studied, the stimulating electrode used to induce LTP, and the recording electrode
used to measure the field EPSP. (B) Prior to beginning the experiment, slices of hippocampal tissue are placed into the small recording chamber. (C) Many researchers
use the in vitro methodology to study LTP induced in neurons in the CA1 region of
the hippocampus. To do this they stimulate the Schaffer collateral fibers and record
field potentials from a recording electrode placed in the CA1 region. SE = stimulating
electrode; RE = recording electrode.

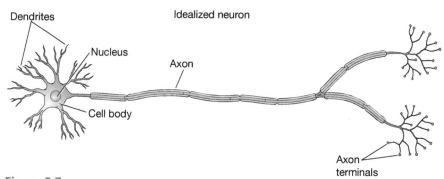

Dendrites

Idealized neuron

Nucleus

Axon

Cell body

Axon
terminals

**Figure 2.7**
A neuron is composed of a cell body (which contains the nucleus), dendrites, an axon, and axon terminals.

## Understanding the Field EPSP

To more fully understand the fEPSP requires a review of the basic structure and function of the neuron and how neurons communicate, as well as a discussion of membrane potential and depolarization.

**STRUCTURE AND FUNCTIONS OF THE NEURON**   An idealized neuron is presented in Figure 2.7, which shows that a neuron is composed of a cell body, **dendrites**, an **axon**, and axon terminals. Neurons are connected in networks and serve many functions. A neuron is:

- an input device that receives chemical and electrical messages from other neurons;

- an integrative device that combines messages received from multiple inputs;

- a conductive–output device that sends information to other neurons, muscles, and organs; and

- a representation device that stores information about past experiences as changes in synaptic strength (Figure 2.8).

The function a particular neuron serves depends on whether it is a presynaptic "sending" neuron or a postsynaptic "receiving" neuron. As noted in the previous chapter, the synapse (Figure 2.8) is the point of contact between the sending and receiving neuron. It is where neurons communicate and information is thought to be stored. The basic components of the synapse are the **presynaptic terminal**, the **postsynaptic dendrite**, and the **synaptic cleft**, which is a small space between the terminal and the spine that contains structures that maintain the connection.

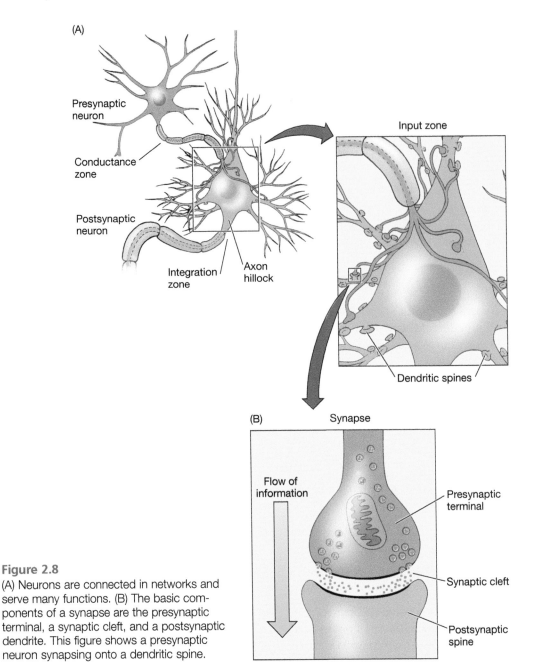

**Figure 2.8**
(A) Neurons are connected in networks and serve many functions. (B) The basic components of a synapse are the presynaptic terminal, a synaptic cleft, and a postsynaptic dendrite. This figure shows a presynaptic neuron synapsing onto a dendritic spine.

**NEURONAL COMMUNICATION** Information transmitted between neurons depends on a combination of electrical events that allow the presynaptic neuron to influence the postsynaptic neuron. Some of the important details of

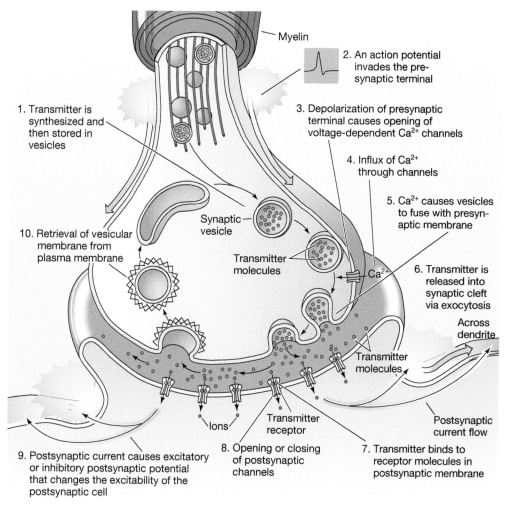

Myelin

2. An action potential invades the pre-synaptic terminal

1. Transmitter is synthesized and then stored in vesicles

3. Depolarization of presynaptic terminal causes opening of voltage-dependent $Ca^{2+}$ channels

4. Influx of $Ca^{2+}$ through channels

5. $Ca^{2+}$ causes vesicles to fuse with presynaptic membrane

Synaptic vesicle

10. Retrieval of vesicular membrane from plasma membrane

Transmitter molecules

$Ca^{2+}$

6. Transmitter is released into synaptic cleft via exocytosis

Across dendrite

Transmitter molecules

Ions

Transmitter receptor

Postsynaptic current flow

9. Postsynaptic current causes excitatory or inhibitory postsynaptic potential that changes the excitability of the postsynaptic cell

8. Opening or closing of postsynaptic channels

7. Transmitter binds to receptor molecules in postsynaptic membrane

**Figure 2.9**
When an action potential arrives in the presynaptic axon terminal, neurotransmitter molecules are released from synaptic vesicles into the synaptic cleft where they bind to specific receptors, causing a chemical or electrical signal in the postsynaptic cell.

this process are shown in Figure 2.9. The general story, however, is that the terminal ending of the sending neuron contains packages of molecules called **neurotransmitters**, which are packaged in structures called **synaptic vesicles**. These molecules are called neurotransmitters because they are the primary communication agent of the sending neuron. When action potentials (spikes of electrical activity that travel along the axon) are generated in the axon of the sending neuron, they can cause the neurotransmitters to be released into the synaptic cleft. The receiving neuron has specialized receptors, generally located

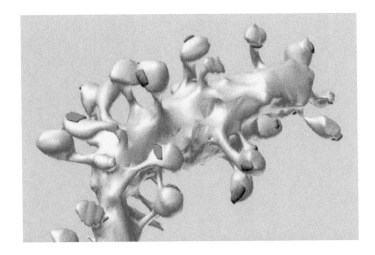

**Figure 2.10**
Dendrites are extensively populated with structures called dendritic spines. A spine
is a small (sub-micrometer) membranous extrusion that protrudes from a dendrite.
This figure illustrates a three dimensional reconstruction of a section of a dendrite with
spines of different shapes and sizes. Dendritic spines are of special interest because
(1) key receptors involved in the regulation of synaptic plasticity are located in spines
and (2) changes in the composition and architecture of the spine are altered by neural
activity. (From *Synapse Web*, Kristen M. Harris, PI, http://synapses.clm.utexas.edu/.)

on the dendrites (Figure 2.10), which are designed to receive the neurotransmitter signals emitted by the sending neuron. After the neurotransmitters are
released, they can bind to receptors located on the dendrites of the receiving
neuron.

When enough receptors are occupied, a brief electrical event called the
**postsynaptic potential** is generated in the postsynaptic neuron. Postsynaptic
potentials occur because activation of the synapse causes a brief change in the
resting membrane potential of the postsynaptic neuron.

MEMBRANE POTENTIAL    There is fluid inside the neurons called intracellular
fluid and neurons are surrounded by what is called extracellular fluid. The
intracellular fluid is separated from the surrounding extracellular fluid by a
cell membrane. Both the intracellular and extracellular fluids contain positively and negatively charged molecules called **ions**. The **membrane potential** is the difference in the electrical charge inside the neuron's cell body
compared to the charge outside the cell body. If the ionic composition of the
intracellular and extracellular fluids were exactly the same, the membrane
potential would be zero. However, the composition is not the same. There are
more negatively charged ions in the intracellular fluid than in the extracellular

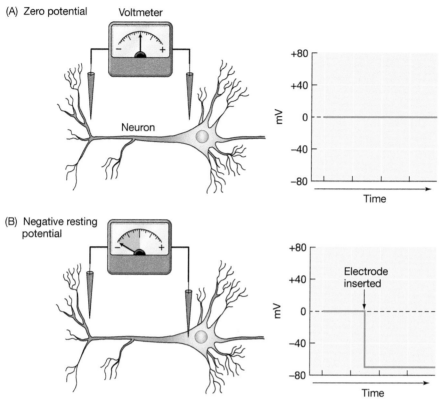

**Figure 2.11**

(A) When two recording electrodes are in the extracellular space surrounding neurons, there is zero potential between them. Likewise, the membrane potential would be zero if the ionic composition of the extracellular and intracellular fluids were exactly the same. (B) However, if one electrode is inserted into the neuron but the other electrode remains in the extracellular space, it would record the resting membrane potential as negative because in the inactive state there are more negatively charged ions in the intracellular fluid than in the extracellular fluid.

fluid. Thus, the membrane potential in the inactive state, that is, the **resting membrane potential**, is negatively charged with respect to the extracellular fluid. The electrical potential is measured in millivolts (mV); each millivolt is 1/1000 of a volt. The resting membrane potential is typically in the range of –50 to –80 mV where the "–" represents a negative potential (Figure 2.11).

DEPOLARIZATION AND HYPERPOLARIZATION    The membrane potential is dynamic and can be driven to become either less negative or more negative. The term **depolarization** represents the case where the membrane potential becomes less negative. When depolarization occurs, the composition of the

**Figure 2.12**
The resting membrane potential is negative. Depolarization occurs when the ionic composition of the intracellular fluid becomes less negative. Hyperpolarization occurs when the ionic composition of the intracellular fluid becomes more negative.

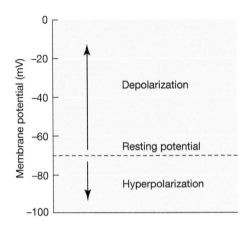

intracellular fluid becomes more like the composition of the extracellular fluid. The term **hyperpolarization** represents the case where the membrane potential becomes more negative. When hyperpolarization occurs, the composition of the intracellular fluid becomes less like the composition of the extracellular fluid. The process of depolarization drives the neuron *towards* generating action potentials, while the process of hyperpolarization drives the neuron *away* from generating action potentials (Figure 2.12).

The electrical stimulation used to produce LTP in the hippocampus generates action potentials in the axons of the sending neurons. As a result, many of the synapses on the postsynaptic neurons will depolarize, that is, positive ions will flow into those neurons. This is called **postsynaptic depolarization.** In principle, postsynaptic potentials can be recorded from either a very small intracellular electrode (an electrode that penetrates the neuron) or from a larger electrode placed in the extracellular fluid in the region where the stimulated axons synapse with the receiving neurons (Figure 2.13). The intracellular electrode would detect positive ions flowing into the neuron, indicating depolarization. However, the extracellular electrode will detect a change in the potential difference between the ionic composition of the extracellular fluid at the recording electrode and another, distant and inactive electrode called the ground electrode. Normally the potential difference between the extracellular recording electrode and ground is zero. As the positive ions flow into the postsynaptic membrane, however, they will flow away from the extracellular recording electrode. This means that the potential between the recording and ground electrodes will become negative. Theoretically, as more synapses contribute to depolarization, the negative potential will increase because more positive ions will flow away from the extracellular recording electrode.

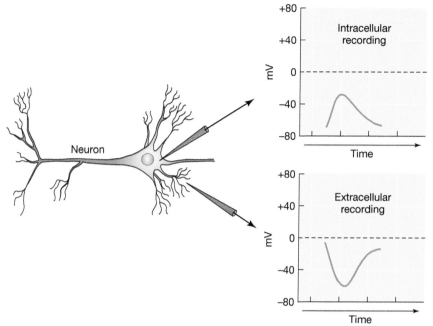

**Figure 2.13**
Postsynaptic potentials can be recorded from either an intracellular electrode that penetrates the neuron or an electrode placed in the extracellular fluid. The intracellular electrode detects positive ions flowing into the neuron, indicating depolarization. The extracellular electrode measures the electrical potential between the extracellular fluid and a ground electrode. When synapses depolarize, positive ions move away from the tip of the electrode into the neuron. This results in the electrical potential between the extracellular fluid and ground electrode becoming negative. Thus, the extracellular recording has a negative slope.

## What is Synaptic Strength?

This discussion of the membrane potential and field potentials provides a foundation for defining **synaptic strength**. In the context of the LTP experiment, synaptic strength is measured by the amount of postsynaptic depolarization produced by the stimulus—how many positive ions flow into the postsynaptic neurons surrounding the extracellular recording electrode. The extracellular electrode reads this as the flow of positive ions away from its tip. Thus, the size of the field EPSP recorded by the extracellular electrode is assumed to indirectly measure the strength of the synaptic connections linking the presynaptic and postsynaptic neuron. The next section describes in more detail how LTP is induced and measured.

## Inducing and Measuring LTP

Figure 2.14 illustrates the delivery of a high-frequency stimulus to Schaffer collateral axons or fibers that synapse onto the CA1 pyramidal neurons. An extracellular recording is positioned to measure the field potential that

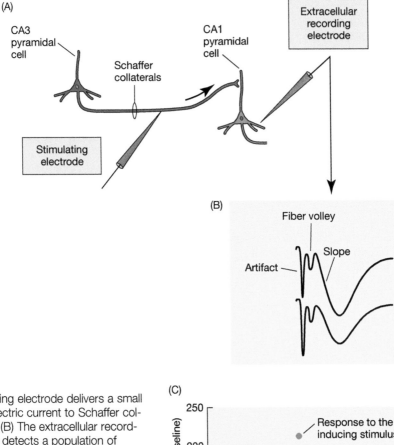

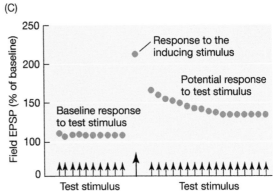

**Figure 2.14**
(A) A stimulating electrode delivers a small amount of electric current to Schaffer collateral fibers. (B) The extracellular recording electrode detects a population of depolarizing synapses in the CA1 region and generates a waveform. The steepness of the slope of the waveform represents the amount of synaptic depolarization around the recording electrode. Thus, more synaptic depolarization is recorded in the top waveform than in the bottom one. (C) A quantitative representation of the results of a typical LTP experiment.

is produced when synapses located on pyramidal neurons depolarize. The waveform produced by the recording electrode is complex because the electrode detects several electrical events. One event is a stimulus artifact associated with simply triggering the current generator that produces the stimulus, another is the **fiber volley** (the action potentials generated by the electrical stimulus), and another is the critical field EPSP. The fiber volley represents the fact that the electrical stimulus applied to the fibers generated action potentials that arrived at the recording site. The field EPSP is detected as the downward slope of the waveform, which measures the rate at which positive ions ($Na^+$) are leaving the recording field and depolarizing synapses. The steepness of the slope is assumed to reflect the amount of postsynaptic depolarization that occurred. A quantitative representation of the results of a typical LTP experiment is provided in Figure 2.14C.

To understand Figure 2.14 it is necessary to describe the details of the LTP experiment. A good place to start is with a discussion of how the independent variable in the LTP experiment—the intensity of the electric current used to evoke the field potential—is determined.

The electrical current applied to the fibers is measured in what are called microamperes, μA. This unit of measure is very small. You would not detect this level of current if it were applied to your finger. Nevertheless, it will generate action potentials in the fibers to which it is applied. It is important to know that in an LTP experiment there are two stimuli: the **test stimulus** and the **inducing stimulus**. The test stimulus is relatively weak and thus evokes a small fEPSP. The inducing stimulus is much stronger and evokes a larger fEPSP.

The intensity of the test stimulus is usually arrived at by preliminary tests in which the intensity of the stimulus is varied, from about 2.5 to 45 μA (Sweat, 2003), and the experimenter measures the amplitude of the fiber volley and the slope of the fEPSP. The goal of this preliminary stage is to find a test stimulus that evokes an fEPSP that is about 35–50% of the maximum response (Figure 2.15).

The test stimulus has two functions. First, it is repeatedly presented to establish a baseline level of synaptic activity, that is, a baseline fEPSP. Once the baseline is established, the strong, inducing stimulus is presented. Its function is to change the strength of the synaptic connections between the stimulated fibers and the receiving neurons. The second function of the test stimulus is to act as a probe to determine if the inducing stimulus changed the strength of connections between the presynaptic fibers and the postsynaptic neurons. Thus, after the inducing stimulus is presented, the test stimulus is repeatedly presented (about every 20 seconds). If the experiment is successful, then the test stimulus will evoke a much larger fEPSP than it did during the baseline period (previously shown in Figure 2.14).

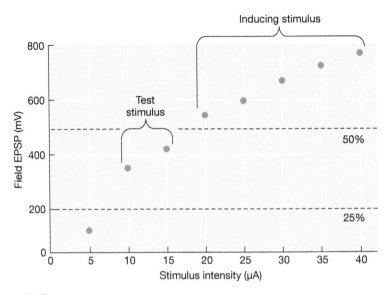

**Figure 2.15**
This figure illustrates a hypothetical relationship between the slope of the field EPSP and the intensity of the stimulus. In this example, either the 10 or 15 μA stimuli might be selected to serve as the baseline test stimulus, and intensities from 20 μA to 40 μA might serve as the inducing stimulus.

The dependent variable shown in Figure 2.14—field EPSP (% of baseline)—represents the difference between the fEPSP produced by the test stimulus during the baseline period prior to when the inducing stimulus is presented (T1), and the response to the test stimulus after the inducing stimulus is presented (T2). To calculate this value, simply divide the value of T2 by the value of T1 and multiply by 100:

$$\text{Field EPSP (\% of baseline)} = \text{T2/T1} \times 100$$

For example, if the average baseline fEPSP (T1) was 350 mV and the fEPSP evoked by the test stimulus after the inducing stimulus was presented (T2) was 500 mV, then the field EPSP (% of baseline) value would be 143%. In order to conclude that the inducing stimulus strengthened the synaptic connections between axon fibers stimulated by the test stimulus and the postsynaptic neurons, that is, that it induced LTP, this value must exceed 100%. Note that the results presented in Figure 2.14 would lead to the conclusion that the strong inducing stimulus had produced LTP.

The inducing stimulus, which generates LTP, is stronger than the test stimulus. Its intensity is also determined from the preliminary tests (see Figure 2.15). If a weak induction protocol is desired, the stimulus might be set to evoke at least half the maximal fEPSP. In this protocol the stimulus would be presented at a high frequency (100 Hz = 100 times in a second) for 1 second. If a stronger protocol is desired, then the intensity of the inducing stimulus might be set to evoke the near maximal response. In the stronger protocol, the stimulus would be presented three times at 100 Hz. The three presentations would be separated by 20 seconds. Researchers often call the inducing stimulus the **high-frequency stimulus (HFS)**.

## Long-Term Depression: The Polar Opposite of LTP

Although experience can strengthen synaptic connections, embedded in the concept of synaptic plasticity is the idea that experience can also weaken synaptic connections. Synaptic plasticity is in fact bidirectional. Depending on the nature of experience-produced synaptic activity, the synaptic connection can be either strengthened or weakened. The term **long-term depression (LTD)** is used to represent the case in which synaptic activity weakens the strength of the synaptic connections. The experimenter uses a high-frequency stimulus protocol to induce LTP. The protocol used to induce LTD, however, is much different (Bear, 2003; Dudek and Bear, 1992). For example, Dudek and Bear discovered that LTD in the hippocampus could be induced by applying 900 pulses of a low-frequency stimulus (1–3 Hz), which takes about 15 minutes. This reduced the field EPSP evoked by the test stimulus for at least an hour (Figure 2.16).

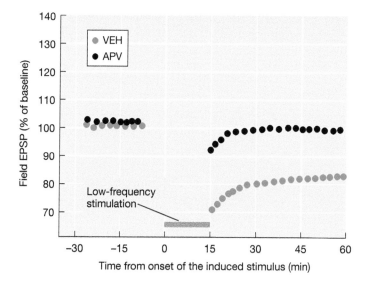

**Figure 2.16**
The delivery of a low-frequency stimulus to Schaffer collateral fibers for about 15 minutes produces a long-term depression in the dendritic field of CA1 neurons. Note that the slope of the field EPSP evoked by the test stimulus is markedly reduced. In addition, this effect is blocked when the NMDA receptor antagonist APV is applied to the slice. (See Chapter 3 for an explanation of NMDA receptor antagonists.) (After Dudek and Bear, 1993.)

## Summary

The idea that experience can be stored by altering the strength of neuron-to-neuron connections is fundamental to the neurobiology of memory. Locating the synapse that contains a memory trace is a difficult task. Neurobiologists have used two general strategies: (1) the simple system approach and (2) a model of plasticity called long-term potentiation.

Neurons communicate through chemical synapses. The release of excitatory neurotransmitters by the presynaptic neuron causes receptors on the postsynaptic neuron to allow positive ions to enter the cell and produce what is called synaptic depolarization—the intracellular fluid become less negative compared to the extracellular fluid.

To produce LTP, the experimenter applies electrical stimulation to axon fibers to cause the release of neurotransmitters to a population of synapses on postsynaptic neurons. An extracellular electrode records positive ions flowing out of the extracellular fluid—the fEPSP. The field potential is assumed to indirectly measure the depolarization of hundreds of synapses on neurons surrounding the recording electrode. LTP is thought to represent the strengthening of synapses activated by the inducing stimulus—an increase in the capacity of these synapses to influx positive ions in response to the test stimulus. The strength of synapses can also be weakened by synaptic activity. This is called long-term depression and is produced by applying long-lasting, low-frequency stimulation.

## References

Bear, M. F. (2003). Bidirectional synaptic plasticity: from theory to reality. *Philosophical Transactions of the Royal Society of London Series B, 358*, 649–655.

Bliss, T. V. and Lomo, T. (1973). Long lasting potentiation of synaptic transmission in the dentate area of the anaesthetized rabbit following stimulation of the perforant path. *Journal of Physiology, 232*, 331–356.

Dudek, S. M. and Bear, M. F. (1992). Homosynaptic long-term depression in area CA1 of hippocampus and effects of N-methyl-D-aspartate receptor blockade. *Proceedings of the National Academy of Sciences, 89*, 4363–4367.

Kandel, E. R. (1976). *Cellular basis of behavior: an introduction to behavioral neurobiology.* San Francisco: W. H. Freeman.

Kandel, E. R. (2001). The molecular biology of memory storage: a dialogue between genes and synapses. *Science, 29*, 1030–1038.

Lashley, K. S. (1950). In search of the engram. *Symposia of the Society for Experimental Biology, 4*, 454–482.

Ramón y Cajal, S. (1894–1904). *Textura del sistema nervioso del hombre y de los vertebrados.* Trans. by N. Swanson and L. W. Swanson as *New ideas on the structure of the nervous system in man and vertebrates.* Cambridge, MA: MIT Press, 1990.

Sweat, J. D. (2003). *Mechanisms of memory.* London: Academic Press.

Teyler, T. J. (1999). Use of brain slices to study long-term potentiation and depression as examples of synaptic plasticity. *Methods, 18,* 109–116.

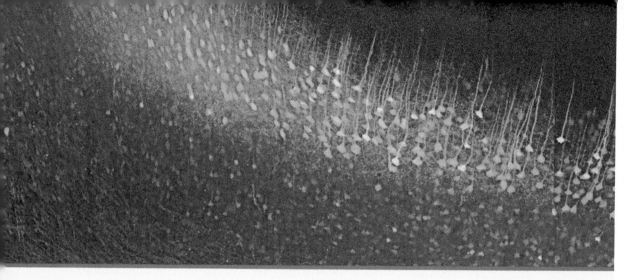

# 3 Modifying Synapses: Central Concepts

The change in synaptic potentials that is produced in an LTP experiment is the product of hundreds of biochemical interactions. These interactions involve processes that modify and rearrange *existing* proteins contained in synapses as well as processes that generate *new* proteins.

The purpose of this chapter is to provide some general ideas that will facilitate an understanding of these processes and what they have to achieve. It begins with a functional description of the synapse as a biochemical factory. It then reviews the key elements of signaling cascades that modify synapses. The central role of glutamate receptors in the induction and expression of LTP is then discussed. The increase in the number of AMPA receptors in the dendritic-spine compartment of the neuron is identified as a fundamental outcome that mediates LTP. The chapter ends by providing an organizing framework for understanding the processes that increase and maintain these receptors in the synapse.

## The Synapse as a Biochemical Factory

A standard view of a synapse is that it comprises three components: (1) a presynaptic component—a terminal ending of an axon of a sending neuron, (2) a postsynaptic component of the receiving neuron, and (3) a synaptic cleft that separates the two primary components. To understand how a synapse can be modified, however, it is useful to think of it as a biochemical factory with each component containing molecules needed to accomplish specific functions. Some of the components and processes involved in the release of neurotransmitters by the presynaptic neuron already have been described (see Figure 2.2). So the primary focus here is on postsynaptic processes.

The synaptic cleft, which separates the pre and post components of the synapse, is occupied by the **extracellular matrix** (**ECM**), illustrated in Figure 3.1. This matrix is composed of molecules synthesized and secreted by neurons and glial cells (Dityateve and Fellin, 2008). The ECM forms a bridge between the pre and postsyanaptic neurons and the molecules it contains interact with the neurons to influence their function.

Changes in synaptic potentials produced by an LTP-inducing stimulus are primarily the result of modifying **excitatory synapses**—synapses whose postsynaptic component is a spiny-like protrusion called a dendritic spine that contains membrane-spanning receptors, called glutamate receptors, that respond to the excitatory neurotransmitter **glutamate**. Synapses that contain dendritic spines are organized both to participate in synaptic transmission and to be modified by synaptic activity. Some general features of an excitatory synapse are shown in Figure 3.1.

### Postsynaptic Density

A major feature of excitatory synapses is a thickening of the postsynaptic membrane termed the **postsynaptic density** (**PSD**). The PSD contains several hundred proteins that include glutamate receptors, ion channels, signaling enzymes, scaffolding proteins, and adhesion molecules (see Figure 3.1). Several core, scaffolding proteins (PSD-95, GKAP, Shank, and Homer) play a key role in organizing the postsynaptic density (Kim and Sheng, 2009; Sheng and Hoogenraad, 2007).

Glutamate receptors located in dendritic spines respond to glutamate released from the presynaptic neuron. The postsynaptic density contributes to this process in two complementary ways. One of its functions is to localize both glutamate receptors and adhesion molecules in the postsynaptic membrane. In this way it facilitates the adhesion of the pre and postsynaptic components and aligns the glutamate receptors with the presynaptic neurotransmitter release zones. This alignment increases the likelihood that

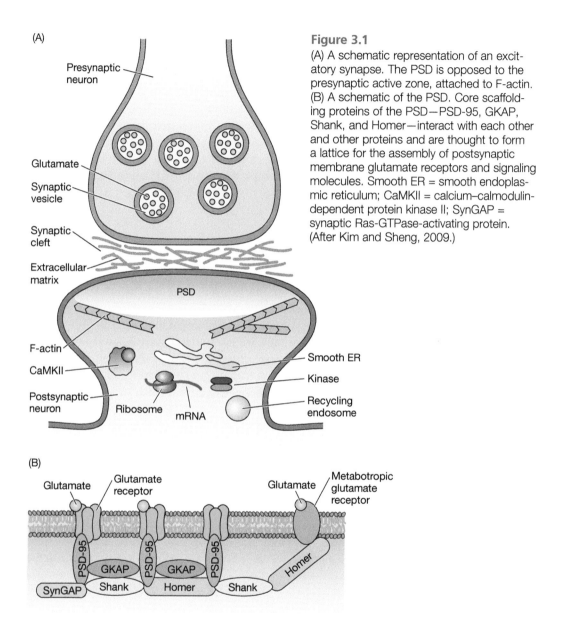

(A)

Presynaptic neuron

Glutamate

Synaptic vesicle

Synaptic cleft

Extracellular matrix

PSD

F-actin

CaMKII

Postsynaptic neuron

Ribosome

mRNA

Smooth ER

Kinase

Recycling endosome

(B)

Glutamate

Glutamate receptor

Glutamate

Metabotropic glutamate receptor

PSD-95

GKAP

SynGAP

Shank

PSD-95

GKAP

Homer

PSD-95

Shank

Homer

**Figure 3.1**
(A) A schematic representation of an excitatory synapse. The PSD is opposed to the presynaptic active zone, attached to F-actin. (B) A schematic of the PSD. Core scaffolding proteins of the PSD—PSD-95, GKAP, Shank, and Homer—interact with each other and other proteins and are thought to form a lattice for the assembly of postsynaptic membrane glutamate receptors and signaling molecules. Smooth ER = smooth endoplasmic reticulum; CaMKII = calcium–calmodulin-dependent protein kinase II; SynGAP = synaptic Ras-GTPase-activating protein. (After Kim and Sheng, 2009.)

glutamate released into the extracellular space will bind to the receptors. Excitatory synapses are plastic—they can be modified when glutamate receptors are activated. This requires the activation of other signaling molecules by the glutamate receptors. A second function of the postsynaptic density is to position these signaling molecules near the glutamate receptors so they can be activated.

## Other Synaptic Proteins

Many other proteins below the PSD are positioned to respond to the activation of glutamate receptors (see Figure 3.1). Many of these are structural proteins, such as **actin**, that provide scaffolding or give the cell its structure. Others are functional proteins—enzymes that catalyze reactions and modify the function of other proteins. In addition there are other complexes such as recycling **endosomes** that transport internalized receptors to and from the plasma membrane, **ribosomes** that are responsible for the translation of new protein, and smooth **endoplasmic reticulum (ER)** that can sequester and release calcium.

# Signaling Cascades

Excitatory synapses are modified by synaptic activity that begins when glutamate is released by the presynaptic neuron. This activity initiates a set of events, signaling cascades that are involved in every aspect of synaptic modification. So it is important to review the fundamental properties of a generic signaling cascade as illustrated in Figure 3.2, which presents the components involved in the cascade—first messenger, second messenger, and target proteins (kinases, phosphatases)—and the sequence of the cascades.

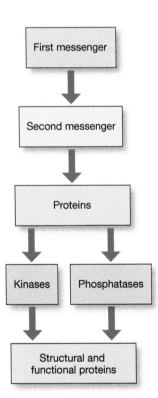

## First and Second Messengers

The signaling cascade is initiated when a **first messenger**— an extracellular substance, such as a neurotransmitter (for example, glutamate) or a hormone—binds to a cell-surface receptor and initiates intracellular activity. The second step in the cascade involves **second messengers**—molecules that relay signals from receptors on the cell surface to target molecules inside the cell. There are several second messengers (see Siegelbaum et al., 2000, for a detailed review), including

**Figure 3.2**
The signaling cascade is initiated when a first messenger—an extracellular substance, such as a neurotransmitter (for example, glutamate) or a hormone—binds to a cell-surface receptor and initiates intracellular activity. The second step in the cascade involves second messengers—molecules that relay signals from receptors on the cell surface to target intracellular protein kinases and phosphatases that then target other proteins.

calcium, cyclic adenosine monophosphates (cAMP), and inositol triphos-phate (IP3).

Second messengers are not proteins. So the number of second messen-ger molecules can be rapidly increased when a neurotransmitter or hormone binds to membrane receptors. This rapid increase is possible because their synthesis does not depend on the relatively slower transcription and transla-tion processes (discussed in Chapter 5). The rapid production of second mes-senger molecules provides a way to amplify the effect of the first messenger inside the cell.

## Protein Kinases and Phosphatases

Once generated, second messengers diffuse and target two classes of proteins, **kinases** and **phosphatases**. A protein kinase is an enzyme that modifies other proteins by chemically adding phosphate groups to them. This process, called **phosphorylation**, can change the protein's cellular location, its ability to asso-ciate with other proteins, or its enzyme activity.

A prototypical protein kinase is composed of two domains—an **inhibi-tory domain** and a **catalytic domain**. The catalytic domain carries out the phosphorylation function of the kinase. However, this activity is normally suppressed by the inhibitory domain. Thus, a kinase can be in two states: (1) it can be inactive and unable to phosphorylate other proteins or (2) it can be active and able to phosphorylate other proteins (including other kinases). To become active the catalytic unit must be released from the inhibitory unit. Sec-ond messengers target the inhibitory domain, unfold it, and thereby expose and activate the catalytic domain (see Figure 3.3). Dissociation of the sec-ond messenger can return the kinase to its inactive state. In this way, second messengers regulate the state (inactive or active) of kinases and thus their function. Second messengers also target proteins called phosphatases. These proteins are designed to remove phosphates from proteins and by doing so play an important role in regulating cellular activity.

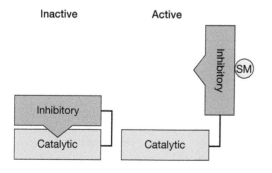

**Inactive**      **Active**

**Figure 3.3**
Kinases are composed of an inhibitory and a cat-alytic domain. In its normal inactive state the cat-alytic unit is unable to phosphorylate other pro-teins. The binding of a second messenger (SM) to the inhibitory domain exposes the catalytic unit and puts the kinase in an active state, enabling it to carry out its phosphorylation function.

## Glutamate Receptors Are Critical to the Induction of LTP

Many of the signaling cascades that are required for long-term potentiation will be described in chapters that follow. It is useful at this point, however, to describe the critical events that initiate LTP—the activation of glutamate receptors. Glutamate is an excitatory neurotransmitter and a primary first messenger for the induction of LTP. It is released into the extracellular space from the presynaptic axon terminals when an LTP-inducing stimulus is applied to the axons of the sending neurons. Some glutamate receptors on the receiving dendritic spines are called **ionotropic receptors** or ligand-gated channels. They are constructed from four or five protein subunits that come together to form a potential channel or pore (Figure 3.4). These receptors span the cell membrane; they protrude outside the cell as well as inside the cell and are positioned to interact with signaling molecules present in both the extracellular space and the **cytosol** (the internal fluid of the neuron). They are called ionotropic receptors because, when their channels open, ions such as Na⁺ (positive sodium ions) or Ca²⁺ (positive calcium ions) can enter the cell.

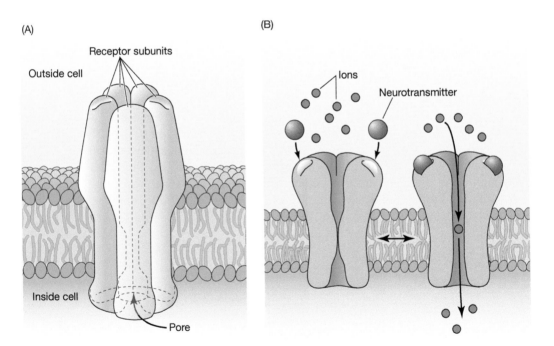

**Figure 3.4**
(A) Ionotropic receptors are located in the plasma membrane. (B) When a neurotransmitter binds to the receptor, the channel or pore opens and allows ions such as Na⁺ and Ca²⁺ to enter the cell.

They are called ligand-gated channels because it is the binding of a **ligand** (an ion, molecule, or molecular group) that opens the channel. Thus, glutamate is a ligand that binds to the site on glutamate receptors and changes the conformation or shape of the receptor so that the channel is briefly open and ions can enter the cell (see Figure 3.4).

## LTP Induction Requires Both NMDA and AMPA Receptors

Glutamate binds to three ionotropic receptors: (1) the a-amino-3-hydroxyl-5-methyl-4-isoxazole-propionate (**AMPA**) **receptor**, (2) the N-methyl-D-aspartate (**NMDA**) **receptor**, and (3) the kainate receptor (Figure 3.5). However, only the AMPA and NMDA receptors are pertinent to this discussion because they are the primary contributors to long-term potentiation.

Understanding of how LTP is induced took a giant step forward when Graham Collingridge (Collingridge et al., 1983) applied a pharmacological agent to the brain called amino-phosphono-valeric acid (abbreviated as APV), a competitive NMDA receptor **antagonist**. Competitive antagonists are molecules that have the property of occupying the receptor site so that the normal binding partner or ligand (in this case glutamate) cannot access

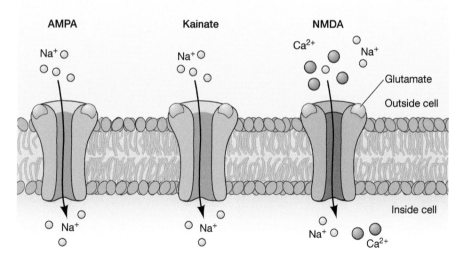

**Figure 3.5**
There are three types of glutamate receptors. AMPA and NMDA receptors, which are located in dendritic spines, play a major role in the induction and expression of LTP. When gluatamate binds to these receptors their channels open and positively charged ions in the extracellular fluid ($Na^+$ and $Ca^{2+}$) enter the neuron.

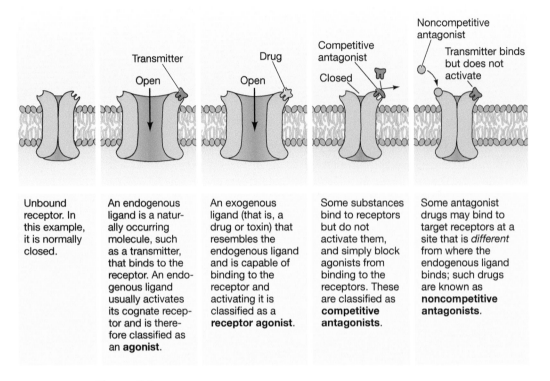

Figure 3.6
The agonistic and antagonistic actions of drugs.

| Unbound receptor. In this example, it is normally closed. | An endogenous ligand is a naturally occurring molecule, such as a transmitter, that binds to the receptor. An endogenous ligand usually activates its cognate receptor and is therefore classified as an **agonist**. | An exogenous ligand (that is, a drug or toxin) that resembles the endogenous ligand and is capable of binding to the receptor and activating it is classified as a **receptor agonist**. | Some substances bind to receptors but do not activate them, and simply block agonists from binding to the receptors. These are classified as **competitive antagonists**. | Some antagonist drugs may bind to target receptors at a site that is *different* from where the endogenous ligand binds; such drugs are known as **noncompetitive antagonists**. |

the site (Figure 3.6). However, the antagonist doesn't fit the site well enough to change the conformation of the receptor: it shields the receptor from its endogenous ligand. Using this methodology, Collingridge made two important observations: (1) applying APV before presenting the high-frequency stimulus prevented the induction of LTP (Figure 3.7), but (2) if APV was applied after LTP had been induced, that is, during the test phase, the test stimulus still evoked a potentiated fEPSP.

These two observations indicate that glutamate must bind to the NMDA receptor to produce the changes in synaptic strength, measured as LTP. But after LTP has been induced, glutamate does not have to bind to the NMDA receptor for LTP to be expressed. Experts say that the NMDA receptor is necessary for the induction of LTP but is not necessary for the expression of LTP. (The expression of LTP is measured as the enhanced field potential compared to baseline). The phrase "NMDA receptor-dependent LTP" is often used to denote the special importance of the NMDA receptor to the induction of LTP.

Graham Collingridge

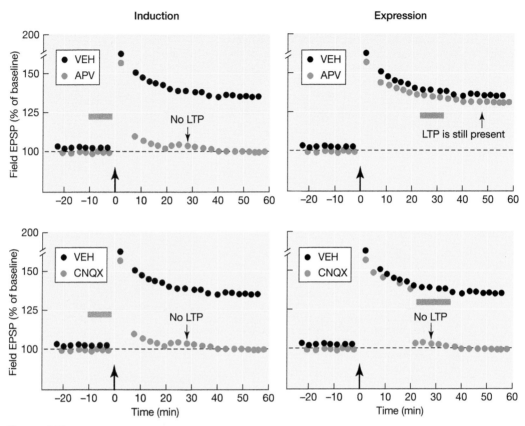

**Figure 3.7**
APV, an NMDA receptor antagonist, prevents the induction of LTP but has no effect on its expression. CNQX, an AMPA receptor antagonist, prevents both the induction and expression of LTP. The bar in each graph represents the application of the drugs—APV and CNQX—or the control vehicle (VEH).

Thus, NMDA receptors are important for only the induction of LTP. In contrast, AMPA receptors are critical for both the induction and expression of LTP. So an AMPA receptor antagonist such as 6-cyano-7-nitroquinoxaline (CNQX) would block both the induction and expression of LTP (see Figure 3.7).

## Two Events Open the NMDA Channel

The NMDA receptor channel is the gateway to the induction of LTP because it allows second-messenger $Ca^{2+}$ into the spine (Dunwiddie and Lynch, 1978). This receptor has two critical binding sites. One site binds to glutamate and the other site binds to magnesium—$Mg^{2+}$. The binding site for

**52** Chapter 3

**Figure 3.8**
(A) The NMDA receptor binds to glutamate. It also binds to Mg$^{2+}$ (sometimes called the magnesium plug) because Mg$^{2+}$ binds to the NMDA channel. (B) The opening of the NMDA receptor requires two events: (1) glutamate must bind to the receptor and (2) the cell must depolarize. When this happens, the magnesium plug is removed and Ca$^{2+}$ can enter the cell.

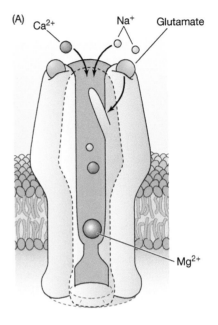

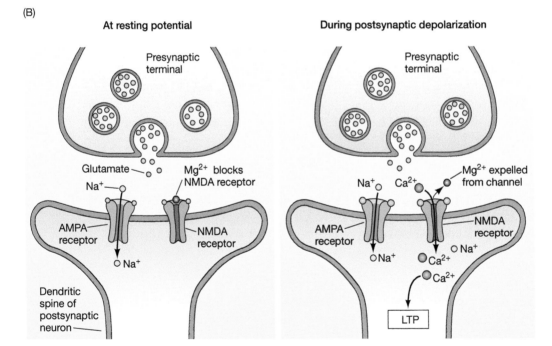

magnesium is in the pore formed by the protein subunits that make up the receptor. Because magnesium binds to a site in the pore, it is sometimes called the $Mg^{2+}$ plug. Calcium cannot enter the cell unless magnesium is removed from the pore. The trick is how to remove the magnesium plug. This outcome requires two events: (1) glutamate has to bind to the NMDA receptor, and (2) the synapse has to depolarize (Figure 3.8). Thus, the binding of glutamate to the NMDA receptor is a necessary but not a sufficient condition to remove the $Mg^{2+}$ plug; the synapse must also depolarize while glutamate is still bound to the receptor. AMPA receptors are critical for LTP induction because the binding of glutamate to these receptors opens the $Na^+$ channel and produces the synaptic depolarization needed to remove the $Mg^{2+}$ plug.

In summary, the induction of LTP occurs when extracellular calcium enters the spine via the NMDA calcium channel. Opening of the calcium channel requires a change in the conformation of the NMDA receptor, produced when glutamate binds to it, coupled with synaptic depolarization that occurs when glutamate binds to AMPA receptors to open sodium channels. Although the opening of the NMDA receptor channel is critical for the induction of LTP, the calcium ions it can influx contribute little or nothing to the expression of LTP. In contrast, the expression of LTP depends completely on sodium ions entering the AMPA receptors.

## Increasing AMPA Receptors Supports the Expression of LTP

The expression of LTP (the slope of the fEPSP) depends exclusively on an increase in the amount of $Na^+$ entering the spine and this depends on AMPA receptors. Consequently, one might infer that the signaling cascades that produce LTP do so by increasing the capacity of AMPA receptors to influx $Na^+$. In fact, nearly 30 years ago, Gary Lynch and Michel Baudry (1984) proposed that LTP (and memory storage) was the result of an increase in the number of glutamate receptors in the spine.

This general idea has proven to be correct (Figure 3.9). Two prominent researchers, Robert Malenka and Mark Bear, concluded: "It now appears safe to state that a major mechanism for the expression of LTP involves increasing the number of AMPA receptors in the plasma membrane at synapses via activity-dependent changes in AMPA receptor trafficking" (Malenka and Bear, 2004, p. 7). This being true, then the fundamental challenge is to understand the biochemical–molecular processes that regulate AMPA receptor function. The following section provides a framework for understanding these processes.

Gary Lynch

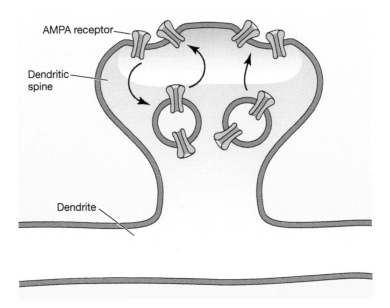

**Figure 3.9**
The complementary ideas that (a) an LTP-inducing stimulus can rapidly increase the number of AMPA receptors in the spines and (b) this is the fundamental outcome that supports the expression of LTP are now central principles of the field. AMPA receptors traffic into and out of dendritic spines. AMPA trafficking is regulated constitutively (double arrows) and by synaptic activity (single arrow). Constitutive trafficking routinely cycles AMPA receptors into and out of dendritic spines, while synaptic activity is thought to deliver new AMPA receptors to them.

## An Organizing Framework: Three Principles

The number of molecules and biochemical interactions that contribute to AMPA receptor regulation is bewildering, and it is far beyond the scope of this book to provide a complete account of what is known. A more modest goal is to identify some of the key outcomes and processes and provide a coherent framework for understanding how this happens.

Three principles help to organize the complexities of the field:

1. The duration of LTP can vary.

2. The duration of LTP is dependent on the extent to which the inducing stimulus initiates the fundamental molecular processes that modify and rearrange existing protein as well as the processes needed to generate new protein.

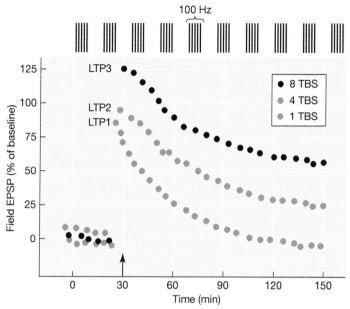

**Figure 3.10**
The number of theta-burst stimuli (TBS) determines the duration of LTP. This family of LTP functions implies that changes in synaptic strength can vary in duration and may have different molecular bases. A fundamental goal of neurobiologists is to understand these differences.

3. Synapses are strengthened and maintained in a sequence of temporal, distinct but overlapping processes.

## The Duration of LTP Can Vary

The duration of long-term potentiation depends on the parameters of the inducing stimulus. Generally speaking, as the intensity of the high-frequency inducing stimulus increases so does the duration of LTP. For example, a **theta-burst stimulation (TBS)** protocol has been used in many important experiments to induce LTP. This protocol is modeled after an increased rate of pyramidal neuronal firing that occurs when a rodent is exploring a novel environment (Larson et al., 1993). One theta burst consists of trains of 10 × 100-Hz bursts (5 pulses per burst) with a 200-millisecond interval between bursts. Figure 3.10 illustrates a family of LTP functions that can be produced by varying the number of theta bursts. Note that the duration of LTP increases with the number of theta bursts. The data illustrated in this figure have two implications: (1) changes in synaptic strength can vary in duration and (2) the molecular basis of these synaptic changes is likely different. This being the case, then an important goal is to discover the different associated molecular processes that are needed to produce this variation.

## Molecular Processes Contribute to LTP Durability

Three general sets of molecular processes contribute to the durability of LTP: (1) post-translation processes, (2) transcription processes, and (3) translation processes (Figure 3.11).

The component proteins needed to change the synapse are already in place at the time glutamate is released. Thus, synaptic activity that induces LTP initiates biochemical processes that work on the already existing parts to modify and assemble them to strengthen synaptic connections. These are post-translation processes because they involve only the modification and rearrangement of existing protein.

Post-translation processes can initially change the strength of synapses. However, the generation of new protein is necessary to ensure these changes will endure. If synaptic activity is sufficiently strong it can initiate transcription processes that generate the messenger ribonucleic acid (mRNA) needed for creating new protein and/or the translation of mRNA into protein, also called protein synthesis. The goal of these processes is to increase the complement of AMPA receptors in the synapses activated by the release of glutamates and to ensure that they will remain there.

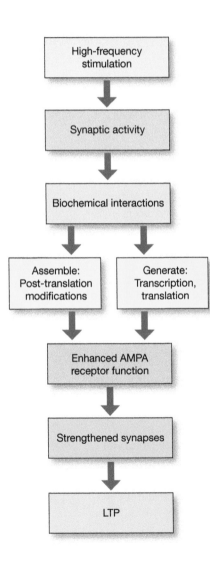

**Figure 3.11**
When high-frequency stimulation generates synaptic activity, biochemical interactions are initiated that lead to several functional outcomes that are critical to the induction of LTP. Post-translation modification processes assemble and rearrange existing proteins. Transcription and translation processes generate new proteins. A major consequence of these processes is that the contribution of AMPA receptors to synaptic depolarization is enhanced, that is, synapses are strengthened.

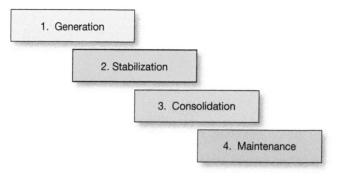

**Figure 3.12**
Changes in synaptic strength that support LTP evolve in stages that can be identified by the unique molecular processes that support each stage.

## Synapses Are Strengthened and Maintained in Stages

Changes in synaptic strength can occur within a minute or so following the induction stimulus. However, these potentiated synapses are not stable and will revert back to their pre-potentiated state unless the inducing stimulus also initiates additional sequences of molecular events (Lynch et al., 2007). This leads to the idea that synapses and memory traces are constructed in stages (as hypothesized by William James; see Chapter 1). Thus, the next chapters in this book will be organized around this idea, and these stages will be referred to as the (a) generation, (b) stabilization, (c) consolidation, and (d) maintenance phases (Figure 3.12). These chapters will reveal that each stage depends on unique molecular processes and that the primary target of these processes is the reorganization of AMPA receptor trafficking and actin cytoskeleton proteins that provide the structural and functional scaffolding needed to maintain the increased number of AMPA receptors.

## Summary

It is useful to think of the components of a synapse as biochemical factors, with each component containing molecules needed to accomplish specific functions. Signaling cascades can modify and rearrange the existing molecules and can generate new molecules through activating translation and transcription processes. The activation of NMDA and AMPA receptors by the release of the first messenger glutamate initiates the processes that potentiate synapses. An end product of the signaling cascades initiated by glutamate binding to NMDA and AMPA receptors is an increase in the number of AMPA receptors in activated synapses. Potentiated synapses can have different durations, which are determined by the molecular processes activated by the inducing stimulus. These processes will be described in the next four chapters within a framework that assumes that synaptic changes evolve in overlapping stages—generation, stabilization, consolidation, and maintenance.

## References

Collingridge, G. L., Kehl, S. J., and McLennan, H. (1983). Excitatory amino acids in synaptic transmission in the Schaffer collateral–commissural pathway of the rat hippocampus. *Journal of Physiology, 34*, 334–345.

Dityateve, A. and Fellin, T. (2008). Extracellular matrix in plasticity and epileptogenesis. *Neuron Glia Biology, 4*, 235–247.

Dunwiddie, T. and Lynch, G. (1978). Long-term potentiation and depression of synaptic responses in the rat hippocampus: localization and frequency dependency. *Journal of Physiology, 276*, 353–367.

Kim, E. and Sheng, M. (2009). The postsynaptic density. *Current Biology, 19*, 723–724.

Larson, J., Xiao, P., and Lynch, G. (1993). Reversal of LTP by theta frequency stimulation. *Brain Research, 600*, 97–102.

Lynch, G. and Baudry, M. (1984). The biochemistry of memory: a new and specific hypothesis. *Science, 224*, 1057–1063.

Lynch, G., Rex, C. S., and Gall, C. M. (2007). LTP consolidation: substrates, explanatory power, and functional significance. *Neuropharmacology, 52*, 12–23.

Malenka, R. C. and Bear, M. F. (2004). LTP and LTD: an embarrassment of riches. *Neuron, 44*, 5–21.

Sheng, M. and Hoogenraad, C. C. (2007). The postsynaptic architecture of excitatory synapses: a more quantitative view. *Annual Review of Biochemistry, 76*, 823–847.

Siegelbaum, S. A., Schwartz, J. H., and Kandel, E. R. (2000). Modulation of synaptic transmission: second messengers. In E. Kandel, J. H. Schwartz, and T. H. Jessell (Eds.), *Principles of neural science, Fourth edition* (pp. 229–239). New York: McGraw-Hill Companies.

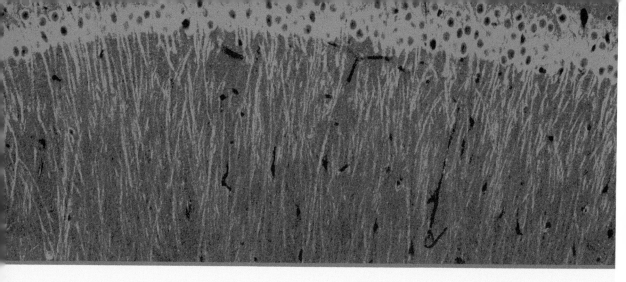

# 4 Generating and Stabilizing the Trace: Post-Translation Processes

Two related ideas are a cornerstone of memory research.

- The memory trace evolves in stages (see Chapter 1).
- During the initial stages the trace is vulnerable to disruption (see Chapter 9).

These ideas derive primarily from the observation that people who suffer a brain concussion often have amnesia for events experienced within a few minutes of the accident but no loss of memory for events that occurred earlier. This observation suggests that newly established memory traces are vulnerable to disruption but over time the traces become stable or consolidated (see Chapter 9).

Changes in synaptic strength that support long-term potentiation go through a similar evolution. LTP can be observed within about a minute after the delivery of a brief, inducing stimulus, but these initial changes are unstable and are easily disrupted (Figure 4.1). For example, this initial potentiation

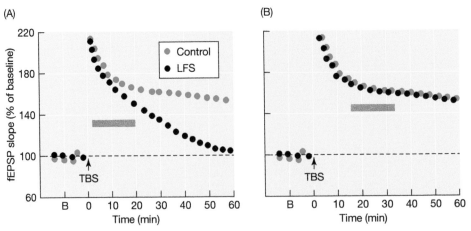

**Figure 4.1**
(A) The delivery of a low-frequency stimulus (LFS, represented by the bar) prevents the development of a lasting LTP when occurring within a minute of the TBS-inducing stimulus. (B) Low-frequency stimulation does not prevent the emergence of a durable LTP when it is delivered at least 10 minutes after TBS stimulation. These findings indicate that the synaptic changes that support LTP are not initially stable, but within about 10 minutes additional processes work to stabilize them and decrease their vulnerability to disruption.

can be reversed if a low-frequency stimulus is applied within 5 minutes after LTP is initially induced, but not if it is applied 30 minutes after LTP induction (Barrionuevo et al., 1980; Larson et al., 1993; Staubli and Chun, 1996; Zhou and Poo, 2005).

That LTP evolves in stages encourages the idea that it is supported by some of the same molecular processes that support memory. It also suggests that the molecular processes recruited to initially strengthen synapses are not sufficient to support lasting changes and must be followed by other molecular events that stabilize the trace. The goal of this chapter is to describe some of the important **post-translation processes** that generate the early phase of LTP and stabilize these changes so that they can later be consolidated.

## Generating the Trace

LTP occurs when synaptic activity engages processes that rapidly deliver more AMPA receptors into the postsynaptic density (PSD). This simple sentence belies the complexity of the molecular machinery responsible for this outcome. Understanding how this result is initially achieved requires some knowledge of: (a) the dynamics of AMPA receptor membrane trafficking and (b) the regulation of the actin cytoskeleton. The discussion below describes how the LTP-inducing stimulus alters the dynamics of ongoing constitutive AMPA trafficking and modifies the actin cytoskeleton complex to rapidly increase the number of AMPA receptors in the postsynaptic density.

## Dynamics of AMPA Receptor Membrane Trafficking

**AMPA receptor trafficking** is continuous and regulated by what are called **constitutive trafficking** processes (Figure 4.2). AMPA receptors are found both in the cell and on the plasma membrane. Some membrane receptors are present in the PSD where they are best positioned to respond to glutamate. Other membrane receptors are not in the PSD and are referred to as nonsynaptic or extrasynaptic receptors. In close proximity to the PSD is a region called the **endocytotic zone** (Petrini et al., 2009) that contains complex molecules

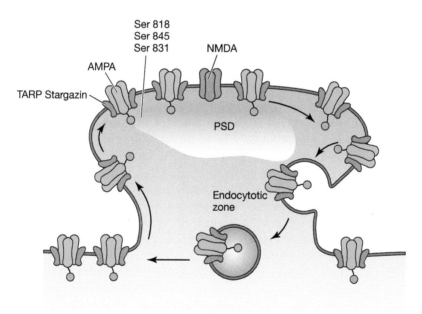

**Figure 4.2**
AMPA receptors are in constant random motion laterally diffusing along the plasma membrane where they enter and leave the PSD. Extrasynaptic receptors are more mobile than those in the PSD. Receptors cycling through the PSD might be captured in the endocytotic zone and packaged for recycling.

designed to capture AMPA receptors leaving the PSD and to repackage them in endosomes for recycling to the membrane.

The role of synaptic activity produced by an LTP-inducing stimulus is to reorganize the constitutive processes to favor increasing the number of AMPA receptors immobilized in the PSD. This requires (a) delivering a pool of these receptors to the extrasynaptic regions and (b) immobilizing or trapping a large number of these receptors in the PSD.

DELIVERING AMPA RECEPTORS   AMPA receptors are delivered to the PSD in three steps (Derkach et al., 2007; Opazo et al., 2010):

- Intracellular vesicles containing AMPA receptors (endosomes) are mobilized to deliver the receptors to the perisynaptic region, a region near the PSD.
- These receptors then diffuse somewhat randomly but laterally along the membrane to enter the PSD.
- Some receptors are trapped in the PSD and immobilized for some period of time and others leave the PSD and are captured in the endocytotic zone for recycling.

The job of constitutive trafficking processes is to ensure that synapses have the necessary supply of AMPA receptors to support synaptic transmission and increase synaptic strength. AMPA receptors can be composed of different subunits (GluA1, GluA2, GluA3, GluA4). Under basal conditions they contain GluA2 subunits. The initial induction of LTP, however, is the result of increasing the number of AMPA receptors composed of GluA1 subunits.

Such GluA1 AMPA receptors have phosphorylation sites (Ser 818, Ser 831, Ser 845) that contribute to this outcome (Figure 4.3). Transmembrane AMPA receptor regulatory proteins, called **TARPs**, also co-assemble with AMPA receptors and are critical to trapping them in the PSD.

The available pool of AMPA receptors containing GluA1 subunits is increased when the Ser 845 site is phosphorylated by protein kinase A (**PKA**). This process moves receptors that are contained in endosomes, located in the intracellular compartment, to the extrasynaptic region where they can laterally diffuse into and out of the PSD. The delivery of GluA1 receptors to the synapse also depends on the phosphorylation of another site on these receptors, Ser 818. This site is phosphorylated by protein kinase C (**PKC**), a kinase that is also activated by second-messenger $Ca^{2+}$. Just how this activity influences the delivery process is less well understood (Boehm et al., 2006).

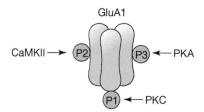

GluA1

CaMKII —▶ P2        P3 ◀— PKA

P1 ◀— PKC

Regulatory function

P1 Ser 818 anchors GluA1 to the PSD

P2 Ser 831 changes GluA1 channel conductance

P3 Ser 845 traffics GluA1 to the extrasynaptic region

**Figure 4.3**
AMPA receptors have serine sites that when phosphorylated by different kinases make different contributions to receptor trafficking and channel conductance. Protein kinase A (PKA) phosphorylates the Ser 845 site to traffic the receptor to the extrasynaptic region. Protein kinase C (PKC) phosphorylates the Ser 818 site and helps to anchor the receptor to the postsynaptic density. CaMKII phosphorylates the Ser 831 site and changes the channel, allowing it to influx calcium as well as sodium.

TRAPPING ADDITIONAL AMPA RECEPTORS   How does the LTP-inducing stimulus increase the number of these AMPA receptors trapped or immobilized in the PSD? Opazo et al. (2010) have described an elegant solution to this question. It requires the interaction of three molecules: (1) an important and unusual kinase called **CaMKII** (see Box 4.1), (2) a TARP called Stargazin, and (3) PSD-95 scaffolding proteins. In their proposal, PSD-95 proteins form potential "slots" for trapping AMPA receptors that are laterally diffusing through the PSD. For the slots to capture the receptors requires that CaMKII phosphorylate serine residues of the AMPA–Stargazin complex. This releases the Stargazin from the membrane and facilitates its binding to PSD-95. It is this binding of Stargazin to PSD-95 that traps additional AMPA receptors in the postsynaptic density. As CaMKII phosphorylates more of the Stargazin serine residues, the receptors become more stable (Figure 4.4).

CaMKII not only participates in increasing the contribution of AMPA receptors to synaptic potentials through its trapping role, it also changes the channel properties of the GluA1 AMPA receptors by phosphorylating the Ser 831 site on the receptor. This event allows the channel to influx calcium as well as Na$^+$. The net result of these effects is a strongly potentiated

## BOX 4.1 CaMKII Autophosphorylates

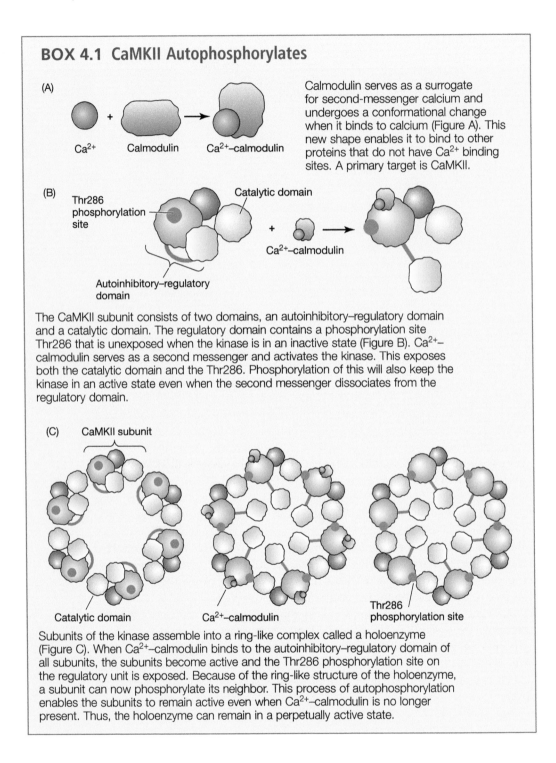

(A)

Ca²⁺    Calmodulin    Ca²⁺–calmodulin

Calmodulin serves as a surrogate for second-messenger calcium and undergoes a conformational change when it binds to calcium (Figure A). This new shape enables it to bind to other proteins that do not have $Ca^{2+}$ binding sites. A primary target is CaMKII.

(B)

Thr286 phosphorylation site

Catalytic domain

+ Ca²⁺–calmodulin

Autoinhibitory–regulatory domain

The CaMKII subunit consists of two domains, an autoinhibitory–regulatory domain and a catalytic domain. The regulatory domain contains a phosphorylation site Thr286 that is unexposed when the kinase is in an inactive state (Figure B). $Ca^{2+}$–calmodulin serves as a second messenger and activates the kinase. This exposes both the catalytic domain and the Thr286. Phosphorylation of this will also keep the kinase in an active state even when the second messenger dissociates from the regulatory domain.

(C)  CaMKII subunit

Catalytic domain    Ca²⁺–calmodulin    Thr286 phosphorylation site

Subunits of the kinase assemble into a ring-like complex called a holoenzyme (Figure C). When $Ca^{2+}$–calmodulin binds to the autoinhibitory–regulatory domain of all subunits, the subunits become active and the Thr286 phosphorylation site on the regulatory unit is exposed. Because of the ring-like structure of the holoenzyme, a subunit can now phosphorylate its neighbor. This process of autophosphorylation enables the subunits to remain active even when $Ca^{2+}$–calmodulin is no longer present. Thus, the holoenzyme can remain in a perpetually active state.

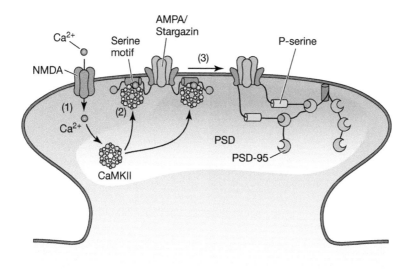

**Figure 4.4**
AMPA receptors become trapped in the PSD when (1) the influx of calcium into the spine via NMDA receptors (2) activates CaMKII. This kinase phosphorylates serine (P-serine) residues on the terminal of the TARP Stargazin. This activity releases the terminal from the membrane and (3) facilitates its binding to PSD-95 complexes, thereby trapping the receptor in the PSD. The stability of the trap increases as CaMKII phosphorylates more of the Stargazin serine residues.

synapse—one whose ability to influx $Na^+$ and $Ca^{2+}$ has been significantly but temporarily enhanced.

## Dynamics of Actin Regulation

The rapid insertion of AMPA receptors into synapses not only requires signaling cascades that reorganize AMPA receptor trafficking but also requires cascades that rapidly disassemble the network of actin proteins that construct the cytoskeleton architecture of the spine (see Gu et al., 2010; Lynch et al., 2007; Ouyang et al., 2005). Disassembling actin cytoskeleton (Figure 4.5) is important because interlaced actin filaments form a meshwork-like structure that presents a potential barrier to the plasma membrane that prevents the delivery and insertion of AMPA receptors and other proteins into the synapse (Gu et al., 2010; Ouyang et al., 2005). Thus, it is necessary to discuss the dynamics of the regulation of actin by signaling cascades that are induced by synaptic activity.

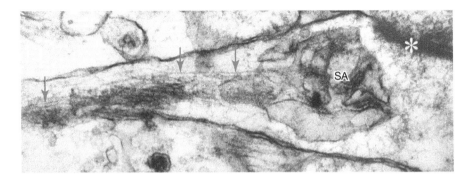

**Figure 4.5**
Actin filaments help form the spine cytoskeleton. Red arrows point to microfilaments of actin running in parallel in the dendritic spine neck. SA = spine apparatus. (From *Synapse Web*, Kristen M. Harris, PI, http://synapses.clm.utexas.edu/.)

Actin exists in two states: **globular actin (G-actin)** and **filament actin (F-actin)**. G-actins are individual subunits of actin that serve as monomer building blocks and assemble into F-actin, a two-stranded helical polymer. A **polymer** is a large organic molecule formed by combining many smaller molecules (monomers); this process is called **polymerization**. F-actin is in a continuous state of turnover, with new subunits added to the barbed end of the strand and older units being removed from the pointed end. The addition and subtraction of the subunits is similar to the action of a treadmill (Figure 4.6).

COFILIN REGULATES ACTIN DYNAMICS   An intercellular protein called actin depolymerization factor–cofilin (hereafter called **cofilin**) regulates the monomer versus filament state of actin. This protein can be in two states. In its normal dephosphorylated state, cofilin actively depolymerizes F-actin (removes monomers from the filament). When phosphorylated on its Ser 3 site, however, cofilin's depolymerizing properties turn off and F-actin becomes more likely to remain in its filament state. However, phosphatases called Slingshot can dephosphorylate cofilin and thereby increase actin depolymerization. Thus, signaling cascades that regulate the state of cofilin determine if actin polymerizes or depolymerizes (Figure 4.7).

DISASSEMBLING ACTIN NETWORKS   Disassembling actin networks involves two pathways critical to the rapid insertion of GluA1 receptors: the **calpain–spectrin pathway** and the **cofilin pathway**. In dendritic spines, polymerized actin can become crosslinked with proteins called **spectrins** that help link the filaments to the plasma membrane and increase their resistance to

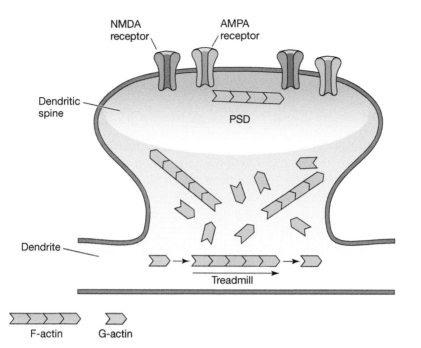

NMDA receptor

AMPA receptor

Dendritic spine

PSD

Dendrite

Treadmill

F-actin

G-actin

**Figure 4.6**
Actin exists in two states. Single arrow tips represent the monomer state, G-actin. Strings of arrows represent filament actin (F-actin), its polymer state. Actin is in a continuous state of turnover similar to a treadmill. Old units are removed from the pointed end and new units are added to the barbed end.

depolymerization. When it was discovered that NMDA-dependent $Ca^{2+}$ was critical to the induction of LTP, Gary Lynch and Michel Baudry (1984) proposed that it did so by activating **calpains**, which belong to a class of enzymes called **proteases** that can degrade proteins. When activated by $Ca^{2+}$, calpains

(A)

(B)

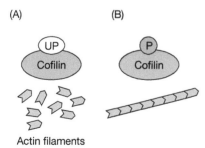

UP

Cofilin

P

Cofilin

Actin filaments

**Figure 4.7**
The state of cofilin regulates actin polymerization. (A) In its normal, unphosphorylated (UP) state, cofilin depolymerizes actin filaments. (B) When phosphorylated (P), cofilin no longer interferes with actin polymerization.

degrade proteins into smaller amino acids with no functional properties. This hypothesis was supported when it was confirmed that calpain degrades spectrins (Simon et al., 1984), and that high-frequency stimulation used to induce LTP initiated calpain activation and spectrin degradation (Lynch et al., 1982). Thus, a $Ca^{2+} \rightarrow$ calpain $\rightarrow$ spectrin degradation signaling cascade provides one route that facilitates disassembling the actin (Lynch et al., 2007; see Figure 4.8).

Recent studies based on the chemical induction of LTP have revealed a second pathway that is critical to the rapid insertion of GluA1 receptors. This pathway depends on the regulation of cofilin (Gu et al., 2010). Specifically, the delivery of GluA1 receptors to the PSD is prevented when cofilin is in the phosphorylated state—the period in which it polymerizes actin. In contrast, when cofilin is in its normal state, actin is depolymerized and AMPA receptors are rapidly delivered. Moreover, during this period when new AMPA receptors are delivered there is no detectable change in the dendritic spine. Thus, it appears that preventing actin polymerization is also an important contributor to the initial insertion of AMPA receptors into the PSD.

### Generating the Trace: Summary

The initial generation of LTP is the result of synergistic signaling cascades that reorganize (a) constitutive AMPA receptor membrane trafficking processes and (b) actin cytoskeleton proteins. These cascades begin when glutamate binds to NMDA and AMPA receptors to open the NMDA calcium channel. $Ca^{2+}$ and its surrogate, $Ca^{2+}$–calmodulin, target key kinases (CaMKII and PKC) that phosphorylate serine sites on the GluA1 receptor complex that includes Stargazin. These processes deliver and trap the GluA1 receptor complex to existing PSD-95 scaffolding proteins and thus disrupt the normal lateral diffusion of these receptors out of the synapse. Calcium-dependent cascades also orchestrate the reorganization of the actin cytoskeleton by activating a calpain–spectrin degradation path. Cofilin further contributes to the disassembling of spine actin cytoskeleton by continuing to depolymerize filament actin. The end product of these cascades is that the number of GluA1 AMPA receptors trapped in the PSD is significantly increased. Thus, the release of glutamate onto these synapses will now produce an enhanced synaptic response—increased synaptic depolarization—and a potentiated fESPS will be detected.

## Stabilizing the Trace

The initial induction of LTP is rapid but the strengthened synapses are unstable and vulnerable to disruption. However, over the next 10 to 15 minutes

(A)

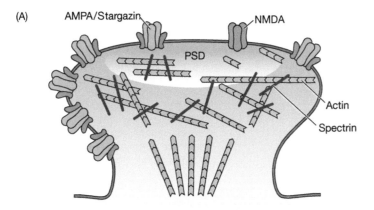

(B)

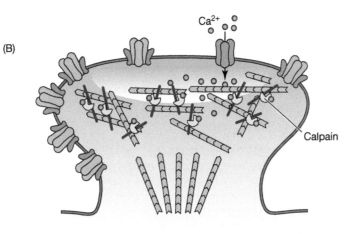

(C)

**Figure 4.8**
(A) Filament actin in the spine head
is crosslinked with spectrins. (B)
The protease calpain is activated
when calcium enters the spine
through the NMDA receptors.
Calpain degrades spectrins and
facilitates the disassembling of
actin. (C) This activity contributes
to the rapid insertion of additional
AMPA receptors in the PSD.

(A)

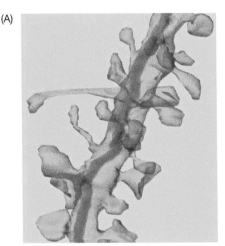

**Figure 4.9**
(A) Spines come in a wide variety of shapes and sizes (from *Synapse Web*, Kristen M. Harris, PI, http://synapses. clm.utexas.edu/). (B) Images of a dendritic branch in a living mouse, captured over six consecutive days. Note the persistent spines are large (yellow arrows) and the transient spines are small (blue arrows). (Image provided by Karel Svoboda; after Holtmaat et al., 2005.)

(B)

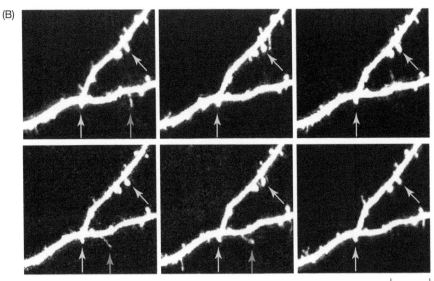

10 µm

after induction, other processes stabilize these synaptic changes and they become more resistant to disruption. The stabilization of synaptic changes depends on the modification of the dendritic spines. Spines come in a wide variety of shapes and sizes (Figure 4.9) and constantly extend out from and retract back into dendrites (Matus, 2000). A spine's size determines how long it exists; large spines endure much longer than small spines (Holtmaat et al., 2005). Modern two-photo microscopy imaging has revealed that in living animals large spines can endure for days (Holtmaat and Svoboda, 2009).

The preferential stability of large spines suggests that processes that create large spines are critical to the stability of synapses that support LTP and memories. This possibility turns out to be the case. Theta-burst stimulation (TBS) that produces enduring LTP also increases spine size. Moreover, these spines have a dense concentration of polymerized actin (Lin et al., 2005). Changes in spine size and stability are the result of many signaling cascades that orchestrate the polymerization and reorganization of actin filaments in spines and processes that enhance the binding of the pre and postsynaptic components of the synapse. This section reviews some of the initial signaling cascades that regulate actin dynamics and then discusses how cell adhesion molecules also contribute to stabilizing the trace.

## Parallel Signaling Cascades Regulate Actin Dynamics

That actin polymerization is critical to the stability of LTP became known when it was discovered that drugs that block actin polymerization, such as latrunculin or cytochalasin, also prevent the emergence of the lasting form of LTP without interfering with its induction (Kim and Lisman, 1999; Krucker et al., 2000). Moreover, within about 10 to 15 minutes following TBS, these drugs no longer disrupt LTP (Figure 4.10). Thus, processes involved in the regulation of actin polymerization and reorganization are central to initially stabilizing synapses that support LTP (Lynch et al., 2007).

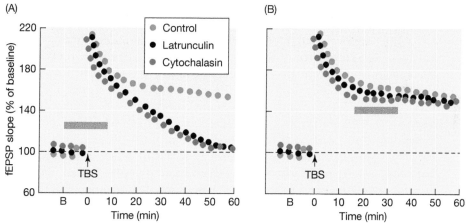

**Figure 4.10**
(A) When drugs such as latrunculin and cytochalasin that prevent actin polymerization are applied before TBS, they do not prevent the induction of LTP, but it rapidly decays. (B) LTP is maintained if these drugs are applied 15 minutes after LTP is induced. The bar represents the application of the drugs.

Signaling cascades that regulate actin dynamics to support LTP accomplish two goals: (1) they shear existing actin filaments into segments that can be repolymerized, and (2) they polymerize and reorganize new actin filaments into complexes that are resistant to depolymerization. Some key elements of these cascades are described below.

EXISTING ACTIN FILAMENTS ARE SHEARED INTO SEGMENTS   Ultimately, new strands of filament actin have to be polymerized to stabilize LTP. Normally actin monomers become available as cofilin depolymerizes existing tread-milling actin filaments. However, the depolymerization function of cofilin is inhibited during the stabilization phase (discussed in the next section). Although the normal role of cofilin is inhibited, additional processes associated with the activation of **myosin IIb**—a motor protein known to play a role in the regulation of neural growth cones (Medeiros et al., 2006)—can shear actin filaments into segments (Rex et al., 2010).

Myosin motor proteins are strongly associated with actin filaments. Actin filaments provide tracks along which these proteins move (Figure 4.11). Rather than removing actin monomers from the point of treadmilling actin filaments, as the myosin IIb motor protein moves it exerts a shearing force on long actin filaments, breaking them into smaller units that can then be reassembled elsewhere in the spine.

Myosin IIb is also activated by a TBS-induced, NMDA-dependent $Ca^{2+}$ signal cascade and has been clearly associated with stabilizing synapses (Rex et al., 2010). For example, inhibiting the activity of myosin IIb prevents the enduring form of LTP but has no effect on its induction. However, inhibiting myosin IIb 10 minutes after TBS has no effect on enduring LTP (see Figure 4.11). The temporal pattern of results associated with inhibiting myosin IIb are the same as those produced by preventing polymerization with the drug latrunculin, and both treatments reduce actin filament levels in spines (Rex et al., 2010).

NEW ACTIN FILAMENTS ARE POLYMERIZED AND REORGANIZED   NMDA-dependent $Ca^{2+}$ associated with theta-burst stimulation sequentially activates two pathways (described below) to polymerize new actin filaments and reorganize them to resist depolymerization. As noted earlier, the state of cofilin regulates actin polymerization and depolymerization and there is strong evidence that cofilin is involved in the regulation of actin dynamics that stabilize LTP:

- TBS greatly increases the number of spines that contain phosphory-lated cofilin (Chen et al., 2007; Rex et al., 2009).

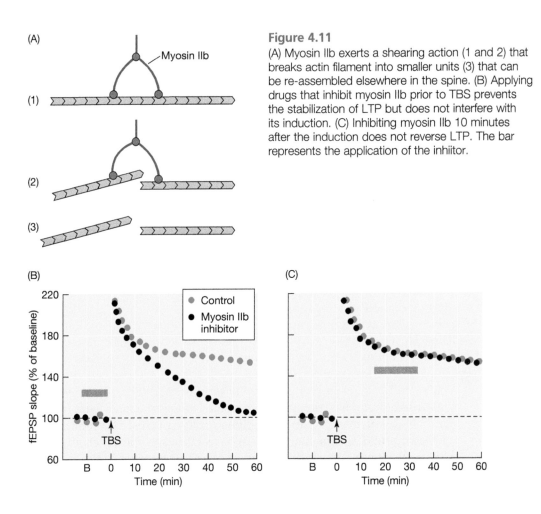

(A) Myosin IIb

(1)

(2)

(3)

**Figure 4.11**
(A) Myosin IIb exerts a shearing action (1 and 2) that breaks actin filament into smaller units (3) that can be re-assembled elsewhere in the spine. (B) Applying drugs that inhibit myosin IIb prior to TBS prevents the stabilization of LTP but does not interfere with its induction. (C) Inhibiting myosin IIb 10 minutes after the induction does not reverse LTP. The bar represents the application of the inhiitor.

(B)

fEPSP slope (% of baseline)

Control
Myosin IIb inhibitor

TBS

Time (min)

(C)

TBS

Time (min)

- The activation of the kinase **LIMK** is a proximal event that phosphorylates cofilin. Interfering with the signaling pathways that activate this kinase prevents the stabilization of LTP but not its induction (Chen et al., 2007; Rex et al., 2009).

Two pathways contribute to actin regulation (Figure 4.12). These pathways are made up of small proteins with enzymatic properties known as **GTPases**. The first GTPase pathway—the **Rho-Rock cascade**—phosphorylates LIMK and enables it to phosphorylate cofilin (Rex et al., 2009), which allows actin to polymerize. As expected, inhibiting this pathway prevents both actin polymerization and enduring LTP from emerging. The second GTPase pathway—the **Rac-PAK cascade**—activates processes that reorganize the actin cytoskeleton

**Figure 4.12**
Calcium entering the synapse through NMDA receptors activates two signaling cascades that regulate actin. Both pathways activate LIMK, a kinase that phosphorylates cofilin and allows actin polymerization. The second pathway, the Rac-PAK cascade, also activates processes that reorganize and crosslink actin filaments to make them resistant to depolymerization.

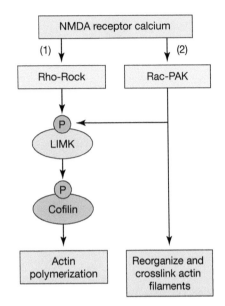

and crosslinking proteins that make the filament actin resistant to depolymerization. When its job is completed, events such as low-frequency electrical stimulation and depolymerization drugs such as latrunculin no longer disrupt LTP.

## Cell Adhesion Molecules Help Stabilize the Trace

The durability of LTP depends on processes that reorganize actin filaments into stable networks that resist depolymerization. As just discussed, many of these intracellular signaling cascades have a relatively direct effect on actin protein contained in dendritic spine regions. However, stabilization also depends on TBS activating cell adhesion molecules—proteins that are located on the cell surface and bind with other cells or with the extracellular matrix. Some of these molecules help cells stick to each other and their surrounds. Many classes of cell adhesion molecules have been identified in synapses (see McGeachie et al., 2011). The discussion below, however, will focus on only two classes—**neural cadherins** (abbreviated as **N-cadherins**) and **integrin receptors**. Both of these have been clearly linked to stabilizing LTP.

NEURAL CADHERINS  Synapses require the coupling of the presynaptic and postsynaptic components so that the postsynaptic component is positioned to respond to glutamate released from the presynaptic neuron. N-cadherins help to couple the pre and postsynaptic components. N-cadherins are calcium-dependent, cell adhesion molecules; they are strands of proteins held together by $Ca^{2+}$ ions. N-cadherins are anchored in the plasma membrane of both the presynaptic terminal and postsynaptic spine. They can exist as either

(A)

(B) (C)

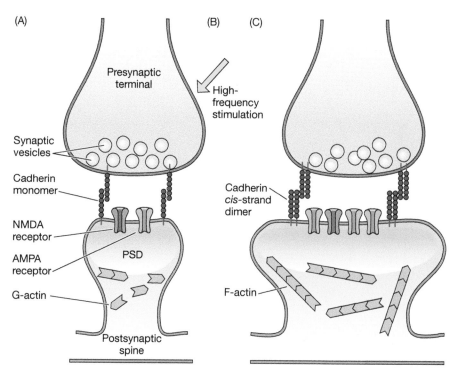

Presynaptic
terminal

High-
frequency
stimulation

Synaptic
vesicles

Cadherin
monomer

Cadherin
*cis*-strand
dimer

NMDA
receptor

AMPA
receptor

PSD

G-actin

F-actin

Postsynaptic
spine

**Figure 4.13**
N-cadherins are reorganized by an LTP-inducing stimulus. (A) Illustration of an unpotentiated synapse with the presynaptic terminal and postsynaptic spine weakly bonded by cadherin monomers. (B) A high-frequency stimulation is delivered to this synapse to induce LTP. (C) The high-frequency stimulus promotes cadherin dimerization so the now-enlarged spine containing additional AMPA receptors is tightly coupled to the presynaptic terminal and well positioned to receive glutamate released from the presynaptic terminal. (After Huntley et al., 2002.)

monomers or cis-stranded dimers (Figure 4.13). The monomer form is weakly adhesive but the cis-stranded or bonded dimers are strongly adhesive. Thus, when a dimer from the presynaptic domain contacts an identical dimer from the postsynaptic domain they form what is sometimes called an "adhesive zipper" that couples the two domains into a stable relationship (Huntley et al., 2002).

N-cadherin complexes respond to synaptic activity (Bozdagi et al., 2000). Several facts point to a critical role of N-cadherins in spine stability. First, TBS selectively promotes the formation of N-cadherin clusters in stimulated spines. This effect requires calcium to enter through NMDA receptors. Second, spines with N-Cadherin clusters are enlarged compared to those without

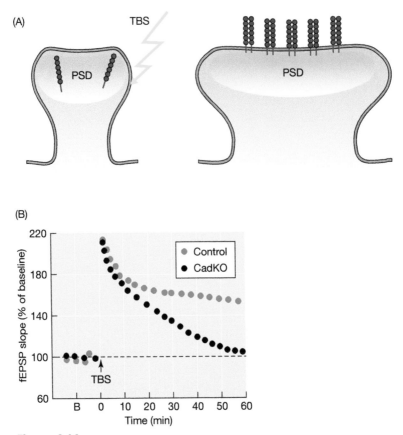

**Figure 4.14**
(A) Spines activated by TBS (lightning bolt) become larger and contain clusters of N-cadherins (Mendez et al., 2010). (B) TBS induces LTP in slices from mice genetically modified to knock out the gene for N-cadherins (CadKO). However, these spines cannot sustain LTP. (After Bozdagi et al., 2010.)

clusters. Third, N-cadherins are not required for the initial induction of LTP but they are critical to enduring LTP and for spines to maintain their size (Bozdagi et al., 2010; Mendez et al., 2010; see Figure 4.14).

N-cadherins are important because (a) they are indirectly anchored to actin filaments and could provide sites for capturing newly generated actin polymers (Honkura et al., 2008), and (b) the larger spines associated with LTP may have an expanded surface and require additional adhesion molecules to keep the pre and postsynaptic components tightly coupled (Murthy et al., 2001).

More tightly coupling the presynaptic and modified postsynaptic components of the synapse could ensure that glutamate released by the presynaptic neuron would be optimally received by receptors on dendritic spines. Thus, this alignment would help to increase the likelihood that the postsynaptic neuron would depolarize in response to a fixed amount of glutamate released by the presynaptic neuron. This coupling could also contribute to increasing the durability of the synapse (see Figure 4.14).

INTEGRIN RECEPTORS    **Integrins** are heterodimer cell adhesion molecules. They are formed from two different subunits called α and β. Integrin receptors respond to molecules in the extracellular space or matrix and to intercellular signals such as calcium (McGeachie et al., 2011). Integrins also are responsive to synaptic activity and regulate actin (Chun et al., 2001; Kramár et al., 2006; Shi and Ethell, 2006).

For integrins to contribute to the regulation of actin dynamics, synaptic activity must increase the contribution of these receptors. Although the precise mechanisms are not yet understood, there is evidence that intracellular integrin receptors can be trafficked into synaptic regions. Recall that the rapid trapping of GluA1 AMPA receptors in the PSD supports the early phase of LTP and that these receptors have special properties—they influx both calcium and sodium. Lin et al. (2005) provided evidence that calcium entering the spine through GluA1 receptors plays an important role in trafficking integrins into the synaptic region. Other sources of calcium (discussed in Chapter 6) might also be important for driving integrins into the synaptic region. However, the general point here is that calcium-dependent signaling cascades enhance the contribution of integrins by increasing their numbers in the synaptic membrane (Figure 4.15).

Integrins respond to ligands contained in the extracellular matrix. However, neutralizing the response of β integrins to these ligands prevents enduring LTP normally produced by TBS, but this has no effect on the initial induction phase (Figure 4.15). TBS that normally produces an enduring LTP also significantly increases the number of spines that contain filament actin. Interfering with the function of β integrins, however, also completely prevents actin filament formation. Kramár et al. (2006) speculated that integrins might participate in the reorganization of actin filaments by attaching crosslinking proteins such as spectrins that increase the resistance of actin filaments to depolymerization. However, there is also evidence that neutralizing β integrins reduces the presence of phosphorylated cofilin (Wang et al., 2008). So these integrins might also participate in the regulation of actin polymerization by activating LIMK, the kinase that phosphorylates cofilin.

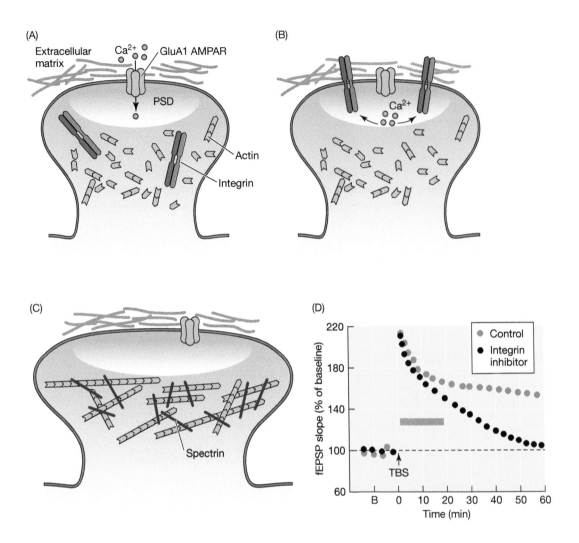

**Figure 4.15**
(A) Calcium enters the spine from GluA1 AMPA receptors. (B) Increased calcium levels traffic integrin receptors in the PSD region, where they bind to ligands in the extracellular matrix (ECM). (C) As a result of activation of the integrin receptors, actin filaments are reorganized to increase their resistance to depolymerization. (D) Inhibiting integrin receptors prevents the late phase of LTP but does not prevent induction. The bar represents the application of the drug.

## Summary

The induction of LTP is fast and depends on (a) the rapid disassembling of the actin cytoskeleton and (b) the trafficking and capturing of GluA1 receptors into the postsynaptic density. For a brief period of time following the induction of LTP the changes in the supporting synapses are unstable and vulnerable to disruption. However, over a relatively brief period—10 to 15 minutes—additional processes are recruited by the influx of calcium into the spine and they rebuild the actin cytoskeleton network by creating additional actin filaments in the spine, reorganizing them, crosslinking the filaments, and securing the pre and postsynaptic elements of the synapse. Although stability has been achieved, it is still relatively temporary.

## References

Barrionuevo, G., Schottler, S., and Lynch, G. (1980). The effects of repetitive low frequency stimulation on control and "potentiated" synaptic responses in the hippocampus. *Life Sciences, 27*, 2385–2391.

Boehm, J., Kang, M., Johnson, R. C., Esteban, J., Huganir, R. L., and Malinow, R. (2006). Synaptic incorporation of AMPA receptors during LTP is controlled by a PKC phosphorylation site on GluR1. *Neuron, 51*, 213–225.

Bozdagi, O., Shan, W., Tanaka, H., Benson, D. L., and Huntley, G. W. (2000). Increasing numbers of synaptic puncta during late-phase LTP: N-cadherin is synthesized, recruited to synaptic sites, and required for potentiation. *Neuron, 28*, 245–259.

Bozdagi, O., Wang, X., Nikitczuk, J. S., Anderson, T. R., Bloss, E. B., Radice, G. L., Benson, D. L., and Huntley, G. W. (2010). Persistence of coordinated long-term potentiation and dendritic spine enlargement at mature hippocampal CA1 synapses requires N-cadherin. *Journal of Neuroscience, 30*, 9984–9989.

Chen, L. Y., Rex, C. S., Casale, M. S., Gall, C. M., and Lynch, G. (2007). Changes in synaptic morphology accompany actin signaling during LTP. *Journal of Neuroscience, 27*, 5363–5372.

Chun, D., Gall, C. M., Bi, X., and Lynch, G. (2001). Evidence that integrins contribute to multiple stages in the consolidation of long-term potentiation. *Neuroscience, 105*, 815–829.

Derkach, V. A., Oh, M. C., Guire, E. S., and Soderling, T. R. (2007). Regulatory mechanisms of AMPA receptors in synaptic plasticity. *Nature Reviews Neuroscience, 8*, 8101–8113.

Gu, J., Lee, C. W., Fan, Y., Komlos, D., Tang, X., Sun, C., Yu, K., Hartzell, H. C., Chen, G., Bamburg, J. R., and Zheng, J. Q. (2010). ADF/cofilin-mediated actin dynamics regulate AMPA receptor trafficking during synaptic plasticity. *Nature Neuroscience, 13*, 1208–1216.

Holtmaat, A. and Svoboda, K. (2009). Experience-dependent structural synaptic plasticity in the mammalian brain. *Nature Reviews Neuroscience, 10*, 647–658.

Holtmaat, A. J., Trachtenberg, J. T., Wilbrecht, L., Shepherd, G. M., Zhang, X., Knott, G. W., and Svoboda, K. (2005). Transient and persistent dendritic spines in the neocortex in vivo. *Neuron, 20*, 279–291.

Honkura, N., Matsuzaki, M., Noguchi, J., Ellis-Davies, G. C., and Kasai, H. (2008). The subspine organization of actin fibers regulates the structure and plasticity of dendritic spines. *Neuron, 57*, 719–729.

Huntley, G. W., Gil, O., and Bozdagi, O. (2002). The cadherin family of cell adhesion molecules: multiple roles in synaptic plasticity. *Neuroscientist, 8*, 221–233.

Kim, C. H. and Lisman, J. E. (1999). A role of actin filament in synaptic transmission and long-term potentiation. *Journal of Neuroscience, 19*, 4314–4324.

Kramár, E. A., Lin, B., Rex, C. S., Gall, C. M., and Lynch, G. (2006). Integrin-driven actin polymerization consolidates long-term potentiation. *Proceedings of the National Academy of Sciences USA, 103* (14), 5579–5584.

Krucker, T., Siggins, G. R., and Halpain, S. (2000). Dynamic actin filaments are required for stable long-term potentiation (LTP) in area CA1 of the hippocampus. *Proceedings of the National Academy of Sciences USA, 6*, 6856–6681.

Larson, J., Xiao, P., and Lynch, G. (1993). Reversal of LTP by theta frequency stimulation. *Brain Research, 600*, 97–102.

Lin, B., Kramár, E. A., Bi, X., Brucher, F. A., Gall, C. M., and Lynch, G. (2005). Theta stimulation polymerizes actin in dendritic spines of hippocampus. *Journal of Neuroscience, 25*, 2062–2069.

Lynch, G. and Baudry, M. (1984). The biochemistry of memory: a new and specific hypothesis. *Science, 224*, 1057–1063.

Lynch, G., Halpain, S., and Baudry, M. (1982). Effects of high-frequency synaptic stimulation on glutamate receptor binding studied with a modified in vitro hippocampal slice preparation. *Brain Research, 244*, 101–111.

Lynch, G., Rex, C. S., and Gall, C. M. (2007). LTP consolidation: substrates, explanatory power, and functional significance. *Neuropharmacology, 52*, 12–23.

Matus, A. (2000). Actin-based plasticity in dendritic spines. *Science, 290*, 754–758.

McGeachie, A. B., Cingolani, L. A, and Goda, Y. (2011). Stabilizing influence: integrins in regulation of synaptic plasticity. *Neuroscience Research, 70*, 24–29.

Medeiros, N. A., Burnette, D. T., and Forscher, P. (2006). Myosin II functions in actin-bundle turnover in neuronal growth cones. *Nature Cell Biology, 8*, 215–226.

Mendez, P., DeRoo, M., Poglia, L., Klauser, P., and Muller, D. (2010). N-cadherin mediates plasticity-induced long-term spine stabilization. *Journal of Cell Biology, 189*, 589–600.

Murthy V. N., Schikorski, T., Stevens C. F., and Zhu, Y. (2001). Inactivity produces increases in neurotransmitter release and synapse size. *Neuron, 32*, 673–682.

Opazo, P., Labrecque, S., Tigaret, C. M., Frouin, A., Wiseman, P. W., De Koninck, P., and Choquet, D. (2010). CaMKII triggers the diffusional trapping of surface AMPARs through phosphorylation of stargazin. *Neuron, 67*, 239–252.

Ouyang, Y., Wong, M., Capani, F., Rensing, N., Lee, C. S., Liu, Q., Neusch, C., Martone, M. E., Wu, J. Y., Yamada, K., Ellisman, M. H., and Choi, D. W. (2005). Transient decrease in F-actin may be necessary for translocation of proteins into dendritic spines. *European Journal of Neuroscience, 22*, 2995–3005.

Petrini, E. M., Lu, J., Cognet, L., Lounis, B., Ehlers, M. D., and Choquet, D. (2009). Endocytic trafficking and recycling maintain a pool of mobile surface AMPA receptors required for synaptic potentiation. *Neuron, 63*, 92–105.

Rex, C. S., Chen, L. Y., Sharma, A., Liu, J., Babayan, A. H., Gall, C. M., and Lynch, G. (2009). Different Rho GTPase-dependent signaling pathways initiate sequential steps in the consolidation of long-term potentiation. *Journal of Cell Biology, 186*, 85–97.

Rex, C. S., Gavin, C. F., Rubio, M. D., Kramár, E., and Rumbaugh, G. (2010). Myosin IIb regulates actin dynamics during synaptic plasticity and memory formation. *Neuron, 67*, 603–617.

Shi, Y. and Ethell, I. M. (2006). Integrins control dendritic spine plasticity in hippocampal neurons through NMDA receptor and $Ca^{2+}$–calmodulin-dependent protein kinase II-mediated actin reorganization. *Journal of Neuroscience, 26* (6), 1813–1822.

Simon, R., Baudry, M., and Lynch, G. (1984). Brain fodrin: substrate for calpain I, an endogenous calcium-activated protease. *Proceedings of the National Academy of Sciences USA, 81*, 3572–3576.

Staubli, U. and Chun, D. (1996). Factors regulating the reversibility of long-term potentiation. *Journal of Neuroscience, 16*, 853–860.

Wang, X. B., Bozdagi, O., Nikitczuk, J. S., Zhai, Z. W., Zhou, Q., and Huntley, G. W. (2008). Extracellular proteolysis by matrix metalloproteinase-9 drives dendritic spine enlargement and long-term potentiation coordinately. *Proceedings of the National Academy of Sciences USA, 105*, 19520–19525.

Zhou, Q. and Poo, M. M. (2005). Reversal and consolidation of activity-induced synaptic modifications. *Trends in Neuroscience, 27*, 378–383.

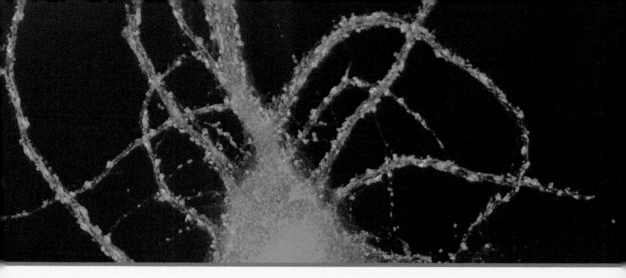

# 5 Consolidating Synaptic Changes: Translation and Transcription

During the initial 10 to 15 minutes after the delivery of the LTP-inducing stimulus, the entry of calcium into the spine engages many signaling cascades that deliver more AMPA receptors into the PSD and orchestrate the rearrangement of actin filaments to broaden the spine head. These signaling cascades modify and rearrange proteins that were already present in the synaptic region. As a consequence, the established LTP becomes resistant to disruption by treatments such as low-frequency stimulation and drugs that prevent polymerization. Nevertheless, there is pressure on strengthened synapses to revert back to their pre-potentiated state. Thus, to ensure that the initial changes endure (consolidate), *new material must be generated*.

Chapter 3 references three sets of molecular processes that contribute to the durability of LTP—post-translation processes, transcription processes, and translation processes—noting that post-translation processes involve only the modification and rearrangement of *existing* protein. The goal of this chapter is to provide an introduction to the two processes that are recruited to generate the *new* material needed for consolidation—**translation** (also known as **protein synthesis**) and **transcription**. Two general hypotheses—*de novo* **protein synthesis** and **genomic signaling**—are described, including a discussion of **local protein synthesis**. Focus then shifts to understanding how synaptic activity initiates transcription, and two signaling models are introduced: (1) the **synapse-to-nucleus** and (2) the **soma-to-nucleus**. The chapter concludes with a discussion of the different sources of calcium and how they determine the duration of LTP.

## The *De Novo* Protein Synthesis Hypothesis

As previously established, post-translation modifications and rearrangement of existing proteins are responsible for the synaptic changes that initially support LTP; however, if these synaptic changes are to resist the pressure to return to their original unpotentiated state, then the inducing stimulus must also initiate translation processes to generate new protein. This view is sometimes referred to as the *de novo* protein synthesis hypothesis.

The idea that enduring long-term memories require synaptic activity to generate new protein emerged over 50 years ago (Roberts and Flexner, 1969). The importance of new protein to enduring LTP was recognized when it was discovered that protein synthesis inhibitors (such as anisomycin) block the development of a long-lasting LTP or **L-LTP** (for example, Frey et al., 1988; Krug et al., 1984). This general finding, illustrated in Figure 5.1, makes the

**Figure 5.1**

A weak high-frequency stimulus (HFS) induces a short-lasting LTP (S-LTP), whereas a strong HFS produces a long-lasting LTP (L-LTP). However, pretreatment (bar) with anisomycin, a protein synthesis inhibitor, prevents the strong stimulus from producing L-LTP but leaves the early-phase, short-lasting component intact. This result indicates that S-LTP produced by the weak stimulus depends only on post-translation modifications and rearrangements of existing protein, but the consolidation of the synaptic changes that support L-LTP requires new protein.

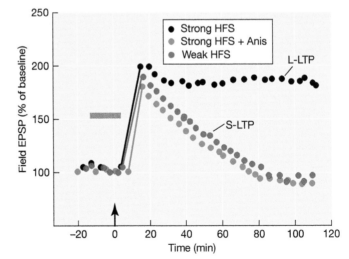

**Figure 5.2**
Long-lasting LTP depends on parallel effects of the LTP-inducing stimulus. It initiates both local translation and genomic signaling cascades (synapse-to-nucleus and soma-to-nucleus signals) that transcribe new mRNA that can then be translated.

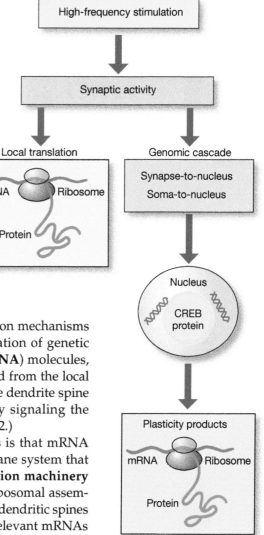

point that when protein synthesis is prevented, the resulting LTP produced by intense, high-frequency stimulation resembles the short-lasting LTP (**S-LTP**) produced by a weak-induction stimulus—the synapses revert back to their original state. Thus, the implication of these results is that enduring synaptic change (**consolidation**) depends on the generation of new protein.

The generation of new protein depends on mechanisms that initiate protein synthesis—the translation of genetic material, **messenger ribonucleic acid (mRNA)** molecules, into protein. New protein can (a) be derived from the local translation of mRNAs already present in the dendrite spine region or (b) result from synaptic activity signaling the genome to transcribe new mRNA (Figure 5.2.)

The standard view of protein synthesis is that mRNA is translated as it passes through a membrane system that surrounds the nucleus. However, **translation machinery** (endoplasmic reticulum, Golgi elements, ribosomal assemblies) is also present locally in the vicinity of dendritic spines (Steward and Schuman, 2001). Moreover, relevant mRNAs are also distributed within the dendrite as well as the cell body of the neuron or soma (Miyashiro et al., 1994). They include mRNAs for proteins that are needed to induce LTP, such as CaMKII and AMPA receptors (Figure 5.3). The presence of translation machinery and mRNA in the local dendritic region suggests the possibility that proteins are translated locally from already existing mRNA (local protein synthesis).

Two research strategies have revealed that local protein synthesis plays an important role in the consolidation of

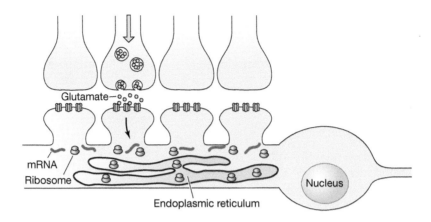

**Figure 5.3**
Messenger RNA and protein translation machinery, such as endoplasmic reticulum (ER) and ribosomes, are present locally in the dendritic spine region. Synaptic activity can activate this machinery and translate this mRNA.

synaptic changes (Sutton and Schuman, 2006). The first involves separating dendrites in the CA1 region of the hippocampus from their cell bodies, making it impossible for proteins that have been newly synthesized in the soma from a genomic cascade to influence synaptic strength (Figure 5.4). Studies with this preparation have observed LTP dependent on protein synthesis (see Kang and Schuman, 1996; Vickers et al., 2005).

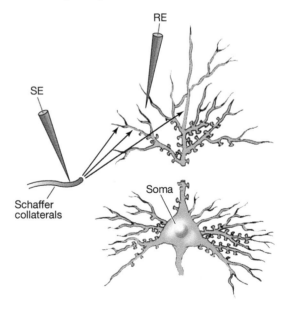

**Figure 5.4**
In this preparation, the dendritic field is surgically separated from the soma. This prevents the delivery to the stimulated synapses of new proteins that were the product of a genomic signaling cascade. Nevertheless, stimulation delivered to the Schaffer collateral fibers can produce a relatively long-lasting LTP. SE = stimulating electrode; RE = recording electrode.

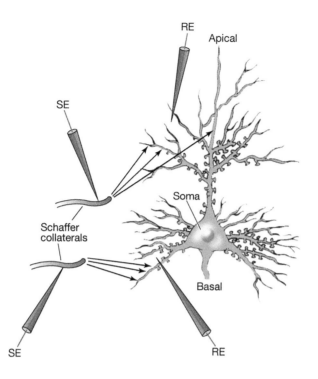

**Figure 5.5**
This figure illustrates the methodology Bradshaw et al. (2003) used to demonstrate the contribution dendritic protein synthesis makes to L-LTP. By stimulating one set of Schaffer collateral fibers they could produce L-LTP in synapses located on dendrites in the apical region of the neuron. By stimulating another set of Schaffer collaterals they could produce L-LTP in synapses located on dendrites in the basal region of the neuron. When the protein synthesis inhibitory emetine was applied to the entire slice, it prevented L-LTP in both dendritic fields. However, when emetine was applied to just the apical dendrites, it blocked L-LTP only in those dendrites, and when applied to just the basal dendrites, it blocked L-LTP only in the basal dendrites. It did not block L-LTP in either region of the dendrites when it was applied to just the soma. These results mean that L-LTP depended on proteins that were translated in the dendrites in response to the LTP-inducing stimulus. SE = stimulating electrode; RE = recording electrode.

The second strategy involves applying protein synthesis inhibitors selectively to the cell bodies and dendritic fields of CA1 pyramidal cells. Bradshaw et al. (2003) took advantage of the fact that pyramidal neurons in this region have both apical and basal dendrites and receive input from different Schaffer collateral fibers (Figure 5.5). Applying the protein synthesis inhibitor emetine selectively to the soma of these cells did not influence L-LTP. In contrast, the application of emetine to the apical dendrites blocked L-LTP in those dendrites but did not block L-LTP in the basal dendrites, while selectively applying emetine to the basal dendrites blocked L-LTP in those dendrites but did not affect L-LTP in the apical dendrites. The observation that a dose of emetine selectively delivered to the soma did not influence L-LTP but did so when delivered to the dendritic fields strongly implicates a role for local protein synthesis in the generation of long-lasting LTP.

## The Genomic Signaling Hypothesis

Not all mRNAs required for producing L-LTP are present locally. They become available later because synaptic activity and neuronal depolarization generate a genomic signaling cascade that results in the transcription of new mRNA. In this case the signaling molecules enter the nucleus to phosphorylate **transcription factors**—proteins that interact with DNA to produce mRNA. This results in the production of mRNAs that subsequently are translated into new proteins (see Figure 5.2).

All parts and functions of a cell depend on ongoing, constitutive transcription and translation processes. The distinguishing feature of the genomic signaling hypothesis is that it assumes that transcripts (mRNA) needed to sustain LTP are produced as a direct consequence of neural activity associated with the stimulus that induces LTP. The new mRNA and protein generated as a result of this neural activity are sometimes called **plasticity products** (**PPs**) because they are involved in changing synapses.

The genomic signaling hypothesis gained support when Nguyen et al. (1994) reported that inhibitors of transcription blocked the development of enduring LTP, but did not interfere with its initial development and stabilization. The hypothesis that L-LTP depends on transcription also gained more specificity when it became known that a transcription factor called cAMP-responsive, element-binding (**CREB**) protein was implicated in both synaptic plasticity and long-term memory (see Figure 5.2 and Nguyen and Woo, 2003; Silva et al., 1998; and Yin and Tully, 1996, for reviews).

It is important to know how CREB protein is activated. Adams and Dudek (2005) have described two general models of how the signals reach the nucleus: synapse-to-nucleus signaling and soma-to-nucleus signaling (Figure 5.6).

### Synapse-to-Nucleus Signaling

The synapse-to-nucleus signaling model is complex. However, the general outline of the process is relatively simple. The stimulation of a postsynaptic neuron first activates second messengers that then activate protein kinases.

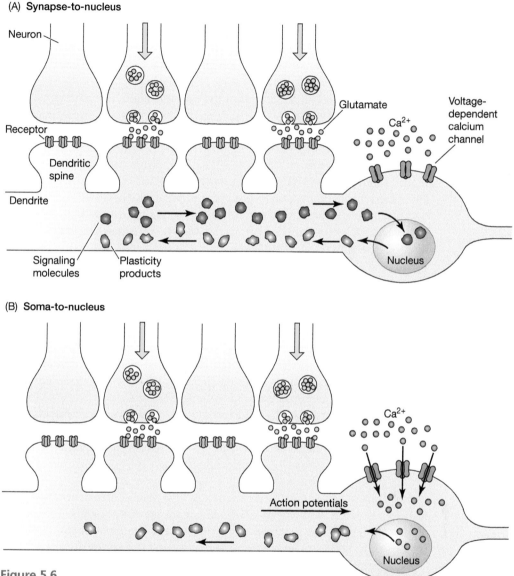

**(A) Synapse-to-nucleus**

Neuron

Glutamate

Ca²⁺

Voltage-dependent calcium channel

Receptor

Dendritic spine

Dendrite

Signaling molecules

Plasticity products

Nucleus

**(B) Soma-to-nucleus**

Ca²⁺

Action potentials

Nucleus

**Figure 5.6**
Synaptic activity can signal the nucleus in two ways. (A) The synapse-to-nucleus signaling model assumes that synaptic activity initiates a cascade that produces signaling molecules that eventually translocate to the nucleus to initiate transcription. (B) The soma-to-nucleus signaling model assumes that, as a result of action potentials produced by synaptic activity, Ca²⁺ enters the soma through voltage-dependent calcium channels (vdCCs) where it can more directly initiate transcription. Note that both of these hypotheses could be true.

Second messengers or their kinase targets translocate into the nucleus where they phosphorylate CREB protein and transcription is initiated. There are multiple intracellular pathways that converge to phosphorylate CREB protein (Figure 5.7). This convergence suggests that CREB protein activation will reflect the combined influence of several sources.

There is no need to discuss all of the possible signaling pathways. However, it is instructive to describe some key ones. One such signaling cascade also involves the activation of PKA. When activated by the second messenger **cAMP**, PKA can translocate to the nucleus to phosphorylate CREB protein and initiate transcription. Moreover, PKA inhibitors can block the development of long-lasting LTP, and this is accompanied by a reduction in genes controlled by CREB protein (Nguygen and Woo, 2003).

Another signaling cascade involves the activation of the kinase complex **ERK–MAPK** (extracellular-regulated kinase–mitogen-activated protein kinase). The activation of this signaling pathway is initiated by **neurotrophic factors**. Neurotrophins are a family of molecules that promote survival of neural tissues and play a critical role in neural development and differentiation. These factors bind to a class of plasma membrane receptors in the tyrosine kinase family called **Trk receptors**.

When activated, both PKA and ERK–MAPK are thought to translocate to the nucleus where they engage transcription factors, including CREB protein, and induce transcription of plasticity-related mRNAs. Stimulation that leads to the induction of long-lasting LTP induces the transcription of CREB-dependent mRNAs. Inhibitors of PKA and ERK–MAPK activation block the transcription of these mRNAs. Moreover, inhibitors of these kinases also block the development of enduring LTP.

## Soma-to-Nucleus Signaling

According to the soma-to-nucleus signaling model, the action potentials produced when a cell depolarizes also can generate a signal. Repetitive action potentials are assumed to open **voltage-dependent calcium channels** (vdCCs) that are located on the plasma membrane of the soma. When these channels open, calcium enters the soma. **Calmodulin** already exists in the nucleus. Thus, when activated by $Ca^{2+}$ it could induce the activation of nuclear enzymes such as CaMKIV that can phosphorylate CREB protein. Activated calmodulin outside of the nucleus also might translocate to the nucleus. This source of $Ca^{2+}$ might also stimulate ERK to translocate to the nucleus to participate in the phosphorylation of CREB protein.

Two arguments support an action-potential, soma-to-nucleus model (Adams and Dudek, 2005). First, the amount of signal generated at single

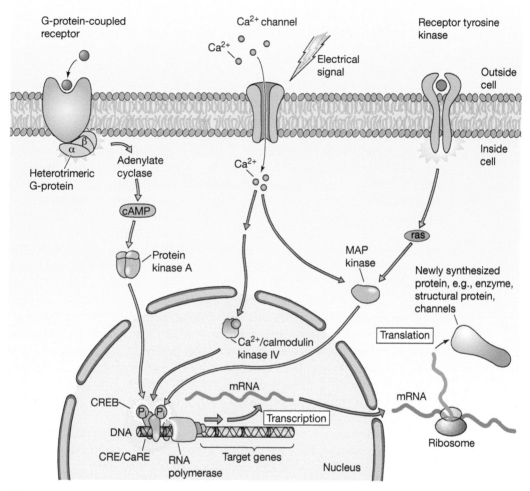

**Figure 5.7**
Transcription occurs in the nucleus where a portion of DNA (deoxyribonucleic acid) is converted into RNA (ribonucleic acid). Transcription then is the transfer of information contained in DNA into mRNA. Ribosomes translate mRNA into protein. This is also called protein synthesis. There are many synapse-to-nucleus signaling pathways that can lead to the phosphorylation of CREB protein and to the production of new mRNA and new proteins that are critical for L-LTP.

synapses that reaches the nucleus may not be enough to initiate transcription. Second, signaling molecules activated by synaptic processes have a long journey to reach the nucleus. So, the time it takes for them to translocate to the nucleus may be too long to allow them to participate in the immediate transcription of genes needed to support L-LTP.

There also is experimental support for the soma-to-nucleus model. A strong prediction from this model is that soma-to-nucleus signaling can substitute for synapse-to-nucleus signaling to produce L-LTP. Dudek and Fields (2002) provided support for this prediction. Recall that a weak stimulus protocol will generate only S-LTP but that a strong stimulus will generate L-LTP (see previous Figure 5.1). A strong stimulus also is likely to produce the action potentials needed to open the calcium channels.

Dudek and Fields reasoned that if action potentials are the critical event for L-LTP, then it should be possible to convert S-LTP into L-LTP by initiating action potentials without strongly stimulating synapses. To do this they weakly stimulated Schaffer collateral input to CA1 neurons and then initiated action potentials in the CA1 cells antidromically (by stimulating from axon to soma in these cells). These action potentials were sufficient to prevent the decay of LTP normally produced by weak stimulation. The action potentials alone also were sufficient to phosphorylate ERK and CREB protein (Figure 5.8).

*A caveat*: Transcription factors such as CREB are proteins. Although they target specific genes for transcription, their activation is the result of post-translation modifications. For example, for CREB protein to be activated, kinases must phosphorylate two sites on this protein.

## Translating Protein Requires Increased Calcium Levels

The above discussion indicates that new protein becomes available in two waves. The initial wave is the result of local synthesis and the second is the result of protein translated from mRNA generated by the genomic signal (Figure 5.9). It is important to note that increased calcium levels are required for both waves.

Calcium entering the neuron through NMDA receptors is critical for the production of LTP but this source of calcium alone may not be sufficient to produce any form of LTP (Morgan and Teyler, 1999; Raymond and Redman, 2006; Sabatini et al., 2001). To mount the signaling cascades needed to produce long-lasting synaptic changes, calcium provided by NMDA receptors needs to be amplified by different sources of $Ca^{2+}$. Thus, it is important to understand the different sources of calcium and some of the complexities associated with their regulation of synaptic activity.

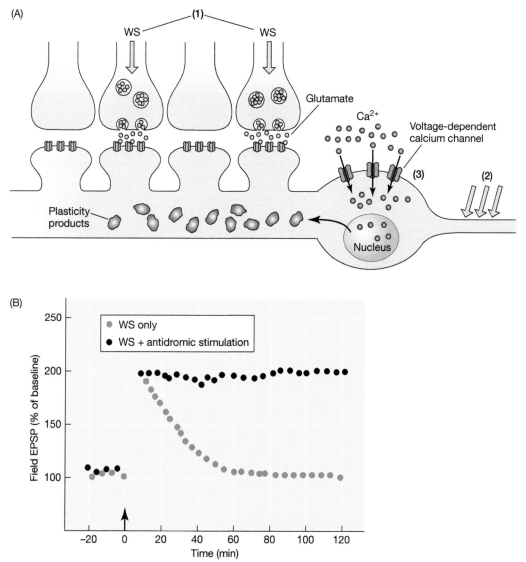

**Figure 5.8**

(A) This figure illustrates how Dudek and Fields (2002) tested the soma-to-nucleus signaling hypotheses. They applied a weak stimulus (WS) to the Schaffer collateral fiber pathway (1). In some slices this was followed by electrical stimulation applied to the axons (called antidromic stimulation) of the CA1 pyramidal cells (2) to produce action potentials in those neurons and allow the influx of $Ca^{2+}$ into the soma and nucleus (3). (B) This figure shows that weak stimulation produced only a short-lasting LTP, but when it was followed by antidromic stimulation L-LTP was induced.

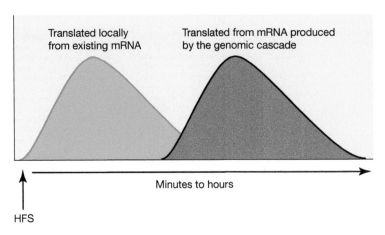

**Figure 5.9**
Strong high-frequency stimulation (HFS) can result in two waves of protein synthesis that may be important for L-LTP. The first wave occurs locally in the dendrites. The second wave occurs when new protein is synthesized from the new mRNA produced by the genomic sigaling cascade. These proteins could be subsequently synthesized in either the soma or dendritic regions.

## Extracellular and Intracellular Sources of Calcium

Two sources of calcium, one extracellular and one intracellular, can influence the induction and duration of LTP (Figure 5.10) (see Baker et al., 2013 for a review). Calcium is contained in the *extracellular* fluid that surrounds the neuron. It can enter the cell through activated NMDA receptors and through

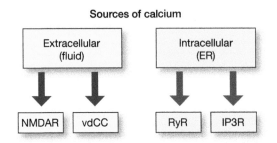

**Figure 5.10**
There are two general sources of calcium that influence LTP. One source is the $Ca^{2+}$ in the extracellular fluid surrounding the neuron. This $Ca^{2+}$ enters the dendritic spines through NMDA receptors and enters the soma through vdCCs. The other calcium source is intracellular. $Ca^{2+}$ is stored in the ER. It can be released when it binds to the RyRs located on the ER in the spine or when IP3 binds to IP3Rs located on the ER in the dendrite.

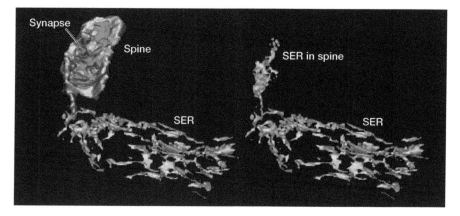

**Figure 5.11**

This figure presents a three-dimensional reconstruction of the endoplasmic reticulum (purple) in a rat hippocampal CA1 dendritic segment. The membrane of the dendrite is not visible, but in the left side of the figure the membrane of the attached spine is present. Note that the ER in the dendrite is contiguous with the ER entering the thin neck of a large dendritic spine (gray). (From *Synapse Web*, Kristen M. Harris, PI, http://synapses.clm.utexas.edu/.) Berridge (1998) has called the ER the "neuron within the neuron" because it is contiguous with the neuron and responds to signaling molecules.

the voltage-dependent calcium channels located on the plasma membrane that surrounds the soma. The vdCCs open and close in response to the depolarizing stimulation associated with action potentials. When they are open, they allow extracellular $Ca^{2+}$ to enter the neuron, thus producing a transient increase in intracellular $Ca^{2+}$ in the soma.

*Intracellular* $Ca^{2+}$ resides in the neuron, stored in what is called the smooth endoplasmic reticulum (ER). For some time, the ER has been recognized as important to $Ca^{2+}$ signaling (Berridge, 1998). The ER network extends continuously throughout the neuron (Droz et al., 1975; Terasaki et al., 1994), even extending into the dendritic spines (Figure 5.11). Because it is continuous within the neuron and responds to signaling events in the cytosol, Berridge (1998) characterized the ER network as the neuron within the neuron. He has proposed that these two membranes, the plasma membrane and the ER, work together to regulate many neuronal processes such as transmitter release, synaptic plasticity, and gene regulation. The ER is important in the context of synaptic plasticity because (1) it is a calcium sink that can rapidly sequester or store free $Ca^{2+}$, and (2) it is a calcium source that can release $Ca^{2+}$ in response to second messengers.

To understand how these different calcium sources influence the processes that support LTP it is useful to think of the neuron as composed of three

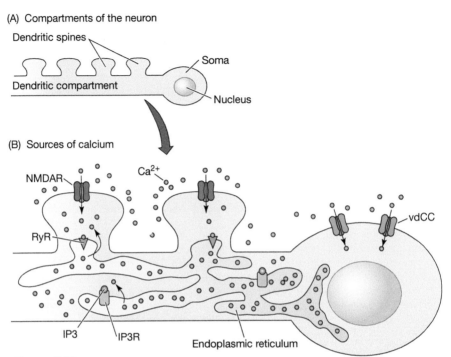

(A) Compartments of the neuron

Dendritic spines

Soma

Dendritic compartment

Nucleus

(B) Sources of calcium

NMDAR

Ca²⁺

vdCC

RyR

IP3

IP3R

Endoplasmic reticulum

**Figure 5.12**
(A) A neuron consists of three compartments: the soma, the dendritic compartment, and dendritic spines. (B) Calcium is present in the extracellular fluid as well as stored intracellularly in the ER. $Ca^{2+}$ levels can increase in each of the three distinct compartments of the neuron. Extracellular $Ca^{2+}$ can enter a dendritic spine through NMDA receptors and can enter the soma through vdCCs. Intracellular $Ca^{2+}$ stored on the ER can be released into dendritic spines when $Ca^{2+}$ binds to RyRs located in dendritic spines or can be released into the dendritic compartment when IP3 binds to IP3Rs.

distinct compartments: (a) dendritic spines, (b) dendritic compartment, and (c) soma or cell body (Figure 5.12).

DENDRITIC SPINE   NMDA receptors are located on the plasma membrane of the dendritic spine compartment, and the ER that protrudes into the spine contains **ryanodine receptors (RyRs)**, which bind to calcium. This spatial proximity of NMDA receptors and RyRs provides the opportunity for what is called **calcium-induced calcium release (CICR)**. It occurs when a small amount of extracellular $Ca^{2+}$ enters through the NMDA receptor and binds to RyRs to release additional $Ca^{2+}$ from the ER (Berridge, 1998). This process—the binding of calcium to RyRs—provides a way to amplify the extracellular

$Ca^{2+}$ entering the spine compartment through NMDA receptors and triggers some of the post-translation modifications (discussed in Chapter 4) that are necessary to induce LTP.

DENDRITIC COMPARTMENT    Endoplasmic reticulum in the dendritic compartment is populated with inositol triphosphate receptors (**IP3Rs**), which respond to the second messenger **IP3**. This second messenger is synthesized when the first messenger glutamate binds to a subtype of **metabotropic receptor** called **mGluR1**, located in the plasma membrane near dendritic spines. In contrast to ionotropic receptors, metabotropic receptors do not form an ion channel pore. Instead, they activate **G-proteins**, which may either alter the opening of a G-protein-gated ion channel or stimulate an effector enzyme that either synthesizes or breaks down a second messenger (Figure 5.13). When second messenger IP3 binds to IP3Rs, calcium is released from the ER in the dendritic compartment. This increase in calcium in the dendritic compartment contributes to the local translation that produces the first wave of new protein.

SOMA COMPARTMENT    The plasma membrane surrounding the soma is populated with vdCCs, and extracellular calcium can enter the soma when action potentials open these channels. As noted above, calcium entering through these channels provides a way to rapidly initiate transcription (see soma-to-nucleus hypothesis) and new mRNA that ultimately is translated to yield the second wave of new protein.

## Recruiting Multiple Calcium Sources Increases LTP Duration

The number of theta-burst stimulation (TBS) trains controls the duration of LTP (see previous Figure 3.10). A single TBS train produces a short-lasting form, LTP1; four trains produce a moderately lasting form, LTP2; and eight trains produce a very long-lasting form, LTP3. Research by Raymond and Redman (2002, 2006) has revealed that the duration of LTP depends on the number of calcium sources recruited by TBS.

- LTP1 depends only on RyRs releasing ER calcium in the dendritic spine compartment.
- LTP2 depends on IP3Rs releasing calcium from the ER in the dendritic compartment.
- LTP 3 depends on calcium entering the soma through vdCCs.

The general point of these observations is that as the number of TBS trains increases, more calcium sources are engaged and they activate transcription and translation processes that increase the stability and consolidation

(A)

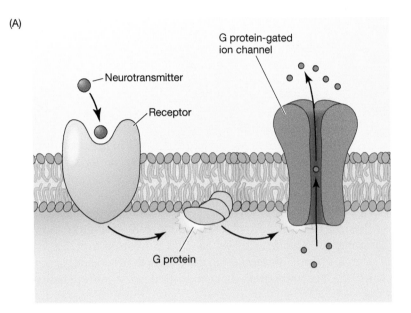

(B)

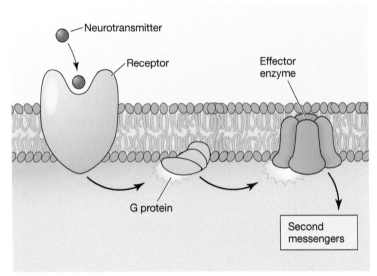

**Figure 5.13**
Metabotropic receptors activate G proteins in the plasma membrane, which may either alter the opening of a G-protein-gated ion channel (A) or stimulate an effector enzyme that either synthesizes or breaks down a second messenger (B).

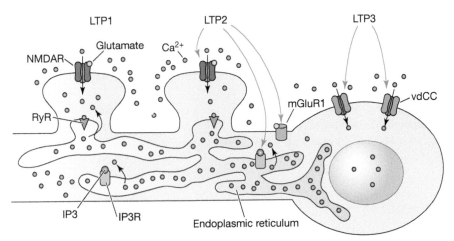

**Figure 5.14**
This figure illustrates how different sources of $Ca^{2+}$ contribute to different forms of LTP. LTP1 is induced when glutamate produced by a weak stimulus (1-train TBS) binds to the NMDA receptor (NMDAR). This results in a modest influx of $Ca^{2+}$ into the spine. Acting as a second messenger, $Ca^{2+}$ binds to the RyRs and causes the ER to release additional $Ca^{2+}$ into the spine. LTP2 is induced when glutamate resulting from stronger stimulation (4-train TBS) binds both to NMDA receptors and to mGluR1s and results in local protein synthesis. LTP3 is produced when the strongest stimulation (8-train TBS) repeatedly opens the vdCCs, and the level of $Ca^{2+}$ in the soma is increased to the point where it can translocate to the nucleus to initiate transcription of genes necessary for the expression of LTP3.

of synaptic changes that support LTP. A summary of how calcium sources influence the induction and persistence of LTP is provided in Figure 5.14.

## Summary

For the initially stabilized synaptic changes to be consolidated, the induction stimulus must be sufficient to activate processes that will generate new proteins. Translation machinery is located in the dendritic spine regions and there is evidence that synaptic activity can induce the synthesis of new proteins from mRNA available in this region. New proteins can also be generated by genomic signaling cascades (synapse-to-nucleus and soma-to-nucleus) that activate transcription factors, such as CREB, to produce mRNA that can then be translated into proteins. To engage translation and transcription processes requires that the induction stimulus recruit multiple sources of calcium. Calcium sources localized to the spine compartment (the CICR cascade) only support short-lasting LTP. Longer-lasting forms of LTP require (a) IP3 to release calcium from the ER in the dendritic compartment and (b) extracellular calcium to enter the soma through vdCCs.

These ideas are important but they leave unanswered questions: What are the special proteins that are translated as a consequence of these signaling processes? And what do they do? These questions will be addressed in the next two chapters.

## References

Adams, J. P. and Dudek, S. M. (2005). Late-phase long-term potentiation: getting to the nucleus. *Nature Reviews Neuroscience, 6*, 737–743.

Baker, K. D., Edwards, T. M., and Rickard, N. S. (2013). Intracellular calcium stores in synaptic plasticity and memory consolidation. *Neuroscience and Biobehavioral Reviews, 37*, 1211–1239.

Berridge, M. J. (1998). Neuronal calcium signaling. *Neuron, 21*, 13–26.

Bradshaw, K. D., Emptage, N. J., and Bliss, T. V. P. (2003). A role for dendritic protein synthesis in hippocampal late LTP. *European Journal of Neuroscience, 18*, 3150–3152.

Droz, B., Rambourt, A., and Koenig, H. L. (1975). The smooth endoplasmic reticulum: structure and role in the renewal of axonal membrane and synaptic vesicles by fast axonal transport. *Brain Research, 93*, 1–13.

Dudek, S. M. and Fields, R. D. (2002). Somatic action potentials are sufficient for late-phase LTP-related cell signaling. *Proceedings of the National Academy of Sciences USA, 99*, 3962–3967.

Frey, U., Krug, M., Reymann, K. G., and Matthies, H. (1988). Anisomycin, an inhibitor of protein synthesis, blocks late phases of LTP phenomena in the hippocampal CA1 region in vitro. *Brain Research, 14*, 135–139.

Kang, H. and Schuman, E. M. (1996). A requirement for local protein synthesis in neurotrophin-induced hippocampal synaptic plasticity. *Science, 273*, 1402–1406.

Krug, M., Lössner, B., and Ott, T. (1984). Anisomycin blocks the late phase of long-term potentiation in the dentate gyrus of freely moving rats. *Brain Research Bulletin, 13*, 39–42.

Miyashiro, K., Dichter, M., and Eberwine, J. (1994). On the nature and differential distribution of mRNAs in hippocampal neurites: implications for neuronal functioning. *Proceedings of the National Academy of Sciences USA, 91*, 10800–10804.

Morgan, S. L. and Teyler, T. J. (1999). VDCCs and NMDARs underlie two forms of LTP in CA1 hippocampus in vivo. *Journal of Neurophysiology, 82*, 736–740.

Nguyen, P. V., Abel, T., and Kandel, E. R. (1994). Requirement of a critical period of transcription for induction of a late phase of LTP. *Science, 265*, 1104–1107.

Nguyen, P. V. and Woo, N. H. (2003). Regulation of hippocampal synaptic plasticity by cyclic AMP-dependent protein kinases. *Progress in Neurobiology, 71,* 401–437.

Raymond, C. R. and Redman, S. J. (2002). Different calcium sources are narrowly tuned to the induction of different forms of LTP. *Journal of Neurophysiology, 88,* 249–255.

Raymond, C. R. and Redman, S. J. (2006). Spatial segregation of neuronal calcium signals encodes different forms of LTP in rat hippocampus. *Journal of Physiology, 570,* 97–111.

Roberts, R. B. and Flexner, L. B. (1969). The biochemical basis of long-term memory. *Quarterly Review of Biophysics, 2,* 135–173.

Sabatini, B. L., Maravall, M., and Svoboda, K. (2001). $Ca^{2+}$ signaling in dendritic spines. *Current Opinion Neurobiology, 11,* 349–356.

Silva, A. J., Giese, K. P., Fedorov, N. B., Frankland, P. W., and Kogan, J. H. (1998). Molecular, cellular, and neuroanatomical substrates of place learning. *Neurobiology of Learning and Memory, 70,* 44–61.

Steward, O. and Schuman, E. M. (2001). Protein synthesis at synaptic sites on dendrites. *Annual Review of Neuroscience, 24,* 299–325.

Sutton, M. A. and Schuman, E. M. (2006). Dendritic protein synthesis, synaptic plasticity, and memory. *Cell, 127,* 49–58.

Terasaki, M., Slater, N. T., Fein, A., Schmidek, A., and Reese, T. S. (1994). Continuous network of endoplasmic reticulum in cerebellar Purkinje neurons. *Proceedings of the National Academy of Sciences USA, 91,* 7510–7514.

Vickers, C. A., Dickson, K. S., and Wyllie, D. J. (2005). Induction and maintenance of late-phase long-term potentiation in isolated dendrites of rat hippocampal CA1 pyramidal neurons. *Journal of Physiology, 568,* 803–813.

Yin, J. and Tully, T. (1996). CREB and the formation of long-term memory. *Current Opinion in Neurobiology, 2,* 264–268.

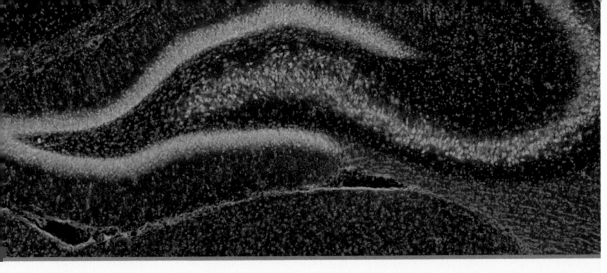

# 6 Consolidating Synaptic Changes: Specific Mechanisms

New protein is needed to consolidate the synaptic changes that support long-lasting LTP. The preceding chapter described research results that link the source of new protein to (a) processes that translate mRNA present locally, (b) the activation of transcription factors by genomic signaling cascades, and (c) the recruitment of multiple calcium sources. This chapter addresses the more detailed questions of (a) what signaling processes are engaged by synaptic activity to initiate local translation, (b) what key new proteins are synthesized, (c) what these new proteins do, and (d) how they find their targets. An important conclusion is that, just as it is critical to the induction and stabilization phases of LTP, the regulation of actin dynamics is also critical to the consolidation stage. Thus, this chapter also discusses the complexities of actin regulation and how real-time images of single synapses have provided insights into these processes. Finally, the role of protein degradation processes in the various stages of LTP is explained.

## Activation of Local Protein Synthesis

The translation of mRNA into protein is complex and tightly regulated (Steward, 2007; Sutton and Schuman, 2005). Normally, the local translation machinery required for new protein is inhibited, and the mRNA that has been transported from the nucleus to the dendrites is packaged to ensure that it is not inadvertently translated along the way. Local synthesis begins when translation machinery in the dendritic spine region is activated. This process, in part, involves the regulation of a class of mRNAs located in the dendritic spine region called **TOP** (terminal oligopyrimidine tracts) mRNAs. For present purposes, it is sufficient to understand that TOP mRNAs encode for proteins such as ribosomal proteins and elongation factors that are part of the translation machinery. Note that proteins encoded by TOP mRNAs themselves do not have specific synaptic functions. They are part of the translation machinery needed to synthesize other proteins that play a more specific role. Thus, when synthesized these proteins *enhance translation capacity* in the region where they are translated (Tsokas et al., 2005, 2007).

### The mTOR–TOP Pathway

The synthesis of TOP mRNAs is regulated by an important kinase called **mTOR** (mammalian target of rapamycin). Exactly how this happens is still a mystery (Thoreen et al., 2012). However, there is little doubt that the activation of the **mTOR–TOP pathway** is critical for synaptic changes supporting LTP to endure. Erin Schuman and her colleagues (Tang et al., 2002) were the first to report this result. Their study showed that rapamycin—a drug that prevents the activation of mTOR—selectively impairs the late phase of LTP without influencing the initial induction. Other laboratories have linked this impaired LTP to the failure of synaptic activity to translate TOP mRNA (Tsokas et al., 2005; 2007). These findings (Figure 6.1) indicate that lasting forms of LTP depend on signaling cascades that activate the mTOR pathway.

### The BDNF–TrkB Receptor Pathway

Synaptic activity that generates lasting LTP produces an increase in the extracellular concentration of the neurotrophin **BDNF** (brain-derived neurotrophic factor) in the region of activity that lasts for about 10 minutes (Aicardi et al., 2004; Patterson et al., 1992). Two facts suggest that BDNF plays a critical role in activating the mTOR–TOP pathway. First, a significant body of research indicates that BDNF is critical to the development of long-lasting LTP (Korte et al.,

Erin Schuman

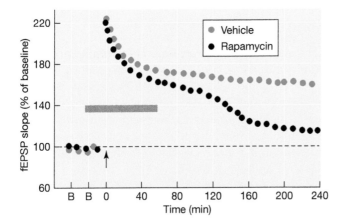

**Figure 6.1**
Application of rapamycin (represented by the bar), which blocks the activation of mTOR kinase, prevents the very late-phase LTP but does not prevent the induction or stabilization phase. The bar represents application of the inhibitor.

1995, 1998). Second, interfering with BDNF signaling prevents the translation of TOP mRNA (Bramham and Messaoudi, 2005; Tang et al., 2002).

BDNF is synthesized, stored, and released from the same neurons that release glutamate (Lessmann et al., 2003), but it can also be released from dendrites. Thus, the exact source of extracellular BDNF in the hippocampus is difficult determine. However, Jia et al. (2010) provided a strong case for presynaptic BDNF release in LTP found in another region of the brain, the striatum. They speculated that the *co-release of glutamate and BDNF from axon terminals might be a ubiquitous requirement for enduring LTP* (Figure 6.2).

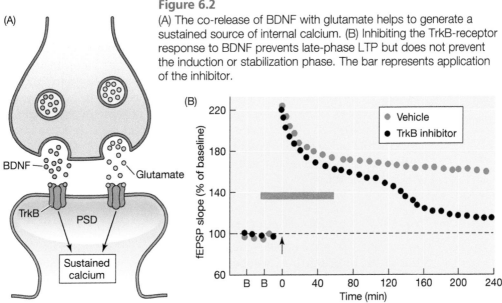

**Figure 6.2**
(A) The co-release of BDNF with glutamate helps to generate a sustained source of internal calcium. (B) Inhibiting the TrkB-receptor response to BDNF prevents late-phase LTP but does not prevent the induction or stabilization phase. The bar represents application of the inhibitor.

The effects of BNDF are mediated by a subset of tyrosine kinase receptors, called **TrkB receptors**. These receptors, co-localized with NMDA receptors in the PSD, have catalytic properties when activated. The binding of BDNF released from presynaptic neurons to TrkB receptors is associated with the additional release of BNDF from the postsynaptic cell. This results in a positive feedback loop that helps sustain BDNF in the local extracellular region. This sustained presence of BDNF promotes the recruitment of intracellular calcium sources (Berninger et al., 1993; Li et al., 1998) and BDNF's contribution to consolidation is prevented in neurons in which these calcium stores have been depleted (Kang and Schuman, 2000).

Pharmacological treatments that prevent BDNF activating TrkB receptors prevent the translation of TOP mRNAs and development of long-lasting LTP (Kang and Schumann, 1996). Thus, it is generally believed that **BDNF–TrkB receptor pathway** signaling is needed to activate the mTOR–TOP system to up-regulate the translation capacity in the local region of synaptic activity (Bramham and Messaoudie, 2005).

## Synthesis of a Key New Protein: Arc

Clive Bramham

The up-regulation of local protein synthesis machinery is a first step toward consolidation of LTP that is dependent on protein synthesis. *But what important new functional–structural proteins does this now active translation machinery synthesize?* Clive Bramham and his colleagues have made a strong case that one such protein is **Arc** (activity-regulated, cytoskeleton-associated protein), also known as Arg3.1 (for example, Bramham, 2008; Bramham et al., 2010; Bramham and Messaoudie, 2005).

Arc is an immediate early gene—a gene that is transcribed rapidly in response to strong synaptic activity because its transcription does not require the prior translation of some other protein. Arc mRNA is quickly transported precisely to the regions of synaptic activity that initiated the transcription signal (Dynes and Steward, 2012). Arc mRNA thus becomes available in local regions at the time the local translation machinery is active.

### Arc Antisense Blocks Long-Lasting LTP

John Guzowski and his colleagues (2000) were the first to identify a contribution of Arc protein to the consolidation of LTP. They used an **antisense** oligonucleotide (a synthesized strand of nucleic acid that will bind to mRNA and

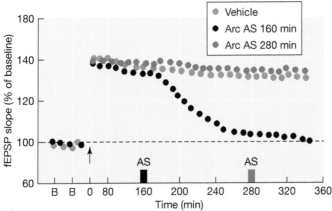

**Figure 6.3**
Arc antisense (AS) reverses a well established LTP when applied about 160 minutes after the inducing stimulus but not when applied 280 minutes later. This indicates that the synaptic changes have been consolidated by 280 minutes. (After Messoudie et al., 2007.)

prevent its translation) to prevent the translation of Arc mRNA into protein. Blocking the translation of Arc mRNA had no effect on the induction of LTP but prevented it from enduring. Consistent with the idea that Arc protein is required for the consolidation of LTP, Messaoudie et al. (2007) reported that Arc antisense rapidly reverses LTP when applied up to 160 minutes, but not when applied 280 minutes, after the induction (Figure 6.3). Thus, it appears that consolidation requires a sustained contribution of Arc translation for several hours following the induction signal. A caveat that may be important is that Messaoudie et al. (2007) measured LTP in the dentate gyrus in living animals.

## BDNF-TrkB Consolidation Depends on Arc

As previously described, the BDNF–TrkB pathway is critical for consolidating the synaptic changes supporting LTP. In fact, applying exogenous BDNF to brain tissue will produce a long-lasting LTP similar to that produced by multiple TBS (for example, Messaoudi et al., 2007). This effect, however, depends on the synthesis of Arc protein because applying antisense to Arc eliminates BDNF-induced potentiation (Figure 6.4). This finding thus potentially links the BDNF→TrkB→mTOR→TOP signaling cascade to the synthesis of Arc and to consolidating synaptic changes that support potentiated synapses. However, BDNF together with NMDA-dependent calcium also activates **ERK**

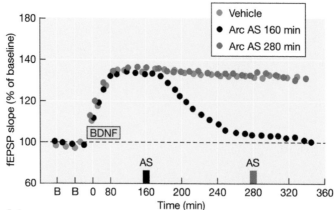

**Figure 6.4**
BDNF alone potentiates synapses. This effect of BDNF depends on the translation of Arc because Arc antisense (AS) reverses this potentiation when applied 160 minutes after BDNF. Arc antisense does not reverse potentiation when applied 280 minutes after BDNF. This indicates that the synaptic changes have been consolidated 280 minutes after BDNF was applied. (After Messoudie et al., 2007.)

(extracellular-regulated kinase), which is also critical for the transcription of Arc mRNA. Thus, the dependency of BDNF-induced LTP on Arc expression also reflects the importance of BDNF to the transcription of Arc mRNA (Bramham et al., 2010).

### Arc Sustains Actin Regulation

Arc protein is a key contributor to consolidating the synaptic changes supporting LTP. Preventing its synthesis within 160 minutes following LTP reverses LTP. This result is associated with two other outcomes. In the absence of Arc protein there is (a) a large reduction in phosphorylated cofilin and (b) a corresponding large loss of new actin filaments (Messaoudie et al., 2007). Thus, the regulation of actin dynamics by phosphorylating cofilin that was initiated almost immediately by the induction stimulus must be sustained for several hours for synaptic changes to be consolidated. Moreover, these processes may depend on the continued transcription and translation of Arc.

## Confirming the Role of Actin Regulation

The regulation of actin dynamics is critical at every stage of LTP—from induction through stabilization and consolidation. Disrupting actin regulation at any stage is fatal to the potentiated synapses. Studies using single-spine imagery have made a significant contribution to confirming the critical role of actin regulation in consolidation of LTP, including the identification of distinct actin pools.

## Contribution of Single-Spine Imaging Studies

Harou Kasai

Harou Kasai's laboratory (Honkura et al., 2008; Matsuzaki et al., 2004; Tanaka et al., 2008) captured images of single spines and how treatments known to potentiate synapses modify actin filaments and spine growth. To do this they labeled actin with a fluorescent protein so that it could be visualized by two-photon, photo activation of the protein. To modify a single spine they released caged glutamate precisely onto that spine. In some experiments (Tanaka et al., 2008) the release of glutamate was accompanied by electrical stimulation of the neuron (a spike-time protocol). In other experiments glutamate was released without spike timing. The change in spine size volume was measured for 60 minutes. These real-time experiments revealed that many of the same processes and functional changes observed or inferred from conventional LTP preparations can be observed in a single spine.

The release of glutamate coupled with spike timing initiated an almost immediate increase in spine volume that continued for about 20 minutes, and this change was sustained for the duration of the experiment (60 minutes). In contrast, the release of glutamate without spike timing produced an initial change in spine volume, but this growth period was truncated and within about a minute spine volume began to return to its pre-stimulated size. Growth associated with either glutamate alone or the combination of glutamate and spike timing was blocked by the application of the NMDA receptor antagonist APV (Figure 6.5). These results indicate that the sustained modification of spine size depends on calcium provided by the NMDA receptors and perhaps by increases in internal calcium provided by the spike-timing protocol.

Other experiments revealed that protein synthesis inhibitors, such as anisomycin, had no effect on initial spine growth but truncated the growth period and its maintenance. In effect, spines in these experiments behaved as if they received only glutamate. Thus, spike timing sustains the growth of spines by initiating processes involved in translation and transcription or both.

A critical role for BNDF in sustaining the growth and maintenance of stimulated spines was also demonstrated. Specifically, inhibiting the TrkB

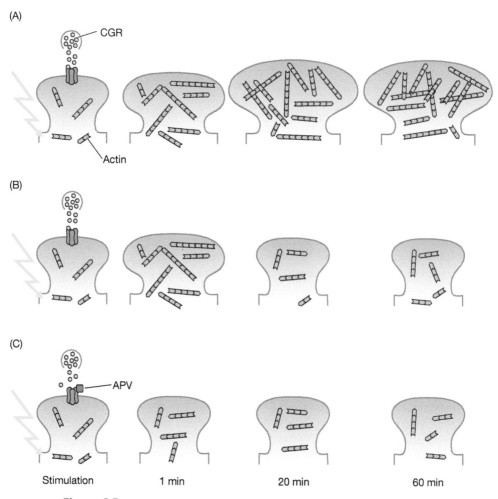

**Figure 6.5**
(A) The release of caged glutamate (CGR) coupled with spike-timed stimulation (lightning bolt) initiates actin polymerization and consequent spine growth that continues for about 20 minutes and persists for the duration of the experiment (60 minutes). (B) Release of caged glutamate alone initiates a brief growth in spine, but this growth is not sustained. (C) The NMDA receptor antagonist APV prevents the changes in actin polymerization and spine growth produced by the glutamate release.

receptor prevented the sustained growth of spines that experienced both glutamate release and spike timing but had no effect on the initial change (Figure 6.6). This result indicated that the spike-timing protocol released endogenous BDNF into the extracellular space where it could bind to the TrkB receptor and contribute to the sustaining spine changes, perhaps by activating

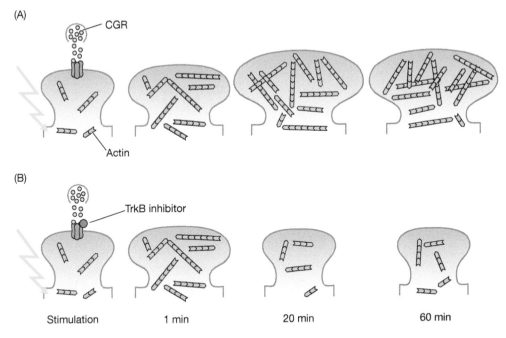

**Figure 6.6**
(A) Release of caged glutamate, coupled with a spike-time protocol, produces sustained growth and maintenance of a single spine. (B) Inhibiting the TrkB response to BDNF prevents sustained growth and maintenance. This result indicates that this protocol releases BDNF into the extracellular space.

Arc transcription factors. However, BDNF's effect on spine enlargement also depended on translation of mRNA into protein because inhibiting protein synthesis also prevented the effects of BDNF.

This remarkable set of experiments confirm at the level of a single spine that a calcium increase in just the spine compartment can initiate but cannot sustain the changes in spine growth that would be needed to support LTP. Sustained change requires additional translation and transcription processes that involve other compartments of the neuron.

## Distinct Actin Pools Regulate Spine Growth

Kasai's laboratory (Honkura et al., 2008) also has used this methodology to provide some insights into why actin dynamics are regulated over a long time period. By imaging actin in spines at rest or spines activated by uncaged glutamate, Kasai's group have identified three pools of actin: (a) a dynamic

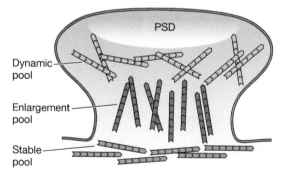

**Figure 6.7**
Three pools of actin have been identified: (1) a dynamic pool, (2) an enlargement pool, and (3) a stable pool. (After Honkura et al., 2009.)

pool that is located in the spine head near the PSD, (b) a stable pool that is located at the base of the spine in the vicinity of the spine neck, and (c) an enlargement pool (Figure 6.7) that is observed by releasing caged glutamate onto the spine.

There is rapid turnover of actin filaments in the dynamic pool compared to the stable pool, and actin in these two pools tends to not overlap. In contrast, nascent actin filaments in the enlargement pool are polymerized as they become distributed throughout the spine. The presence of separate pools of actin filaments offer some clues as to why actin has to be regulated at different time points. Recall that the initial induction of LTP requires a rapid disassembling of actin filaments followed by rapid reassembling in order to initially trap new AMPA receptors. These first steps likely involve regulation of the dynamic actin pool in the spine head. The continued growth of the spine head then occurs as a result of mechanical forces generated by the nascent actin from the enlargement pool as it distributes throughout the spine.

One of the remarkable observations by Honkura et al. (2008) was that actin filaments provided by the enlargement pool rapidly vacate the spine through the spine neck and the spine returns to its original size. Functionally, this would mean that changes in synaptic strength would be lost. These researchers speculate that confinement of the enlargement pool requires processes that aggregate or crosslink actin fibers there so as to prevent the enlargement pool from escaping through the narrow and rigid spine neck. These processes are known to depend on CaMKII (Matsuzaki et al., 2004).

Nevertheless, even under optimal conditions the enlargement actin pool will slowly exit the spine in about 15 minutes. So unless other processes are activated to continue to reinforce actin polymerization, the actin scaffold will collapse and synaptic changes will be lost. It is possible that it is the continuing source of actin polymerization provided by the BDNF→TrkB receptor→Arc pathway that is needed for the spine to retain its newly acquired actin filaments. This final consolidation phase also likely involves the crosslinking of filament actin with spectrins that help trap the new actin filaments in the spine.

## Targeting Plasticity Products

Arc's role in consolidating synaptic changes raises an important general question. Newly transcribed Arc mRNAs are transported from the nucleus selectively to dendritic regions containing the spines that were stimulated to initiate the transcription. *How do mRNAs transcribed in response to synaptic activity find their way to the correct synapses?* Julietta Frey and Richard Morris (1998) addressed this question and proposed what is now called the **synaptic tag and capture hypothesis**. The basic ideas in their proposal are illustrated in Figure 6.8 and in the following explanation.

Julietta Frey

1. Synaptic activity that potentiates synapses has two general effects: (a) it can generate a synaptic tag, which will allow the stimulated spine to subsequently capture newly transcribed plasticity molecules such as Arc, and (b) it can engage the translation and transcription machinery to generate new plasticity products (PPs).

2. Relatively weak stimulation (such as that needed to produce a short-lasting LTP) can create synaptic tags but will not engage the translation and transcription machinery.

3. Relatively strong stimulation will create synaptic tags and also engage the translation and transcription machinery.

4. Newly generated PPs can be captured by any tagged synapses but untagged synapses are not eligible to receive new PPs.

5. Over time, synapses will lose their tag and return to their initial state.

6. Over time, the supply of new PPs will deplete.

7. To capture the PPs, the tags and new PPs must overlap in time.

This hypothesis makes an important prediction: weakly stimulated synapses can capture PPs that were generated by strongly stimulating other synapses belonging to the same neuron. This is because the tags generated by weak stimulation makes these synapses eligible to capture new PPs, even though these synapses did not participate in generating the new PPs (Frey

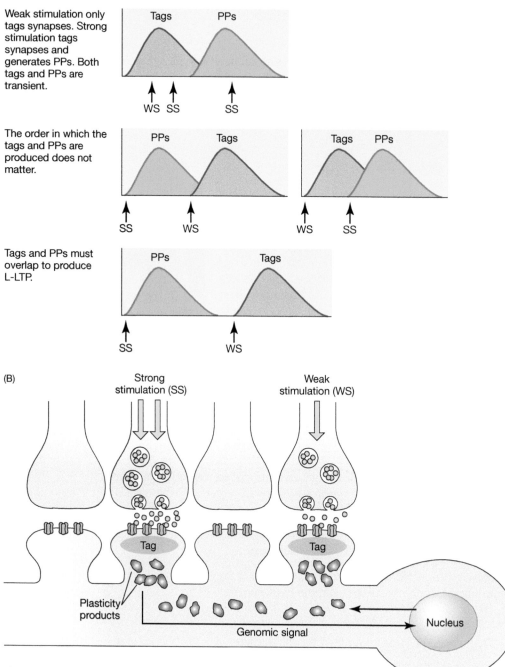

**Figure 6.8**

(A) The synaptic tag and capture hypothesis is based on three assumptions. (B) A strong stimulus (SS) both tags a synapse and generates a genomic signaling cascade that leads to transcription and translation of proteins (plasticity products or PPs) used to support L-LTP. The function of the tag is to capture the protein. A weak stimulus (WS) will not generate a genomic signaling cascade. However, it can tag synapses and these synapses capture PPs produced by a strong stimulus providing the timing is correct. Note that untagged synapses do not capture PPs.

and Morris, 1998). This important prediction has received experimental support (Figure 6.9).

The synaptic tag and capture hypothesis raises an important question: *what is the molecular basis of the synaptic tag?* The fate of synaptic changes that

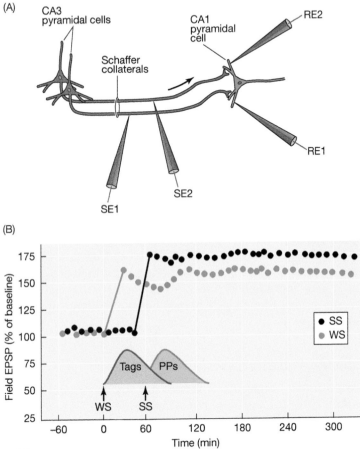

**Figure 6.9**
(A) This schematic illustrates the procedure Frey and Morris (1997, 1998) used to test the synaptic tag and capture hypothesis. It shows that separate sets of Schaffer collateral fibers can synapse on dendrites belonging to the same CA1 neurons. Stimulating electrodes (SE1 and SE2) can generate field EPSPs in the dendritic fields that can be recorded by the extracellular recording electrodes (RE1 and RE2). By controlling the intensity of the stimulation delivered by the stimulating electrodes, it is possible to generate either a short-lasting or long-lasting LTP on synapses belonging to the same neuron. (B) A weak stimulus (WS) that normally would produce a short-lasting LTP will produce a long-lasting LTP if a strong stimulus (SS) is delivered to synapses belonging to the same neuron. Theoretically, this happens because the synaptic tags produced by the weak stimulus will capture plasticity products (PPs) generated by the strong stimulus.

support LTP depends on the extensive regulation of actin filaments and the structural changes in the dendritic spines it supports. Thus, it is reasonable to suppose that changes in functional and structural properties of spines that depend on actin filaments are a major component of the tagging operation. Given the importance of actin regulation to LTP, it is not surprising that Redondo and Morris (2010) suggested that the reconfiguration of the cytoskeleton is a crucial component of the tag. They also proposed that the tag should be considered a state of the synapse and not a product of a single molecule or the state of a particular molecule.

## Protein Degradation and LTP

For more than 50 years the idea that consolidation depends on the synthesis of new proteins has been central to the thinking about how synapse memories are consolidated. However, it is now clear that a complementary set of processes *that degrade existing protein* is just as important to LTP as the synthesis of new protein (Bingol et al., 2010; Cajigas et al., 2010; Fonseca et al., 2006; Hegde, 2010). The contribution of protein degradation processes to LTP is addressed in this section, beginning with an explanation of the ubiquitin proteasome system and its contribution to the initial and later stages of LTP. The implication of these findings is discussed and placed in the context of viewing the neuron as composed of a set of distinct compartments in which the system serves different functions that may be regulated by different sources of calcium.

### The Ubiquitin Proteasome System

There are a number of specific processes devoted to protein degradation (Bingol et al., 2010; Tai and Schuman, 2008). However, it is the **ubiquitin proteasome system** (**UPS**) that is most important to the regulation of synaptic plasticity. The signaling cascades that regulate this system are complex (for example, Hegde, 2010) but the general operating principles are easily understood (Figure 6.10).

The system is composed of small proteins called ubiquitin and larger protein complexes called proteasomes. Ubiquitin identifies proteins that need to be degraded. A process called **ubiquitination** accomplishes this goal. It begins when post-translation modifications bond a single ubiquitin molecule to a protein. Additional ubiquitin molecules then can be added, and this process yields a **polyubiquitin chain** (Tai and Schuman, 2008). Proteins tagged with a polyubiquitin chain are directed to proteasomes for degradation.

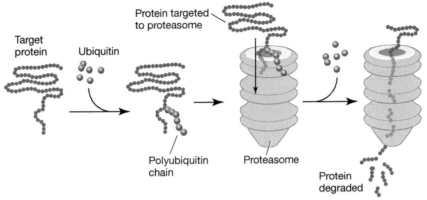

**Figure 6.10**
This figure illustrates the general principles of the UPS. Post-translation modifications bond a ubiquitin molecule to a protein (ubiquitination). A polyubiquitin chain marks the protein for delivery to the proteasome and protein degradation.

The general importance of the UPS was recognized in the award of the 2004 Nobel Prize in Chemistry to Aron Ciechanover, Avran Hershko, and Irwin Rose. Ashok Hegde was the first to discover a role for the UPS system in synaptic plasticity (Hegde et al., 1993). Contemporary researchers have revealed that protein degradation regulates several stages of LTP.

Components of the UPS are localized in dendrites, synapses (Ehlers, 2003; Patrick et al., 2003), and the nucleus. Glutamate transmission activates the ubiquitination processes (Bingol and Schuman, 2006; Ehlers, 2003; Guo and Wang, 2007) and the activation of CaMKII plays a critical role in recruiting proteasome into dendritic spines (Bingol et al., 2010). Moreover, stimulation that induces LTP activates this system and results in protein degradation (Ehlers, 2003; Karpova et al., 2006; Lee et al., 2008).

To study the UPS pathway researchers apply drugs such as β-lactone and epoxomycin that inhibit or prevent proteasomes from degrading protein. Under these conditions, even if it is tagged with ubiquitin, protein will not be degraded. If a proteasome inhibitor alters a functional outcome (such as enhancing the duration of LTP), it would be concluded that the normal function depends on the UPS degrading protein.

## Protein Degradation Influences Three Phases of LTP

The preceding chapters established that synaptic changes that support LTP evolve in several stages: (a) an early stage that involves only post-translation

Ashok Hegde

modifications, (b) a later stage that depends on local protein synthesis in dendritic-spine regions, and (c) a second wave of proteins synthesized from new mRNA that is a product of genomic signaling cascades. Hegde and his colleagues have shown that the UPS contributes to the regulation of each stage (Dong et al., 2008).

INHIBITING THE UPS ENHANCES EARLY PHASE LTP   A weak stimulus protocol normally produces a short-lasting LTP that does not require protein synthesis. If the UPS is inhibited the resulting LTP is enhanced (Figure 6.11). However, this form of LTP does not endure and returns to a basal state in about 30 minutes.

Given this result, one should conclude that protein degradation is designed to limit initial potentiation. The early induction phase depends only on post-translation process. Thus, it is likely that existing proteins localized in dendritic spines are degraded. One might speculate that the UPS normally degrades GluA1 AMPA receptors, since reducing their number would downregulate potentiated synapses (Burbea et al., 2002; Turrigiano, 2002). Other targets might be scaffolding proteins (for example, Shank and GKAP) located in the PSD. If key scaffolding proteins are lost, then support for the postsynaptic density protein PSD-95, which provides docking sights for GluA1 receptors, would collapse and the synapses would de-potentiate (Ehlers, 2003).

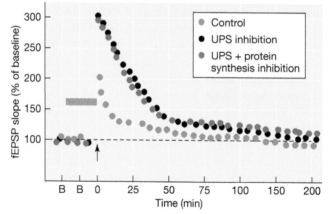

**Figure 6.11**
Inhibiting the UPS enhances the initial induction of LTP produced by a weak induction stimulus. Note that this enhancement occurred even when protein synthesis was also blocked. The bar represents delivery of the proteasome inhibitor or its vehicle. This result indicates that the UPS normally degrades already existing proteins during the initial induction of LTP.

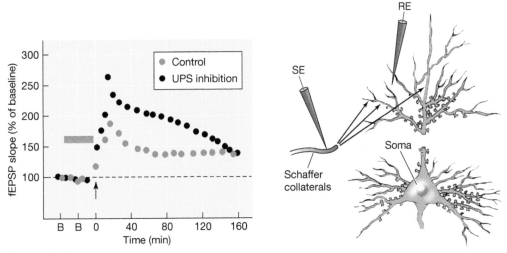

**Figure 6.12**
Inhibiting the UPS in the isolated dendritic field preparation enhances LTP supported locally by the translation of new protein from mRNA already in the dendritic-spine region. The bar represents delivery of the proteasome inhibitor or its control vehicle. These results indicate that the UPS system normally degrades some of these locally synthesized new proteins.

**INHIBITING THE UPS ENHANCES LTP THAT DEPENDS ON LOCAL PROTEIN SYN-THESIS**    Synaptic changes that support LTP also depend on protein synthesis occurring locally in the dendritic-spine region. Recall that support for this claim comes from a slice preparation in which dendritic fields are isolated from the cell body and thus from the influence of transcription processes. An LTP depending on protein synthesis can be generated in isolated dendrites (Vickers et al., 2005). Blocking the UPS enhances the expression of LTP observed for about an hour when this preparation is employed (Figure 6.12). This enhanced expression is also observed when transcription is inhibited in an intact preparation. However, if protein synthesis is inhibited in conjunction with inhibiting the UPS, this enhancement is markedly reduced.

These results suggest that protein degradation processes operating in the dendritic-spine region also are designed to limit potentiation (Dong et al., 2008). To be more specific, recall that activation of the mTOR pathway initiates the synthesis of proteins that facilitate the local translation of other proteins. The fact that inhibiting the UPS enhances LTP supported by local protein synthesis in isolated dendrites suggests that under normal conditions newly synthesized proteins are over-expressed and must be down-regulated. These new proteins could be glutamate receptor subunits, scaffolding proteins such as Shank or GKAP, or kinases such as CaMKII (Dong et al., 2008; Guo and Wang, 2007).

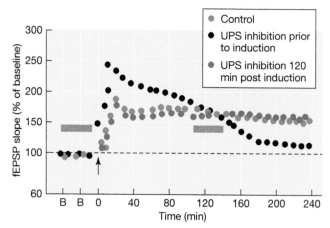

**Figure 6.13**

Inhibiting the UPS prior to induction enhances the early phases of LTP but prevents LTP from enduring. However, inhibiting the UPS 120 minutes after induction does not prevent LTP from enduring. These results suggest that the late enduring phase of LTP requires the degradation of proteins that repress the transcription processes. The bars indicate when the UPS inhibitor was applied.

INHIBITING THE UPS PREVENTS THE LATE ENDURING PHASE OF LTP   To generate an enduring LTP requires a strong inducing stimulus. Although UPS inhibition enhances the early phases of LTP, paradoxically it prevents LTP from enduring (Figure 6.13). However, the contribution of the UPS to the late-lasting phase is temporally limited: inhibiting the UPS 120 minutes after the induction stimulus does not reverse established LTP.

One explanation for this finding involves a class of proteins called **transcription repressor proteins** that normally interfere with transcription. These proteins must be degraded for transcription to occur (Dong et al., 2008). Thus, the late enduring phase of LTP may be impaired because inhibiting the UPS prevents the degradation of transcription repressor proteins and consequently the availability of critical plasticity proteins needed to support enduring LTP. In support of this idea, Dong and his colleagues (2008) reported that a protein that represses CREB-mediated transcription (ATF4) is degraded during LTP and that inhibiting the UPS prevents degradation of this repressor protein.

## Compartment-Specific Protein Degradation

Chapter 5 suggested that to understand how calcium regulates LTP it was important to view the neuron as organized into a set of specialized compartments—the spine, dendrite and soma. This view also is also useful for

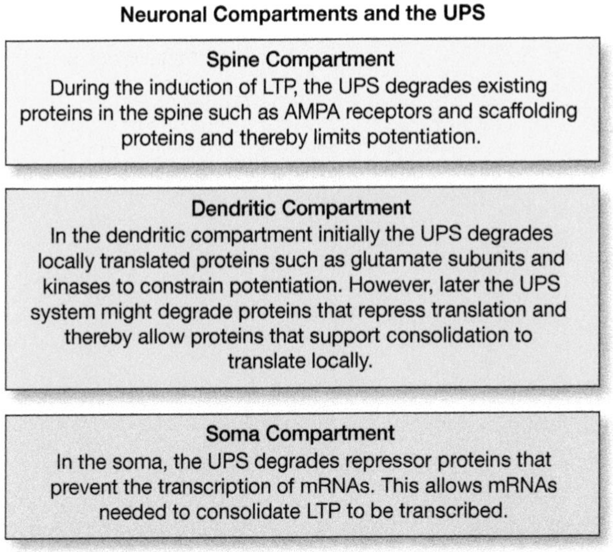

**Neuronal Compartments and the UPS**

**Spine Compartment**
During the induction of LTP, the UPS degrades existing
proteins in the spine such as AMPA receptors and scaffolding
proteins and thereby limits potentiation.

**Dendritic Compartment**
In the dendritic compartment initially the UPS degrades
locally translated proteins such as glutamate subunits and
kinases to constrain potentiation. However, later the UPS
system might degrade proteins that repress translation and
thereby allow proteins that support consolidation to
translate locally.

**Soma Compartment**
In the soma, the UPS degrades repressor proteins that
prevent the transcription of mRNAs. This allows mRNAs
needed to consolidate LTP to be transcribed.

**Figure 6.14**
The functions of the UPS during LTP depend on the neuronal compartment in which
it is activated. It is possible that different sources of calcium regulate these functions.

understanding how protein degradation contributes to LTP. Protein degradation processes serve different functions depending on the compartment in
which they are activated. In the spine compartment the UPS interacts with
other post-translation processes to down-regulate existing proteins and prevent hyperpotentiated synapses. In the dendritic compartment protein degradation processes likely degrade new locally translated protein and thereby
limit the magnitude and duration of LTP. Finally, protein degradation processes operate in the soma where the nucleus is located. In this compartment
these processes appear to degrade repressor proteins that prevent the transcription of mRNAs needed to consolidate the synaptic changes that support
LTP (Figure 6.14). Given that different calcium sources operate in each compartment, one might speculate that these specific calcium sources also regulate
the compartment-specific functions of the UPS system.

## Summary

The consolidation of synaptic changes requires the generation of new protein.
Figure 6.15 provides a general summary of some of the major signaling pathways that contribute to this outcome.

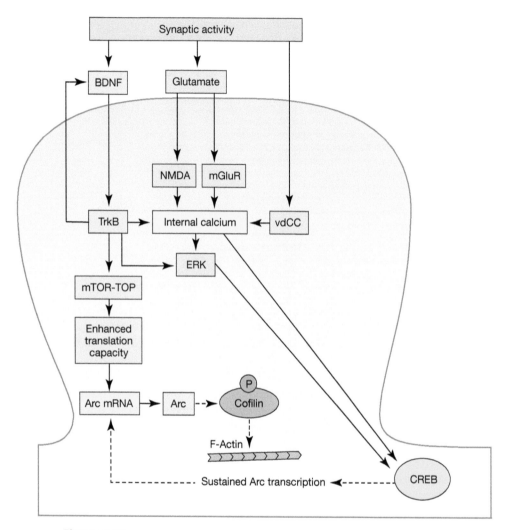

**Figure 6.15**
This figure provides a summary of the processes that contribute to consolidating synaptic changes. The release of glutamate and BDNF initiates a set of signaling cascades designed to enhance translation machinery in dendritic spines and to signal the genome to continuously transcribe new Arc mRNA. Arc mRNA is targeted back to synapses that have been tagged by recent synaptic activity where it translated. Arc protein then contributes to the phosphorylation of cofilin and the polymerization of Actin.

Consolidation requires that the induction stimulus must be sufficient to cause the presynaptic terminals to release both glutamate and BDNF. An important outcome of the co-release of glutamate and BNDF is a sustained increase in intracellular second-messenger calcium levels. This sustained pool of calcium supports (a) processes that increase translation capacity in stimulated dendritic-spine regions and (b) signaling cascades involving ERK and vdCCs that activate transcription factors such as CREB. Consequently, Arc mRNA is continuously transcribed (perhaps for several hours) and transported to dendritic regions where the translation machinery has been up-regulated.

Stimulated synapses acquire a property called a tag that enables them to capture newly transcribed Arc and other mRNAs. Translated Arc protein then ensures the continued phosphorylation of cofilin and a nascent supply of filament actin. Interruption of any of these processes in principle could prevent consolidation.

After 3 hours the consolidation phase winds down. Functionally this means that LTP will no longer be reversed by (a) preventing protein synthesis, (b) preventing the activation of the mTOR–TOP pathway, (c) inhibiting the TrkB-receptor response to BDNF, (d) interfering with CREB-mediated transcription, or (e) preventing the translation of Arc mRNA. Even so, the processes described here will not ensure that the synaptic changes will be maintained for days.

Paradoxically, the consolidation of synaptic changes that support enduring LTP also depends on protein degradation. The UPS is designed to degrade protein and is regulated by synaptic activity induced by LTP. Enduring LTP, but not the initial induction of LTP, is prevented if proteasomes are inhibited prior to the induction stimulus, but not if they are inhibited about 3 hours after the induction stimulus. This contribution of the UPS supports consolidation by degrading transcription repressor proteins so that new mRNA can be transcribed.

## References

Aicardi, G., Argilli, E., Cappello, S., Santi, S., Riccio, M., Thoenen, H., and Canossa, M. (2004). Induction of long-term potentiation and depression is reflected by corresponding changes in secretion of endogenous brain-derived neurotrophic factor. *Proceedings of the National Academy of Sciences USA*, *101*, 15788–15792.

Berninger, B., Garcia, D. E., Inagaki, N., Hahnel, C., and Lindholm, D. (1993). BDNF and NT-3 induce intracellular Ca2I elevation in hippocampal neurons. *NeuroReport*, *4*, 1303–1306.

Bingol, B. and Schuman, E. M. (2006). Activity-dependent dynamics and sequestration of proteasomes in dendritic spines. *Nature*, *441*, 1144–1148.

Bingol, B., Wang, C. F., Arnott, D., Cheng, D., Peng, J., and Sheng, M. (2010). Autophosphorylated CaMKIIa acts as a scaffold to recruit proteasomes to dendritic spines. *Cell*, *140*, 567–578.

Bramham, C. R. (2008). Local protein synthesis, actin dynamics, and LTP consolidation. *Current Opinion in Neurobiology*, *18*, 524–531.

Bramham, C. R., Alme, M. N., Bittins, M., Kuipers, S. D., Nair, R. R., Pai, B., Panja, D., Schubert, M., Soule, J., Tiron, A., and Wibrand, K. (2010). The Arc of synaptic memory. *Experimental Brain Research*, *2*, 125–140.

Bramham, C. and Messaoudi, E. (2005). BDNF function in adult synaptic plasticity: the synaptic consolidation hypothesis. *Progress in Neurobiology*, *76*, 99–125.

Burbea, M., Dreier, L., Dittman, J. S., Grunwald, M. E., and Kaplan, J. M. (2002). Ubiquitin and AP180 regulate the abundance of GLR-1 glutamate receptors at postsynaptic elements in *C. elegans*. *Neuron*, *35*, 107–120.

Cajigas, I. J., Will, T., and Schuman, E. M. (2010). Protein homeostasis and synaptic plasticity. *The EMBO Journal*, *18*, 2746–2752.

Dong, C., Upadhya, S. C., Ding, L., Smith, T. K., and Hegde, A. N. (2008). Proteasome inhibition enhances the induction and impairs the maintenance of late-phase long-term potentiation. *Learning and Memory*, *15*, 335–347.

Dynes, J. L. and Steward, O. (2012). Arc mRNA docks precisely at the base of individual dendritic spines indicating the existence of a specialized microdomain for synapse-specific mRNA translation. *The Journal of Comparative Neurology*, *26*, 433–437.

Ehlers, M. D. (2003). Activity level controls postsynaptic composition and signaling via the ubiquitin-proteasome system. *Nature Neuroscience*, *6*, 231–242.

Fonseca, R., Vabulas, R. M., Hartl, F. U., Bonhoeffer, T., and Nagerl, U. V. (2006). A balance of protein synthesis and proteasome-dependent degradation determines the maintenance of LTP. *Neuron*, *52*, 239–245.

Frey, U. and Morris, R. G. (1997). Synaptic tagging and long-term potentiation. *Nature*, *385*, 533–536.

Frey, U. and Morris, R. G. (1998). Synaptic tagging: implications for late maintenance of hippocampal long-term potentiation. *Trends in Neurosciences*, *21*, 181–188.

Guo, L. and Wang, Y. (2007). Glutamate stimulates glutamate receptor interacting protein 1 degradation by ubiquitin–proteasome system to regulate surface expression of GluR2. *Neuroscience*, *145*, 100–109.

Guzowski, J. F., Lyford, G. L., Stevenson, G. D., Houston, F. P., McGaugh, J. L., Worley, P. F., and Barnes, C. A. (2000). Inhibition of activity-dependent arc protein expression in the rat hippocampus impairs the maintenance of long-term potentiation and the consolidation of long-term memory. *Journal of Neuroscience*, *20*, 3993–4001.

Hegde, A. N. (2010). The ubiquitin-proteasome pathway and synaptic plasticity. *Learning and Memory*, *17*, 314–327.

Hegde, A. N., Goldberg, A. L., and Schwartz, J. H. (1993). Regulatory subunits of cAMP-dependent protein kinases are degraded after conjugation to ubiquitin: a molecular mechanism underlying long-term synaptic plasticity. *Proceedings of the National Academy of Sciences USA*, *90*, 7436–7440.

Honkura, N., Matsuzaki, M., Noguchi, J., Ellis-Davies, G. C. R., and Kasai, H. (2008). The subspine organization of actin fibers regulates the structure and plasticity of dendritic spines. *Neuron, 57,* 719–729.

Jia, Y., Gall, C. M., and Lynch, G. (2010). Presynaptic BDNF promotes postsynaptic long-term potentiation in the dorsal striatum. *Journal of Neuroscience, 30,* 14440–14445.

Kang, H. and Schuman, E. M. (1996). A requirement for local protein synthesis in neurotrophin-induced synaptic plasticity. *Science, 273,* 1402–1406.

Kang, H. and Schuman, E. M. (2000). Intracellular Ca$^{(2+)}$ signaling is required for neurotrophin-induced potentiation in the adult rat hippocampus. *Neuroscience Letters, 282,* 141–141.

Karpova, A., Mikhaylova, M., Thomas, U., Knopfel, T., and Behnisch, T. (2006). Involvement of protein synthesis and degradation in long-term potentiation of Schaffer collateral CA1 synapses. *Journal of Neuroscience, 26,* 4949–4955.

Korte, M., Carroll, P., Wolf, E., Brem, G., Thoenen, H., and Bonhoeffe, T. (1995). Hippocampal long-term potentiation is impaired in mice lacking brain-derived neurotrophic factor. *Proceedings of the National Academy of Sciences USA, 92,* 8856–8860.

Korte, M., Kang, H., Bonhoeffer, T., and Schuman, E. (1998). A role for BDNF in the late phase of hippocampal long-term potentiation. *Neuropharmacology, 37,* 553–559.

Lee, S. H., Choi, J. H., Lee, N., Lee, H. R., Kim, J. I., Yu, N. K., Choi, S. L., Lee, S. H., Kim, H., and Kaang, B. K. (2008). Synaptic protein degradation underlies destabilization of retrieved fear memory. *Science, 319,* 1253–1256.

Lessmann, V., Gottmann, K., and Malcangio, M. (2003). Neurotrophin secretion: current facts and future prospects. *Progress in Neurobiology, 69,* 341–374.

Li, Y. X., Lester, H. A., Schuman, E. M., and Davidson, N. (1998). Enhancement of neurotransmitter release induced by brain-derived neurotrophic factor in cultured hippcampal neurons. *Journal of Neuroscience, 18,* 10231–10240.

Matsuzaki, M., Honkura, N., Ellis-Davies, G. C., and Kasai, H. (2004). Structural basis of long-term potentiation in single dendritic spines. *Nature, 429,* 761–766.

Messaoudi, E., Kanhema, T., Soule, J., Tiron, A., Dagyte, G., da Silva, B., and Bramham, C. R. (2007). Sustained Arc/Arg3.1 synthesis controls long-term potentiation consolidation through regulation of local actin polymerization in the dentate gyrus in vivo. *Journal of Neuroscience, 27,* 10445–10455.

Patrick, G. N., Bingol, B., Weld, H. A., and Schuman, E. M. (2003). Ubiquitin-mediated proteasome activity is required for agonist-induced endocytosis of GluRs. *Current Biology, 13,* 2073–2081.

Patterson, S. L., Grover, L. M., Schwartzkroin, P. A., and Bothwell, M. (1992). Neurotrophin expression in rat hippocampal slices a stimulus paradigm inducing LTP in CA1 evokes increases in BDNF and NT-3 mRNAs. *Neuron, 9,* 1081–1088.

Redondo, R. L. and Morris, R. G. (2011). Making memories last: the synaptic tagging and capture hypothesis. *Nature Reviews Neuroscience, 12,* 17–30.

Steward, O. (2007). Protein synthesis at synaptic sites on dendrites. In Able Lajtha (Editor), *Handbook of neurochemistry and molecular neurobiology* (pp. 169–195). Netherlands: Springer.

Sutton, M. A. and Schuman, E. R. (2005). Local translational control in dendrites and its role in long-term synaptic plasticity. *Journal of Neurobiology, 64* (1), 116–131.

Tai, H. C. and Schuman, E. M. (2008). Ubiquitin, the proteasome and protein degradation in neuronal function and dysfunction. *Nature Reviews Neuroscience, 9*, 826–838.

Tanaka, J., Horiike, Y., Matsuzaki, M., Miyazaki, T., Ellis-Davies, G. C. R., and Kasai, H. (2008). Protein synthesis and neurotrophin-dependent structural plasticity of single dendritic spines. *Science, 319*, 1683–1687.

Tang, S. J., Reis, G., Kang, H, Gingras, A. C., Sonenberg, N., and Schuman, E. M. (2002). A rapamycin-sensitive signaling pathway contributes to long-term synaptic plasticity in the hippocampus. *Proceedings of the National Academy of Sciences USA, 99*, 467–72.

Thoreen, C. C., Chantranupong, L., Keys, H. R., Wang, T., Gray, N. S., and Sabatini, D. M. (2012). A unifying model for mTORC1-mediated regulation of mRNA translation. *Nature, 48* (7396), 109–113.

Tsokas, P., Grace, E. A., Chan, P., Ma, T., Sealfon, S. C., Iyengar, R., Landau, E. M., and Blitzer, R. D. (2005). Local protein synthesis mediates a rapid increase in dendritic elongation factor 1A after induction of late long-term potentiation. *Journal of Neuroscience, 25*, 5833–5843.

Tsokas, P., Ma, T., Iyengar, R., Landau, E. M., and Blitzer, R. D. (2007). Mitogen-activated protein kinase upregulates the dendritic translation machinery in long-term potentiation by controlling the mammalian target of rapamycin pathway. *Journal of Neuroscience, 27*, 5885–5894.

Turrigiano, G. G. (2002). A recipe for ridding synapses of the ubiquitous AMPA receptor. *Trends in Neurosciences, 25*, 597–598.

Vickers, C. A., Dickson, K. S., and Wyllie, D. J. (2005). Induction and maintenance of late-phase long-term potentiation in isolated dendrites of rat hippocampal CA1 pyramidal neurons. *Journal of Physiology, 568*, 803–813.

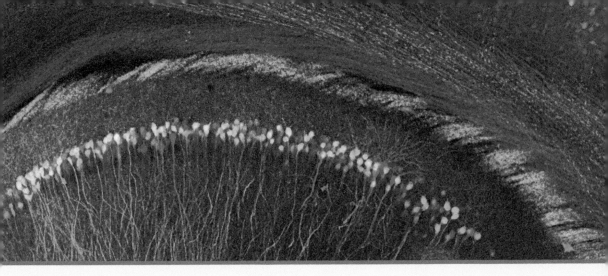

# 7 Maintaining the Consolidated Trace

As the significance of molecular biology and biochemistry for neurobiology was becoming clear, Francis Crick, co-discoverer of the structure DNA, raised a daunting issue—*the molecular turnover problem*. The synaptic molecules that support memory traces are short-lived in comparison to the duration of our memories. Thus, a fundamental problem is to understand how the strengthened synapses that support memories can outlive the molecules from which they are made. As Crick (1984, page 101) put it: "How then is memory stored in the brain so that its trace is relatively immune to molecular turnover?"

The previous chapters revealed that much is known about the molecular processes that support the generation, stabilization, and consolidation of the synaptic changes that support LTP (and by inference memories), but they did not answer this question. Crick, however, suggested a general answer: "… the molecules in synapses interact in such a way that they can be replaced with new material, one at a time, without altering the overall

Francis Crick

state of the structure." Crick's suggestion is likely correct. The goal of this chapter is to describe recent progress toward providing specific answers to the question, *how is the consolidated memory trace maintained*?

As noted, for potentiated synapses to endure, they must be reconstructed to resist pressure to return to their basal unpotentiated state. Two forces operate to return synapses to their original state: (1) molecular degradation, which Crick identified (Figure 7.1) and (2) constitutive, endocytic (molecule engulfing)

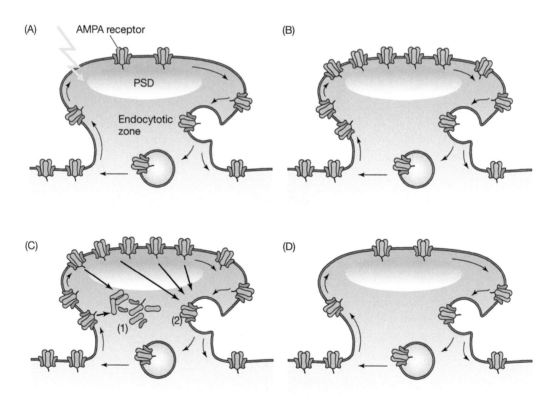

**Figure 7.1**
(A) An unpotentiated synapse is depolarized. (B) As the synapse is potentiated, AMPA receptors are added to the postsynaptic density. (C) Two processes—(1) degradation of AMPA receptors and (2) receptor endocytosis—then pressure the synapse to (D) return to its pre-potentiated state.

processes that operate to cycle AMPA receptors out of the synaptic region (Sacktor, 2011). Left unchecked, both of these processes will gradually return the potentiated synapses to their basal state. Thus, the question is, *what molecular processes are engaged that counter these forces and maintain the potentiated synapses?*

## PKMζ: A Promising Maintenance Molecule

The general idea that AMPA receptors diffuse around the plasma membrane to cycle into and out of the postsynaptic density was described in Chapter 4. That chapter also introduced the view that the immediate induction of LTP was due to trapping GluA1 type AMPA receptors in the PSD. It is important to know that AMPA receptors containing GluA2 soon replace GluA1 receptors. To understand how consolidated synapses are maintained requires knowing (a) how GluA2s replace GluA1s and (b) how they are then maintained in the synapse.

Todd Sacktor and his colleagues (see Sacktor, 2011) have argued that the protein kinase M zeta (**PKMζ**) has properties that may solve these two problems. Unlike PKC it lacks an inhibitory domain, so once translated it is persistently active because it does not require a second messenger to be in an active, catalytic state. PKMζ mRNA is found in regions of dendritic spines and is locally translated in the dendritic spine region. The initial translation of PKMζ requires the activity of several kinases, including CaMKII, P13, MAPK, PKA, mTOR, and actin filaments (Figure 7.2). Newly synthesized PKMζ becomes available within about 10 minutes following a strong LTP-inducing stimulus.

Given that all proteins will degrade, maintaining strengthened synapses requires at least one molecule that has the property of self-perpetuation. Once translated into protein, PKMζ has self-perpetuating properties. Normally, the PKMζ mRNA is protected from translation by a **translator repressor protein** (Osten et al., 1996). PKMζ self perpetuates by interacting with other proteins to remove this repressor, which facilitates the translation of additional PKMζ (see Figure 7.2). In this way, PKMζ participates in a positive feedback loop that continuously translates PKMζ mRNA into protein in dendritic spine regions where it was initially translated.

Todd Sacktor

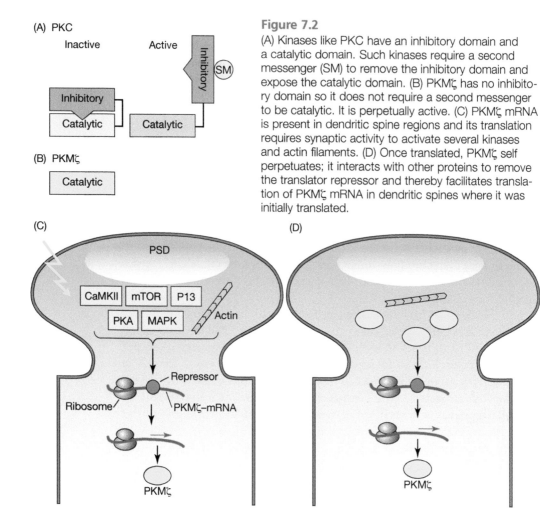

(A) PKC

Inactive   Active

Inhibitory

Catalytic   Catalytic

(B) PKMζ

Catalytic

(C)

PSD

CaMKII   mTOR   P13

PKA   MAPK   Actin

Repressor

Ribosome   PKMζ–mRNA

PKMζ

(D)

PKMζ

**Figure 7.2**
(A) Kinases like PKC have an inhibitory domain and a catalytic domain. Such kinases require a second messenger (SM) to remove the inhibitory domain and expose the catalytic domain. (B) PKMζ has no inhibitory domain so it does not require a second messenger to be catalytic. It is perpetually active. (C) PKMζ mRNA is present in dendritic spine regions and its translation requires synaptic activity to activate several kinases and actin filaments. (D) Once translated, PKMζ self perpetuates; it interacts with other proteins to remove the translator repressor and thereby facilitates translation of PKMζ mRNA in dendritic spines where it was initially translated.

## Inhibiting PKMζ Prevents LTP Maintenance

As noted, PKMζ does not have an inhibitory domain; however, it does have a potential binding site for an inhibitory domain. The development of **ZIP** (zeta inhibitory peptide) made it possible to examine the role of PKMζ in LTP (Laudanna et al., 1998). ZIP functions as the missing inhibitory domain for PKMζ and thus can return it to an inactive, non-catalytic state in which it no longer can phosphorylate other proteins.

Applying ZIP to hippocampal slices prior to the induction of LTP had no effect on the expression of the early form of LTP, although it did prevent the late phase (Figure 7.3). The unique finding was that the application of ZIP reversed the potentiated response even when it was applied 2 or 5 hours after LTP was induced. For comparison, other molecules known to be involved in LTP (for example, CaMKII, MAPK, and PKC) are required for a much shorter time after LTP is induced (Serrano et al., 2005). In addition, as previously mentioned Arc antisense did not reverse LTP when applied 4 hours after induction. Thus, PKMζ is important to maintaining potentiated synapses.

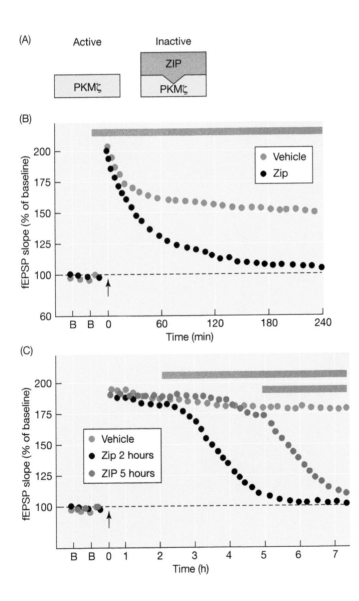

**Figure 7.3**
(A) As noted, PKMζ has no inhibitory domain; however, the peptide ZIP functions as an inhibitory domain and inactivates it. (B) ZIP applied to a slice prior to the inducing stimulus does not affect the early induction phase of LTP but does prevent the late phase. (C) ZIP applied 2 or 5 hours following induction reverses late-phase LTP. The bars represent when ZIP was applied. (After Serrano et al., 2005.)

## PKMζ Releases and Maintains GluA2 AMPA Receptors

As noted, GluA1 receptors are responsible for the initial potentiation of synapses but are replaced by GluA2 receptors. PKMζ contributes to this outcome. First, the application of PKMζ to hippocampal slices produces potentiated synapses (Ling et al., 2002, 2006), while inhibiting PKMζ prevents this potentiation (Figure 7.4). This result implies that PKMζ can traffic AMPA receptors into the PSD, and this implication has been confirmed (Ling et al., 2006).

There is a pool of GluA2 receptors maintained outside of the synapse by binding to a protein interacting with C kinase 1 called PICK1. This protein is involved in the removal of GluA2 receptors from synapses and is part of the machinery that constitutively regulates AMPA receptor trafficking. The release of this pool of GluA2s for insertion into the synapse depends in

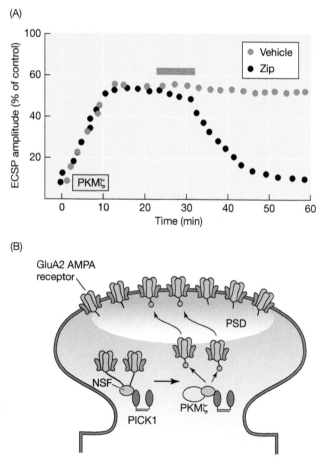

**Figure 7.4**

(A) PKMζ potentiates synapses and the application of a PKMζ inhibitor (gray bar) reverses this effect. Note in this example the data are from intracellular recordings (EPSC). (B) A pool of GluA2 AMPA receptors is trapped outside of the synapse by protein interacting with C kinase 1 (PICK1). Release of this pool depends on a trafficking protein enzyme, NSF. When PKMζ interacts with the NSF–PICK1 complex, the receptors are released for entry into the PSD.

part on a trafficking protein enzyme called NSF (N-ethylmaleimide-sensitive factor). PKMζ forms a complex with NSF and PICK1, which facilitates the disruption of the PICK1–GluA2 complex, releasing the GluA2 receptors into the PSD and potentiating the synapse (Sacktor, 2011; Yao et al., 2008). See Figure 7.4 for an illustration of this process, through which PKMζ can ensure continuous delivery of GluA2 AMPA receptors to the PSD.

There is continuous pressure to recycle AMPA receptors out of synapses and, left unopposed, the endocytic cycle will remove additional GluA2 receptors and return the synapse to its unpotentiated state (Sacktor, 2011). The underlying endocytotic processes are not completely understood. However, when Trk receptors—a class of membrane spanning tyrosine kinase receptors that have enzymatic properties—are activated, they selectively phosphorylate sites on GluA2 AMPA receptors. These receptors are not removed if this process is prevented by genetic deletion of these phosphorylation sites. So the activation of this Trk receptor pathway is a likely contributor to the endocytosis of GluA2 receptors (Ahmadian et al., 2004; Fox et al., 2007).

Sacktor (2011) has proposed that PKMζ disrupts the normal endocytosis of GluA2 receptors (Figure 7.5). His hypothesis is based on two facts: (1) normally when ZIP reverses LTP maintenance GluA2 receptors are removed from the PSD, and (2) the peptide GluR23Y, which also interferes with the removal of GluA2 receptors (Ahmadian et al., 2004), prevents ZIP from removing these receptors (Migues et al., 2010). These results imply that

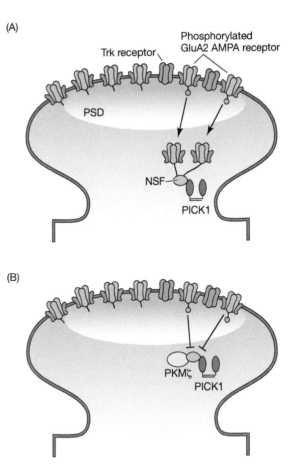

**Figure 7.5**
(A) The activation of Trk (tyrosine kinase) receptors phosphorylates tyrosine sites on GluA2 AMPA receptors. This activity releases the receptors from the PSD into the endocytotic zone where they bond with the NSF–PICK1 complex for recycling. (B) The presence of PKMζ disrupts the normal endocytic cycle—the receptors remain trapped in the PSD and the synapse remains potentiated.

PKMζ contributes to maintaining LTP by disrupting the removal of GluA2 receptors from the PSD.

## Two Key Contributions of PKMζ

The important general conclusion from these experiments is that PKMζ maintains potentiated synapses through two parallel and complementary actions: (1) it facilitates the release of non-synaptic pools of GluA2 AMPA receptors for insertion into the PSD and (2) it interferes with the endocytic cycle that normally removes these receptors from the synapse (Figure 7.6). The combined effects of these two processes thus enable synapses to maintain the number of AMPA receptors required to support a potentiated synaptic response to glutamate release. Inhibiting the catalytic properties of PKMζ by ZIP in principle disrupts both of these functions and returns these synapses to their unpotentiated state.

## Trapping PKMζ

PKMζ is a powerful kinase. As noted earlier, the application of PKMζ to a slice of hippocampal tissue rapidly potentiates synapses by releasing GluA2 AMPA receptors into the PSD (see Figure 7.4). So when synaptic activity initiates the local synthesis of PKMζ there is the possibility it will spread beyond the specific spine compartments that were initially stimulated. As a consequence, PKMζ might eventually potentiate all synapses along a dendrite and the specificity of the inducing signal would be lost. Thus, it is important that PKMζ is trapped in the spine compartments in which it is synthesized.

Sacktor (2011) has proposed that this happens because GluA2 serves as an "autotag" to capture and retain PKMζ in the spine compartments (Figure 7.7). The autotag operates as the GluA2s are being recycled (released) into the PSD by the phosphorylation activity of PKMζ on the NSF–PICK1 complex. When phosphatases remove the phosphates from GluA2 receptors, they are free to recapture the PKMζ–PICK1 complex. Re-phosphorylation by PKMζ then blocks the endocytic removal of the GluA2s. In this way PKMζ is trapped in

**Figure 7.6**
PKMζ maintains potentiated synapses through two parallel and complementary actions: (1) it facilitates the release of non-synaptic pools of GluA2 receptors to replace GluA1 receptors and (2) it interferes with the endocytic cycle that normally removes GluA2s from the synapse.

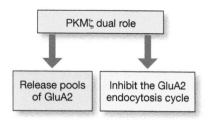

(A) PKMζ can spread to other spine compartments

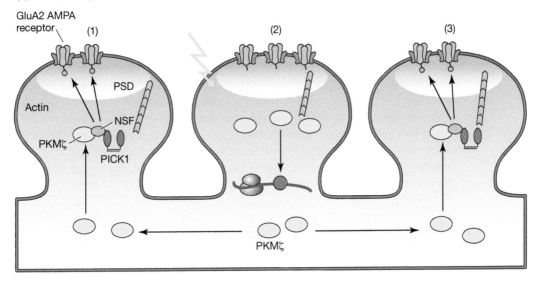

(B) GluA2 AMPA receptors serve as an "autotag" to trap the PMKζ–PICK1 complex

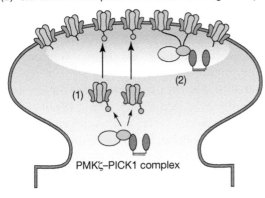

**Figure 7.7**
(A) Once synaptic activity induces PKMζ synthesis in a spine compartment (spine 2, above) in response to synaptic activity, continued synthesis could lead to PKMζ spreading from the original compartment to neighboring spines (1 and 3), where it could potentiate these spines by releasing GluA2 receptors (not shown). (B) The spread of PKMζ is minimized because once the GluA2 receptors are released into the spine (1) they are free to recapture the PKMζ–PICK1 complex (2). In principle this autotagging process traps PKMζ in the spines where it was synthesized. Because PKMζ disrupts the endocytic cycle, an additional outcome is that GluA2s remain in the PSD region and the spine remains potentiated.

the synapse. Moreover, the added GluA2s are maintained in the PSD and the synapses remain potentiated.

The GluA2 autotag is capable of regulating the location of PKMζ. However, recent experiments have also revealed that PKMζ is a plasticity product that can be captured by weakly stimulated synapses (Sajikumar and Korte, 2011). In the previous chapter the synaptic tag and capture idea was introduced, and supported by the result that weakly stimulated synapses could capture plasticity products generated by strongly stimulating other synapses belonging to the same neuron. Recent experiments indicate that PKMζ is one of the important proteins captured by tagged synapses. This is because if ZIP is applied to the slice, it prevents strong stimulation from enhancing the LTP associated with weak stimulation. Thus, it is likely that PKMζ is an important plasticity product that is available to be captured outside of the region where it was initially synthesized.

## Genetic Engineering Reveals Additional Maintenance Molecules

The emergence of PKMζ as a critical contributor to the maintenance of potentiated synapses has raised an important question—*is it the memory maintenance molecule?* In considering this question, it should be appreciated that much of the evidence implicating PKMζ is based on a pharmacological strategy in which ZIP was the major agent used to inactivate PKMζ. The underlying assumption in all of these experiments is that ZIP selectively targets only PKMζ.

Recently, a genetic engineering strategy was used to evaluate the importance of PKMζ. Mice were genetically modified to lack PKMζ (Volk et al., 2013). If PKMζ is critical for the maintenance of LTP, one would expect that hippocampal slices from these mice would not be able to maintain LTP. However, established LTP was maintained and, moreover, ZIP reversed the LTP maintenance.

These unexpected results support three conclusions: (1) enduring memories and LTP can be established independent of the presence of PKMζ, that is, the maintenance of LTP does not require PKMζ, (2) ZIP is not selective for PKMζ as it also interacts with other molecules, and (3) there must be other kinases or other molecules that can participate in the maintenance of LTP and memories. There are at least two alternative explanations of these data.

- PKMζ is the primary memory maintenance molecule in normal rats, and the genetic studies have uncovered redundant compensatory molecules whose contribution is masked by the normal presence of PKMζ.

- PKMζ is not involved in the maintenance of LTP and maintenance depends on other kinase targets of ZIP.

These new results and surrounding controversy (Frankland and Josselyn, 2013) have created uncertainty about the current understanding of how synaptic changes are maintained. However, it is important to appreciate that this is how the scientific process works. Ideas emerge, hypotheses are tested, and new results raise new questions that if answered can lead to a deeper understanding of how nature solved an important problem—in this case the maintenance problem.

The field will now need to answer several questions:

- What are these new targets of ZIP that must be engaged to support maintenance?
- Are the processes these new targets regulate redundant with PKMζ?
- What if any role does PKMζ play in maintenance?

Until these questions are answered it may be appropriate to conclude that PKMζ and other kinase targets of ZIP maintain the synaptic changes that support LTP.

## Summary

Consolidated synapses face the molecular turnover problem. They have to be maintained in the face of forces that (a) degrade the molecules that strengthen them and (b) are designed to remove the GluA2 receptors from the synapses. PKMζ may play a major role in maintaining strengthened synapse because it has several important properties:

- It lacks an inhibitory unit and is persistently active.
- PKMζ mRNA is available in dendritic spine regions.
- Once translated it can self perpetuate.
- It releases pools of GluA2 receptors from the extrasynaptic region.
- It disrupts the endocytic cycle that normally would remove GluA2 receptors from the synapse.
- Inhibiting its catalytic function with ZIP reverses potentiation produced by an LTP-inducing stimulus.

Nevertheless, recent evidence based on the genetic knockout approach suggests that other, unknown kinase targets of ZIP may either be the primary mediators of effects previously assigned to PKMζ or may compensate for the absence of PKMζ.

# References

Ahmadian, G., Ju, W., Liu, L., Wysznski, M., Lee, S. H., Dunah, A. W., Taghibiglou, C., Wang, Y., Lu, J., Wong, T. P., Sheng, M., and Wang, Y. T. (2004). Tyrosine phosphorylation of GluR2 is required for insulin-stimulated AMPA receptor endocytosis and LTD. *EMBO Journal, 23*, 1040–1050.

Crick, F. (1984). Memory and molecular turnover. *Nature, 312,* 101.

Fox, C. J., Russell, K., Titterness, A. K., Wang, Y. T., and Christie, B. R. (2007). Tyrosine phosphorylation of the GluR2 subunit is required for long-term depression of synaptic efficacy in young animals in vivo. *Hippocampus, 17*, 600–605.

Frankland, P. W. and Josselyn, S. A. (2013). Neuroscience: memory and the single molecule. *Nature, 493*, 312–313.

Laudanna, C., Mochly-Rosen, D., Liron, T., Constantin, G., and Butcher, E. C. (1998). Evidence of zeta protein kinase C involvement in polymorphonuclear neutrophil integrin-dependent adhesion and chemotaxis. *Journal of Biological Chemistry, 273*, 30306–30315.

Ling, D. S., Benardo, L. S., and Sacktor, T. C. (2006). Protein kinase Mζ enhances excitatory synaptic transmission by increasing the number of active postsynaptic AMPA receptors. *Hippocampus, 16*, 443–452.

Ling, D. S., Benardo, L. S., Serrano, P. A., Blace, N., Kelly, M. T., Crary, J. F., and Sacktor, T. C. (2002). Protein kinase Mζ is necessary and sufficient for LTP maintenance. *Nature Neuroscience, 5*, 295–296.

Migues, P. V., Hardt, O., Wu, D. C., Gamache, K., Sacktor, T. C., Wang, Y. T., and Nader, K. (2010). PKMζ maintains memories by regulating GluR2-dependent AMPA receptor trafficking. *Nature Neuroscience, 13,* 630–634.

Osten, P., Valsamis, L., Harris, A., and Sacktor, T. C. (1996). Protein synthesis-dependent formation of protein kinase Mζ in LTP. *Journal of Neuroscience, 16*, 2444–2451.

Sacktor, T. C. (2011). How does PKMζ maintain long-term memory? *Nature Reviews Neuroscience, 12*, 9–15.

Sajikumar, S. and Korte. M. (2011). Metaplasticity governs compartmentalization of synaptic tagging and capture through brain-derived neurotrophic factor (BDNF) and protein kinase Mζ (PKMζ). *Proceedings of the National Academy of Sciences USA, 108*, 2551–2556.

Serrano, P., Yao, Y., and Sacktor, T. C. (2005). Persistent phosphorylation by protein kinase Mζ maintains late-phase long-term potentiation. *Journal of Neuroscience, 25*, 1979–1984.

Volk, L. J., Bachman, J. L., Johnson, R., Yu, Y., and Huganir, R. L. (2013). PKMζ is not required for hippocampal synaptic plasticity, learning and memory. *Nature, 493*, 420–423.

Yao, Y., Kelly, M. T., Sajikumar, S., Serrano, P., Tian, D., Bergold, P. J., Frey, J. U., and Sacktor, T. C. (2008). PKM zeta maintains late long-term potentiation by N-ethylmaleimide-sensitive factor/GluR2-dependent trafficking of postsynaptic AMPA receptors. *Journal of Neuroscience, 28* (31), 7820–7827.

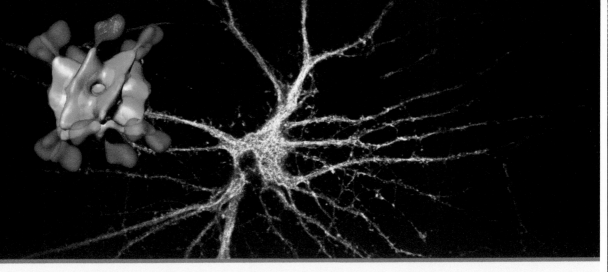

# 8 Toward a Synthesis

Some of the molecular events that are engaged by an LTP-inducing stimulus have now been described. These processes were organized into a framework that assumes that changes in synaptic strength evolve over four distinct but overlapping stages: trace generation, trace stabilization, trace consolidation, and trace maintenance. The goal of this chapter is to summarize the major points that have been presented and discuss some of the issues and implications they raise.

## Generation

Potentiating a synapse happens rapidly and depends on increasing calcium levels in the spine (Figure 8.1). This is accomplished when glutamate binds to AMPA and NMDA receptors and the resulting synaptic depolarization removes the $Mg^+$ from NMDA receptors. A small influx of calcium via NMDA receptors is amplified by calcium released from the endoplasmic reticulum when

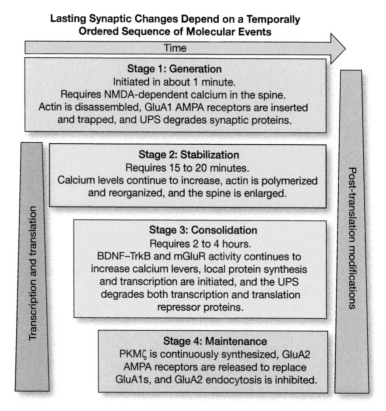

**Figure 8.1**
Synapses are strengthened in four overlapping stages. This figure illustrates the approximate duration of each stage and important events that occur during each stage. Note that all stages depend on the activation of post-translation processes that modify and rearrange existing proteins. Translation and transcription processes are initiated within minutes of strong synaptic activity. The consolidation phase uniquely depends on signal cascades that translate local proteins and initiate transcription.

calcium binds to rynadine receptors. This increase in calcium modifies calmodulin so that it can then place CaMKII into a persistently active state. One important consequence is that CaMKII phosphorylates the TARP Stargazin, associated with GluA1 AMPA subunits. This modification releases Stargazin from the plasma membrane so that it can bind to PSD-95 proteins and trap these GluA1 receptors in the postsynaptic density. Another consequence is that CaMKII phosphorylates GluA1 receptors, enabling them to influx calcium.

In parallel with this activity, the increase in calcium levels activates calpain proteins that degrade spectrins that crosslink actin filaments. Additionally, the depolymerization properties of cofilin are temporarily enhanced. Together, these processes in a sense function to clear a path for the rapid insertion of GluA1 AMPA receptors into the PSD. All of this takes place in about a minute and is not accompanied by an increase in spine size. These initial changes result in a potentiated synapse, but they are transient and subject to reversal by low-frequency stimulation.

This initial stage does not depend on either the transcription of new mRNA or the translation of new proteins. However, in response to calcium signaling produced by glutamate, the ubiquitin proteasome system (UPS) is activated in the dendritic spine compartment where it degrades proteins that are part of the scaffolding matrix in the PSD and where it may also degrade GluA1 AMPA receptors. Degrading these proteins limits the extent to which synapses are potentiated.

It is relatively easy to potentiate a synapse. All that is required is enough glutamate to depolarize the synapse, cause a brief increase in the calcium content in a spine, and trap additional AMPA receptors in the PSD. That being so, one can imagine that intrinsic neural activity as well as neural activity generated by sensory input are constantly potentiating the synapses they activate. However, there are endogenous mechanisms in play that are designed to remove these receptors and return the synapses to their pre-potentiated state. Thus, these synapses are only temporarily potentiated.

## Stabilization

If potentiated synapses are to endure, the inducing stimulus must recruit additional processes. Actin proteins are the primary targets of these processes. Thus, the release of glutamate onto a spine also engages processes that polymerize actin filaments to produce driving forces that enlarge the spine and change its geometry. These processes depend on calcium levels that (a) activate myosin IIb motor proteins that shear existing actin filaments into smaller units that can then provide the basis for building many actin filament strands, and (b) activate other enzymes that phosphorylate LIMK and thus increase actin polymerization and the crosslinkage of actin filaments to make these new filaments resistant to depolymerization.

These activities are further reinforced by the activation of integrin receptors that respond to molecules in the extracellular matrix and contribute to crosslinking actin filaments and to deactivating cofilin. These processes require about 15 minutes to complete. If any of these pathways are inhibited during this time period, potentiated synapses will return to their initial baseline state. However, the same inhibitory treatments have no effect when applied 15 minutes after the induction stimulus. From these observations one can conclude that the induction stimulus sets in motion a set of processes that modify and rearrange existing proteins, and this all takes place in about 15 minutes.

## Consolidation

The initial stages take advantage of already existing structural and functional proteins—they depend only on post-translation processes. Additional AMPA receptors are trafficked into the PSD, and the expansion and reorganization of actin filaments sets the stage for consolidating the net gain in AMPA receptors. The consolidation phase centers on processes that synthesize *new* proteins. Thus, transcription and translation inhibitors that do not influence the initial induction and stabilization phase prevent potentiated synapses from enduring for more than about an hour.

The activation of transcription and translation processes depends on additional processes that can sustain increased calcium levels in the dendritic spine region and in the soma. These are brought about by the presynaptic neuron releasing (a) enough glutamate to open the NMDA calcium channel and to activate G-protein-coupled mGluR receptors, and (b) BDNF. BDNF binds to TrkB receptors that are co-localized with AMPA and NMDA receptors. The activation of these receptors results in the postsynaptic neuron also releasing BDNF into the extracellular fluid. This positive feedback loop keeps the TrkB receptors in a catalytic state and further reinforces the release of calcium stored in the ER. One important outcome of the BDNF–TrkB signaling cascade is the activation of the mTOR pathway and the translation of TOP mRNAs. This facilitates interactions between ribosomes and mRNAs and enables the local translation of other mRNAs that code for important proteins such as CaMKII, Arc, and PKMζ.

This sustained increase in intracellular calcium associated with the BDNF–TrkB pathway also intiates signaling cascades that translocate into the nucleus to activate transcription machinery. This leads to the production of mRNA that codes for Arc and other plasticity products. This transcription activity is sustained for about 2 hours, and blocking the translation of Arc mRNA during this period will return potentiated synapses to their pre-potentiated state. During this time period, Arc participates in processes that continue to phosphorylate cofilin and ensure the polymerization of actin.

The UPS also plays a critical role during the consolidation stage. It initially operates to regulate the level of protein translated locally to ensure that synapses are not overly potentiated. This system is also engaged in the nucleus where it degrades proteins that normally prevent transcription of mRNAs that are needed for enduring LTP.

About 4 hours following the initial induction of LTP, synaptic changes are consolidated. Functionally, this means that disrupting protein synthesis, transcription, the BDNF–TrkB pathway, or the translation of Arc into protein no longer reverses potentiated synapses.

## Maintenance

The processes just described are important for establishing an enlarged, well-formed spine that contains enough new AMPA receptors in the PSD to support a potentiated synaptic depolarization response to glutamate. However, for the potentiated synapse to persist for days requires the initiation of processes that must perpetuate these changes. PKMζ has emerged as a potential orchestrator of the maintenance of potentiated spines. An induction stimulus that is strong enough to support potentiation into the consolidation phase also initiates the maintenance phase. Within about 5 minutes after induction, PKMζ mRNA is translated locally in dendritic spine compartments that were stimulated by the release of glutamate. PKMζ is an atypical kinase that has no inhibitory domain and is continuously in a catalytic state. It also has the capacity to self perpetuate by facilitating additional translation of mRNA that codes for PKMζ. Once translated, PKMζ reconfigures the trafficking of GluA2 AMPA receptors. It does this by stimulating the release of pools of GluA2 receptors into the PSD and by inhibiting the endocytic processes that are designed to pull GluA2s from the PSD. It must be appreciated, however, that the evidence implicating PKMζ derives primarily from the application of ZIP and the assumption that it selectively inhibits PKMζ. Results from the genetic knockout approach have challenged the idea that PKMζ is unique in the maintenance domain. Thus, one can expect that new molecular targets of ZIP will be identified in the future.

## Issues and Implications

The previous sections summarized some of the basic steps in the evolution of synaptic changes that support LTP. This section discusses some issues and implications of this summary, in particular the importance of actin regulation and the relationship between synaptic plasticity and memory.

### The Importance of Actin Regulation

A striking and surprising conclusion is that *every stage in the evolution of the synaptic basis of LTP depends on the regulation of actin proteins*. The generation stage requires disassembling the actin cytoskeleton in order to allow more AMPA receptors and perhaps other molecules to enter the PSD. Thereafter, for about 2 to 4 hours as the potentiated synapses stabilize and consolidate, actin is continuously polymerized. Processes that reorganize and crosslink actin filaments increase the size of the spine and stabilize its new geometry. Moreover, this new geometry is critical for the maintenance of potentiated synapses. Why are so many signaling processes devoted to creating an actin cytoskeleton that sustains an enlarged spine? There is very little information available that speaks directly to the functional significance of an enlarged spine. However, some speculative answers are provided below.

**ACTIN FILAMENTS PROVIDE TRACKS FOR MOTOR PROTEINS** AMPA receptors are continuously recycled (Park et al., 2006). As they leave the postsynaptic density they are repackaged into endosomes. The redelivery of these AMPA receptors to the extrasynaptic region depends on calcium signaling pathways that modify myosin motor proteins so they can attach to the endosome. As shown in Figure 8.2, these motor proteins then use the actin filaments as a substrate to deliver the AMPA receptors to the extracellular region (Wang et al., 2008). Thus, one might imagine that a well-organized actin cytoskeleton would benefit the trafficking of AMPA receptors during the maintenance phase. More generally, actin networks and their associated myosin motor

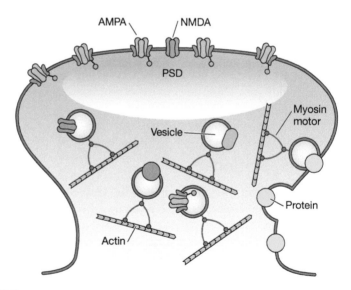

**Figure 8.2**
Actin filaments provide support for myosin motor proteins to deliver vesicle-bound proteins to the plasma membrane.

proteins may be critical for targeting many vesicle-bound membrane proteins to their proper locations, and these vesicles will be more effectively delivered to spines that have well-formed actin networks (Semenova et al., 2008).

LARGE SPINES COMPETE SUCCESSFULLY FOR KEY MOLECULES    Molecules that make up key components of a synapse are dynamic, so much so that it has been suggested that the "the entire complement of synaptic proteins in mature neural circuits are replaced multiple times a day" (Ehlers, 2003, p. 800). For example, fluorescent PSD-95 has been observed to circulate among neighboring spines. The principle determiner of where it goes and how long it stays is spine size, which is largely determined by the actin cytoskeleton (Gray et al., 2006). Large spines are more successful than smaller spines in both attracting and maintaining PSD-95 proteins. Without maintaining the needed complement of such proteins, the structural basis for trapping AMPA receptors would be lost and potentiated synapses would revert back to their baseline state.

ACTIN FILAMENTS ARE NECESSARY FOR THE INITIAL SYNTHESIS OF PKMζ    Maintenance of potentiated synapses depends on PKMζ delivering GluA2 receptors to the postsynaptic density and inhibiting the endocytosis of these receptors (Kelly et al., 2007). Given that the synthesis of PKMζ requires a developed actin network, then interfering with actin regulation processes that establish this network would be fatal to maintenance.

## Synaptic Plasticity and Memory

Everyone agrees that memories are stored in the brain. Moreover, since Ramón y Cajal put forth the synaptic plasticity hypothesis (see Chapter 1), neurobiologists believe that the synapse is the fundamental information storage element in the brain. Information storage devices should have two important properties: they should be modifiable and the resulting modification should be stable. The synapse meets the modifiability criterion because experience can alter the strength of the connections linking the presynaptic and postsynaptic neurons. Synapses are plastic. This property, however, is just the opposite of the stability requirement. If modified synapses are to maintain newly acquired information they should be stable—resistant to change. From this point of view, *synaptic plasticity is the enemy of memory stability*. Some have argued, however, that the changes in spine morphology alter the plasticity of synapses.

SPINE MORPHOLOGY AND SYNAPTIC STABILITY    The shape of dendritic spines can change dramatically in response to the high-frequency stimulus that produces LTP. A general feature of potentiated spines is that they have broader heads and shorter necks. This is brought about by the reorganization of the actin cytoskeleton. Moreover, large spines are more stable than small ones. Some researchers have proposed that this altered structure changes the spine's functional properties so that it becomes resistant to further modification (Hayashi and Majewska, 2005; Kasai et al., 2003; Matsuzaki et al., 2001). Thus, stability might be preserved because the structure of the spine is also modified by synaptic activity.

How might this happen? One idea is that once the morphology of the spine is changed the regulation of calcium is altered. Specifically, the new spine morphology—broad head and short neck—allows the spine to more rapidly diffuse or eliminate the increased calcium resulting from NMDA receptor activation (Hayashi and Majewska, 2005; Noguchi et al., 2005; O'Donnell et al., 2011). Thus, even though these spines would contribute to exciting the neuron (because they allow more sodium to enter it), they would be resistant to modification by calcium-induced plasticity processes (Figure 8.3). Thus, the stability of the spine may emerge in part because actin proteins have been reorganized to create a large mushroom shape.

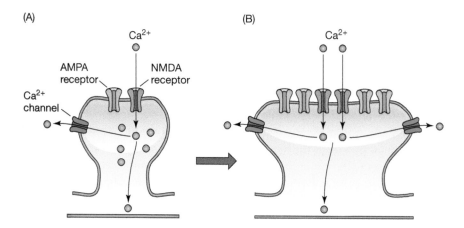

**Figure 8.3**
A spine's structure determines its stability and resistance to modification. High-frequency stimulation induces a cascade of biochemical processes that (1) change the morphology of the spine by broadening its head and (2) result in the insertion of disproportionately more AMPA than NMDA receptors into the head. The changes in the spine structure are thought to make the spine resistant to future changes that might occur in response to glutamate by increasing the capacity of the spine to diffuse $Ca^{2+}$ out of the head into extracellular space and into the dendrites. (A) Thus, in the smaller spine, $Ca^{2+}$ accumulates in the head in sufficient quantity to initiate the biochemical cascades needed to alter synaptic strength. (B) However, the potentiated spine with a broader head and wider neck allows $Ca^{2+}$ to rapidly efflux out of the head without initiating these cascades. (After Hayashi and Majewska, 2005.)

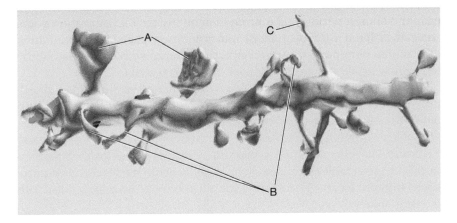

**Figure 8.4**
This figure illustrates a three-dimensional reconstruction of a dendritic section of a CA1 pyramidal cell (from *Synapse Web*, Kristen M. Harris, PI, http://synapses.clm.utexas.edu/). (A) Large spines may no longer be plastic and modifiable. (B) Small spines may be plastic and modifiable. (C) Small filopodium-like spines are unstable and withdraw within about 3 days unless they synapse with a presynaptic partner. The constant generation of new spines may be the dendrite's solution to maintaining storage capacity.

**SOME SPINES LEARN AND OTHERS REMEMBER**    Spines are dynamic and in many cases quite unstable; they can come and go (Figure 8.4). However, synaptic activity alters this dynamic and creates spines that are much more likely to survive. As noted, these spines are often large and mushroom-shaped. It is possible that such spines hold information about our past experiences that can subsequently be retrieved. However, as just discussed, these large spines may no longer be eligible to be modified. They are not very plastic. In principle, one could imagine that eventually all spines might become large and stable and the brain would lose its capacity to store new information. Dendrites would become saturated with spines that are no longer plastic and new information could not be stored.

Neurons have evolved a strategy to counter the saturation problem. Processes are operating in dendrites to constantly generate new spines that can become eligible for modification provided that they find a proper presynaptic partner to pair up with. Karel Svoboda and his colleagues (Knott et al., 2006) have directly monitored this process in the cortex of mice and found that spine-like filopodia are continuously

Karel Svoboda

growing out of dendrites and may be looking to pair with presynaptic elements. If within 2 to 3 days they do not form a synapse with a presynaptic element they disappear. However, if they do pair up with a presynaptic element, a new weakly connected synapse becomes available.

These facts suggest that spines can be categorized as "learning spines" and "memory spines" (Bourne and Harris, 2007). Learning spines are thin spines that can concentrate biochemical signals, such as calcium and its targets, which can modify synapses. In contrast, memory spines are large and mushroom-shaped—designed to capture products needed for their maintenance and to be stable (protected from modification). The biochemical interactions engaged by an LTP-inducing stimulus convert "learning spines" into "memory spines."

## Summary

Changes in synaptic strength are the result of an LTP-inducing stimulus initiating an overlapping, temporally organized sequence of molecular events that occur in four stages: generation, stabilization, consolidation, and maintenance. Trace generation is rapid and followed by a stabilization phase that requires about 15 minutes. Processes that consolidate synaptic changes require approximately 2 to 3 hours. The consolidation stage ends when LTP is no longer disrupted by agents that interrupt the transcription and translation processes initiated by the inducing stimulus. A primary goal of these three stages is to drive additional AMPA receptors into the postsynaptic density and build the infrastructure for their maintenance. The role of the maintenance stage is to reconfigure the trafficking of AMPA receptors containing GluA2 subunits so that potentiated synapses will retain these receptors. This process depends on the unique kinase PKMζ and other, yet to be identified molecules.

Much of the biochemistry engaged by the LTP-inducing stimulus is targeted at the trafficking of AMPA receptors. The regulation of actin filaments is a second major target. Induction requires the disassembling of filament actin. Stabilization and consolidation depend on the continuous polymerization and reorganization of actin filaments to create a large spine that provides an infrastructure for the potentiated spine to compete successfully for the molecules it will need to persist and to transport these molecules to the postsynaptic density.

A spine's size determines its stability. Relatively small thin spines are not likely to endure compared to large spines. However, small spines that find a presynaptic binding partner are quite plastic and can be converted into large spines by an LTP-inducing stimulus. The stability of large spines and the plastic properties of small spines suggest that large spines can be thought of as "memory spines" that hold information and small spines as "learning spines" that can acquire new information.

## References

Bourne, J. and Harris, K. M. (2007). Do thin spines learn to be mushroom spines that remember? *Current Opinion Neurobiology*, *17*, 381–386.

Ehlers, M. (2003). Ubiquitin and the deconstruction of synapses. *Science*, *302*, 800–801.

Gray, N. W., Weimer, R. M., Bureau, I., and Svoboda, K. (2006). Rapid redistribution of synaptic PSD-95 in the neocortex in vivo. *PLoS Biol*, *4*, 265–275.

Hayashi, Y. and Majewska, A. K. (2005). Dendritic spine geometry: functional implication and regulation. *Neuron*, *46*, 529–532.

Kasai, H., Matsuzaki, M., Noguchi, J., Yasumatsu, N., and Nakahara, H. (2003). Structure-stability-function relationships of dendritic spines. *Trends in Neurosciences*, *26*, 360–368.

Kelly, M. T., Yudong, Y., Sondhi, R., and Sacktor, T. C. (2007). Actin polymerization regulates the synthesis of PKMzeta in LTP. *Neuropharmacology*, *52*, 41–45.

Knott, G. W., Holtmaat, A., Wilbrecht, L., Welker, E., and Svoboda, K. (2006). Spine growth precedes synapse formation in the adult neocortex in vivo. *Nature Neuroscience*, *9*, 1117–1124.

Matsuzaki, M., Ellis-Davies, G. C., Nemoto, T., Miyashita, Y., Iino, M., and Kasai, H. (2001). Dendritic spine geometry is critical for AMPA receptor expression in hippocampal CA1 pyramidal neurons. *Nature Neuroscience*, *4*, 1086–1092.

Noguchi, J., Matsuzaki, M., Ellis-Davies, G. C., and Kasai, H. (2005). Spine-neck geometry determines NMDA receptor-dependent $Ca^{2+}$ signaling in dendrites. *Neuron*, *46*, 609–622.

O'Donnell, C., Nolan, M. F., and van Rossum, M. C. W. (2011). Dendritic spine dynamics regulate the long-term stability of synaptic plasticity. *Journal of Neuroscience*, *31*, 16142–16156.

Park, M., Salgado, J. M., Ostroff, L., Helton, T. D., Robinson, C. G., Harris, K. M., and Ehlers, M. D. (2006). Recyling endosomes supply AMPA receptors for LTP. *Neuron*, *52*, 817–830.

Semenova, I., Burakov, A., Berardone, N., Zaliapin, I., Slepchenko, B., Svitkina, T., Kashina, A., and Rodionov, V. (2008). Actin dynamics is essential for myosin-based transport of membrane organelles. *Current Biology*, *18*, 1581–1586.

Wang, Z., Edwards, J. G., Riley, N., Provance, D. W., Karcher, R., Li, X-d., Davison, I. G., Ikebe, M., Mercer, J. A., Kauer, J. A., and Ehlers, M. D. (2008). Myosin Vb mobilizes recycling endosomes for postsynaptic plasticity. *Cell*, *135*, 535–548.

# PART 2
## Molecules and Memories

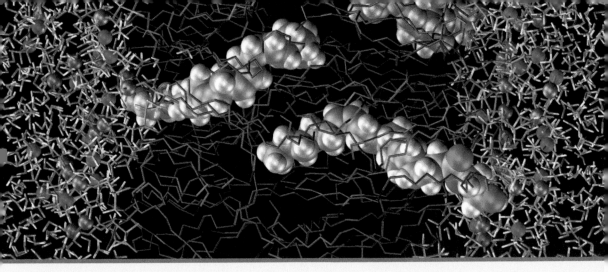

# 9 Making Memories: Conceptual Issues and Methods

A fundamental question for many students of memory is, *how is information contained in a behavioral experience stored in the brain*? Many researchers believe that the synapse is the basic information storage unit, and previous chapters have described some of the essential findings and ideas about how synapses can be modified. This chapter uses this foundation to explore how memories might be made.

In studies of synaptic plasticity, the stimulus that modified synapses was high-frequency electrical stimulation. Memories, however, are established as a result of a behavioral experience, that is, a behaving organism interacting with its environment. This experience is assumed to produce changes in synaptic strength in regions of the brain that store the experience. Memory researchers are thus in the difficult position of connecting the mechanisms of synaptic plasticity to behavioral experience. To do this, the researcher has to navigate a number of difficult conceptual and interpretive issues and the research requires behavioral and brain methodologies that have not yet been discussed. Thus, the goal of this chapter is to provide an understanding of some of these issues and methodologies.

## LTP and Memory

If the synapse is the fundamental storage unit in the brain, and if studies of LTP have produced a complete understanding of how synapses are modified (which they have not), then one might argue that we already know how memories are made. The problem with this argument is that the information acquired by studying LTP comes from a highly artificial preparation.

First, the experience used to induce LTP is a low-intensity, high-frequency electrical event that bypasses all the sensory inputs that normally bring environmental information into the brain. No one has any firm idea about exactly how the pattern of electrical stimulation used to produce LTP corresponds to the pattern of neural activity generated by normal sensory stimulation that initiates the formation of a memory trace in a behaving organism. It should be appreciated that a slightly more intense inducing stimulus would generate seizure activity in a normal brain. Second, the modified synapses typically are in slices of brain tissue that are maintained in a chemical cocktail to keep them functional. There are consequences associated with the removal of the tissue, which requires a number of preparatory steps just to get a functional preparation. In short, to produce LTP an unnatural stimulus is often delivered to an abnormal neural preparation. So in principle all the results and ideas that we have discussed might have no relevance to how a normal brain stores the information contained in natural experiences.

Fortunately, even though there are enormous differences between the sensory consequences of a behavioral experience arriving into an intact brain and the electrical stimulation arriving into a population of neurons, studies of LTP have yielded important ideas about how memories are formed. Thus, although the synaptic changes that are recorded as LTP do not constitute a memory, studies of synaptic plasticity are the fundamental source of hypotheses about how the brain makes memories. So much of what has already been presented will help in understanding the molecules that make memories.

## Behavior and Memory

As previously stated, memories are the product of behaving organisms interacting with their environments. Chapter 1 made the point that memory is a concept offered to explain why behavioral experiences can influence

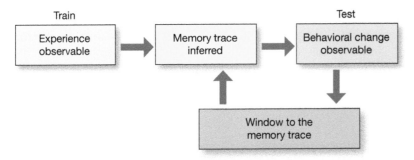

**Figure 9.1**
All experimental investigations of memory require a training phase to establish a memory and a test phase to detect the memory. The existence of a memory trace is inferred when the training experience influences behavior. Thus, test behavior can be thought of as the window to the memory trace.

subsequent behavioral responses to the environment. No one has ever directly observed a memory. This state of affairs has important implications for trying to understand the biological basis of memory. In reality, the effort requires trying to link some physical properties of the brain to an abstract, unobservable concept. To approach this endeavor requires some discussion about the relationship between memory and behavior.

To start the discussion, consider the basic paradigm used in all studies of learning and memory (Figure 9.1). The inference that a memory has been established requires that the subject in the experiment have a particular experience and then be tested with some component of that experience. If the experience influences the behavioral test, then one might infer that a memory has been established. Recall, for example, that Ebbinghaus trained himself on lists of nonsense syllables and then tested himself to see if he remembered them.

## Test Behavior: The Window to the Memory Trace

Given that Ebbinghaus recalled the nonsense syllables, one might infer that a memory was established. However, this was because his past behavioral experience influenced his test behavior. The memory was not observed. What was observed was that studying the lists influenced his recall of the nonsense syllables. Note that without a measurable behavioral test response, there would be no evidence that his studying produced a memory trace. Thus, one might conclude that test behavior is the window to the memory trace. Unless the researcher can demonstrate that experience alters test behavior, there is no basis to say it established a memory.

If memory were the only thing that influenced behavior, the study of the biological basis of learning and memory would still be difficult, but far simpler. Unfortunately, this is not the case; a measurable behavior is the final product of many different component processes (Figure 9.2). To list just a few, there are:

- sensory, attention, and perceptual processes that determine what the subject experiences at the time of training and testing;
- motivational processes that determine the subject's willingness to initiate a response;
- emotional processes that can interfere with the subject's ability to access stored information;
- motor systems that provide the basis for the behavioral response to be expressed; and
- a memory system that stores the experience.

What are the implications of this state of affairs? In studying the biological basis of memory, neurobiologists use a variety of methods to influence brain function. They include:

- experimentally damaging a particular region of the brain;
- injecting drugs into the brain that are designed to influence some aspect of neural function; and
- genetic engineering to increase or decrease the expression of some potential memory molecule.

These methods are discussed in greater detail later in this chapter. To interpret the results produced by any of these methods, the researcher has to confront the possibility that the treatment influenced behavior by its effect on one or more of the component processes listed above.

To illustrate this point, consider the hypothesis that a specific region of the brain stores the memory for some particular experience. To test this hypothesis the experimenter would damage this region and then provide the subjects with a learning experience. The results would be stunningly clear: compared to control subjects that had no brain damage, subjects with brain damage would display no behavioral evidence that they ever had the training experience. They would behave as if they had no memory for the experience. What can be concluded from this outcome?

The proper conclusion would be simply that the data are consistent with the hypothesis. Unfortunately, the results would also be consistent with other explanations. Before anyone would believe that the damaged region was critical to memory formation, additional experiments would need to be performed to rule out alternative explanations. The lesion might have impaired

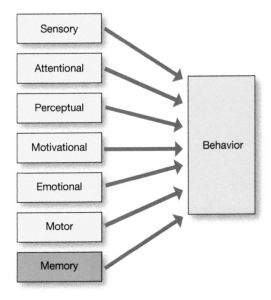

**Figure 9.2**
An organism's behavioral response is determined by the interaction of many different component processes. Thus, before one can conclude that some biological manipulation influenced some aspect of memory, one has to be sure that it did not influence some other component that influences behavior.

(1) sensory–attention or perceptual processes, (2) motivation or emotional processes, or (3) motor processes. Thus, the experimenter's work would have just begun. This caveat applies to the interpretation of any manipulation of brain processes that alters the behavioral measure of memory.

### The Learning–Performance Distinction

Successful inroads into understanding the biological basis of memory depend on researchers establishing a strong basis for their conclusions. They must be able to show that the brain manipulation in their experiment influenced behavior by selectively influencing the unobservable memory component and not by affecting some other component process. Psychologists call this problem the **learning–performance distinction**. It recognizes that the researcher has to be sure that the treatment exerted its effect by its influence on the memory component and not on some other component process that could also influence performance. To rule out the possibility that the brain manipulation did not influence other component processes is a daunting task. In spite of these complexities, however, memory researchers have made significant advances in this area.

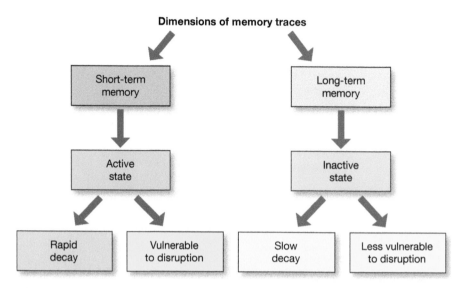

**Figure 9.3**
Memory traces can differ on at least three dimensions: duration, state, and vulnerability to disruption.

## Dimensions of Memory Traces

At least since William James's treatise on psychology, some memory researchers have believed that behavioral experience produces a succession of memory traces in the brain. How many traces are created is a matter of debate that does not need to be considered here. However, most researchers who study the biological basis of memory agree that experience initiates at least two memory traces: a **short-term memory trace** that decays relatively quickly and a more stable, **long-term memory trace** that has a much slower decay rate (Figure 9.3). Because this distinction is so important to neurobiological memory research, it is important to discuss it more fully.

The idea that short-term and long-term memory traces have different decay rates is important. This duration distinction also is tied to two other dimensions: the state of the memory trace (active versus inactive) and its vulnerability to disruption. For example, a football player who receives a blow to the head may not recall any events he experienced several minutes prior to the blow but he may have full recall of everything that happened in the locker room before the game started. The blow to the head produced a very time-limited retrograde amnesia (a failure to remember an experience that happened prior to the occurrence of the disrupting event). Not all memories were lost; the amnesia was limited only to events that occurred just before the causal event, that is, the blow to the head. One explanation for the limited

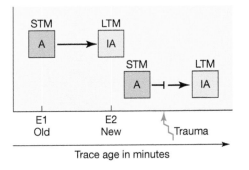

**Figure 9.4**
A football player has two sets of experiences. E1 represents the locker room experiences prior to the game. E2 represents experiences just prior to the head trauma. Thus, the E1 memories are older than the E2 memories. The trauma produces amnesia only for the newer E2 memories because they are still in an active state at the time the trauma occurs. The E1 memories are not affected because they had achieved the inactive, long-term memory state. STM = short-term memory; LTM = long-term memory; A = active state; IA = inactive state; E1 = experience 1; E2 = experience 2.

retrograde amnesia is that the blow only affected the memory traces in the active state. Memories that had achieved long-term memory status and were not in the active state at the time of the trauma were not lost. This point is illustrated in Figure 9.4.

## The Concept of Memory Consolidation

Following a learning experience, the memory trace is vulnerable to disruption. With the passage of time, the trace becomes more stable and resistant to memory disruption. This outcome is attributed to a process called **memory consolidation**, a concept introduced over 100 years ago by Müeller and Pilzecker (1900). This concept is illustrated in Figure 9.5.

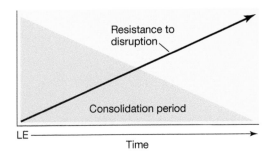

**Figure 9.5**
This figure illustrates the concept of memory consolidation. Following a learning experience (LE), a memory trace is vulnerable to disruption. With the passage of time, resistance to memory disruption increases and the trace becomes more stable. The term memory consolidation is used to describe this change from vulnerable to less vulnerable. The consolidation period is the time it takes to achieve this outcome.

*Electroconvulsive Shock and Memory Disruption*

Experimental investigations of memory disruption associated with brain trauma did not emerge until nearly half a century after Müeller and Pilzecker's research (see McGaugh, 2003, for a review of the history of this development). In the late 1930s, two Italian physicians, Ugo Cerletti and Lucio Bini, began to use **electroconvulsive shock** (**ECS**) to treat psychiatric disorders (Cerletti and Bini, 1938). Clinical observations indicated that patients treated with ECS often did not recall their experiences in the time period leading up to the treatment. A decade later, Carl Duncan (1949) recognized that ECS might be a useful tool for experimentally producing amnesia in animals. He trained rats and administered ECS within a minute or so of training, or an hour later. Rats that received ECS shortly after training displayed a memory impairment. Dozens of experiments were subsequently conducted that used the ECS methodology. Unfortunately, however, this research did not answer any fundamental questions about memory consolidation (McGaugh, 2003). In essence, based on clinical examples, it was already known that brain trauma can disrupt recently established memories and the ECS methodology did not advance understanding beyond this point.

*Memory Disruption: A Storage or Retrieval Failure?*

In the preceding discussion, the term memory disruption was used to describe the vulnerability of newly established memory traces. Sergei Korsakoff (1897) recognized that memory can be disrupted for two reasons (see Chapter 1).

- The impairment is a **storage failure**. According to this hypothesis, the agent that produces amnesia, for example a blow to the head, interferes with the processes responsible for storing the memory. The implication of this idea is that events experienced prior to the trauma will never be remembered. A memory not stored can never be recovered.

- The impairment is a **retrieval failure**. According to this hypothesis the memory is stored but cannot be accessed. The agent that produces amnesia in some way disrupts the neural pathways that enable the memory to be retrieved. The implication of this idea is that the memory loss is temporary. Even without trauma, we often have retrieval failures. For example, it is common to forget the location of a book or a coffee cup, only later to remember it. In this case the information had been stored but for some reason could not be accessed or retrieved (Figure 9.6).

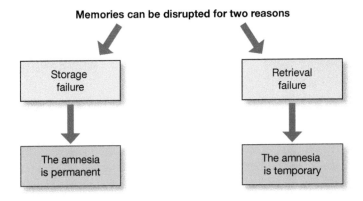

**Figure 9.6**
A disrupting event can interfere with the storage of the memory trace or it can interfere with processes involved in retrieval.

The ECS methodology contributed very little to the understanding of how memories are formed. However, it sensitized researchers to the idea that memory failures produced by brain trauma can be either a storage failure or retrieval failure. For a time, research on memory consolidation stalled because researchers using this methodology could not resolve the question of whether or not an event that produces a memory impairment interfered with storage or retrieval. The possibility that a memory impairment can be due to retrieval failures must always be considered when someone claims that their brain manipulation interferes with the consolidation processes that store the memory. The retrieval hypothesis is diabolical because it is impossible to completely disprove. It can never be proved that a memory will not recover with time. The question is, *how much time must be allowed before concluding that the impairment is due to a storage failure: a day, a week, a month?* There is no good answer to this question except that longer is better.

## Some Behavioral Test Methods for Studying Memory

Memory researchers use a wide variety of behavioral test methods to study the biological basis of memory. It would be impossible to cover even a small fraction of what is known in this area, so choices have to be made. Much of what we know about the biological basis of memory can be illustrated by initially focusing on results and ideas that have emerged from three extensively used methods: (1) inhibitory avoidance conditioning, (2) fear conditioning, and (3) spatial learning in a water-escape task. This section describes these methods and some of the advantages they have for memory research. Other methods are described in subsequent sections.

## Inhibitory Avoidance Conditioning

An illustration of the apparatus used to study **inhibitory avoidance conditioning** is shown in Figure 9.7. The basic procedure is simple. A rodent (rat or mouse) is placed in the bright side of the apparatus. Rodents generally prefer to be in dimmer environments, so within 10 seconds or so, it will cross over to the dark side. When this occurs, a brief electrical shock is applied to its feet and the subject is removed. Some time later the rodent is again placed in the bright side of the apparatus, and the experimenter measures the time it takes the rodent to enter the dark side of the compartment. The expectation is that if the rodent remembers that it was shocked in the dark side, it will be reluctant to cross over. So the latency to cross over to the dark side should

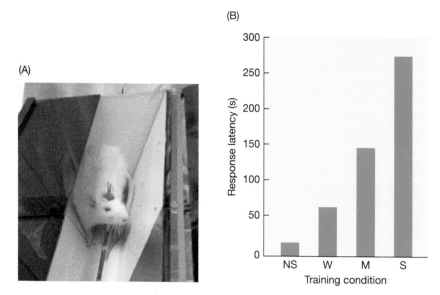

**Figure 9.7**
(A) A photograph of an apparatus used to study inhibitory avoidance learning. The rat is placed in the bright end of the apparatus. When it crosses to the dark side, it receives an electric shock across its feet. To assess the memory for this experience, the rat is placed again in the bright end and the time it takes to cross to the dark side (crossover latency) is measured. (B) The graph illustrates the effect of increasing shock intensity on response latency. Note that as shock intensity increases, so does response latency. NS = no shock; W = weak shock; M = moderate shock; S = strong shock. (Photo courtesy of James L. McGaugh.)

increase. This methodology is called inhibitory avoidance because the rodent has to inhibit its tendency to cross over and thus avoid the place where it was shocked. Note that in using this task, the researcher assumes that the strength of the memory trace is reflected in the response latency, that is, longer latencies reflect a stronger memory trace.

Inhibitory avoidance conditioning has two important attributes. First, only one training trial is required to produce a memory for the experience, although more trials can be given. Second, the rodent's crossover latency is quite sensitive to the intensity of the shock. As shock intensity is increased, the latency to cross over also increases.

Experimental treatments may be hypothesized to either increase or decrease the strength of the memory. So when investigating a drug or some other manipulation that is hypothesized to strengthen a memory trace, a low-intensity shock should be used. This is because if a strong shock is used, the rodent's crossover latency would be so long that it might obscure the possibility of seeing the enhanced latency predicted by the hypothesis. This outcome is called a **ceiling effect** because if the response measure is at the maximum (ceiling), there is no way to see the influence of some other manipulation.

In contrast, if the treatment is hypothesized to impair the memory processes that produce avoidance behavior, then a somewhat higher level of shock that produces a long latency would be used. If a weak shock that produces a short crossover latency is used, it may not be possible to observe the predicted decrease in performance. This outcome is called a **floor effect** because the performance measure is too low to be further reduced by the drug.

## Fear Conditioning

**Fear conditioning** has become a very popular method for studying the biological basis of memory. The basic methodology, illustrated in Figure 9.8, is a version of Pavlovian conditioning described in Chapter 1. Some time after a rodent is placed into what is called a conditioning chamber, an auditory stimulus (the conditioned stimulus) is presented. About 10 to 15 seconds after the onset of the auditory stimulus, electrical shock (the unconditioned stimulus) is delivered to the rodent's feet. One can administer one or several training trials. An innate defensive response called **freezing** (see Chapter 19) is a conditioned response that is often used to assess the rodent's memory for the experience. In the presence of a danger signal, such as the sight or sounds of a predator, rodents instinctively become still or immobile. This behavior has survival advantages because a moving animal is more likely to be detected by a predator than a still one.

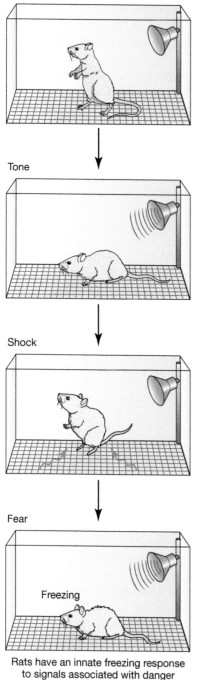

Exploration

Tone

Shock

Fear

Freezing

Rats have an innate freezing response
to signals associated with danger

The fear conditioning procedure also has important advantages. It allows the experimenter very precise control over factors that might influence the strength of a memory such as (1) the intensity of the CS and US, (2) the time separating the CS and US, and (3) the number of training trials. The innate freezing response that is the CR is easy to measure. Usually the experimenter will observe the rodent and determine the time it spends freezing. However, there are automated methods available to measure this behavior. The basic assumption is that the duration of the freezing response is an indicator of the strength of the memory.

## Spatial Learning in a Water-Escape Task

**Spatial learning** in a water-escape task is a far more complex behavioral test method than the other two described above. The water-escape task was developed by Richard Morris (1981) to allow researchers a method for studying how animals acquire map-like representations of their environments. Essentially, a small platform is located in a large, circular pool of water into which rodents are placed and then tested on finding the location of the platform (Figure 9.9). There are two versions of the water-escape task: the place-learning task and the visible-platform task.

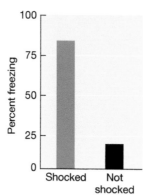

**Figure 9.8**
In fear conditioning, after the rat has explored the conditioning context, an auditory cue (tone) is presented for about 15 seconds. Shock is delivered when the tone terminates. Rats are then tested for their fear of the context–place where shock occurred and later for their fear of the tone. Shocked rats display more freezing than rats that were not shocked.

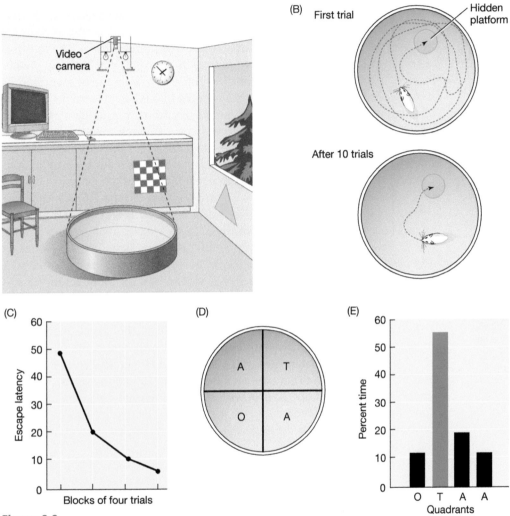

**Figure 9.9**
The place-learning version of the Morris water-escape task. (A) A circular swimming pool in the laboratory. (B) On the first trial, the rodent swims a long distance before it locates the platform. After several trials, it learns to swim directly to the platform. (C) Escape latency, the time it takes the rat to find the hidden platform, decreases as a function of training trials. (D) A schematic of the swimming pool that divides it into four quadrants: T = the training quadrant; A = the two adjacent quadrants; O = the quadrant opposite the training quadrant. (E) The results of a probe trial with the platform removed from the pool. Note that the rats spend more time swimming in the training quadrant than in the other quadrants.

PLACE-LEARNING TASK   To create the **place-learning task**, the platform is placed in the pool just below the surface of the water but invisible to the rodent. The rodent is placed in the water at the edge of the pool and is released. It can escape from the pool by finding the invisible platform. Note that a special property of this basic task is that the platform remains in the same location of the pool over a block of training trials. The location is specified in relationship to the features of the room in which the pool is located. Typically, the rodent is started randomly from one of several locations inside the side of the pool. This ensures that it has to learn the location of the platform and does not learn just to swim in a particular direction in relationship to some single feature in the room. Rodents are excellent swimmers and, even though the platform is invisible, once the rodent habituates to the surprise of being in the water, it takes very few trials for it to learn to swim quickly and directly to the platform. Successful performance on this task is measured in several ways. During training, **escape latency** (the time it takes to find the platform) decreases dramatically. The distance the rodent swims before it finds the platform, called **path length**, also improves. With practice the rodents swim directly to the platform. Usually escape latency and path length are highly connected because, other things being equal, on a trial when the rodent swims a short distance to find the platform the escape latency will be shorter than when it swims a long distance before locating the platform.

Researchers use what is called a **probe trial** to further assess the rodent's memory for the location of the platform. On a probe trial, the platform is removed from the pool and the rodent is placed in the pool and allowed to search for it. The duration of the search can vary (20 to 60 seconds), depending on the experimenter. The rodent's performance can be videotaped or a special camera that feeds data into a computer for further processing can capture it. In either case the experimenter collects information about where the rodent swims.

One standard measure of performance in this task is called **quadrant search time**. The pool is divided conceptually into four equal quadrants. During training the platform is in one quadrant. A rodent that has stored a memory of the location of the platform will spend more of its search time in the training quadrant than it will in the other quadrants. Another performance measure is called **annulus crossings**. In this case, the measure is how many times during the probe trial the animal actually crosses the exact place where the platform is located compared to how many times it crosses the equivalent area in the other quadrants.

VISIBLE-PLATFORM TASK   The **visible-platform task** is often used as a control task to evaluate alternative interpretations of the effect of some brain manipulation on performance in the place-learning task. In this task the platform sets above the water surface and usually is painted to make it contrast with the water. The platform location usually varies on each trial. If some drug, genetic manipulation, or lesion disrupts performance on the place-learning version of the task, one would want to know that this treatment did not disrupt sensory, motivational–emotional, or motor systems. If the treatment has no effect on performance on the visible-platform task, then one would be more confident about concluding that the treatment influenced some aspect of memory. If, however, the same treatment disrupted performance on this task, then it would be difficult to conclude that the treatment affected memory.

### Why These Three Behavioral Test Methods?

These three test methods—inhibitory avoidance conditioning, fear conditioning, and spatial learning in a water-escape task—initially are the center of focus because many researchers who study memory molecules have targeted treatments to two regions of the brain, the **hippocampus** and **amygdala**. The hippocampus is targeted because, as will later be discussed, it makes a critical contribution to what is called episodic memory (see Chapters 16 and 17) and because the bulk of the LTP literature comes from slices taken from the hippocampus. The amygdala is targeted because it is thought to be critically involved in the storage of emotional memories (see Chapter 19). The amygdala is targeted also because it is a region of the brain where LTP is studied. Other behavioral paradigms will be introduced in subsequent chapters.

## Methods for Manipulating Brain Function

Our understanding of how memories are made in the brain requires that the researcher be able to manipulate the brain to determine if a particular region or molecule is critical to creating a memory. This section addresses two general ways this is accomplished. One method, based on damaging or chemically altering neurons in a specific region of the brain, depends on stereotaxic surgery. The other method utilizes genetic engineering techniques to target specific genes.

### Stereotaxic Surgery

**Stereotaxic surgery** uses a coordinate system to locate specific targets inside the brain to enable some procedure to be carried out on them (for example, a lesion, injection, or implantation). As illustrated in Figure 9.10, a stereotaxic surgery device allows the researcher to lower a fine wire, called an **electrode**, into a precise region of the brain. By passing electric current through the tip of this wire, the researcher can damage neurons in the region of the electrode tip. The device can also be used to position a small injection needle (often referred to as a **cannula**) into a precise brain region so that the researcher can inject into that region a chemical solution that can also damage neurons. Both of these methods are used to damage a particular brain region.

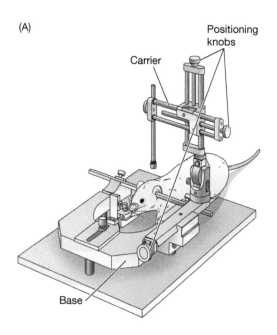

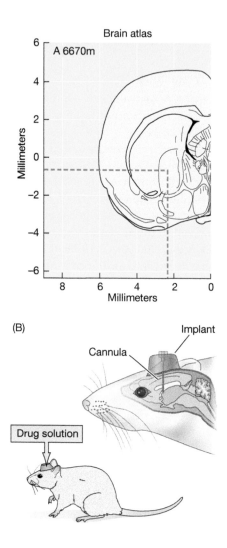

**Figure 9.10**
(A) A stereotaxic device is used during surgery for precise placement of a fine wire (electrode) or a small injection needle (cannula) for targeting electrical current or a chemical solution into a specific region of the brain. The base holds the anesthetized animal's head and neck in a stationary position. The carrier portion places the electrode or cannula in a precise location based on the coordinates of the target area identified with a brain atlas. (B) A cannula guide is implanted deep into the rat's brain. Drugs can then be delivered to specific regions of the brain of an awake and moving rat by inserting a cannula into the guide.

## Genetic Engineering

Pharmacological agents have been used with much success in elucidating some of the major molecules that contribute to memory. However, drugs are often "dirty," meaning they are not highly selective to the intended target. This state of affairs can have unintended consequences that can make it difficult to interpret results. Moreover, controlling the spread of the drug to other regions is also difficult and presents other interpretative problems.

**Genetic engineering** methods permit much more precise targeting of specific molecules that might play a role in making memories. By using biotechnology to directly influence the genome, it is possible to modify or delete the gene for a particular protein or to transfer new genes into the genome. These methods have made it possible to alter the DNA in a fertilized egg and thereby alter specific genes. Moreover, because this occurs in the fertilized egg, which is then implanted back into the pseudo pregnant animal, this experimentally induced mutation will be carried by the offspring. In general, a particular gene can be removed or "knocked out" or a transgenic animal can be produced, in which case a replacement gene is substituted for the original gene (Figure 9.11).

Researchers often apply genetic engineering methods to mice to study learning and memory. In the first generation of genetically engineered mice, the offspring develop with the mutation and, since a given gene can play an important role in many different functions of the organism, even if the animal survives it might be abnormal in many ways that make it quite difficult to determine the importance of the gene for learning and memory.

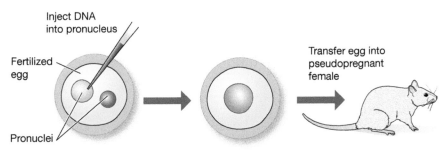

**Figure 9.11**
DNA is injected into a pronucleus from a fertilized egg. This DNA can be designed to replace or knock out a particular gene or it can substitute for another gene.

However, genetic engineering methods have become much more sophisticated. So there now exists what is called a **conditional knockout methodology**. Under the right conditions, this methodology allows the experimenter to knock out a particular gene in a very well specified region of the brain, such as the CA1 region of the hippocampus, and to do this at different times in development. Moreover, the results of these new techniques can be reversed. Thus, a given gene might be turned off for some period of time and then turned back on, so one can study the same animal with a particular gene knocked out or with that gene functioning.

VIRAL VECTOR SYSTEM   Regional and temporal specificity also have been improved by the use of **viral vector systems**—the use of viruses to deliver new genetic material into specific cells (Waehler et al., 2007). Viruses contain genetic material that provides the basic instructions for self-replication. However, they do not have the machinery and metabolism to replicate. Thus, to replicate they must invade a host and hijack the host machinery for this purpose. Viruses can be modified to deliver desired genes into host cells. This is accomplished by deleteing some or all of the coding regions of the viral genome and replacing them with a genetic construct that contains the desired new genetic material—the vector genome—and additional genetic elements that control the expression of the gene. This is called a promoter sequence. When the virus is injected into target neurons, the vector genome will then be expressed (Figure 9.12). It is also possible to associate the vector genome with a green fluorescent protein (GFP), a protein that displays bright green fluorescence when exposed to light in the blue-to-ultraviolet ranges. This enables the researcher to identify cells that have been infected by the virus.

OPTOGENETICS   As the name **optogenetics** implies, this methodology combines genetic engineering with optics, the branch of physics that studies the properties of light, to provide a way to control the activity of individual neurons (Deisseroth, 2011; Fenno et al., 2011). Although signaling cascades that regulate neuroplasticity involve interactions among molecules in single neurons, brain functions (vision, motor behaviors, emotional behaviors, and memories) are ultimately the product of neurons communicating with each other. Thus, a fundamental challenge to brain science is to identify the specific neurons and their contribution to the basic brain functions. To do this requires a method that allows scientists to control one type of cell without altering other types. Existing techniques, based on electrical or chemical stimulation, do not allow this type of control. Francis Crick (1979) suggested that light might be able to control neurons with the temporal and regional specificity needed to map out complex functional circuits of the brain. The development of optogenetics has proven Crick correct.

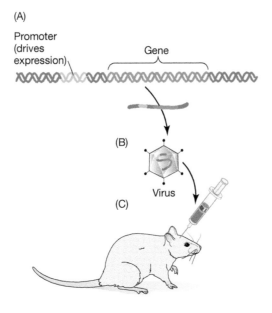

**Figure 9.12**
This figure illustrates a viral vector system used to deliver new genes to neurons where they will be expressed in neurons infected by the viruses. (A) A genetic construct is made that contains the relevant new genetic material and genes for a promoter that drives expression of the gene-infected neurons. (B) This genetic construct is then packaged into the virus and (C) and injected into targeted neurons.

The discovery that some microorganisms produce proteins that in response to light can regulate the flow of ions across the membrane was fundamental to this development. The genes that code for these proteins are called **opsins**. In 2005, Karl Deisseroth and his colleagues reported that, by using the just described viral vector methodology, genes that code for a class of opsins, called channelrhodopsin, could be targeted to hippocampal neurons and would be expressed (Boyden et al., 2005). When activated by blue light, these channel proteins could be stimulated to open and close with millisecond precision and conduct positive ions with the result of depolarizing the neuron. To provide the light source (either with laser light or with light emitting diodes) optical fibers are implanted into the brain region thought to express the protein, and light will activate only those neurons expressing channelrhodopsin. Another class of opsins, called halorhodopsin, has the opposite effect—when stimulated with green

Karl Deisseroth

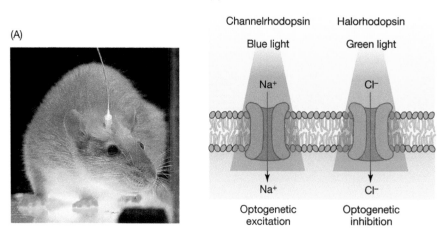

**Figure 9.13**
After rhodopsin genes have been expressed on membranes, they can be activated by light to excite neurons (channelrhodopsin) or to inhibit neurons (halorhodopsin). Channelrhodopsin is activated by blue light and halorhodopsin is activated by green light.

light they conduct negatively charged chloride ions and thereby hyperpolarize the neuron (Figure 9.13) With these tools, the experimenter can excite or inhibit the firing of specific neurons.

## Summary

Memory researchers must confront a number of conceptual and interpretative issues. Memories cannot be directly observed, so behavior has to be tested in order to infer that a memory has been established. However, behavior is the final product of many different processes. This problem is recognized as the learning–performance distinction. Alternative explanations of the results have to be eliminated before it can be concluded that some brain manipulation influenced memory processes and not some other components that influence behavior. Two ideas are fundamental to confronting these issues: (1) experience can produce memory traces with different properties and (2) memory traces need to consolidate. Interpreting memory impairments is difficult because the experimental treatment can impair processes that store the memory trace (storage failure) or processes that retrieve the memory trace (retrieval failure). Memory researchers depend upon behavioral procedures such as inhibitory avoidance, fear conditioning, and place learning to measure memory, and they depend on methods such as stereotaxic surgery, pharmacology, and genetic engineering to manipulate the brain.

## References

Boyden, E. S., Zhang, F., Bamberg, E., Nagel, G., and Deisseroth, K. (2005). Millisecond-timescale, genetically targeted optical control of neural activity. *Nature Neuroscience, 8,* 1263–1268.

Cerletti, U. and Bini, L. (1938). Electric shock treatment. *Bollettino Reale Accademia Medico, Roma, 64,* 136–138.

Crick F. H. (1979). Thinking about the brain. *Scientific American, 241,* 219–232.

Deisseroth K. (2011). Optogenetics. *Nature Methods, 8,* 26–29.

Duncan, C. P. (1949). The retroactive effect of electroshock on learning. *Journal of Comparative and Physiological Psychology, 42,* 332–344.

Fenno, L., Yizhar, O., and Deisseroth, K. (2011). The development and application of optogenetics. *Annual Review of Neuroscience, 34,* 389–412.

Korsakoff, S. S. (1897). Disturbance of psychic function in alcoholic paralysis and its relation to the disturbance of the psychic sphere in multiple neuritis of nonalchoholic origins. *Vesin. Psychiatrii 4:* fascicle 2.

McGaugh, J. L. (2003). Memory and emotion. New York: Columbia University Press.

Morris, R. G. M. (1981). Spatial localization does not depend on the presence of local cues. *Learning and Motivation, 12,* 239–260.

Müeller, G. E. and Pilzecker, A. (1900). Experimentalle beitrage zur lehre vom gedachtinis. *Zeitschrift für Psychologie und Physiologie der Sinnesorgane, I,* 1–288.

Waehler, R., Russell, S. J., and Curiel, D. T. (2007). Engineering targeted viral vectors for gene therapy. *Nature Reviews: Genetics, 8,* 573–587.

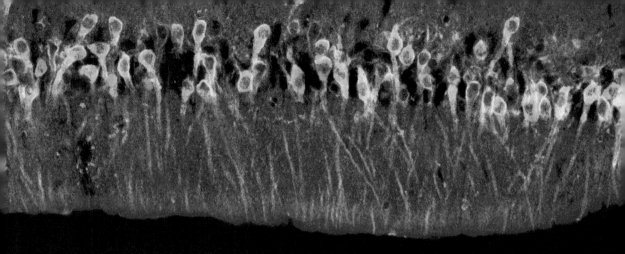

# 10 Memory Formation: Early Stages

Memories are produced by experience. The goal of this and the next three chapters is to discuss some of the important cellular–molecular processes that translate experience into memories. These chapters are organized around three basic ideas already presented in the chapters on synaptic plasticity: (1) synaptic changes supporting LTP depend on the binding of glutamate to NMDA and AMPA receptors, (2) post-translation processes can support short-lasting LTP, (3) but long-lasting LTP requires new protein that results from transcription and translation processes. From the perspective of how memories are made, these ideas suggest that post-translation processes can establish a short-term memory trace but experience has to engage transcription and translation processes if the memory is to endure.

It is generally assumed that the formation of a memory trace begins when a behavioral experience activates an ensemble of neurons that might potentially represent the content of the experience. Activated neurons then release

(A)

Behavioral experience

(B)

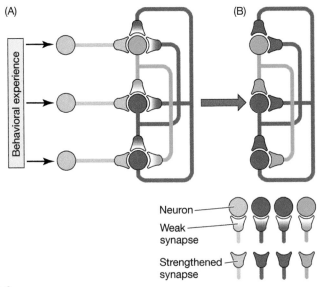

Neuron

Weak synapse

Strengthened synapse

**Figure 10.1**
(A) The formation of a memory trace begins when a behavioral experience activates a set of weakly connected neurons. (B) The cellular–molecular processes activated in these neurons strengthen their synaptic connections, thereby creating a neural representation of the behavioral experience, called a memory trace.

glutamate onto the postsynaptic sites and initiate the cascade of cellular–molecular events that strengthen synaptic connections among this set of neurons (Figure 10.1). The signaling cascades that lead to memory formation begin with the release of the first messenger glutamate and the activation of glutamate receptors—a good place to begin the discussion of the early stages of memory formation.

This chapter first addresses the contribution of glutamate receptors (NMDA and AMPA) to memory formation, acquisition, and retrieval; then examines the roles of CaMKII and actin regulation in memory formation; and concludes with a discussion of the dependence of working and reference memory on glutamate receptors.

## NMDA Receptors and Memory Formation

Given the critical contribution NMDA receptors make in the initiation of processes that strengthen synapses, one would expect that these receptors are also important for the initiation of memories for behavioral experience.

Researchers have used both pharmacological and genetic engineering methodologies to test this hypothesis.

## Pharmacological Alteration

Richard Morris (Morris et al., 1986) was the first researcher to experimentally test the hypothesis that the initial formation of a memory trace depends on the activation of NMDA receptors. To do this he implanted a cannula to deliver the NMDA receptor antagonist APV into the ventricular system of a rat's brain where it would enter the cerebral spinal fluid. Cerebral spinal fluid is the substance that covers the brain and spinal cord and cushions them against impact. It also provides them with oxygen and nutrients and removes waste products (Figure 10.2).

Richard Morris

Morris reasoned that APV injected into this fluid would widely diffuse and occupy NMDA receptors throughout the brain. If NMDA receptors are involved in creating memories for behavioral experiences, then blocking glutamate's access to these receptors at the time of the learning experience should impair memory formation. Morris infused APV dissolved in a vehicle solution into the brain for several days in order to ensure that it occupied NMDA receptors. Control rats were infused with just the vehicle solution. He then trained these rats in the place-learning version of the water-escape task (see Chapter 9).

Morris's experiments revealed that APV prevented the induction of LTP in the dentate gyrus of the hippocampus and, more importantly, dramatically impaired the rat's ability to learn the location of the hidden platform. Morris thus provided the first evidence that NMDA receptors, which are critical to the induction of LTP, may also participate in the initiation of a memory trace. Since Morris et al.'s original publication, there have been a large number of studies using APV to successfully implicate a role for NMDA receptors in memory formation (for example, Campeau et al., 1992; Fanselow and Kim, 1994; Matus-Amat et al., 2007; Morris et al., 1990; Stote and Fanselow, 2004).

## Genetic Engineering

Results provided by the genetic engineering approach (see Chapter 9) have strengthened and extended conclusions based on pharmacology. By using these techniques, researchers are able to selectively delete or selectively over-express the gene for a particular molecule that might be important for making

(A)

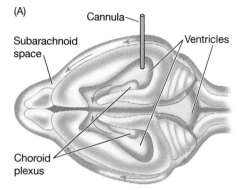

(C) LTP in dentate gyrus

(B)

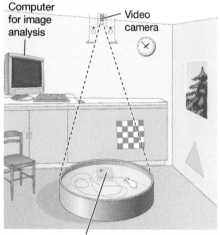

Submerged escape platform

**Figure 10.2**

This figure illustrates the components of the classic Morris experiment. (A) A cannula was implanted into the ventricles of the rat's brain and attached to a time-release pellet that contained the NMDA receptor antagonist APV. (B) Rats were trained on the place-learning version of the water-escape task. (C) Rats infused with APV could not sustain LTP in the dentate gyrus. (D) Rats infused with APV were impaired in learning the location of the hidden platform. (E) Control rats selectively searched the quadrant that contained the platform during training, but rats infused with APV did not. T = training quadrant; A = adjacent quadrant; O = opposite quadrant.

(D)

(E)

NMDA receptor subtypes

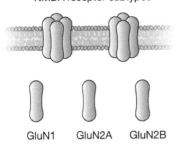

GluN1      GluN2A      GluN2B

**Figure 10.3**
NMDA receptors are composed of four sub-units. All functional NMDA receptors contain GluN1 subunits. There are a variety of GluN2 subunits. This figure illustrates NMDA receptor complexes composed of GluN1–GluN2A and GluN1–GluN2B subunits.

memories. Before considering some of the key findings, however, the composition of the NMDA receptor needs to be more fully described.

The NMDA receptor is composed of four subunits (Figure 10.3). The subunits can be divided into two classes: GluN1 and GluN2. There are several subtypes of GluN2 receptors, designated GluN2A, GluN2B, GluN2C, and GluN2D. All NMDA-receptor complexes contain the GluN1 subunit, but a combination of both GluN1 and GluN2 subunits is required to form a functional channel that can open to allow calcium ($Ca^{2+}$) into the neuron. Researchers interested in the contribution of NMDA receptors to memory have taken advantage of their structure and used genetic engineering methods to selectively delete or overexpress one of these subunits in mice.

DELETION   Susumu Tonegawa and his colleagues (Tsien et al., 1996) were able to selectively delete the GluN1 subunit in pyramidal cells in the CA1 field of the mouse hippocampus. This mouse is called a CA1 knockout (CA1KO). These researchers then stimulated the Schaffer collateral fibers and recorded field potentials in slices taken from the CA1KO mice. As one would expect, since the GluN1 subunit is needed to form a functional NMDA receptor, LTP could not be induced in the CA1 field. Note, however, that GluN1 subunits were expressed in neurons in the dentate gyrus (the location where LTP was discov-

Susumu Tonegawa

ered by Bliss and Lomo; see Chapter 2). Thus, NMDA receptors in this region should be functional, and it was possible to induce LTP in CA1KO mice by stimulating the perforant path and recording field potentials in the dentate gyrus (Figure 10.4).

The most important results, however, were those that demonstrated that the NMDA receptors in the CA1 field were critical for memory. The researchers tested the CA1KO mice in both the place-learning and visible-platform

(A)

Normal                CA1KO

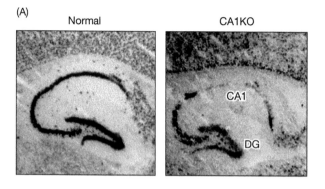

**Figure 10.4**
(A) This photomicrograph shows a section of a normal hippocampus that has been stained to reveal the presence of the GluN1 subunit. Note that the GluN1 subunit is absent in the CA1 region of the section taken from the genetically engineered mouse, called a CA1 knockout or CA1KO, but is present in the dentate gyrus (DG). (B) LTP cannot be induced in CA1 in slices taken from mice lacking the GluN1 subunit. (C) LTP can be induced in the dentate gyrus in slices taken from the genetically engineered mice because the GluN1 subunit is still present. (D) The CA1KO mice are impaired on the place-learning version of the Morris water-escape task. (E) These mice also do not selectively search the training quadrant on the probe trial. (After Tsien et al., 1996.)

(B) LTP in CA1

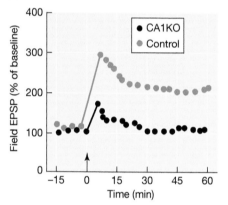

(C) LTP in DG

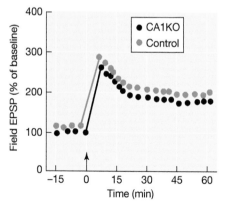

(D)

(E)

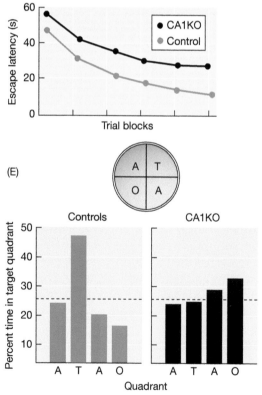

versions of the Morris water-escape task. These mice were very impaired in acquiring the memory for the location of the hidden platform but were able to learn to swim directly to the visible platform.

Tonegawa and his colleagues (Nakazawa et al., 2003) have also deleted the GluN1 receptor from the CA3 region of the hippocampus. Mice with this deletion were not impaired on the standard place-learning task. However, these researchers also employed a modified version of this task that required mice to learn the location of the platform in one trial. In this study, the mice received four training trials daily, but the platform was moved to a new location each day. Normal mice showed that they acquired the memory for the platform in one trial because their escape latency decreased dramatically between Trial 1 and Trial 2. The escape latency of mice with the GluN1 subunit deleted in CA3, however, did not show a change between the two trials. Thus, this experiment implied that the GluN1 subunit in the CA3 region is necessary for one-trial place learning but not for learning the location of the platform when it remained in the same location every trial.

OVEREXPRESSION    Results of studies discussed thus far indicate that if NMDA receptor function is compromised either by a pharmacological blockade or a genetic deletion of one of its subunits, memory formation can be impaired. Joe Tsien and his colleagues (Tang et al., 1999), however, asked a different question: *can memory formation be improved by enhancing NMDA function?*

During the development of the nervous system, the composition of the NMDA subunits changes. Early in development when the nervous system is being assembled, the GluN2B subunits are dominant, but later these subunits tend to be replaced by GluN2A subunits (Figure 10.5). This shift in the ratio of NMDA receptors containing GluN2B and GluN2A subunits is also associated with different channel-opening properties. NMDA receptor complexes

Joe Tsien

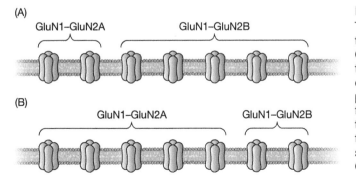

**Figure 10.5**

This figure illustrates the shift in the ratio of GluN1–GluN2A and GluN1–GluN2B NMDA receptors that takes place as the brain develops. (A) During the early postnatal period there are relatively more GluN1–GluN2B receptor complexes. (B) With maturation there is a shift in the balance so that there are more GluN1–GluN2A receptor complexes.

that contain GluN2B subunits remain open longer than those that contain GluN2A subunits and presumably permit more $Ca^{2+}$ to enter the spine. When the GluN2B subunits dominate, it is easier to induce LTP than when GluN2A subunits dominate.

Based on these findings, Tsien reasoned that if one could genetically modify mice to overexpress the GluN2B subunits, it might be possible to improve memory formation. Tsien was successful in engineering this specific overexpression in the cortex and hippocampus of mice in his study. As expected, these mice showed enhanced LTP compared to control mice. The exciting result, however, was that, in addition to enhanced LTP, these mice also demonstrated enhanced memory formation. Their performance in the place-learning version of the water maze was superior to the control mice. They displayed enhanced place learning as well as stronger contextual and auditory-cue fear conditioning, and their object-recognition memory was improved. Tsien called the smart mice Doogie mice after an intellectually precocious teenage character in a once popular television show (Figure 10.6).

## Cautions and Caveats

Pharmacological and genetic alterations of the NMDA receptor complex provide evidence that the NMDA receptor can make an important contribution to memory function and thus can play an important role in memory formation. However, it is also important to note that: (a) the interpretation of some of these results has been challenged, and (b) there have been reports that memories can be formed even in the face of a strong pharmacological block of NMDA receptors (for example, Cain et al., 1997; Niewoehner et al., 2007; Saucier and Cain, 1995). The classic Morris et al. (1986) paper reporting that blocking the NMDA receptor with APV impaired the rat's performance on the place-learning task can serve to illustrate this issue. This result is, of course, consistent with the idea that NMDA receptors are important in memory formation.

It is often the case that when important new results are reported, the scientific community greets them with caution and skepticism. A number of researchers initially challenged the conclusion that APV impaired performance on this task because it interfered with a process critical to memory formation. As stated previously, any brain manipulation that alters performance can do so for many reasons. Some researchers believe that APV impaired the processes that support the sensory and motor requirements of the task (Bannerman et al., 2006; Cain, 1997; Keith and Rudy, 1990).

In fact Saucier and Cain (1995) reported that if rats are provided with the experience of swimming in a pool before training on the place-learning task,

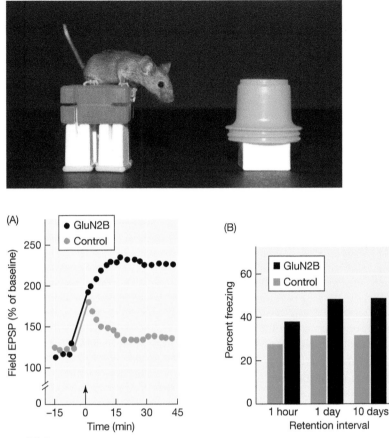

**Figure 10.6**

In the Doogie mouse, the GluN1–GluN2B NMDA complex is overexpressed in several regions of the brain, including the cortex, hippocampus, and amygdala (photo courtesy of J. Z. Tsien). (A) Slices from the Doogie mouse show enhanced LTP. (B) The Doogie mouse shows a stable and enhanced memory for a contextual fear-conditioning experience.

blocking NMDA receptors and LTP in the dentate gyrus has no effect on performance. Bannerman and his colleagues (2006) have discussed many other examples.

Moreover, Brian Wiltgen and his colleagues (2010) have reported that mice can learn to fear a new context paired with shock even when NMDA receptors in the hippocampus are pharmacologically inhibited by APV. However, this happens only if the mice were recently conditioned to another similar context. These findings imply that experience can modify the dependency of learning on NMDA receptors and enhance the ability of calcium from other sources to compensate for calcium influxed through NMDA receptors (Tayler et al., 2011; Wiltgen et al., 2010).

There are several lessons to be taken from this discussion:

- Drugs and genetic manipulations can modify behavior without affecting learning and memory.
- These agents can have multiple effects. Even if the targeted molecule or receptor does make a contribution to memory, it might be involved in some other component system that influences behavior.
- Memory formation may take place without the contribution of NMDA receptors.

There is also a more general point that is worth making. As noted, Saucier and Cain (1995) reported that once sensory–motor impairments were reduced, rats easily learned to find the hidden platform even when NMDA receptors were blocked. What should one conclude from this finding? It is tempting to conclude that NMDA receptors do not participate in establishing a memory for the location of the platform, but that would be wrong. Saucier and Cain's observation may mean that there are other mechanisms that can produce memories when NMDA receptors are not functional. They do not, however, exclude the possibility that NMDA receptors normally contribute to creating place memories.

The general point is that when a component of the brain is removed and this has no effect on memory formation, one cannot say the component (for example, brain region, cell, or molecule) is not involved in memory formation when it is normally present. The brain has redundant mechanisms that might substitute for each other. So the absence of an effect primarily reveals what the brain can do without the component. It does not reveal what that component does in the normal brain.

## AMPA Receptors and Memory Formation

AMPA receptors play a major role in strengthening synapses. By participating in depolarizing the neuron, they contribute to opening the NMDA calcium channel and thus to initiating intracellular events that strengthen synapses. Moreover, the end product of the biochemical changes that produce LTP is an increase in AMPA receptor function. Existing receptors may stay open longer and more of them are present in the PSD.

Based on these facts one should expect to find evidence that AMPA receptors are involved in both the formation and retrieval of a memory. Indeed, there is evidence that supports this prediction. For example, it is known that object-recognition memory critically depends on a cortical region adjacent to the hippocampus called **perirhinal cortex**. Winters and Bussey (2005) infused the AMPA receptor antagonist CNQX (6-cyano-7-nitroquinoxaline) into the perirhinal cortex of rats to temporarily reduce AMPA receptor function. Infusing this drug before training prevented the rats from forming a memory of the object, while injecting the drug before testing prevented them from retrieving the memory.

## Fear Conditioning Drives GluA1 AMPA Receptors into Spines

It is generally accepted that long-term potentiation is the result of the induction stimulus engaging processes that drive additional GluA1 AMPA receptors into the dendritic spines. One might expect that if memory formation depends on the synaptic changes that support LTP, then behavioral experiences that produce memories also should traffic additional GluA1 AMPA receptors into spines. In a remarkable set of experiments, Roberto Malinow and his colleagues (Rumpel et al., 2005) provided evidence that this occurs. They used genetic engineering methods to create GluA1 AMPA receptors and then injected these receptors into the amygdala. Green fluorescent protein was also expressed by the receptors and allowed neurons that contained these receptors to be visualized (Figure 10.7). They used a fear-conditioning procedure to establish a memory—the rats received several pairings of an auditory CS with shock. After the rats were tested for their fear response, they were sacrificed and slices of brain tissue from the basolateral amygdala were prepared to determine if the behavioral training had driven GluA1 receptors into the spines.

Malinow's group was able to detect the presence of these receptors in synapses because when glutamate binds to them electrical current can be detected that is slightly different from that produced by endogenous GluA1 receptors. To activate these synapses they stimulated the auditory pathway in the thalamus that projects to the amygdala. These experiments revealed that the conditioning experience had driven the GluA1 receptors into the dendritic spines because they were able to detect an increase in the signature response of synapses belonging to the neurons that fluoresced.

Roberto Malinow

## Preventing AMPA Receptor Trafficking Impairs Fear Conditioning

If the GluA1 AMPA receptor plays a critical role in the support of the fear memory, then it follows that if trafficking this receptor into the spine is

**Figure 10.7**
LTP studies have shown that GluA1 AMPA receptors are inserted into the plasma membrane of dendritic spines in response to synaptic activity. Malinow and his colleagues used a special technique to insert modified glutamate receptors, GluA1s, into the lateral amygdala. (A) These receptors were labeled with a fluorescent molecule and could be visualized. (B) Rats with these fluorescent AMPA receptors were tested for fear of a tone paired with shock or tested for fear of a tone unpaired with shock. Rats in the paired condition displayed fear to the tone. The rats were then sacrificed and slices were taken from their brains. An analysis of these slices revealed fear conditioning had driven the GluA1 AMPA receptors into the spines. (C) Schematic representation of the distribution of the GluA1 receptors prior to training. (D) After the training, rats in the paired condition had more GluA1 receptors trafficked into the plasma membrane than rats in the unpaired condition. These results indicate that a behavioral experience that produces fear conditioning also drives AMPA receptors into the synapse. (After Rumpel et al., 2005.)

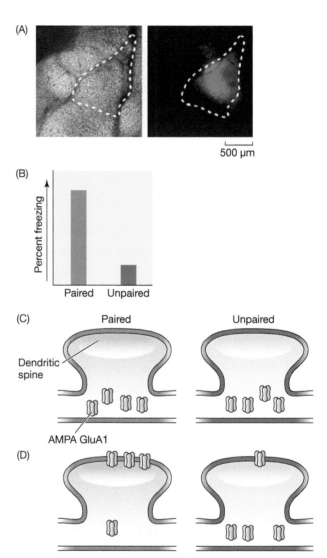

prevented, the fear memory should be weak. Malinow's group also used genetic engineering to test this hypothesis. They created and injected a nonfunctional version of the GluA1 subunit receptor that would compete with the functional receptors for delivery to the membrane. This nonfunctional unit could be driven into the spine but would not respond properly to glutamate release. It might be thought of as a dummy receptor. The experiments revealed that rats with neurons that contained nonfunctional receptors displayed a reduced fear memory (Figure 10.8). This means that the memory for the fear experience, as measured by the rat's freezing response, depends

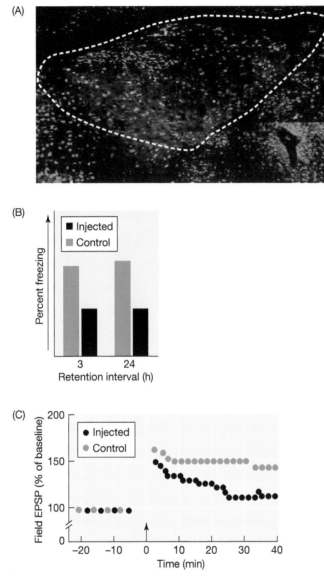

**Figure 10.8**
(A) Modified nonfunctional GluA1 receptors are injected into the lateral amygdala.
These modified receptors compete with endogenous functional GluA1 receptors for
trafficking into spines. (B) Rats injected with this receptor display impaired fear conditioning to a tone paired with shock. (C) Slices from animals injected with the modified
receptor cannot sustain LTP induced in the lateral amygdala. (After Rumpel et al.,
2005.)

on trafficking AMPA receptors with functional GluA1 subunits into the membrane.

## Ampakines and Cognitive Enhancement

AMPA receptors play a critical role in initiating the processes that strengthen synapses. The resulting up-regulation of these receptors that also occurs is largely responsible for the enhanced synaptic response recorded as LTP (Figure 10.9). The empirical facts behind these conclusions have made AMPA receptors attractive candidates for the development of therapeutics designed to enhance memory and other complex forms of cognition. Gary Lynch and his colleagues have developed a class of drugs called **ampakines** that may enhance cognitive function (Baudry et al., 2012; Lynch and Gall, 2006).

Ampakines cross the blood–brain barrier and bind to a site on the AMPA receptor. However, they function as neither agonists nor antagonists. Their

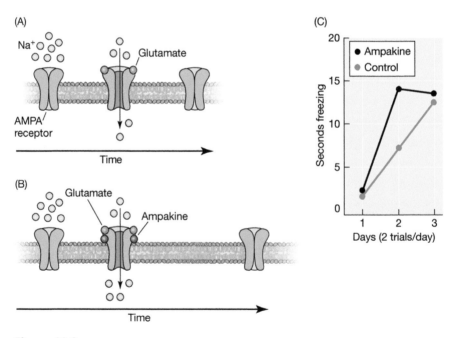

**Figure 10.9**
(A) When glutamate binds to AMPA receptors the conductance channel is briefly opened and this allows positive ions to enter. (B) When ampakines and glutamate both bind to the AMPA receptor, the channel stays open longer and therefore more ions enter and the synaptic response is enhanced. (C) Ampakines enhance the rate of auditory fear conditioning.

influence is observed when glutamate binds to the receptor. As previously learned, when glutamate binds to an AMPA receptor a channel opens and $Na^+$ enters the cell. Normally this channel rapidly closes. However, when an ampakine also binds to the AMPA receptor it slows down the deactivation or closure of the channel. Functionally, what this means is that when an ampakine is present there will be a prolonged current flow and enhanced synaptic responses. Thus, the neuron will more likely depolarize (which should facilitate the opening of the NMDA receptor channel) and will also be more likely to release neurotransmitters onto other neurons to which it is connected.

There are a number of reports that ampakines can enhance learning (see Lynch and Gall, 2006, for a review). For example, Rogan et al. (1997) treated rats with an ampakine prior to fear conditioning to a tone paired with very mild shock. They reported that it enhanced the rate at which conditioned fear was established (see Figure 10.9). There is also evidence that ampakines may be used to ameliorate mild memory impairments that develop with age.

## NMDA and AMPA Receptors: Acquisition and Retrieval

When the NMDA receptor's contribution to LTP was discovered in the hippocampus, researchers found that APV, the NMDA receptor antagonist, blocked the induction but not the expression of LTP (see Chapter 3). This means that when APV was administered prior to the induction stimulus it prevented LTP, but when it was administered after LTP was established, it had no effect. In contrast, AMPA receptors have been shown to be important in both the induction and expression of LTP.

In the context of building memories, these findings suggest that NMDA and AMPA receptors might make different contributions to the acquisition and retrieval of memories. Specifically, as suggested earlier, NMDA receptors should be critical for the acquisition of the memory but not for its retrieval. AMPA receptors, however, should be important for both the acquisition and retrieval of the memory.

Morris and his colleagues (Day et al., 2003) used a clever one-trial memory task to test this hypothesis. Training occurred in a large open arena that featured two landmarks, a pyramid, and a stack of golf balls (Figure 10.10). Rats were first allowed to learn the layout of the arena. The floor of the arena had many small holes that could be filled with either just sand or sand and a food pellet. During the acquisition phase of training, the rat was released into the area twice. Each time it explored the area until it found an uncovered sand well that contained a distinctive food pellet (for example, a banana or cinnamon flavored pellet). The rat's task was to remember the location of the sand wells and the flavor of the pellets they contained.

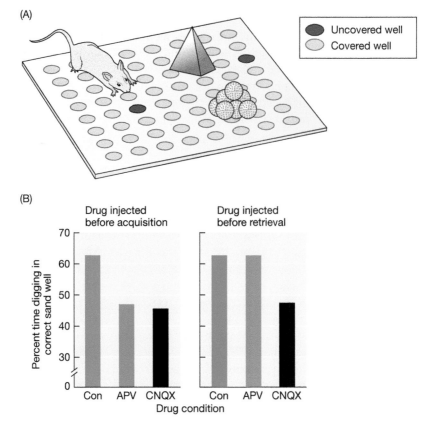

**Figure 10.10**
(A) This graphic is a schematic of the arena Morris and his colleagues used to study the role of glutamate receptors in the acquisition and retrieval of a memory for the location of flavored food pellets. On the retrieval test, the two sand wells that contained the flavored pellets on the acquisition trial were uncovered. The rat was fed one of the pellets in the release point. Its task was to remember which sand well contained that pellet during acquisition. (B) When given before acquisition, both APV and CNQX interfered with establishing the food-location memory. However, only CNQX, the AMPA receptor antagonist, interfered with the retrieval of the memory. Con = control group. (After Day et al., 2003.)

To determine if the rat remembered the sand-well locations that contained the pellets, it was returned to one of four release points and fed one of the pellets (for example, banana). It was released into the arena, where the two sand wells that had contained food pellets in the acquisition phase were uncovered. Digging in the sand well that contained banana pellets, it would be rewarded with another banana pellet. However, digging in the other sand well would not yield a food pellet. Each day a new set of flavors was used, and the rats easily learned to dig in the sand well that contained the flavor pellet that they were fed at the release point. About 2 hours separated the acquisition and retrieval phase of the experiment.

After the rats had learned the task, Morris evaluated the role of NMDA and AMPA receptors in the acquisition and retrieval of the memory of the flavor location. To do this, either the NMDA antagonist APV or the AMPA receptor antagonist CNQX was injected into the hippocampus. These drugs were injected either before the acquisition phase or before the retrieval phase of the experiment.

Morris found that APV impaired performance when it was injected before the acquisition phase but had no effect when it was injected prior to the retrieval phase. Note that because the rats were not impaired when APV was injected prior to retrieval, one can be confident that the drug did not impair sensory, motor, or motivational processes that are essential to performance. In contrast, CNQX impaired performance when it was injected both prior to the acquisition phase and prior to the retrieval phase. Recall that Winters and Bussey (2005) reported that AMPA receptors were critical to both the acquisition and retrieval of memories for objects. These results bore out the hypothesis that NMDA and AMPA glutamate receptors can play a role in the acquisition and retrieval of a memory similar to the role they play in the induction and expression of LTP—that NMDA receptors are critical only for acquisition while AMPA receptors contribute both to acquisition and retrieval.

## CaMKII and Memory Formation

Studies of synaptic plasticity suggest that NMDA and AMPA receptors are important because the opening of the NMDA calcium channel allows a spike of **$Ca^{2+}$** to enter the spine. $Ca^{2+}$ is a second messenger that activates another messenger protein, calmodulin, which binds to the kinase CaMKII. This protein plays a critical role in establishing LTP, so one would expect that it also plays an important role in memory formation. Much of what is known about what CaMKII contributes to memory formation comes from studies with genetically engineered mice. The general strategy has been to either remove the CaMKII gene or to overexpress the active form of CaMKII.

Alcino Silva

The first application of genetic engineering to the study of memory molecules was directed at CaMKII. Alcino Silva and his colleagues successfully deleted the CaMKII gene (Silva, Paylor et al., 1992; Silva, Stevens et al., 1992). LTP could not be induced in the CaMKII knockout mice (CaMKII KO) and these mice were severely

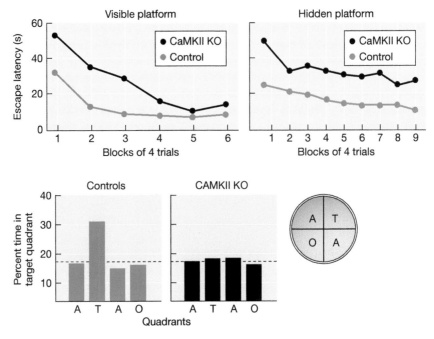

**Figure 10.11**
The CaMKII-deficient mouse (CaMKII KO) can learn to swim to the visible platform but cannot learn the location of the hidden platform. Note that control mice selectively search the target quadrant on a probe trial while the defective CaMKII KO mice do not. T = training quadrant; A = adjacent quadrant; O = opposite quadrant. (After Silva, Paylor et al., 1992.)

impaired in both the visible-platform and place-learning versions of the Morris water-escape task (Figure 10.11). These were exciting results. Nevertheless, this pioneering work was also criticized for not completely ruling out the possibility that the mutation caused sensory motor impairments that were responsible for their poor performance.

## Preventing Autophosphorylation of CaMKII Impairs Learning

One of the important properties of CaMKII is its capacity to autophosphorylate and remain in an active state in the absence of calcium–calmodulin. Given the importance of autophosphorylated CaMKII to synaptic plasticity, Peter Giese and his colleagues (Giese et al., 1998; Irvine, Danhiez et al., 2011; Irvine, Maunganidze et al., 2011; Irvine et al., 2006) have studied mice that have been genetically engineered to be deficient in **autophosphorylation**. Synaptic plasticity studies of these animals indicate that LTP cannot be induced in the CA1

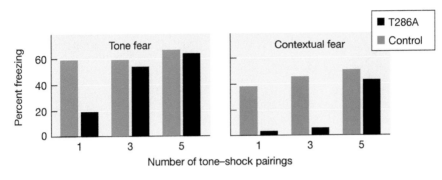

**Figure 10.12**
Autophosphorylation is critical for rapid formation of a fear memory but not essential for memories produced with multiple training trials. In this experiment, mice genetically engineered to impair autophosphorylation of CaMKII (T286A mice) and control mice received 1, 3, or 5 pairings of a tone and shock. Control mice acquired fear to the context and to the tone after only one pairing; however, the defective mice required several pairings to acquire the fear memory. (After Irvine et al., 2006.)

field by stimulating the Schaffer collateral fibers but that it can be induced in the dentate gyrus by stimulating the perforant path (Cooke et al., 2006; Irvine, Danhiez et al., 2011; Irvine, Maunganidze et al., 2011).

Under limited training conditions (one trial), these autophosphorylation-deficient mice showed a deficit in inhibitory avoidance learning and in contextual and auditory-cue fear conditioning. However, if they were given just a few extra trials, they were completely normal (Figure 10.12). Thus, suppressing the autophosphorylation of CaMKII has a significant but limited effect on the formation of memories that support these behaviors (Irvine, Danhiez et al., 2011; Irvine, Maunganidze et al., 2011; Irvine et al., 2006). The finding that with additional training these animals acquired a memory for these tasks suggests that the one-trial impairment is unlikely due to sensory or motor impairment. One important implication of this work is that the autophosphorylation of CaMKII may be critical for the rapid (one-trial) formation of a memory but that other processes can compensate for this contribution (Radwanska et al., 2011) when multiple training trials occur. It should be noted, however, that even though mice deficient in CaMKII autophosphorylation can learn under certain conditions, they are not normal.

## CaMKII and Fear Memories

Sarina Rodrigues and her colleagues (Rodrigues et al., 2004) have provided some of the most convincing evidence that CaMKII can play a critical role in the formation of a fear memory. These researchers found that CaMKII was

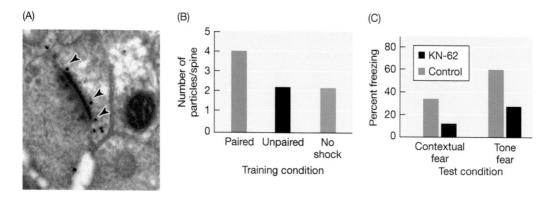

**Figure 10.13**
Fear conditioning produces increased phosphorylated CaMKII in dendritic spines in the amygdala. (A) A micrograph showing particles of phosphorylated CaMKII in a spine. (B) Rats that received paired presentations of a tone and shock have more particles of phosphorylated CaMKII in spines than control animals that received either no shock or unpaired presentations of the tone and shock. (C) The drug KN-62, which inhibits the phosphorylation of CaMKII, impairs both contextual and tone–fear conditioning. (After Rodrigues et al., 2004.)

present in synapses with NMDA receptors that contained GluN2B subunits. They then found that fear conditioning increased the presence of phosphorylated CaMKII in dendritic spines, indicating that the conditioning experience activated this kinase. In addition, they observed that a drug (KN-62) that inhibits CaMKII activation blocked the acquisition of both contextual and auditory fear conditioning and also prevented LTP in this region of the brain (Figure 10.13). This is exactly the pattern of results one would expect based on the role of CaMKII in synaptic plasticity. Note the basolateral amygdala is believed to be a critical memory site for fear conditioning.

## Actin Dynamics and Memory Formation

Studies of LTP established that actin regulation is critical to the evolution of the synaptic changes that support LTP (see Chapters 3 to 7). Thus, it is not surprising that behavioral studies reveal that actin regulation is also critical for producing memories (Lamprecht, 2011). Some evidence for this claim follows.

A primary regulator of actin dynamics is cofilin (see Chapter 4). In its normal active state cofilin interferes with actin polymerization. In its phosphorylated state, however, the depolymerization property of cofilin is turned off. Given that synaptic changes supporting LTP require actin polymerization, one would expect that a behavioral experience that produces a memory would engage signaling pathways such as LIMK that would phosphorylate cofilin. This implication has been confirmed. For example, the training procedure used to produce an object–place recognition memory increases the ratio of phosphorylated cofilin to total cofilin in the hippocampus, a region of the brain that supports object–place memory (Britta et al., 2012). Moreover, interfering with actin polymerization by infusing latrunculin into the hippocampus prevents the formation of the memory needed to perform the task.

Different regions of the brain support different types of memories. For example, the basolateral amygdala region and prelimbic cortex provide critical support of fear memories but are not critical for a learned taste aversion that is acquired when one gets sick following the consumption of a novel food. Taste aversion memories are supported by neurons in the insular cortex. Thus, one would expect that the training procedure that produces a learned taste aversion would selectively activate actin regulation processes in the insular cortex but not in the basolateral amgydala. This predicted result has been confirmed. First, training that produces a learned taste aversion increases the length of the post-synaptic density in spines located in the insular cortex but has no effect on spines located in the basolateral amygdala or prelimbic cortex. Second, cytochalasin D, which interferes with actin polymerization, prevents the lengthening of the PSD in spines in the insular cortex and prevents the formation of the taste aversion memory (Bi et al., 2010).

## Working and Reference Memory Depend on Glutamate Receptors

At least since the writings of William James, memory researchers have been influenced by the idea that a memory trace induced by a new experience evolves in stages (see Chapter 1). An initial trace is formed that is labile and subject to rapid decay. However, during this period other processes are at work to yield a more enduring and stable trace that represents the information contained in the experience. This idea informed the chapters on synaptic plasticity and will be further explored in Chapter 11.

It is also the case that everyday experiences support the idea that information can intentionally be held in memory and manipulated to solve a particular problem or achieve a particular goal. For example, you enter a grocery store with the intent of purchasing a few items (bread, milk, eggs, coffee, cheese, steak, and cake). Assuming you did not create a written list then you will have to maintain this information in memory until you complete your shopping. Once your shopping is complete there is no further need to maintain this information in memory. Psychologists refer to this category of memory as **working memory** (see Baddeley, 1986; Baddeley et al., 2009).

## An Animal Model

Psychologists have developed a variety of tasks that can be used to study working memory in animals (Sanderson and Bannerman, 2012). David Olton introduced the radial arm maze methodology that has proven to be quite useful (Olton and Samuelson, 1976). It is called a radial maze because it has a number of arms radiating out from the center (Figure 10.14). To create a working memory task each arm is baited with a food reward and the rodent is released from the center and allowed to collect all of the rewards. Once visited an arm is not re-baited. So the most efficient strategy is for the rodent to avoid reentering arms that have already have been visited. This requires that the animal "remember" the arms that no longer contain food—it is a

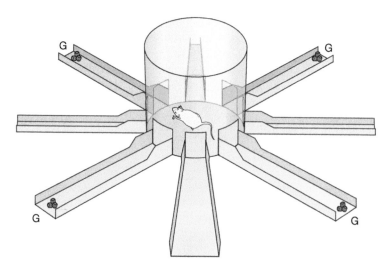

**Figure 10.14**
The radial maze can be used to study both working memory and reference memory. A trial begins when the rodent is placed in the center of the maze. It ends when the animal has retrieved the food reward from all baited arms. Only four of the eight arms are baited but the same four arms are baited on each trial. The rat has to learn which four arms are never baited (the reference memory component) and to remember which arms it previously visited (the working memory component). The rat can now make two types of errors on a trial: (1) a working memory error—it enters a previously sampled arm, and (2) a reference memory error—it enters an arm that was never baited. G = goal.

working memory task. Radial arm mazes with up to 16 arms have been used, and rats are remarkably successful in this task. Once experienced with the procedure, rodents rarely make a working memory error and revisit a previously sampled arm.

A variation of this task allows the researcher to study both working memory and what is called **reference memory**. In this variation the maze typically has eight arms but only four are baited. The same four arms are baited on each trial. Now the rat not only has to remember which arms it visited but also has to learn and remember which arms are baited and which are never baited. This part of the task is called the reference memory component of the task. The rat can now make two types of errors on a trial: (1) a working memory error—it enters a previously sampled arm, and (2) a reference memory error—it enters arms that are never baited. Trained rats perform very well on this task, making almost no working or reference memory errors.

## Glutamate Receptor Composition Is Critical to Working Memory

The availability of such tasks has allowed neurobiologists to discover some of the molecular events that support working and reference memory. Remarkably, the subunit composition of AMPA and NMDA receptors determines whether or not rodents are successful on working memory and reference memory tasks. However, before this evidence is discussed, it is useful to briefly return to the LTP experiment.

The point was made in Chapter 3 that the initial short-lasting, early phase of LTP depends on the rapid insertion of GluA1 AMPA receptors. Researchers using genetically altered mice have provided direct support for this view (Romberg et al., 2009). When a weak TBS is used, slices from control mice display a short-lasting LTP, but slices from mice that lack the gene for the GluA1 subunit (called GluA1 KO) do not express this short-lasting potential. Nevertheless, when stimulated by a stronger theta-burst protocol, slices from the GluA1 KO mice display an enduring LTP, equivalent to control mice, even though they do not display the early, short-lasting phase (Figure 10.15). These results indicate that GluA1 subunits are required for the initial early phase of LTP but not for the later developing phase, which likely requires GluA2 AMPA receptors. They also reveal that an enduring LTP can be established independent of any contribution from GluA1 receptors.

David Bannerman and his colleagues (Bannerman, 2009; Sanderson and Bannerman, 2012; Schmitt et al., 2003) have studied the performance of GluA1 KO mice in the radial arm maze. Unlike control mice the KO mice made numerous working memory errors—revisiting the previously baited arms. This result implies that synaptic changes that support working memory require the rapid addition of GluA1 receptors into the postsynaptic density.

**Figure 10.15**
(A) GluA1 knockout (KO) mice do not express early-phase, short-lasting LTP but do express late-phase, enduring LTP. (After Romberg et al., 2009.) (B) The GluA1 KO mice do not differ from control mice in learning the reference memory component of the radial maze task but display severely impaired working memory. (After Sanderson and Bannerman, 2012.)

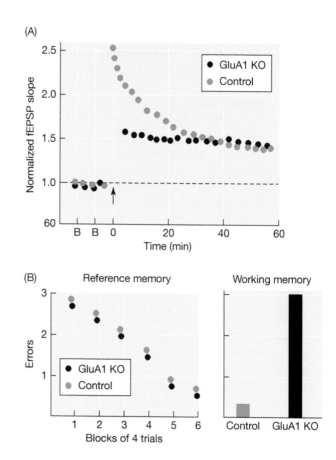

Additional support for this conclusion is that both the LTP impairment and the working memory impairment displayed by GluA1 KO mice can be rescued by transferring a GluA1 expression system into these mice (Schmitt et al., 2005). This form of genetic engineering restores the ability of some neurons to express the gene for the GluA1 subunit.

To master the reference memory component of the task—learning to discriminate which set of arms are baited and which are not—requires many training trials. Mice lacking GluA1 receptors learn this discrimination. This fact suggests that the synaptic changes that support this learning depend on some of the processes that produce the enduring form of LTP that the GluA1 KO mice display. One might speculate that repeated training can engage the processes that traffic GluA2 AMPA receptors.

Different subunits of the NMDA receptor also contribute selectively to working and reference memory. Specifically, the NMDA receptors composed of the GluN1 and GluN2A subunits are required for working memory but not for reference memory. Given this pattern of results, one might speculate that calcium influx through NMDA receptors composed of GluN1–GluN2A subunits contributes to the rapid insertion of GluA1 AMPA receptors. It is not yet clear just what if any NMDA receptor subunit combination is needed to support reference memory (Bannerman, 2009). However, there is no evidence that it depends on the GluN1–GluN2B subtype. The fact is that very little is yet known about how repeated training alters the basic processes involved in learning and memory.

The general conclusion from this discussion of working and reference memory is that the subunit composition of both AMPA and NMDA receptors is critical for working memory. It depends on processes that rapidly insert GluA1 AMPA receptors into the synapse. The insertion of these receptors depends in part on NMDA receptors composed of GluN1 and GluN2A subunits. In contrast, neither enduring LTP nor reference memory requires GluA1 receptors. Given the established role of GluA2 AMPA receptors in the maintenance of LTP, it is reasonable to speculate that reference memory depends on processes that regulate the trafficking of these receptors.

## Summary

Studies of synaptic plasticity have strongly implicated glutamate receptors (NMDA and AMPA receptors) and CaMKII as major components in the signaling cascades that lead to strengthening of synapses. Both pharmacological and genetic engineering methodologies have been used to determine if these molecules are also critical to memory formation.

There are a large number of reports that NMDA receptors make a critical contribution to the acquisition, but not the retrieval, of some forms of memory. Such studies have revealed that interfering with the contribution of these receptors can impair memory formation, while enhancing the NMDA calcium channel function can enhance memory formation.

Studies of AMPA receptors have revealed that they play a critical role in both the acquisition and retrieval of memories. Particularly striking is that just as they can be driven into synapses by high-frequency stimulation used in LTP experiments, they can also be driven into spines by fear conditioning. Moreover, if normal AMPA receptors are not driven into spines, the acquisition of a fear memory is impaired. In addition, delaying the closure of AMPA receptor channels with ampakines appears to provide a potential therapy for enhancing the laying down of memory traces.

The regulation of actin that is so critical to each stage of LTP is also critical to the initial construction of memory traces that support learned behaviors. Behavioral experiences that generate new memories also engage processes that regulate actin, and construction of these memory traces is impaired when actin polymerization is prevented.

Studies of working and reference memory have revealed that these two types of memory depend on different subunit compositions of AMPA and NMDA receptors. Working memory requires the rapid insertion of GluA1 AMPA receptors and this depends on NMDA receptors composed of GluN1 and GluN2A subunits. Reference memory does not require GluA1 AMPA receptors but may depend on AMPA receptors containing GluA2 subunits.

## References

Baddeley, A. D. (1986). *Working memory*. New York: Oxford University Press.

Baddeley, A., Eysenck, M. W., and Anderson, M. C. (2009). *Memory*. Hove and New York: Psychology Press.

Bannerman, D. M. (2009). Fractionating spatial memory with glutamate receptor subunit-knockout mice. *Biochemical Society Transactions, 37*, 1323–1327.

Bannerman, D. M., Rawlins, J. N., and Good, M. A. (2006). The drugs don't work—or do they? Pharmacological and transgenic studies of the contribution of NMDA and GluRA-containing AMPA receptors to hippocampal-dependent memory. *Psychopharmacology, 8*, 533–566.

Baudry, M., Kramar, E., Xu, X., Zadran, H., Moreno, S., Lynch, G., Gall, C., and Bi, X. (2012). Ampakines promote spine actin polymerization, long-term potentiation, and learning in a mouse model of Angelman syndrome. *Neurobiology of Disease, 47*, 210–215.

Bi, A. L., Wang, Y., Li, B. Q., Wang, Q. Q., Ma, L., Yu, H., Zhao, L., and Chen, Z. Y. (2010). Region-specific involvement of actin rearrangement-related synaptic structure alterations in conditioned taste aversion memory. *Learning and Memory, 17* (9), 420–427.

Britta, S., Nelson, A., Christine, F., Witty, A., Elizabeth, A., Williamson, A., Jill, M., and Daniel, A. (2012). A role for hippocampal actin rearrangement in object placement memory in female rats. *Neurobiology of Learning and Memory, 98* (3), 284–290.

Cain, D. P. (1997). LTP, NMDA, genes and learning. *Current Opinion in Neurobiology, 7*, 235–242.

Cain, D. P., Saucier, D., and Boon, F. (1997). Testing hypotheses of spatial learning: the role of NMDA receptors and NMDA-mediated long-term potentiation. *Behavioral Brain Research, 84*, 179–193.

Campeau, S., Miserendino, M. J., and Davis, M. (1992). Intra-amygdala infusion of the N-methyl-D-aspartate receptor antagonist AP5 blocks acquisition but not expression of fear-potentiated startle to an auditory conditioned stimulus. *Behavioral Neuroscience,* *106,* 569–574.

Cooke, S. F., Wu, J., Plattner, F., Errington, M., Rowan, M., Peters, M., Hirano, A., Bradshaw, K. D., Anwyl, R., Bliss, T. V., and Giese, K. P. (2006). Autophosphorylation of alphaCaMKII is not a general requirement for NMDA receptor-dependent LTP in the adult mouse. *Journal of Physiology, 574,* 805–818.

Day, M. R., Langston, R., and Morris, R. G. (2003). Glutamate-receptor-mediated encoding and retrieval of paired-associate learning. *Nature, 424,* 205–209.

Fanselow, M. S. and Kim, J. J. (1994). Acquisition of contextual Pavlovian fear conditioning is blocked by application of an NMDA receptor antagonist D,L-2-amino-5-phosphonovaleric acid to the basolateral amygdala. *Behavioral Neuroscience, 108,* 210–212.

Giese, K. P., Fedorov, N. B., Filipkowski, R. K., and Silva, A. J. (1998). Autophosphorylation at Thr286 of the alpha calcium-calmodulin kinase II in LTP and learning. *Science, 279,* 870–873.

Irvine, E. E., Danhiez, A., Radwanska, K., Nassim, C., Lucchesi, W., Godaux, E., Ris, L., Giese, K. P. (2011). Properties of contextual memory formed in the absence of αCaMKII autophosphorylation. *Molecular Brain, 28,* 4–8.

Irvine, E. E., Maunganidze, N. S., Pyza, M., Ris, L., Szymańska, M., Lipiński, M., Kaczmarek, L., Stewart, M. G., and Giese, K. P. (2011). Mechanism for long-term memory formation when synaptic strengthening is impaired. *Proceedings of the National Academy of Sciences USA, 108,* 18471–18475.

Irvine, E. E., von Hertzen, L. S., Plattner, F., and Giese, K. P. (2006). AlphaCaMKII autophosphorylation: a fast track to memory. *Trends in Neurosciences, 8,* 459–465.

Keith, J. R. and Rudy, J. W. (1990). Why NMDA receptor-dependent long-term potentiation may not be a mechanism of learning and memory: reappraisal of the NMDA receptor blockade strategy. *Psychobiology, 18,* 251–257.

Lamprecht, R. (2011). The roles of the actin cytoskeleton in fear memory formation. *Frontiers in Behavioral Neuroscience, 5,* 39.

Lynch, G. and Gall, C. M. (2006). Ampakines and the threefold path to cognitive enhancement. *Trends in Neurosciences, 10,* 554–562.

Matus-Amat, P., Higgins, E. A., Sprunger, D., Wright-Hardesty, K., and Rudy, J. W. (2007). The role of dorsal hippocampus and basolateral amygdala NMDA receptors in the acquisition and retrieval of context and contextual fear memories. *Behavioral Neuroscience, 12,* 721–731.

Morris, R. G., Anderson E., Lynch, G. S., and Baudry, M. (1986). Selective impairment of learning and blockade of long-term potentiation by an N-methyl-D-aspartate receptor antagonist, AP5. *Nature, 319,* 774–776.

Morris, R. G., Davis, S., and Butcher, S. P. (1990). Hippocampal synaptic plasticity and NMDA receptors: A role in information storage? *Philosophical Transactions of the Royal Society Series B, 329,* 187–204.

Nakazawa, K., Sun, L. D., Quirk, M. C., Rondi-Reig, L., Wilson, M. A., and Tonegawa, S. (2003). Hippocampal CA3 NMDA receptors are crucial for memory acquisition of one-time experience. *Neuron, 38,* 305–315.

Niewoehner, B., Single, F. N., Hvalby, O., Jensen, V., Borgloh, S. M., Seeburg, P. H., Rawlins, J. N., Sprengel, R., and Bannerman, D. M. (2007). Impaired spatial working memory but spared spatial reference memory following functional loss of NMDA receptors in the dentate gyrus. *European Journal of Neuroscience, 25,* 837–846.

Olton, D. S. and Samuelson, R. J. (1976). Remembrance of places passed: spatial memory in rats. *Journal of Experimental Psychology: Animal Behavior Processes, 2,* 97–116.

Radwanska, K., Medvedev, N. I., Pereira, G .S., Engmann, O., Thiede, N., Moraes, M. F., Villers, A., Irvine, E. E., Kaczmarek, L., Stewart, M. G., Giese, K. P. (2011). Mechanism for long-term memory formation when synaptic strengthening is impaired. *Proceedings of the National Academy of Science USA, 108,* 18471–18475.

Rodrigues, S. M., Farb, C. R., Bauer, E. P., LeDoux, J. E., and Schafe, G. E. (2004). Pavlovian fear conditioning regulates Thr286 autophosphorylation of $Ca^{2+}$/calmodulin-dependent protein kinase II at lateral amygdala synapses. *Journal of Neuroscience, 24,* 3281–3288.

Rogan, M. T., Stäubli, U. V., and LeDoux, J. E. (1997). AMPA receptor facilitation accelerates fear learning without altering the level of conditioned fear acquired. *Journal of Neuroscience, 17,* 5928–5935.

Romberg, C., Raffel, J., Martin, L., Sprengel, R., Seeburg, P. H., Rawlins, J. N., Bannerman, D. M., and Paulsen, O. (2009). Induction and expression of GluA1 (GluR-A)-independent LTP in the hippocampus. *European Journal Neuroscience, 29,* 1141–1152.

Rumpel, S., LeDoux, J. E., Zador, A., and Malinow, R. (2005). Postsynaptic receptor trafficking underlying a form of associative learning. *Science, 308,* 83–88.

Sanderson, D. J. and Bannerman, D. M. (2012). The role of habituation in hippocampus-dependent spatial working memory tasks: evidence from GluA1 AMPA receptor subunit knockout mice. *Hippocampus, 22,* 981–994.

Saucier, D. and Cain, D. P. (1995). Spatial learning without NMDA receptor-dependent long-term potentiation. *Nature, 378,* 186–184.

Schmitt, W. B., Deacon, R. M., Seeburg, P. H., Rawlins, J. N., and Bannerman, D. M. (2003). A within-subjects, within-task demonstration of intact spatial reference memory and impaired spatial working memory in glutamate receptor-A-deficient mice. *Journal of Neuroscience, 23,* 3953–3959.

Schmitt, W. B., Sprengel, R., Mack, V., Draft, R. W., Seeburg, P. H., Deacon, R. M., Rawlins, J. N., and Bannerman, D. M. (2005). Restoration of spatial working memory by genetic rescue of GluR-A-deficient mice. *Nature Neuroscience, 8,* 270–272.

Silva, A. J., Paylor, R., Wehner, J. M., and Tonegawa, S. (1992). Impaired spatial learning in alpha-calcium-calmodulin kinase II mutant mice. *Science, 257,* 206–211.

Silva, A. J., Stevens, C. F., Tonegawa, S., and Wang, Y. (1992). Deficient hippocampal long-term potentiation in alpha-calcium-calmodulin kinase II mutant mice. *Science, 257,* 201–206.

Stote, D. L. and Fanselow, M. S. (2004). NMDA receptor modulation of incidental learning in Pavlovian context conditioning. *Behavioral Neuroscience, 118*, 253–257.

Tang, Y. P., Shimizu, E., Dube, G. R., Rampon, C., Kerchner, G. A., Zhuo, M., Liu, G., and Tsien, J. Z. (1999). Genetic enhancement of learning and memory in mice. *Nature, 401*, 63–69.

Tayler, K. K., Lowry, E., Tanaka, K., Levy, B., Reijmers, L., Mayford, M., and Wiltgen, B. J. (2011). Characterization of NMDAR-independent learning in the hippocampus. *Frontiers of Behavioral Neuroscience, 5*, 1–12.

Tsien, J. Z., Huerta, P. T., and Tonegawa, S. (1996). The essential role of hippocampal CA1 NMDA receptor-dependent synaptic plasticity in spatial memory. *Cell, 87*, 1327–1338.

Wiltgen, B. J., Royle, G., Gray, E. E., Abdipranoto, A., Thangthaeng, N., Jacobs, N., Saab, F., Tonegawa, S., Heinemann, S. F., O'Dell, T. J., Fanselow, M. S., and Vissel, B. (2010). A role for calcium-permeable AMPA receptors in synaptic plasticity and learning. *PLoS ONE, (5)* 9, e12818.

Winters, B. D. and Bussey, T. J. (2005). Glutamate receptors in perirhinal cortex mediate encoding, retrieval, and consolidation of object recognition memory. *Journal of Neuroscience, 25*, 4243–4251.

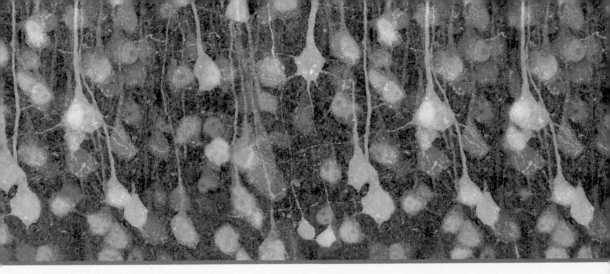

# 11 Memory Consolidation

The initial creation of a memory is rapid and depends only on post-translation processes. However, it is unlikely to endure unless other processes are recruited and continue long after the initiating behavioral experience. The perspective introduced in Chapter 9 has helped to guide neurobiologists attempting to uncover the molecular processes that create enduring memories (Figure 11.1). It assumes that a behavioral experience quickly establishes a short-term memory (STM) trace that can evolve into a long-term memory (LTM) trace.

The evolution and consolidation of the LTM trace requires time and depends on processes that operate for hours following the initiating behavioral experience. The goal of this chapter is to describe some of the consolidation processes that establish long-term memories. Two important principles will emerge:

- Enduring memories require that behavior initiate processes that generate new protein and thus depend on transcription and translation.

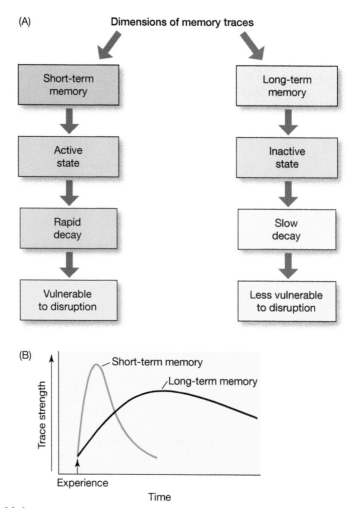

(A) Dimensions of memory traces

(B)

Figure 11.1
Shortly after an experience, memory retrieval is supported by an active short-term trace. As this trace decays, a more stable, long-term memory trace is generated that can support memory retrieval for a much longer period of time.

- These consolidation processes occur in multiple waves that can continue for at least 24 hours.

First, the logic of the research paradigm used to study these issues is presented. Next, the general role of transcription processes in making long-term memories is described, focusing on the transcription factor CREB and exploring some of the memory genes that are transcribed. Translation processes are then discussed with respect to long-term memories, specifically the *de novo* protein synthesis hypothesis and the role of some of the signaling cascades and various other proteins. The chapter concludes with a brief consideration of the contribution of protein degradation processes to memory consolidation and a discussion of duration of the consolidation window—how long it takes to consolidate a memory.

## The Research Paradigm

Researchers often use the experimental strategy described in Figure 11.2 to uncover the molecular–cellular processes that contribute to memory consolidation. Typically, the subject is trained on a task such as fear conditioning or inhibitory avoidance learning. Two variables are included in the experiment. The first is a drug or genetic manipulation designed to influence some target molecule that has been hypothesized as important for memory; a drug treatment can be delivered either before or some time after training. The second variable is called the **retention interval**—the time between the training experience that establishes the memory and the test used to retrieve the memory. The assumption is that test performance at short retention intervals (usually less than 4 hours) is supported by the short-term memory test but that test performance at longer retention intervals requires a consolidated long-term memory.

The logic of this strategy can be further understood by considering a hypothetical experiment in which a drug is used to evaluate the contribution of some particular molecule ($M_x$) to memory consolidation. The drug is thought to degrade the contribution $M_x$ makes to memory consolidation and, in this case, is infused into the brain prior to training. Figure 11.3 shows two possible outcomes produced by the drug. The outcome in Figure 11.3A indicates that the drug impaired performance at the long, 24-hour retention interval but had no effect on performance at the short, 1-hour retention interval. These results would be consistent with the hypothesis that

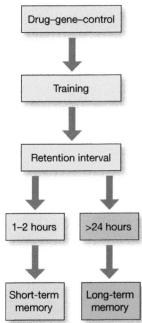

**Figure 11.2**
This figure illustrates the generic research design for determining the contribution of a particular molecule(s) to memory storage. A drug or gene is evaluated by assessing its effect on memory at two retention intervals—a short interval (1 to 2 hours) designed to assess short-term memory (STM) and a longer interval, usually about 24 hours, designed to assess long-term memory (LTM).

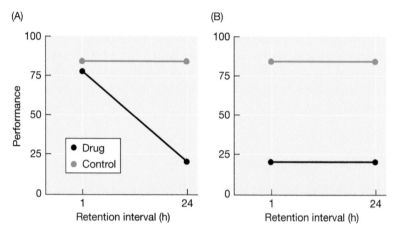

**Figure 11.3**
(A) The drug targeted at $M_x$ impaired performance at the 24-hour retention interval but had no effect at the 1-hour retention interval. This result is consistent with the hypothesis that $M_x$ is important for the consolidation of the long-term memory trace and is not critical for the short-term memory trace. (B) The treatment impaired performance at both the 1-hour and 24-hour retention intervals. This result is consistent with the hypothesis that $M_x$ contributes to both short-term and long-term memory but is also consistent with other interpretations.

$M_x$ contributes to the consolidation of the long-term memory trace. They also support an even stronger conclusion—that the short-term memory trace did not depend on a contribution from $M_x$. This is because the drug did not impair retention at the short interval. Thus, the results shown in Figure 11.3A will be the signature pattern required to support the hypothesis that a targeted molecule or signaling cascade contributes to memory consolidation and not to memory formation. This pattern has been observed in many experiments.

In contrast, Figure 11.3B shows that the drug impaired performance at both the short and long retention intervals. These data are more difficult to interpret. They could mean that the generation of both the STM and the LTM traces requires a contribution from $M_x$. However, these data are also consistent with the hypothesis that the drug used to influence $M_x$ interfered with how the animal normally sampled the environment (see Chapter 7). If one repeated the experiment but infused the drug immediately after training and obtained the same result, then this interpretation could be ruled out.

## Transcription and Enduring Memories

Strong synaptic activity initiates genomic signaling cascades that are critical for consolidating synaptic changes that support long-lasting LTP (see Chapter

5). Enduring memories also depend on what can be called a behaviorally induced genomic cascade (Figure 11.4) that leads to the transcription of new mRNAs (see Alberini, 2009).

The first evidence that LTM might depend on behavior initiating a genomic cascade came from researchers who used the simple system approach (see Chapter 2). Eric Kandel's laboratory demonstrated that transcription inhibitors blocked Aplysia's LTM but not STM for a tail-shock experience, and specifically implicated a role in this process for the transcription factor CREB (cAMP-responsive element-binding protein). (See Chapter 5 as well as Kandel, 2001, for a summary of some of this work.) Genetic and behavioral research using the fruit fly has also played an important role in these ideas (Yin and Tully, 1996).

## The Importance of CREB

As is the case for LTP, memory researchers have been driven by the more specific hypothesis that CREB is important in the production of memory genes (Silva et al., 1998). So this protein must be a primary focus of discussion. Several research strategies have revealed the importance of CREB to memory: (a) genetic deletion of CREB, (b) CREB antisense, (c) genetic overexpression of CREB, and (d) CREB selection of neurons that participate in the memory trace.

CREB DELETION    The idea that long-term memory may depend on the transcription of memory genes regulated by CREB received a major boost when Rusiko Bourtchouladze and Alcino Silva and their colleagues (Bourtchouladze et al., 1994) reported that mice genetically engineered to repress CREB (CREB knockout mice) displayed normal fear conditioning when the retention interval was short but were impaired when the retention interval was

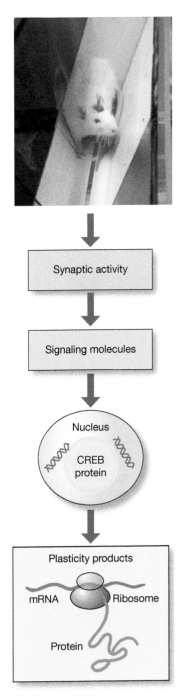

**Figure 11.4**
A behavioral experience such as inhibitory avoidance training initiates a genomic signaling cascade that results in new plasticity products (mRNA and protein) needed to consolidate the memory for the experience. (Photo courtesy of James McGaugh.)

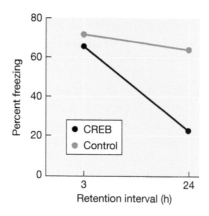

**Figure 11.5**
Mice genetically engineered to repress CREB display fear when tested 3 hours after training but not when tested 24 hours after training. These results are consistent with the hypothesis that long-term memory but not short-term memory requires plasticity products transcribed by CREB. (After Bourtchouladze et al., 1994.)

Rusiko Bourtchouladze

John Guzowski

long (Figure 11.5). These mice also were severely impaired when required to learn the place-learning version of the Morris water-escape task.

CREB ANTISENSE    Other researchers have used a more regional and temporally specific methodology for targeting the disruption of CREB protein levels to study its role in memory storage. John Guzowski (Guzowski and McGaugh, 1997) used the antisense methodology (discussed in Chapter 6) to disrupt CREB protein level. Antisense oligodeoxynucleotides (ODNs) can be made that interfere with the translation of particular proteins and injected into regions of the brain thought to be memory storage sites. The rationale is that if the antisense is administered long enough before a behavioral experience, no CREB protein will be available to target the transcription of the new mRNAs needed to produce the enduring memory. Guzowski infused antisense ODNs for CREB into the dorsal hippocampus and 6 hours later trained rats on the place-learning version of the Morris water-escape task. He reasoned that if memory genes are targeted by CREB protein, then reducing available CREB by blocking its translation should impair LTM but not STM. Consistent with this reasoning, his rats were normal when tested 30 minutes after training but were markedly impaired when tested 3 days after training (Figure 11.6).

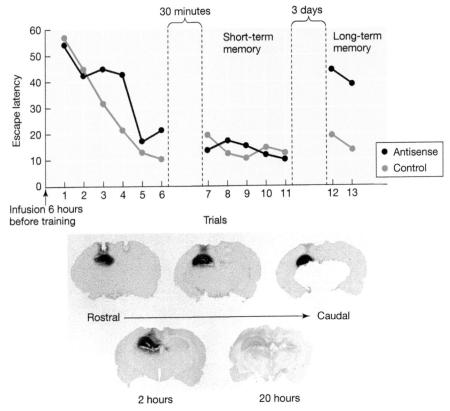

**Figure 11.6**
Infusing an antisense DNA that blocks CREB translation leads to impaired long-term memory for place learning in the Morris water-escape task, but does not affect short-term memory. Note that rats injected with the antisense performed as well as the control rats when the retention interval was only 30 minutes but displayed much longer escape latencies than controls when the retention interval was 3 days. The photograph shows the extent and duration of the antisense. Note that the antisense was no longer present 20 hours after training. (After Guzowski and McGaugh, 1997; photo courtesy of John Guzowski.)

**CREB OVEREXPRESSION**  Under some conditions of training, normal rats fail to display a long-term fear memory to a visual cue (such as light) that has been paired with shock. This can happen when the **inter-trial interval (ITI)**—the time between the light–shock pairings—is very short (3 to 15 seconds). When the inter-trial interval is short, rats display a short-term but not long-term memory for the conditioning experience (Figure 11.7A). However, Sheena Josselyn and her colleagues (Josselyn et al., 2001) were able to prevent the long-term memory impairment associated with the short inter-trial interval.

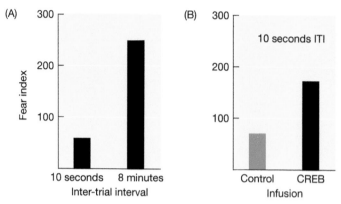

**Figure 11.7**
This graph illustrates the results of a long-term memory test when the inter-trial interval (ITI)—the time separating light–shock conditioning trials—was either 10 seconds or 8 minutes. Note that long-term memory was poor when the ITI was 10 seconds compared to when the ITI was 8 minutes. (B) This graph shows that injecting a virus that expresses CREB into the lateral amygdala (LA) prior to the conditioning trials can eliminate the impaired long-term memory normally found when the ITI is only 10 seconds.

Sheena Josselyn

They used a viral vector to deliver CREB into the lateral amygdala (LA) so that CREB was overexpressed in the region where the memory is stored. These rats were able to acquire a long-term memory of the light–shock experience (Figure 11.7B).

**CREB NEURON SELECTION** As illustrated, CREB activation is important for memory consolidation. In addition, Josselyn discovered that the level of CREB expressed in a neuron determines if it will be recruited in the neuronal ensemble that supports the memory (Josselyn, 2010). A fear memory is supported in part by neurons in the LA. Although many of these neurons receive the sensory inputs provided by the fear-conditioning experience, only about 20% of them actually become part of the memory trace.

Josselyn and her colleagues speculated that this might reflect competition among the neurons for participating in the memory-supporting ensemble. To test this hypothesis, they used a combination of approaches. They used a herpes viral vector to infect neurons in the LA with CREB (to manipulate its level of expression of CREB) and a selective neural toxin, diptheria, which selectively killed only these neurons (Figure 11.8). This approach produced two remarkable findings: (1) neurons that overexpressed CREB were preferentially selected to become part of the neural ensemble supporting the fear

(A) Some neurons (red) in lateral amygdala are infected with CREB

(B) Fear conditioning selects neurons (yellow) over-expressing CREB

(C) A neurotoxin designed to target cells that overexpress CREB erases the fear memory

(D)

**Figure 11.8**
(A) Herpes simplex viral vector infects some neurons in the lateral amygdala with CREB. (B) These neurons that now over-express CREB are preferentially selected to become part of the engram or memory trace that supports the fear memory. (C) Diptheria neurotoxin (NT) selectively kills the neurons that overexpress CREB. (D) The results of the fear-conditioning experiment revealed that the diptheria treatment that selec-tively killed neurons overexpressing CREB also erased the fear memory. These results indicate that (a) neurons in the lateral amygdala compete to participate in the neuron ensemble that supports the fear memory, and (b) neurons expressing high lev-els of CREB at the time of fear conditioning win the competition. (After Josselyn, 2010.)

memory, and (2) the established fear memory was erased when the neural toxin killed those neurons (Han et al., 2007).

## Some Memory Genes

CREB targets a vast array of genes, so it is important to ask, *which genes transcribed by CREB make a significant contribu-tion to memory consolidation?* To constrain this topic, this section focuses on three immediate early genes—genes that are transcribed rapidly because they do not require the prior translation of other proteins (Figure 11.9). Two of these genes, BDNF and Arc, code for proteins discussed in previous chapters. The third gene, C/EBPβ (CCAAT/ enhancer binding protein), is discussed in detail below.

BDNF and Arc are critical to the consolidation of LTP (see Chapter 6). Both are also transcribed in response to behavioral experiences that can produce enduring memories. For example, Arc is rapidly transcribed in the

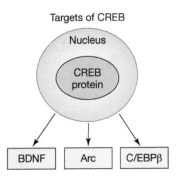

**Figure 11.9**
CREB mediates transcription of memory genes—BDNF, Arc, and C/EBPβ.

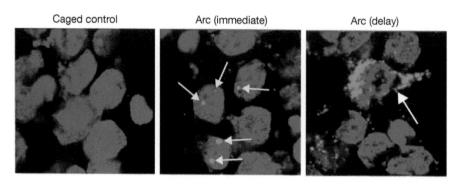

Caged control          Arc (immediate)          Arc (delay)

**Figure 11.10**
Exploring a novel context activates the immediate early gene Arc in the CA1 region of the hippocampus. Note that Arc is initially seen in the nucleus of the cell (immediate) but when rats are sacrificed 20 minutes after exploration (delay), Arc can be seen in the cytoplasm. (Photo provided by John Guzowski et al., 2001.)

hippocampus when rats (1) explore novel environments (Guzowski et al., 1999; Huff et al., 2006), (2) are required to learn the location of the hidden platform in the Morris water-escape task (Guzowski et al., 2001), or (3) are exposed to a fear-conditioning procedure (Ploski et al., 2008). Moreover, rapidly transcribed Arc translocates from the nucleus to the cytoplasm within about 15 to 20 minutes of the inducing behavioral experience (Figure 11.10). Similarly, memory-producing behavioral experiences up-regulate the expression of BDNF mRNA in both the hippocampus (Falkenberg et al., 1992; Tyler et al., 2002) and basolateral amygdala (for example, Ou and Gean, 2007).

C/EBPβ is important because it is a transcription factor and can target the transcription of other genes that may be needed to establish enduring memories. As one might expect, given that CREB targets C/EBPβ for transcription, CREB must be phosphorylated before C/EBPβ is transcribed. What might not be expected is that a detectable increase in C/EBPβ mRNA is not observed until hours after CREB is phosphorylated (Figure 11.11). Note that immediately following inhibitory avoidance training, phosphorylated CREB is observed in the CA1 field of the hippocampus and remains at a high level for at least 20 hours. In contrast, increased levels of C/EBPβ mRNA are not observed until 9 hours after training (Taubenfeld, Wiig et al., 2001).

The late emergence of C/EBPβ mRNA suggests that the construction of the memory trace may continue for a much longer period than one would anticipate from in vitro LTP experiments. Consistent with this view, the use of antisense ODNs to prevent C/EBPβ translation into protein does not interfere with inhibitory avoidance learning when infused into the hippocampus 1 hour prior to training, but it dramatically impairs performance if infused

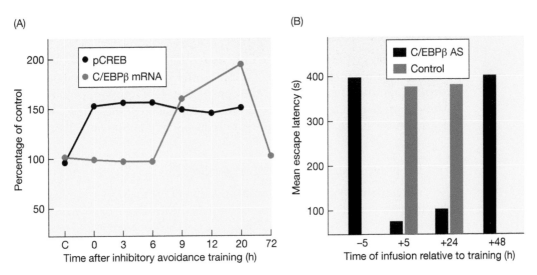

**Figure 11.11**
(A) Increased levels of phosphorylated CREB (pCREB) are present in the hippocampus shortly after training and remain high for at least 20 hours. In contrast, increased levels of C/EBPβ mRNA are not observed until 9 hours after training. (B) C/EBPβ antisense infused into the hippocampus 5 and 24 hours after training impaired retention of the inhibitory avoidance memory. Rats were tested 48 hours after training. These results indicate that C/EBPβ-protein-dependent processes operate at least 24 hours following training. (After Taubenfeld, Milekic et al., 2001.)

5 or 24 hours after training. Thus, not only is C/EBPβ mRNA elevated in response to training, its translation into protein is needed to secure the memory (Taubenfeld, Milekic et al., 2001).

## *Summary of Transcription*

The idea that the construction of long-term memories depends on molecular products resulting from transcription emerged directly from studies of LTP. Much research has focused on the transcription factor CREB. Several research strategies have confirmed a role for CREB in the construction of enduring memories. Moreover, a number of genes identified as important for enduring LTP, especially Arc and BDNF, are transcribed in response to behavioral experiences that generate long-lasting memories. In addition to targeting genes for proteins that are immediately involved in modifying synapses (such as Arc and BDNF), CREB also targets another transcription factor, C/EBPβ, that targets the expression of other mRNAs that become important many hours after the behavioral experience.

## Translation and Enduring Memories

Transcription processes generate only new mRNA. To function, however, these transcripts must be translated into protein. The idea that translation (protein synthesis) is critical for the consolidation of long-term memories is often referred to as the *de novo* protein synthesis hypothesis (previously described in Chapter 5 with regard to the consolidation of synaptic changes).

### The De Novo *Protein Synthesis Hypothesis*

According to this hypothesis, the consolidation of the memory trace requires that the to-be-remembered experience initiate the synthesis of new proteins. Flexner et al. (1963) put forth this hypothesis long before anything was known about mechanisms of synaptic plasticity, and hundreds of studies were published in the 1960s and 1970s on this topic (Davis and Squire, 1984).

The *de novo* protein synthesis hypothesis has two important implications:

- Protein synthesis is critical for the formation of the long-term memory trace but not for the induction of the short-term memory trace.

- It is the synthesis of new proteins induced by the training experience, not just the level of protein, that is critical for consolidation. This means that the protein synthesis inhibitor must be administered around the time of the behavioral experience if it is to prevent the consolidation of the LTM trace. Delaying the administration of the inhibitor for several hours should have no effect on memory retention because the trace will have been consolidated.

A study by Bourtchouladze and her colleagues (1998) illustrates how these hypotheses are tested. The protein synthesis inhibitor anisomycin was injected systemically (into the body cavity) prior to fear conditioning. The rats were tested at several different times after training. The results for 1-, 6-, and 24-hour retention tests are presented in Figure 11.12A. Note that the drug had no effect at the 1-hour retention interval but impaired retention at the longer, 6- and 24-hour tests. These results are consistent with the idea that a short-term memory trace can be formed that does not depend on protein synthesis, while a long-term memory trace requires new proteins.

Bourtchouladze and her colleagues also varied the interval between training and the delivery of anisomycin and found that anisomycin was effective when it was given immediately after training but had no effect when given either 3 or 24 hours later (Figure 11.12B). Their results imply that:

- memories can be retrieved from a short-term memory trace or a long-term memory trace;

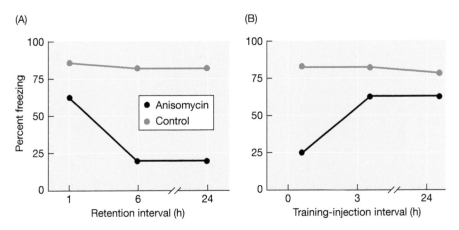

**Figure 11.12**
(A) Anisomycin injected immediately after training disrupts retention performance at the 6- and 24-hour retention intervals but not at the 1-hour interval. (B) The effect of anisomycin depends on the interval between training and the injection. It interfered with memory formation only when it was given immediately (0 hour) after training. This result indicates that the consolidation process was about 3 hours. (After Bourtchouladze et al., 1998.)

- the two traces have different molecular requirements: the long-term trace but not the short-term trace requires new proteins, synthesized in response to neural activity induced by the training experience; and

- blocking protein synthesis per se is not important; it must be blocked shortly after the behavioral experience.

## Methodological Issues

Bourtchouladze's results are subject to the same criticisms that were leveled at many previous studies based on systemic injections of protein synthesis inhibitors (Davis and Squire, 1984). No one doubts that drugs like anisomycin, when given in large amounts, can profoundly block the synthesis of new proteins. Nor does anyone doubt that they can disturb memory storage. However, protein synthesis inhibitors are also toxic and have many side effects (Figure 11.13), including making the animal ill. Thus, the question becomes, *did the drug impair long-term memory because it inhibited protein synthesis or because it disrupted other processes needed to consolidate the memory?* (Gold, 2006).

**Figure 11.13**
In addition to blocking protein synthesis, anisomycin has other effects on neurons. The drug is toxic and can kill neurons. It also causes an excessive release of neurotransmitters in the region of the injection and induces genomic signaling cascades in the neuron that result in an overproduction of mRNAs. These additional effects make it difficult to accept the conclusion that the reason anisomycin disrupts memory consolidation is that it inhibits protein synthesis.

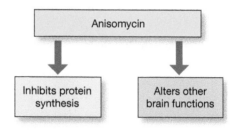

To avoid some of the problems associated with the systemic injection of protein synthesis inhibitors, researchers now often inject the drug directly into a region of the brain that is thought to contain the synapses that hold the memory trace. For example, Schafe and his colleagues (1999) injected anisomycin directly into the basolateral amygdala (BLA) where a fear memory trace is believed to be stored (see Chapter 19). Anisomycin was injected into the BLA just after rats were conditioned to an auditory cue paired with shock. These rats displayed normal freezing at a 1-hour testing interval but very little freezing when they were tested 24 hours later (Figure 11.14).

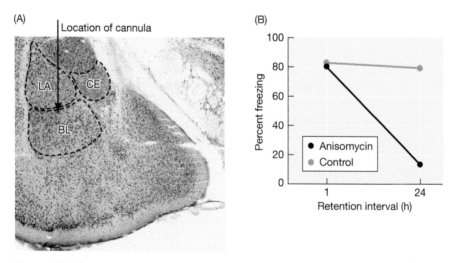

**Figure 11.14**
(A) This figure shows a section of the amygdala and illustrates the location of the cannula in the basolateral amygdala through which anisomycin was injected (photo courtesy of Serge Campeau and Cher Masini). (B) Anisomycin did not impair performance when the retention test was given 1 hour after training but did impair performance when the retention interval was 24 hours. These results are thus consistent with the *de novo* protein synthesis hypothesis. LA = Lateral amygdala; BL = Basal amygdala; CE = Central amygdala. (After Schafe et al., 1999.)

The pattern of results produced by direct infusions of protein synthesis inhibitors into the brain is consistent with the idea that the long-term memory trace requires the synthesis of new proteins but the short-term memory trace does not. However, there also are problems associated with this approach. For example, anisomycin delivered into the BLA dramatically increases the extracellular concentration of several important neurotransmitters—norepinephrine, serotonin, and dopamine (Canal et al., 2007). These drugs also initiate a process called **gene superconductance**—a genomic signaling cascade that causes an overproduction of mRNAs (Radulovic and Tronson, 2008). Abnormal levels of neurotransmitters and mRNAs can interfere with the normal molecular processes that store the memory trace. Moreover, when anisomycin and cycloheximide are infused into the brain, the neurons in that region exhibit no electrical activity for over 2 hours (Sharma et al., 2012).

The side effects associated with the use of broad-scale protein synthesis inhibitors make it difficult to conclude that they produce amnesia because they prevent protein synthesis (Gold, 2006; Routtenberg and Rekert, 2005; Rudy, 2008). However, studies using these protein synthesis inhibitors do permit strong conclusions. Specifically, because they do not interfere with performance at short retention tests, one can confidently conclude that *short-term memory does not require new protein but depends only on post-translation modifications*.

## Multiple Rounds of Protein Synthesis

While there are problems associated with the use of nonselective protein synthesis inhibitors, a more modern approach—using more selective pharmacological agents and genetic techniques that can target more specific proteins—has provided much stronger support for the *de novo* protein synthesis hypothesis. To organize this modern approach, it is important to note that studies of LTP have led to the conclusion that strong synaptic activity can initiate at least two rounds of protein synthesis—an early round that occurs locally in the dendritic spine region and a late round that occurs after new mRNAs have been transcribed and trafficked out of the nucleus.

Research discussed in this section supports the view that enduring memories can depend on the behavioral experience generating multiple rounds of protein synthesis. The discussion focuses on the importance of the mTOR pathway and the translation of three proteins that contribute to this outcome—BDNF, Arc, and insulin growth factor-II (IGF-2).

THE mTOR PATHWAY  Studies of LTP have clearly identified a role for mTOR (mammalian target of rapamycin) in enduring LTP. This protein kinase is more complex than previously described in Chapter 6. It forms two functionally

Fred Helmstetter

distinct multiple protein complexes. One complex, called mTOR complex 1 (mTORC1), is sensitive to (inhibited by) rapamycin, while the other, mTOR complex 2 (mTORC2), is insensitive to rapamycin.

The rapamycin-sensitive mTORC1 is important for local protein synthesis and regulates mRNA translation through activating downstream targets such as p70s6 kinase (p70s6k) and the elongation-factor-binding protein 4E-BP (see Hoeffer and Klann, 2010, for a review). Thus, one might expect that interfering with this pathway should disrupt memory consolidation processes. Consistent with this hypothesis, Fred Helmstetter and his colleagues have reported that contextual fear conditioning is normally associated with increased phosphorylation of p70s6k in the amygdala and dorsal hippocampus. However, when the rapamycin is infused into these regions to inhibit mTORC1, both the level of phosphorylated p70s6k and fear conditioning are reduced (Gafford et al., 2011; Parsons et al., 2006).

Moreover, studies using the inhibitory avoidance procedure revealed that rapamycin selectively impaired performance when the retention interval was 24 hours but not when it was only 3 hours (Figure 11.15). This result is important because it indicates that proteins translated in response to the mTORC1 signaling are important for the consolidation of long-term memory but not for producing a short-term memory (Bekinschtein et al., 2007; Jobim et al., 2012).

mTORC2 is insensitive to rapamycin and has been studied by genetic deletion of one of its components called rictor (rapamycin-insensitive companion of TOR) in neurons in the forebrain. This deletion reduces the activity of mTORC2. Studies of mice with this genetic deletion (called rictor KO) found that mTORC2 contributes to long-term memory but does not influence short-term memory (Huang et al., 2013). These results were obtained using both the fear-conditioning (Figure 11.16A) and Morris place-learning tasks. Moreover, a rapidly emerging short-lasting LTP could be generated in slices from rictor KO mice but a long-lasting LTP could not be produced (Figure 11.16B). Huang et al. (2013) also found that deletion of rictor disrupted signaling cascades that are critical

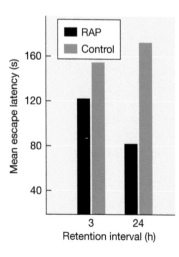

**Figure 11.15**
Rapamycin inhibits mTORC1. When it is infused into the basolateral amygdala prior to inhibitory avoidance training it does not interfere with performance when the retention interval is 3 hours but impairs test performance when the retention interval is 24 hours. These results suggest that signaling cascades regulated by mTORC1 are important for memory consolidation. (After Jobim et al., 2012.)

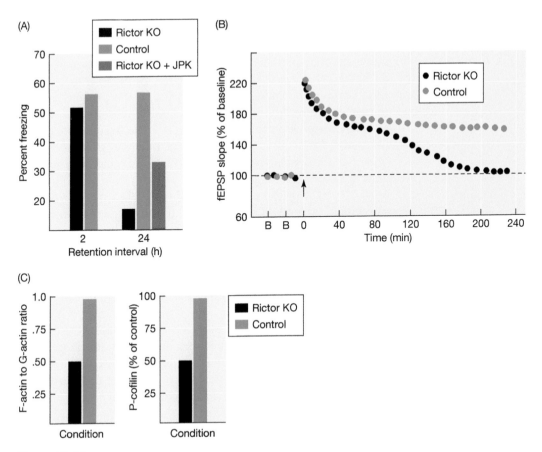

**Figure 11.16**
mTORC2 is important for long-term memory and enduring LTP. It contributes to long-term changes in synaptic strength by regulating actin dynamics. (A) rictor KO mice display normal short-term memory (2-hour retention test) for a contextual fear-conditioning experience but impaired long-term memory (24-hour retention test). This impairment is partially rescued by infusing an agent, jasplakinolide (JPK), which promotes actin polymerization. (B) Theta-burst stimulation (4 × 100Hz) induces early-phase, short-lasting LTP in rictor KO mice but does not induce the late-phase, long-lasting LTP in these mice. (C) The regulation of actin dynamics and signaling is disrupted in rictor KO mice. The ratio of F-actin to G-actin is a measure of the level of actin polymerization. It is reduced in the rictor KO mice. Phosphorylated cofilin (p-cofilin) is required for actin polymerization. It is reduced in the rictor KO mice. These data indicate that the long-term but not short-term memory depends on signaling cascades regulated by mTORC2. Impaired long-term memory and LTP are due in part to impaired actin regulation in the rictor KO mice. (After Huang et al., 2013.)

to actin polymerization (such as phosphorylation of cofilin) and the ratio of F-actin to G-actin. (Figure 11.16C). In addition, treatments that directly promote actin polymerization partially rescue the memory deficit associated with the rictor KO factor.

In summary, signaling cascades regulated by the mTOR protein complex contribute to memory consolidation in two ways. mTORC1 regulates signaling cascades that increase local protein synthesis, whereas mTORC2 regulates processes that contribute to the regulation of actin. Disrupting either of these functions will impair the development of long-term memory but have no influence on the formation of a short-term memory.

BDNF   As previously learned, BDNF is critical to the consolidation of synaptic changes that support enduring LTP (see Chapter 6). Its role is complex because in response to a strong inducing stimulus an increased level of BDNF contributes to the activation of the mTOR signaling cascade by binding to TrkB receptors. As a consequence of subsequent CREB activation, additional BDNF mRNA and protein become available to participate in the further strengthening of synaptic connections.

A large literature indicates that BDNF plays a prominent role in the consolidation of memories (see Rattiner, Davis, French et al., 2004; Rattiner, Davis, and Ressler, 2004; Tyler et al., 2002). For example, BDNF protein levels are increased in the hippocampus by contextual fear conditioning and place learning and in the BLA by fear conditioning. Moreover, treatments that interfere with BDNF function impair long-term memory.

It has been known for some time that BDNF protein levels in the BLA dramatically increase during the first hour following auditory-cue fear conditioning but then return to baseline (Ou and Gean, 2006; Rattiner, Davis, and Ressler, 2004). However, Po-Wu Gean and his colleagues (Ou et al., 2009) expanded the time period over which BDNF was measured and discovered two distinct peak levels of BDNF expression. One peak of BDNF occurred 1 hour after training but the other did not occur until 12 hours later, and BDNF did not return to its pre-training baseline level until 30 hours after training (Figure 11.17A).

To determine if these peaks were functionally significant, Ou et al. (2009) infused the BDNF scavenger TrkB–IgG or the TrkB receptor antagonist K252a into the BLA, either 1 or 9 hours prior to fear conditioning. TrkB–IgGs are nonfunctional TrkB receptors that compete with endogenous TrkB receptors for BDNF. Their presence depletes the availability of extracellular BDNF to bind to the functional TrkB receptors. Rats were tested at two retention intervals—1 day or 7 days after training. Interfering with BDNF function by either method impaired the development of long-term memory. Interference 30 minutes before training markedly reduced the fear expressed at both the 1-day and 7-day retention test. However, eliminating BDNF function 9 hours

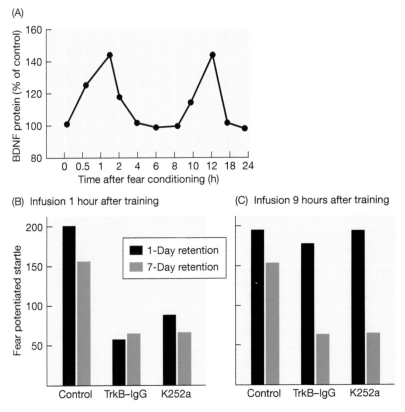

**Figure 11.17**
(A) BDNF protein levels peak at 1 and 12 hours following fear conditioning. (B) Impairing BDNF function 1 hour after training with either the BDNF scavenger TrkB–IgG or the TrkB antagonist K252a impairs the fear response at both the 1-day and 7-day retention intervals. (C) In contrast, administering these treatments 9 hours after training impairs the fear response only on the 7-day retention test. The measure of fear was the fear-potentiated startle response. Rats startle more to a brief loud noise in the presence of a fear stimulus. These results indicate that the first peak of BDNF is critical for the memory expressed on both the 1- and 7-day retention tests. However, the second peak is required only to support the memory expressed on the 7-day retention test. (After Ou et al., 2009.)

after training reduced the fear expressed only 7 days after training (Figures 11.17B and 11.17C).

These results are important because they indicate that (a) the processes needed to secure this long-lasting fear memory (for at least 7 days) operate for 9 hours and perhaps longer, and (b) separate BDNF-dependent processes support retention at the 1- and 7-day retention intervals. The processes that support 1-day retention do not depend on BDNF expressed 12 hours after training, but the processes that support 7-day retention depend on BDNF translated during both peak periods. It is also tempting to conclude that the second peak of BDNF is dependent on processes mediated by the first wave.

The idea that discrete waves of BDNF protein contribute to long-term memory is also supported by the research of Slipczuk and his colleagues (2009). They reported that BDNF antibodies infused into the dorsal hippocampus can impair retention of the memory for inhibitory avoidance training when they are infused 15 minutes prior to training or 3 hours after training. However, the antibodies had no effect when infused 1 hour or 9 hours after training. The antibodies also prevented the training experience from activating mTOR when administered 15 minutes or 3 hours after training, thus linking the memory impairment to BDNF's effect on mTOR.

Although the time courses vary, either because different tasks were used or different brain regions were sampled, the studies by Ou et al. (2009) and Slipczuk et al. (2009) suggest an important conclusion—the processes supporting consolidation operate over long periods of time and likely involve multiple waves of new proteins. Some of these proteins are likely translated within minutes of training. Others proteins are translated later, after behaviorally induced transcription processes have produced new mRNA.

ARC PROTEIN    Arc protein also is important for memory consolidation. This conclusion is based on two general observations. First, behavioral experiences that produce memories increase the levels of Arc protein in brain regions (Ploski et al., 2008; Ramírez-Amaya et al., 2005). For example, Ploski et al. (2008) reported that fear conditioning increased Arc mRNA and protein levels in the lateral amygdala. Second, antisense ODNs have been used to prevent the translation of Arc mRNA. John Guzowski and his colleagues (Guzowski et al., 2000) were the first to use this strategy. They reported that when Arc antisense ODN was infused into the hippocampus, rats were able to learn the location of the hidden platform in the Morris water-escape task and remembered that location following a 30-minute retention interval. However, these rats did not remember the location when tested 2 days following training. Ploski et al. (2008) reported that Arc antisense infused into the lateral amygdala (a) reduced Arc protein and (b) impaired memory for a fear-conditioning experience when the retention interval was 24 hours but not when the interval was 3 hours (Figure 11.18).

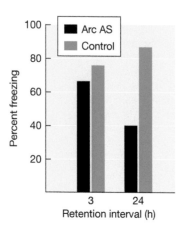

**Figure 11.18**
Arc antisense ODN impairs long-term memory (24-hour retention interval) but not short-term memory (3-hour retention interval). (After Ploski et al., 2008.)

IGF-2 PROTEIN    **Insulin growth factor-II (IGF-2)** is a protein that belongs to a system that is important for normal somatic growth and development, tissue repair, and regeneration (Alberini and Chen, 2012). In the brain its highest level of expression is in the hippocampus. The mRNA for this protein is targeted for transcription by the previously mentioned transcription factor C/EBPβ. Christina Alberini and her colleagues (Chen et al., 2011) reported that inhibitory avoidance training dramatically increases expression of IGF-2 mRNA but not until about 20 hours after training, and it remains elevated for 36 hours. Moreover, antisense to C/EBPβ blocked IGF-2 expression, which confirmed that IGF-2 is transcribed by C/EBPβ.

Christina Alberini

Alberini and her colleagues also confirmed that this protein plays a critical role in consolidating the inhibitory avoidance memory. To do this they infused IGF-2 antisense into the hippocampus at several times following training. Their experiment revealed that antisense infused within 8 hours of training impaired performance when the retention interval was 24 hours, and antisense infused up to 36 hours following training impaired performance when the retention interval was 48 hours. However, antisense applied about 104 hours following training did not impair performance when the retention interval was 120 hours. Moreover, the impairment produced by the IGF-2 antisense could be rescued by a co-infusion of IGF-2 in the hippocampus. These results indicated that the IGF-2 continues to contribute to memory consolidation for over 24 hours (Figure 11.19).

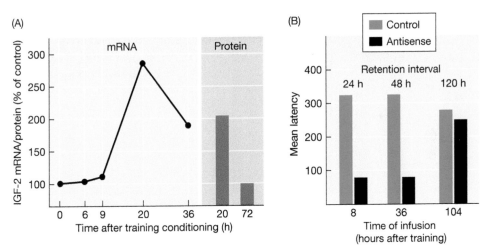

**Figure 11.19**
(A) Inhibitory avoidance training induces CREB-dependent transcription of IGF-2 mRNA and protein. Note that the mRNA level does not increase until about 20 hours after training. Protein level is also high 20 hours after training but not 72 hours later. (B) The consolidation of the inhibitory avoidance memory remains dependent on IGF-2 for at least 36 hours. IGF-2 antisense was infused into the hippocampus 8, 36, or 104 hours after training. (After Chen et al., 2011.)

To add to the importance of IGF-2 to memory consolidation processes, Alberini's group demonstrated that injecting IGF-2 into the hippocampus following training enhanced retention performance when rats were tested 1, 7, or 21 days following training. Just how IGF-2 contributes to consolidation is not well understood (see Alberini and Chen, 2012). However, it is known that its contribution depends on Arc protein because when Arc antisense was co-infused with IGF-2 antisense, IGF-2 did not enhance memory retention. Given that Arc regulates actin polymerization, it is possible that IGF-2 is another contributor to processes regulating actin.

## Protein Degradation Processes

Just as there is evidence that protein degradation contributes to establishing long-lasting LTP (see Chapter 6), a case can be made that protein degradation mediated by the ubiquitin proteasome system (UPS) is critical for establishing enduring memories.

Several lines of evidence indicate that the UPS is involved in memory consolidation. First, behavioral experiences that induce lasting memories increase ubiquitination and proteasome activity (Artinian et al., 2008; Lopez-Salon et

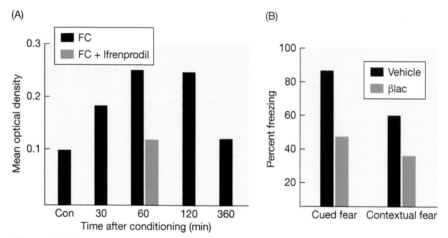

**Figure 11.20**
Protein degradation is important for long-term fear memories. (A) Fear conditioning (FC) induces polyubiquitination in the amygdala. This process is prevented by the NMDA antagonist ifrenprodil. (B) The proteasome inhibitor βlactone (βlac) impairs both cued and contextual fear conditioning. These results indicate that protein degradation is critical for consolidating long-term fear memories. (After Jarome et al., 2011.)

al., 2001). Fred Helmstetter's group (Jarome et al., 2011) found that fear conditioning rapidly ubiquitinates scaffolding proteins in the postsynaptic density of neurons in the amygdala. Moreover, antagonizing NMDA receptors prevents ubiquitination, suggesting that the UPS operates in parallel with the calcium-dependent processes needed to generate new protein (Figure 11.20A).

Second, drugs that block proteasome activity also prevent long-term memory formation (Artinian et al., 2008; Jarome et al., 2011; Lopez-Salon et al., 2001). For example, Jarome et al. (2011) reported that inhibiting the proteasome function (thereby preventing degradation of ubiquitin-tagged proteins) in the amygdala impaired long-term memory for both cued and contextual fear (Figure 11.20B). Similarly, Lopez-Salon et al. (2001) reported that blocking proteasome function in the hippocampus prevented the formation of a long-term memory for an inhibitory avoidance experience.

## Defining the Consolidation Window

When the memory trace is formed it is unstable and vulnerable to disruption. The concept of consolidation was introduced because the memory trace stabilizes over time. How long does it take a memory trace to consolidate? The answer to this question depends in part on specifying criteria for concluding when the trace is consolidated. A general criterion is that the window of vulnerability to disruption by some agent must be time limited (Dudai, 2004). This is because at some point in time the trace has consolidated. However, this criterion is not adequate because, as discussed above, the retention interval is also important (for example, 1 versus 7 days), and several windows of vulnerability have been observed when the retention interval is 7 days. The motivating question is addressed in this context.

Agents that prevent transcription and translation (such as antisense to CREB, BDNF, Arc, C/EBPβ, and IGF-2, and less selective agents like anisomycin) have time-limited effects on memory. In addition, a number of nuances have been discovered. Specifically, in the intact animal, processes that consolidate memories do not operate in a continuous manner but in discrete waves. The first wave occurs during the first hour or so following training. In about 3 hours a new round of consolidation takes place and persists perhaps for about 8 to 9 hours. These two waves of consolidation are dependent on the BDNF–mTOR pathway (see Slipczuk et al., 2009) and retention at 1 day depends on both waves. A third wave of consolidation also has been identified. It depends on the transcription factor C/EBPβ and one of its gene targets, IGF-2. Antisense to either C/EBPβ or IGF-2 impairs memory even when it is infused 24 hours following training. Based on these observations,

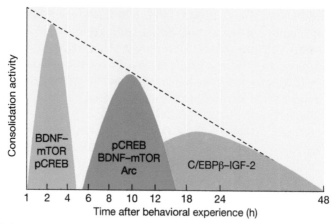

**Figure 11.21**

In the intact animal, memory consolidation processes operate in at least three waves. The first wave occurs rapidly and involves the local translation of new protein regulated by the BDNF–mTOR signaling pathway. During this initial period genomic signaling processes are also activated to phosphorylate CREB to transcribe new BDNF and Arc so that in about 3 hours a new wave of consolidation takes place and persists perhaps for about 8 to 9 hours. The second round is also dependent on the BDNF–mTOR pathway and retention at 1 day depends on both waves. The third wave depends on the activity of the transcription factor C/EBPβ and one of its known gene targets—IGF-2. The third wave is active for about 24 hours. Little is known about the downstream targets of IGF-2. Based on this summary one would assume that the consolidation period in some cases could last over 30 hours.

consolidation processes operate for at least 24 hours and within this period there are multiple windows of vulnerability. These ideas are summarized in Figure 11.21.

In considering the full implications of this discussion, however, it must be noted that the conclusions are based on studies in which a key component of the experience is an aversive, highly arousing event (shock), and these kinds of single experiences are the ones that are most likely to produce memories that last for days and weeks. A different profile might emerge for studies of less arousing experiences, such as memory for objects or a context and event such as what you had for breakfast.

## Summary

The initial STM trace depends only on the post-translation modification and rearrangement of existing protein. However, it is unstable and vulnerable to disruption. Over a period of about 24 hours, transcription and translation processes engaged by the memory-producing experience operate to consolidate a more robust LTM trace that is more stable and harder to disrupt. The transcription factor CREB targets the transcription mRNA for proteins such as BDNF, Arc, C/EBPβ, and IGF-2 that are important for consolidation. If the translation of these genes is prevented, the memory trace will not endure. The translation of these proteins depends on the initial activation of the mTOR pathway and protein degradation processes. The supply of new proteins needed to consolidate memories is not continuous. Instead, proteins such as BDNF, C/EBPβ, and IGF-2 come in discrete waves. This leads to the idea that consolidation occurs in overlapping stages, with each stage depending on different molecules. However, within about 24 hours the consolidation period comes to an end and the memory trace is no longer vulnerable to potential disrupting events such as protein synthesis inhibitors and antisense to CREB, BDNF, Arc, C/EBPβ, and IGF-2, and less selective agents like anisomycin.

# References

Alberini, C. M. (2009). Transcription factors in long-term memory and synaptic plasticity. *Physiological Reviews*, *89*, 121–145.

Alberini, C. M. and Chen, D. Y. (2012). Memory enhancement: consolidation, reconsolidation and insulin-like growth factor 2. *Trends in Neuroscience*, *35*, 274–283.

Artinian, J., McGauran, A. M., De Jaeger, X., Mouledous, L., Frances, B., and Roullet, P. (2008). Protein degradation, as with protein synthesis, is required during not only long-term spatial memory consolidation but also reconsolidation. *European Journal Neuroscience*, *11*, 3009–3019.

Bekinschtein, P., Katche, C., Slipczuk, L. N., Igaz, L. M., Cammarota, M., Izquierdo, I., and Medina, J. H. (2007). mTOR signaling in the hippocampus is necessary for memory formation. *Neurobiology of Learning and Memory*, *87*, 303–307.

Bourtchouladze, R., Abel, T., Berman, N., Gordon, R., Lapidus, K., and Kandel, E. R. (1998). Different training procedures recruit either one or two critical periods for contextual memory consolidation, each of which requires protein synthesis and PKA. *Learning and Memory*, *5*, 365–367.

Bourtchuladze, R., Frenguelli, B., Blendy, J., Cioffi, D., Schutz, G., and Silva, A. J. (1994). Deficient long-term memory in mice with a targeted mutation of the cAMP-responsive element-binding protein. *Cell*, *79*, 59–68.

Canal, C. E., Chang, Q., and Gold, P. E. (2007). Amnesia produced by altered release of neurotransmitters after intra-amygdala injections of a protein synthesis inhibitor. *Proceedings of the National Academy of Sciences*, *104*, 12500–12505.

Chen, D. Y., Stern, S. A., Garcia-Osta, A., Saunier-Rebori, B., Pollonini, G., Bambah-Mukku, D., Blitzer, R. D., and Alberini, C. M. (2011). A critical role for IGF-II in memory consolidation and enhancement. *Nature*, *469*, 491–497.

Davis, H. P. and Squire, L. R. (1984). Protein synthesis and memory: a review. *Psychological Bulletin, 96*, 518–559.

Dudai, Y. (2004). The neurobiology of consolidation, or, how stable is the engram. *Annual Review of Psychology, 55*, 51–86.

Falkenberg, T., Mohammed, A. K., Henriksson, B., Persson, H., Winblad, B., and Lindefors, N. (1992). Increased expression of brain-derived neurotrophic factor mRNA in rat hippocampus is associated with improved spatial memory and enriched environment. *Neuroscience Letters, 138*, 153–156.

Flexner, J. B., Flexner, L. B., and Stellar, E. (1963). Memory in mice as affected by intracerebral puromycin. *Science, 141*, 57–59.

Gafford, G. M., Parsons, R. G., and Helmstetter, F. J. (2011). Consolidation and reconsolidation of contextual fear memory requires mammalian target of rapamycin-dependent translation in the dorsal hippocampus. *Neuroscience, 19*, 98–104.

Gold, P. E. (2006). The many faces of amnesia. *Learning and Memory, 13*, 506–514.

Guzowski, J. F., Lyford, G. L., Stevenson, G. D., Houston, F. P., McGaugh, J. L., Worley, P. F., and Barnes, C. A. (2000). Inhibition of activity-dependent arc protein expression in the rat hippocampus impairs the maintenance of long-term potentiation and the consolidation of long-term memory. *Journal of Neuroscience, 20*, 3993–4001.

Guzowski, J. F. and McGaugh, J. L. (1997). Antisense oligodeoxynucleotide-mediated disruption of hippocampal cAMP response element binding protein levels impairs consolidation of memory for water maze training. *Proceedings of the National Academy of Sciences, 18*, 2693–2698.

Guzowski, J. F., McNaughton, B. L., Barnes, C. A., and Worley, P. F. (1999). Environment-specific expression of the immediate early gene Arc in hippocampal neuronal ensembles. *Nature Neuroscience, 2*, 1120–1124.

Guzowski, J. F., McNaughton, B. L., Barnes, C. A., and Worley, P. F. (2001). Imaging neural activity with temporal and cellular resolution using FISH. *Current Opinion in Neurobiology, 5*, 579–584.

Han, J. H., Kushner, S. A., Yiu, A. P., Cole, C. J., Matynia, A., Brown, R. A., Neve, R. L., Guzowski, J. F., Silva, A. J., and Josselyn, S. A. (2007). Neuronal competition and selection during memory formation. *Science, 316*, 457–460.

Hoeffer, C. A. and Klann, E. (2010). mTOR signaling: at the crossroads of plasticity, memory and disease. *Trends in Neuroscience, 33*, 67–75.

Huang, W., Zhu, P. J., Zhang, S., Zhou, H., Stoica, L., Galiano, M., Krnjević, K., Roman, G., and Costa-Mattioli, M. (2013). mTORC2 controls actin polymerization required for consolidation of long-term memory. *Nature Neuroscience, 16*, 441–448.

Huff, N. C., Frank, M., Wright-Hardesty, K., Sprunger, D., Matus-Amat, P., Higgins, E., and Rudy, J. W. (2006). Amygdala regulation of immediate early gene expression in hippocampus induced by contextual fear conditioning. *Journal of Neuroscience, 26*, 1616–1623.

Jarome, T. J, Werner, C. T., Kwapis, J. L., and Helmstetter, F. J. (2011). Activity dependent protein degradation is critical for the formation and stability of fear memory in the amygdala. *PLoS One, 6* e24349.

Jobim, P. F., Pedroso, T. R., Werenicz, A., Christoff, R. R., Maurmann, N., Reolon, G. K., Schröder, N., and Roesler, R. (2012). Impairment of object recognition memory by rapamycin inhibition of mTOR in the amygdala or hippocampus around the time of learning or reactivation. *Behavioral Brain Research, 228,* 151–158.

Josselyn, S. A. (2010) Continuing the search for the engram: examining the mechanisms of fear memories. *Journal of Psychiatry and Neuroscience, 35,* 221–228.

Josselyn, S. A., Shi, C., Carlezon, W. A. Jr., Neve, R. L., Nestler, E. J., and Davis, M. (2001). Long-term memory is facilitated by cAMP response element-binding protein overexpression in the amygdala. *Journal of Neuroscience, 21,* 2404–2412.

Kandel, E. R. (2001). The molecular biology of memory storage: a dialogue between genes and synapses. *Science, 29,* 1030–1038.

Lopez-Salon, M., Alonso, M., Vianna, M. R., Viola, H., Mello, E., and Souza, T. (2001). The ubiquitin-proteasome cascade is required for mammalian long-term memory formation. *European Journal of Neuroscience, 14,* 1820–1826.

Ou, L. C. and Gean, P. W. (2006). Regulation of amygdala-dependent learning by brain derived neurotrophic factor is mediated by extracellular signal-regulated kinase and phosphatidylinositol-3-kinase. *Neuropsychopharmacology, 31,* 287–296.

Ou, L. C. and Gean, P. W. (2007). Transcriptional regulation of brain-derived neurotrophic factor in the amygdala during consolidation of fear memory. *Molecular Pharmacology, 72,* 350–358.

Ou, L. C, Yeh, S. H., and Gean, P. W. (2009). Late expression of brain-derived neurotrophic factor in the amygdala is required for persistence of fear memory. *Neurobiology of Learning and Memory, 93,* 372–382.

Parsons, R. G., Gafford, G. M., and Helmstetter, F. J. (2006). Translational control via the mammalian target of rapamycin pathway is critical for the formation and stability of long-term fear memory in amygdala neurons. *Journal of Neuroscience, 26,* 12977–12983.

Ploski, J. E., Pierrre, V. J., Smucny, J., Park, K., Monsey, M. S., Overeem, K. A., and Schafe, G. E. (2008). The activity-regulated cytoskeletal-associated protein (Arc/Arg3.1) is required for memory consolidation of pavlovian fear conditioning in the lateral amygdala. *Journal of Neuroscience, 28* (47), 12383–12395.

Radulovic, J. and Transon, N. C. (2008). Protein synthesis inhibitors, gene superinduction and memory: too little or too much protein? *Neurobiology of Learning and Memory, 89*(3), 212–218.

Ramírez-Amaya, V., Vazdarjanova, A., Mikhael, D., Rosi, S., Worley, P. F., and Barnes, C. A. (2005). Spatial exploration-induced Arc mRNA and protein expression: evidence for selective, network-specific reactivation. *Journal of Neuroscience, 25,* 1761–1768.

Rattiner, L. M., Davis, M., French, C. T., and Ressler, K. J. (2004). Brain-derived neurotrophic factor and tyrosine kinase receptor B involvement in amygdala-dependent fear conditioning. *Journal of Neuroscience, 24,* 4796–4806.

Rattiner, L. M., Davis, M., and Ressler, K. J. (2004). Differential regulation of brain-derived neurotrophic factor transcripts during the consolidation of fear learning. *Learning and Memory, 11,* 727–731.

Routtenberg, A. and Rekart, J. (2005). Post-translational protein modifications as the substrate for long-lasting memory. *Trends in Neurosciences, 28,* 12–19.

Rudy, J. W. (2008.) Is there a baby in the bathwater? Maybe: some methodological issues for the de novo protein synthesis hypothesis. *Neurobiology of Learning and Memory, 89,* 219–224.

Schafe, G. E., Nadel, N. V., Sullivan, G. M., Harris, A., and LeDoux, J. E. (1999). Memory consolidation for contextual and auditory fear conditioning is dependent on protein synthesis, PKA, and MAP kinase. *Learning and Memory, 6,* 97–110.

Sharma, A. V., Frank, E., Nargang, F. E., and, Dickson, T. C. (2012). Neurosilence: profound suppression of neural activity following intracerebral administration of the protein synthesis inhibitor anisomycin. *Journal of Neuroscience, 32,* 2377–2387.

Silva, A. J., Kogan, J. H., Frankland, P. W., and Kida, S. (1998). CREB and memory. *Annual Review Neuroscience, 2,* 127–148.

Slipczuk, L., Bekinschtein, P., Katche, C., Cammarota, M., Izquierdo, I., and Medina, J. (2009). BDNF activates mTOR to regulate GluR1 expression required for memory formation. *PLoS ONE, 4* (6), e6007.

Taubenfeld, S. M., Milekic, M. H., Monti, B., and Alberini, C. M. (2001). The consolidation of new but not reactivated memory requires hippocampal C/EBPβ. *Nature Neuroscience, 4,* 813–818.

Taubenfeld, S. M., Wiig, K. A., Monti, B., Dolan, B., Pollonini, G., and Alberini, C. M. (2001). Fornix-dependent induction of hippocampal CCAAT enhancer-binding protein and co-localizes with phosphorylated cAMP response element binding protein and accompanies long- term memory consolidation. *Journal of Neuroscience, 21,* 84–91.

Tyler, W. J., Alonso, M., Bramham, C. R., and Pozzo-Miller, L. D. (2002). From acquisition to consolidation: on the role of brain-derived neurotrophic factor signaling in hippocampal dependent learning. *Learning and Memory, 9,* 224–237.

Yin, J. and Tully, T. (1996). CREB and the formation of long-term memory. *Current Opinion in Neurobiology, 2,* 264–268.

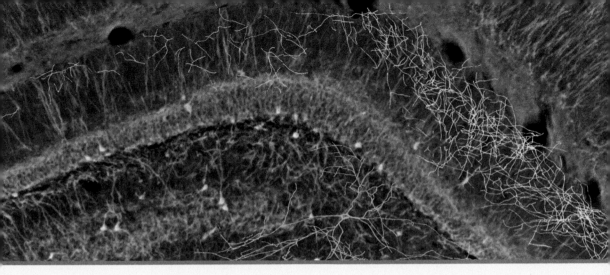

# 12 Memory Maintenance and Forgetting

The consolidation period ends when the memory trace is no longer vulnerable to the disruption of transcription and translation processes that were initiated by the memory-producing behavior. This requires about 24 hours. However, the consolidated memory trace must still be maintained in the face of molecular turnover (see Chapter 7). Since maintenance processes must operate over the life of the memory, they must be regulated by molecular events that operate continuously. Moreover, the disruption of a memory maintenance process any time following consolidation should (a) erase the memory and (b) do so without altering the ability of those neurons to relearn. This chapter first examines the role of PKMζ in memory maintenance and then touches on theories of forgetting and the concept of active decay as they relate to the preservation of memories.

## PKMζ and Memory Maintenance

Given the discussion of the role of PKMζ in maintaining LTP in Chapter 7, it should come as no surprise that this kinase has been extensively investigated for its potential role in memory maintenance. As was the case for LTP, the primary strategy has been to inactivate PKMζ with zeta inhibitory protein (ZIP). Given that ZIP reverses well-established LTP, then the prediction is that it also should erase well consolidated memories. In fact spatial memories, fear memories, inhibitory avoidance memories, instrumental response memories, object-location memories, and taste-aversion memories have all been erased by injecting ZIP into the relevant storage sites (Hardt et al., 2013; Kwapis et al., 2012; Pastalkova et al., 2006; Pauli et al., 2012; Sacktor, 2011; Serrano et al., 2008; Shema et al., 2007). So the idea that PKMζ is an important memory maintenance molecule has considerable support.

### Interfering with PKMζ Erases a Taste-Aversion Memory

The work of Yadin Dudai and his colleagues provides an excellent example of the strategy of inactivating PKMζ with ZIP (Shema et al., 2007). They asked if the maintenance of the memory for an acquired taste aversion depends on PKMζ (Figure 12.1). They injected ZIP into insular cortex, which previous studies had identified as a storage site for taste-aversion memories. A single injection of ZIP into insular neocortex either 3, 7, or 25 days after training erased the memory. It is important to note that there was no time window constraining the effects of ZIP. The taste-aversion memory was erased even when it was 25 days old. In contrast, when it was injected into the hippocampus, which is not a storage site for the taste-aversion memory, ZIP had no effect. Moreover, even though ZIP erased old established taste memories, it did not alter the acquisition of a new taste aversion.

Dudai's group (Shema et al., 2011) also confirmed the importance of PKMζ

Yadin Dudai

with another strategy. They infected neurons in insular cortex with a lentivirus designed to transfect these neurons with a dominant negative gene ($LV_{DN}$) that coded for an inactive form of PKMζ. This mRNA would compete with existing PKMζ for translation but the resulting protein would not be functional, so the predicted outcome was that rats treated with $LV_{DN}$ would not maintain an established taste-aversion memory. The virus was injected 5 days following the acquisition of the memory. Consistent with the prediction, rats injected with the virus displayed a markedly reduced taste aversion when tested 6 days later (Figure 12.1C).

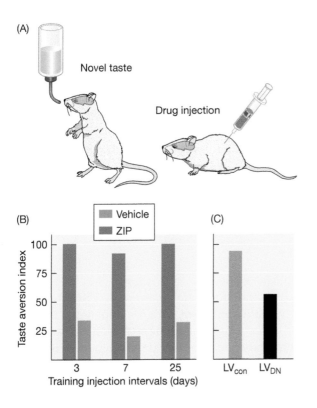

(A)

Novel taste

Drug injection

(B)

Taste aversion index

Vehicle
ZIP

Training injection intervals (days)

(C)

LV_con    LV_DN

**Figure 12.1**
(A, B) Rodents will acquire an aversion to novel taste that is followed by a drug that induces a temporary illness. A single injection of ZIP into insular cortex will greatly reduce a well consolidated taste-aversion memory. (C) The lentivirus dominant negative PKMζ (LV_DN) construct competes with PKMζ for expression. If it is injected into insular cortex 5 days following the acquisition of a taste-aversion memory, the memory is weakened.

## PKMζ Strengthens New Memories and Prevents Forgetting

Dudai's group also used the lentivirus approach to reveal that PKMζ *can enhance established memories*. In this case they asked two questions: (1) could PKMζ convert a weak memory trace into a stronger one, and (2) could it prevent the forgetting that normally occurs? To do this they designed lentiviruses to deliver the gene for PKMζ (LV_PKMζ) or a control construct (LV_con) that did not contain the gene. To determine if PKMζ could strengthen a weak memory, rats were trained with a taste-aversion protocol designed to produce a weak taste aversion. Remarkably, injecting LV_PKMζ into insular cortex 5 days prior to this training enhanced the memory for that experience—it converted a weak memory into a strong one. To determine if PKMζ could rescue an older fading memory, rats were not tested until 9 days after training. Injecting LV_PKMζ 6 days following training prevented normal forgetting.

## PKMζ KO Mice Learn and Remember

The results summarized above support the hypothesis that PKMζ makes a critical contribution to the maintenance of consolidated memories.

However, just as in the case for LTP (see Chapter 7), it has been reported that mice genetically engineered to knock out PKMζ (PKMζ KO) can acquire and maintain fear memories and place-learning memories. Moreover, even though these mice did not express PKMζ, injecting ZIP into the relevant brain sites erased these memories (Lee et al., 2013). Such results question the conclusion that PKMζ is essential for memory maintenance. However, these results are also consistent with the hypotheses that (a) there are redundant, perhaps compensatory molecules that can substitute for the absence of PKMζ (Frankland and Josselyn, 2013; Hardt et al., 2013; Price and Ghosh, 2013) and (b) these substitute kinases can be targets of ZIP. Future research is needed to identify these other memory maintenance molecules that are targets of ZIP.

### Interpretive Caveat

A general interpretative point is embedded in this issue. Specifically, the observation that the removal of a brain substrate (for example, PKMζ) impairs performance on the memory test is consistent with the hypothesis that the substrate contributes to some process important for memory (such as maintenance). However, the interpretation is uncertain if the removal of the substrate does not disrupt performance process. One cannot conclude that the targeted substrate does not normally play its assigned role. However, such a result does reveal what the brain can do in the absence of that substrate.

## Toward a Neurobiology of Forgetting

After a memory trace is consolidated, molecular processes featuring PKMζ and other targets of ZIP kinase are recruited to allow the potentiated GluA2 synapses supporting the trace to resist de-potentiation and thus maintain the trace. Such mechanisms may be sufficient to maintain the trace for a long period of time. As Hardt et al. (2013) noted, however, in many cases an initially formed memory may have no functional significance and thus no reason to be preserved. For example, there is no reason to remember what you had for lunch a week ago. Memories are most likely preserved when (a) the behavioral experience is repeated or (b) when the memory is recalled (Hardt et al., 2013). In both cases new related memory traces are added and/or the existing memory trace is refreshed. The memory trace is also more likely to be preserved if the behavioral experience contains events that are arousing. Much will be said about these topics in later chapters.

Nevertheless, memories for much of what we have experienced are forgotten. Historically, the dominant idea is that forgetting is primarily due to our

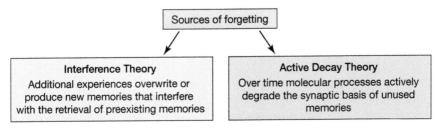

**Figure 12.2**
Two theories of forgetting.

additional experiences overwriting existing memories or producing new memories that interfere with the retrieval of the older memories. This idea is generally referred to as the **interference theory of forgetting**, and it has empirical support (Wixted, 2004). Oliver Hardt and his colleagues (Hardt et al., 2013), however, have argued that interference theory cannot explain all forgetting and there are many reasons to believe that unused dormant traces likely decay. Moreover, they suggest that there is an active molecular basis for decay—**active decay theory** (Figure 12.2).

Oliver Hardt

Given that memories are established by processes that traffic additional AMPA receptors into synapses and maintain their presence, then it is quite reasonable to assume that if these additional AMPA receptors are removed the memory will be lost. In the earlier chapters on LTP, it was emphasized that endocytic processes operate to de-potentiate synapses by actively removing newly trafficked AMPA receptors from the PSD. It was also noted that an important way in which PKMζ maintains potentiated synapses is by reconfiguring the endocytic processes to interfere with removal of AMPA receptors.

It is possible that unused memories might ultimately decay because there is some degradation in the PKMζ maintenance signaling cascades. The finding that PKMζ can prevent forgetting provides support for this idea. Another possibility is that decay of the memory trace is an active process used by the brain to clear out unneeded memories (Hardt et al., 2013). This hypothesis is supported by the findings that both the decay of LTP in the dentate gyrus and the forgetting of a spatial memory are prevented by continuously antagonizing NMDA receptors during the retention interval (Villarreal et al., 2002; Figure 12.3). Such results suggest that small amounts of calcium entering the potentiated synapses might serve as a signal to internalize AMPA receptors, perhaps by degrading PKMζ (Hrabetova and Sacktor, 2001).

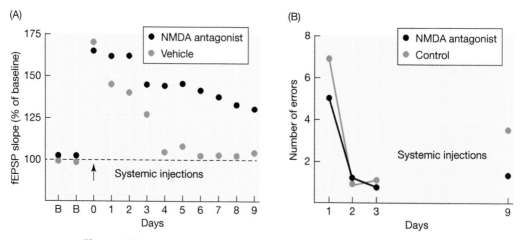

**Figure 12.3**
(A) Theta-burst stimulation was applied to the perforant pathway to induce LTP in dentate gyrus of intact rats. Within about 4 days it decayed to baseline in vehicle-treated rats, but this decay was prevented by daily systemic injections of an NMDA antagonist. (B) Rats learned a working memory task (see Chapter 11). After a 5-day retention interval, rats in the vehicle condition had forgotten the task. However, daily systemic injections of an NMDA antagonist prevented forgetting. (After Villarreal et al., 2002.) These results support the hypothesis that active molecular events initiated by small amounts of calcium actively de-potentiate the synapses that support the memory trace.

These ideas about forgetting are largely speculative. However, forgetting is the flip side of memory maintenance. Thus, as the understanding of the molecular basis of memory maintenance advances, one might hope that more insights into the molecular basis of forgetting will be acquired. This topic will likely be addressed in future research.

## Summary

Consolidated memories no longer need new protein generated by the memory-producing experience. However, they must be maintained in the face of molecular turnover, and maintenance processes must operate over the duration of the memory trace. Two sources of evidence support the hypothesis that PKMζ contributes to memory maintenance.

- Treatments designed to interfere with the contribution of PKMζ—the application of ZIP and the dominant negative lentivirus approach—both erase well consolidated memories.

- Overexpression of PKMζ by the lentivirus approach reveals that PKMζ enhances the strength of the memory trace.

Testing the hypothesis that PKMζ is essential to the maintenance of consolidated memories has led to the discovery that there are other molecules that contribute to memory maintenance. Their identity is not yet known but they are also targets of ZIP.

Forgetting is the converse of memory maintenance. Recent insights into the molecular basis of maintenance encourage the idea that some forgetting may be the product of ongoing endocytic processes that remove AMPA receptors from synapses supporting memories for insignificant events.

# References

Frankland, P. W. and Josselyn, S. A. (2013). Neuroscience: Memory and the single molecule. *Nature, 493,* 312–313.

Hardt, O., Nader, K., and Nadel, L. (2013). Decay happens: the role of active forgetting in memory. *Trends in Cognitive Neuroscience, 17,* 111–120.

Hrabetova, S. and Sacktor, T. C. (2001). Transient translocation of conventional protein kinase C isoforms and persistent downregulation of atypical protein kinase Mzeta in long-term depression. *Molecular Brain Research, 95,* 146–152.

Kwapis, J. L., Jarome, T. J., Gilmartin, M. R., and Helmstetter, F. J. (2012). Intra-amygdala infusion of the protein kinase Mzeta inhibitor ZIP disrupts foreground context fear memory. *Neurobiology of Learning and Memory, 98,* 148–153.

Lee, A. M., Kanter, B. R., Wang, D., Lim, J. P., Zou, M. E., Qiu, C., McMahon, T., Dadgar, J., Fischbach-Weiss, S. C., and Messing, R. O. (2013). Prkcz null mice show normal learning and memory. *Nature, 493,* 416–419.

Pastalkova, E., Serrano, P., Pinkhasova, D., Wallace, E., Fenton, A. A., and Sacktor, T. C. (2006). Storage of spatial information by the maintenance mechanism of LTP. *Science, 313,* 1141–1144.

Pauli, W. M., Clark, A. D., Guenther, H. J., O'Reilly, R. C., and Rudy, J. W. (2012). Inhibiting PKMζ reveals dorsal lateral and dorsal medial striatum store the different memories needed to support adaptive behavior. *Learning and Memory, 19,* 307–314.

Price, T. J. and Ghosh, S. (2013). ZIPping to pain relief: the role (or not) of PKMzeta in chronic pain. *Molecular Pain, 9:* 6.

Sacktor, T. C. (2011). How does PKMζ maintain long-term memory? *Nature Reviews Neuroscience, 12,* 9–15.

Serrano, P., Friedman, E. L., Kenney, J., Taubenfeld, S. M., Zimmerman, J. M., Hanna, J., Alberini, C., Kelley, A. E., Maren, S., Rudy, J. W., Yin, J. C., Sacktor, T. C., and Fenton, A. A. (2008). PKMζ maintains spatial, instrumental, and classically conditioned long-memories. *PLoS Biology, 6,* 2698–2706.

Shema, R., Haramati, S., Ron, S., Hazvi, S., Chen, A., Sacktor, T. C., and Dudai, Y. (2011). Enhancement of consolidated long-term memory by overexpression of protein kinase Mzeta in the neocortex. *Science, 331,* 1207–1210.

Shema, R., Sacktor, T. C. and Dudai, Y. (2007). Rapid erasure of long-term memory associations in cortex by an inhibitor of PKMζ. *Science, 317,* 951–953.

Villarreal, D. M., Do, V., Haddad, E., and Derrick, B. E. (2002). NMDA receptor antagonists sustain LTP and spatial memory: active processes mediate LTP decay. *Nature Neuroscience, 5,* 48–52.

Wixted, J. T. (2004). The psychology and neuroscience of forgetting. *Annual Review of Psychology, 55,* 235–269.

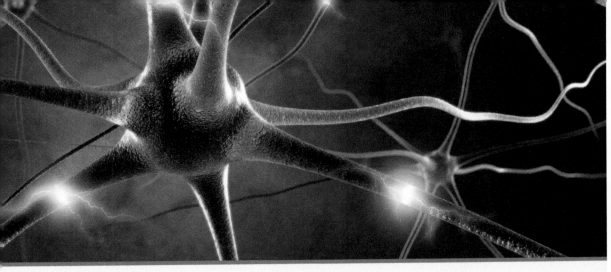

# 13 Memory Modulation Systems

About 15 years ago my friend Wayne and I were out for a walk with his dogs. Basically, it was like any other walk—uneventful, filled with the usual banter. But that changed when suddenly one of the dogs, Poco, leaped in the air, followed by the sound of a rattlesnake. This was an arousing event. I vividly remember Poco's reaction, and that we had to coax the dogs past this point in the road. This is one of the few things that I remember with any detail from our many walks. Something about arousing events makes them memorable.

The goal of this chapter is provide an understanding of why this happens. It is organized around the idea that neural and hormonal processes that are activated by arousal can influence the cellular–molecular processes that consolidate memory. These neuro-hormonal events modulate the activity of neurons in the memory storage sites. First the memory modulation framework is described. Evidence indicating that the basolateral amygdala makes a critical contribution to memory modulation is then presented. Next, two general ways in which memory storage is influenced by the adrenal hormone **epinephrine** (released by the adrenal medulla) and its related neurotransmitter **norepinephrene** are described. The chapter ends with a brief discussion of how glucocorticoids, the other adrenal hormone, influence memory storage.

## Memory Modulation Framework

The **memory modulation framework** illustrated in Figure 13.1 is the product of James L. McGaugh, his students, and collaborators. The important assumptions of this framework are:

1. A behavioral experience can have two independent effects: it can activate specific sets of neurons that represent and store the content of the experience, and it can activate hormonal and other neural systems that can influence the mechanisms that store the memory.

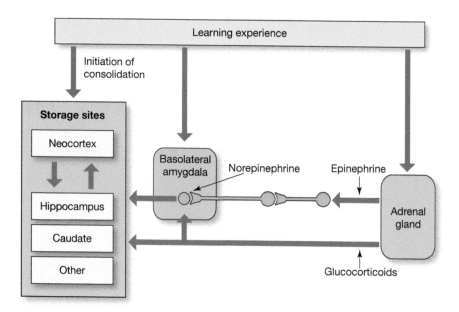

**Figure 13.1**

The figure illustrates the memory modulation framework. Experience has two independent effects. It can initiate the acquisition and storage of the memory trace and it can activate the release of adrenal hormones that can modulate the processes that store the memory. (After McGaugh et al., 2002.)

2. These hormonal and other neural systems are called **memory modulators**. They are not part of the storage system, but they can influence the synapses that store the memory.

3. Memory modulators have a time-limited role and influence only the storage of very recently acquired memories. They operate during a period of time shortly after the behavioral experience when the trace is being consolidated.

4. The neural systems that modulate memory strength are not necessary for the retrieval of the memory.

The basis for the memory modulation idea emerged when McGaugh was a graduate student (McGaugh, 1959, 2003; McGaugh and Petrinovich, 1959) and discovered that Karl Lashley (1917) had improved the rate at which rats learned a complicated maze by injecting them with a low dose of strychnine before training. Strychnine can be a lethal poison. However, at a low dose it is a stimulant and produces a state of arousal. McGaugh's insight was that the state of arousal created by strychnine might influence the processes that consolidate memory traces. To evaluate his idea, he injected the drug immediately after the rats had been trained and found improved retention performance. However, it had no effect on performance when administered before the retention test.

James McGaugh

McGaugh and his colleagues subsequently found that strychnine given after training enhanced memories produced by a variety of behavioral experiences. The implication of these findings was unmistakable: *there is a brief period of time shortly after the memory-inducing behavioral experience when the strength of the memory trace can be modified*. McGaugh's early work was important because it established this idea.

The state of arousal generated by the behavioral experiences influences memory strength. This happens because arousing stimuli (such as encountering a rattlesnake) can stimulate the **adrenal gland**, specifically the adrenal medulla, to secrete a hormone or molecule into the blood stream called **adrenaline**. One general role of this hormone is to mobilize us for behavioral action. The expression "it gave me an adrenaline rush" relates to this effect. Adrenaline is often called epinephrine, and that is the name used in this discussion. Epinephrine belongs to a class of catecholamine hormones that bind to receptors called **adrenergic receptors**. It is closely related to norepinephrine, also secreted by the adrenal medulla but in much smaller quantities, which can act as a neurotransmitter in the brain. In addition to its energizing effects, epinephrine can have a second effect—it can influence the strength of a memory trace.

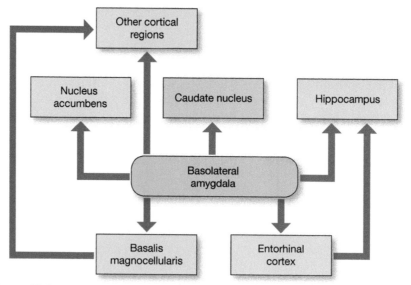

**Figure 13.2**
The amygdala is anatomically connected to many regions of the brain that are likely storage sites for different types of memories. Thus, it is in a position to influence or modulate storage processes in other regions of the brain. (After McGaugh, 2002.)

## The Great Modulator: The Basolateral Amygdala

The **basolateral amygdala** (**BLA**) is now thought to be the primary mediator of epinephrine's influence on memory (McGaugh, 2002, 2004). It has anatomical connections with many other regions of the brain that store memories, so it is in a position to influence the memory storage processes in these other regions (Figure 13.2). There is an extensive literature supporting this idea (see McGaugh, 2004; McIntyre et al., 2012). Some examples are described below.

To establish that the amygdala modulates memory storage in other regions of the brain, it must be shown that the amygdala is not itself a storage site for the memory. This means that the memory can be retrieved even if the amygdala is removed. For example, both the place-learning and visible-platform versions of the Morris water-escape task can be learned and remembered even when the amygdala is significantly damaged (Sutherland and McDonald, 1990). Thus the amygdala is not a critical storage site for these memories. Instead, the hippocampus (see Chapters 15 and 16) is a key storage area for the place-learning memory, and the caudate (see Chapter 18) is thought to be important for the acquisition and storage of the memory for the

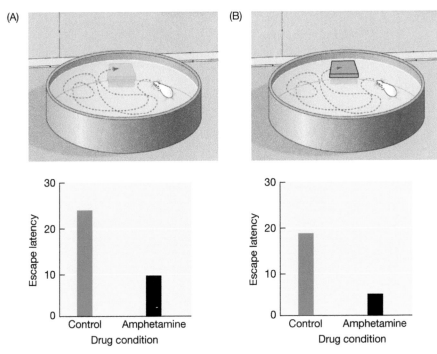

**Figure 13.3**
(A) Injecting the stimulant amphetamine into the amygdala following training on the place-learning version of the Morris water-escape task improved retention performance. (B) Injecting the amphetamine following training on the visible-platform task improved retention performance. (Short latency indicates better retention.) The hippocampus is thought to be a critical storage site for place learning and the caudate is thought to be critical for the visible-platform task. (After Packard and Teather, 1998.)

visible-platform task. Nevertheless, as shown in Figure 13.3, if amphetamine, a stimulant drug, is injected into the amygdala following training, retention performance on both versions of the task is enhanced (Packard et al., 1994; Packard and Teather, 1998). Thus, the amygdala facilitates the storage of these memories but is not needed to retain the memory.

The amygdala is not a unitary structure but consists of many subnuclei (Figure 13.4). Further research has revealed that neurons in the BLA are the critical mediator of the memory modulation properties of this region of the brain. This conclusion is based on experiments in which drugs that influence modulation were injected into specific subnuclei of the amygdala (McGaugh et al., 2000). For example, if lidocaine (a drug that temporarily suppresses neuronal activity) is injected into the BLA, memory retention is impaired

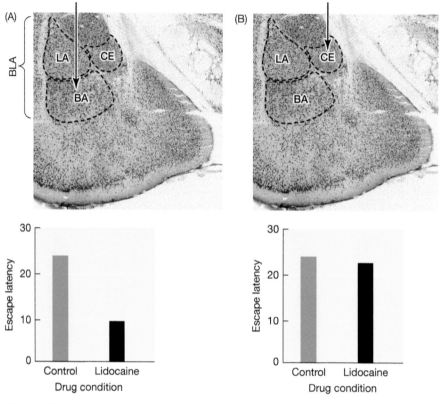

**Figure 13.4**
(A) An injection of lidocaine into the basolateral amygdala (BLA) following avoidance training impaired the retention of the inhibitory avoidance response. (B) Lidocaine had no effect when it was injected into the central nucleus (CE) of the amygdala. LA = lateral nucleus; BA = basal nucleus. (After Parent and McGaugh, 1994.)

(Figure 13.4A), but if it is injected into the central nucleus of the amygdala (Figure 13.4B), it has no effect on retention (Parent and McGaugh, 1994). These data establish that the BLA is likely the major brain region mediating the effects of epinephrine.

## The Role of Epinephrine

The adrenal medulla hormone epinephrine is now recognized as a major contributor to memory modulation processes. Paul Gold (Gold and Van Buskirk, 1975) provided the first direct evidence that it can strengthen memory traces.

In this study, rats were given a single trial of inhibitory avoidance training with a low-intensity shock that was designed to be minimally arousing. These animals were then injected with epinephrine at different times after training. The basic idea was to inject a dose of epinephrine that would mimic what the adrenal gland would naturally release in response to a stronger, more arousing shock. Remarkably, the avoidance behavior of rats injected with the adrenal hormone was dramatically increased. The effect also was time dependent because the hormone had to be injected shortly after training (Figure 13.5). Epinephrine also influences the strength of human memories. Larry Cahill, for example, showed people a series of slides containing visual scenes (Cahill and Alkire, 2003). Some of these subjects were injected with epinephrine immediately following exposure to the scenes. A week later, these subjects were able to recall the scenes better than subjects injected with just the vehicle.

To influence neurons, molecules in the blood vesicles have to diffuse through the blood–brain barrier, which is designed to separate circulating blood from the brain's extracellular fluid. This barrier protects the brain from potentially harmful molecules. Even though they influence memory, epinephrine molecules are too large to cross the blood–brain barrier. So how does epinephrine released into blood vesicles influence amygdala function? The

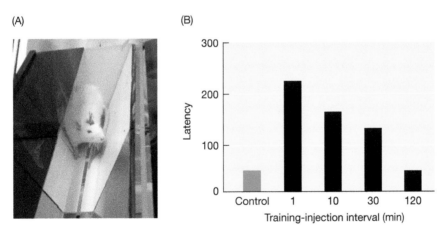

(A)          (B)

**Figure 13.5**
On the training trial, rats received a mild shock when they crossed to the dark side of the apparatus. Compared to control rats injected with the saline vehicle, rats that were injected with a dose of epinephrine—calculated to mimic the level of epinephrine that would naturally be released from the adrenal gland if the animals had received a strong shock—displayed enhanced inhibitory avoidance. The enhancing effect of epinephrine, however, was time dependent. It was more effective when it was given shortly after the training trial. (After Gold and Van Buskirk, 1975.)

answer is that it exerts its influence on memory in two distinct ways. One path starts with epinephrine binding to receptors on the vagal nerve and ends with the release of the neurotransmitter norepinephrine into the BLA. The other path starts with epinephrine's influence on glucose release by liver cells. These two pathways and some of their influences are described in the sections that follow.

## The Epinephrine Vagus Connection

In this section, the neuro-hormonal circuit linking epinephrine to the BLA is described and some of the supporting evidence is reviewed. The focus then turns to the influence of norepinephrine on memory processing. When epinephrine is released in the blood stream, it binds to adrenergic receptors located on a major cranial nerve, the **vagus** or vagal nerve (Figure 13.6). This

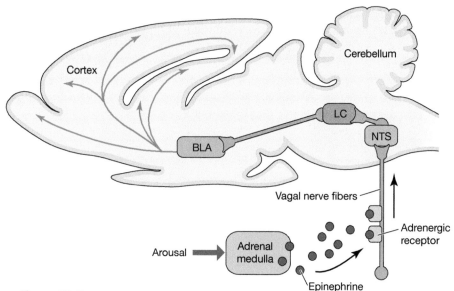

**Figure 13.6**
Epinephrine does not cross the blood–brain barrier. However, when it is released from the adrenal medulla it binds to adrenergic receptors on the vagal nerve. In response to activation, the vagal nerve releases glutamate on neurons in the solitary tract nucleus (NTS). Activated NTS neurons release glutamate onto neurons in the locus coeruleus, which in turn release norepinephrine that binds to adrenergic receptors in the baso-lateral amygdala (BLA). Disrupting any component of this neuro-hormonal circuit will prevent arousal from enhancing memory.

nerve carries information about the body into the brain, and synapses on a brain-stem region called the **solitary tract nucleus** or NTS (Hassert et al., 2004; Miyashita and Williams, 2006). Neurons from the NTS synapse on a small collection of neurons (less than 2,000) in the brain stem called the **locus coeruleus** (**LC**). Neurons in the LC project widely to distant brain regions, including the forebrain, hippocampus, and amygdala. When activated, these neurons release the neurotransmitter norepinephrine onto their target neurons. The release of norepinephrine into the BLA is the key outcome of the vagus connection (McIntyre et al., 2012).

Several lines of evidence support the existence of this neuro-hormonal circuit (McIntyre et al., 2012). For example, when epinephrine is administered to anesthetized rats it activates the vagal nerve. However, this outcome is prevented by the beta-adrenergic receptor antagonist sotalol (Miyashita and Williams, 2006). This result supports the hypothesis that epinephrine binds to beta-adrenergic receptors on the vagal nerve. Epinephrine in the periphery also increases the firing rate of neurons in the LC, and the temporary inactivation of neurons in the NTS reduces memory enhancement by a peripheral injection of epinephrine (Williams and McGaugh, 1993). These results indicate that epinephrine in the periphery activates LC through the NTS.

Direct electrical stimulation of ascending vagal fibers increases glutamate levels in the NTS. Thus, as one might expect, antagonizing AMPA receptors (the mediators of synaptic transmission) in the NTS prevents epinephrine from enhancing memory (King and Williams, 2009). Finally, there is evidence that stimulating the ascending vagal fibers produces burst firing in neurons in the locus coeruleus (Dorr and Debonnel, 2006) and that stimulating the vagus nerve following inhibitory avoidance training can enhance the memory (Clark et al., 1998).

Training experiences that produce strong memories do so because epinephrine released from the adrenal gland ultimately results in release of norepinephrine into the BLA. If this is true one should be able to detect increases in the level of norepinephrine in the BLA when rats are shocked after crossing to the dark side of the avoidance apparatus. Quirarte and his colleagues (Quirarte et al., 1998) used a methodology called microdialysis (Figure 13.7) to observe this increase, which is shown in Figure 13.8A.

There is another interesting fact associated with this set of events. By itself, electric shock, the stimulus typically used to produce inhibitory avoidance learning, does not cause norepinephrine to be released in the amygdala. Rats have to both explore the environment and then receive shock for norepinephrine to be released in the amygdala (McIntyre et al., 2002). It is as if the amygdala is designed to detect the coincidence of a novel behavioral experience and an arousing event (Figure 13.8B).

(A)

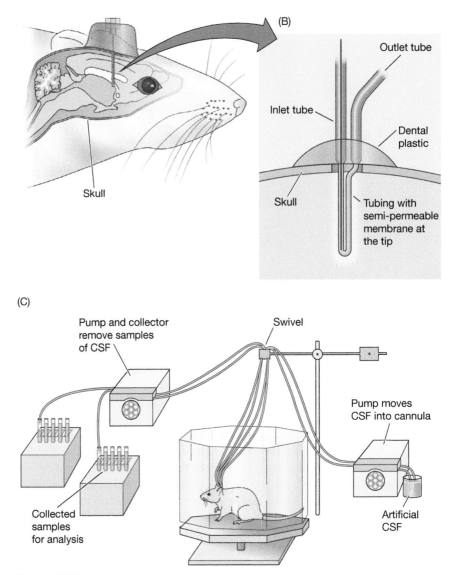

(B)

Outlet tube

Inlet tube

Dental plastic

Skull

Skull

Tubing with semi-permeable membrane at the tip

(C)

Pump and collector remove samples of CSF

Swivel

Pump moves CSF into cannula

Collected samples for analysis

Artificial CSF

**Figure 13.7**
Microdialysis allows extracellular fluid to be collected from deep within the brain. (A) A rat with a specially designed microdialysis probe implanted in the brain. (B) A detail of the microdialysis probe. (C) A freely moving rat connected to the instrumentation designed to extract a very small quantity of extracellular fluid. The content of this fluid can then be analyzed for its composition. CSF = cerebral spinal fluid.

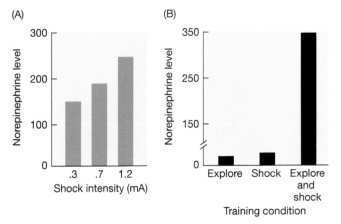

**Figure 13.8**
The microdialysis methodology was used to extract norepinephrine from the extracellular brain fluid. (A) The level of norepinephrine released into the extracellular fluid in avoidance training is determined by the intensity of the shock. (After Quirarte et al., 1998.) (B) Just shocking a rat or allowing it to explore the avoidance training apparatus does not increase the level of norepinephrine. That requires the rat both to explore the novel apparatus and to be shocked. (After McIntyre et al., 2002).

## Norepinephrine Enhances Memories

If LC neurons release norepinephrine into the amygdala and this event enhances memory storage, then one can make two predictions:

1. Injecting norepinephrine into the BLA following training should enhance the memory.

2. Injecting the beta-adrenergic-receptor antagonist, propranolol, into the BLA should attenuate the memory resulting from an arousing behavioral experience.

   These predictions have been confirmed. Figure 13.9A shows that injecting norepinephrine into the BLA following training on the place-learning version of the Morris water task improves the rat's retention of the location of the hidden platform. In contrast, injecting propranolol into the amygdala following training impairs retention of the platform location (Hatfield and McGaugh, 1999). Figure 13.9B shows that injecting norepinephrine into the amygdala following avoidance training with a weak shock enhances retention of the avoidance response. However, if propranolol is injected after avoidance training with an arousing strong shock, the avoidance response is reduced (Gallagher et al., 1977; Liang et al., 1986).

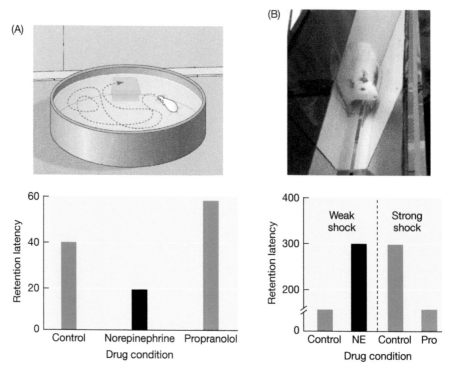

**Figure 13.9**
(A) The injection of norepinephrine into the amygdala following place learning enhanced the rat's retention of the platform location, but when propranolol was injected, retention was impaired. (B) Norepinepherine (NE) injected into the amygdala following inhibitory avoidance training with a weak shock enhanced retention performance. Propranolol (Pro) injected into the amygdala following inhibitory avoidance training with strong shock impaired retention. (After Hatfield and McGaugh, 1999.)

## Norepinephrine Enhances Glutamate Release and Arc Translation

Researchers now have a good understanding of the primary factors involved in initiating amygdala-dependent memory modulation.

1. An arousing behavioral event induces the adrenal gland to release epinephrine into the blood stream.

2. Epinephrine binds to receptors on the vagal nerve.

3. The vagal nerve transmits a signal into the NTS that is conveyed to the amygdala as the release of norepinephrine from the locus coeruleus.

This sequence of events raises two questions: (1) how does the release of norepinephrine influence their target BLA neurons? and (2) what is the downstream influence of BLA output on their target neurons, that is, how does this output strengthen memories?

Neurons in the amygdala release glutamate. So the answers to these questions center on how norepinephrine influences glutamate release and how it then influences the signaling mechanisms in the downstream target neurons that store the memory. Adrenergic receptors in the amygdala are metabotropic—they are coupled to a G-protein complex. This complex becomes active and one of its protein subunits activates the effector protein, adenylyl cyclase, which then catalyzes the formation of the second messenger cAMP (cyclic adenosine monophosphate). The kinase target of cAMP is PKA. The upshot of this cascade is that amygdala neurons in the BLA generate a sustained release of glutamate onto neurons in the target storage sites.

Given that glutamate receptors are a primary mediator of intracellular signaling events that alter synaptic strength, then one would expect that additional glutamate released by BLA neurons would enhance these events. This would most likely result from calcium released from endoplasmic stores. For example, additional glutamate would be expected to activate the mGluR→IP3→IP3R pathway to release calcium from the endoplasmic reticulum and facilitate local protein synthesis (see Chapter 5).

Christa McIntyre and her colleagues were among the first to address the downstream effects of the BLA signal. For example, they reported that inhibitory avoidance training normally leads to the increased translation of Arc in the hippocampus (McIntyre et al., 2005). However, when lidocaine, a drug that inactivates neurons, is injected into the BLA prior to training, the level of Arc protein in the hippocampus is reduced and the memory for the inhibitory avoidance experience is impaired. In contrast, when clenbuterol, an adrenergic receptor agonist, is injected into the BLA, the level of Arc protein in the hippocampus is increased and the memory for the training experience is strengthened.

Christa McIntyre

These results (Figure 13.10) indicate that activity in the BLA produced by inhibitory avoidance training modulates the level of Arc protein in another area of the brain, the hippocampus, and that the level of Arc protein correlates with the strength of the memory. Additional work from this group has extended this paradigm to show that (a) the amygdala signal enhances both Arc protein and CaMKII levels in another storage area (rostral anterior cingular cortex) for the inhibitory avoidance memory, and (b) inactivating the neurons in the BLA reduces memory and the expression of Arc and CaMKII (Holloway and McIntyre, 2011; Holloway-Erickson et al., 2012). McReynolds and McIntyre (2012) have described a variety of other ways in which the BLA signal can influence memory storages processes.

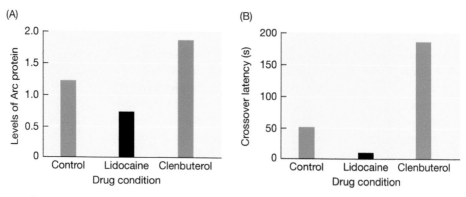

**Figure 13.10**
(A) This graph illustrates the effect of injecting lidocaine and clenbuterol into the BLA on the level of Arc protein in the hippocampus following inhibitory avoidance learning. (B) This graph illustrates the effect of these drugs on inhibitory avoidance. Note that lidocaine reduced the level of Arc protein in the hippocampus and decreased inhibitory avoidance. In contrast, clenbuterol increased the level of Arc protein and enhanced inhibitory avoidance. (After McIntyre et al., 2005.) These results suggest that the BLA might modulate memory by influencing the level of Arc protein in the hippocampus.

## The Norepinephrine Signal in Other Storage Areas

There is enhanced release of norepinephrine in the BLA as a result of the epinephrine–NTS–LC pathway (illustrated in Figure 13.6). However, LC neurons also project to other areas of the brain that store memories. For example, studies of LTP have reported that norepinephrine contributes to LTP in the hippocampus (Gelinas and Nguyen, 2005; Katsuki et al., 1997). Roberto Malinow and his colleagues (Hu et al., 2007) have discovered that norepinephrine facilitates LTP and memory of an explored context by facilitating trafficking of GluA1 AMPA receptors (see Chapter 4). This happens because when norepinephrine binds to adrenergic receptors the cAMP–PKA pathway is activated. PKA then phosphorylates two sites, Ser 831 and Ser 845, and facilitates trafficking of these receptors into the PSD, under weak training conditions (Figure 13.11)

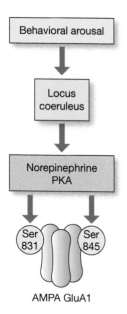

**Figure 13.11**
When norepinephrine is released into the hippocampus, PKA is activated and phosphorylates two sites (Ser 831 and Ser 845) on the GluA1 AMPA receptor subunit. This facilitates the trafficking of GluA1s into the dendritic spine and increases memory strength.

## The Epinephrine Liver–Glucose Connection

The second general way in which epinephrine can modulate memory storage, even though it does not cross the blood–brain barrier, is by its influence on the liver. The importance of this pathway is described below, beginning with a brief discussion of bioenergenics followed by a description of some of the evidence that glucose modulates memory storage and is especially important as we age. Finally, the influence of glucose levels on transcription is discussed.

### Bioenergenics and the Brain

Translation and transcription processes that generate new protein and processes that distribute and arrange the new protein can last for many hours and require considerable energy. Initial changes in the underlying synapses are rapid and can rely on existing energy sources. However, available energy sources may not be sufficient to support transcription and translation processes that generate new protein. The flow of energy in cells is called **bioenergenics**, and the primary source of energy is glucose that enters the brain via the cerebral vasculature. Paul Gold and his colleagues have provided a large body of work that leads to the conclusion that epinephrine also enhances memory by its influence on glucose (Gold, 2005; Gold and Korol, 2012).

Paul Gold

The most general function associated with the adrenal medulla is complementing the sympathetic nervous system in orchestrating the so-called "flight-or-fight" reaction. It contributes to this reaction by its interaction with the liver. A major function of the liver is to remove glucose from blood and convert it to glycogen, where it is stored in preparation for future use. Cells in the liver contain adrenergic receptors. So when an arousing event is experienced, epinephrine is released and transported in blood to the liver where it binds to these receptors and initiates signaling that results in the liver secreting glucose into the blood (Figure 13.12). This increase in glucose provides energy to cells in the periphery that participate in the flight-or-flight response. In addition, glucose in the blood can enter the brain where it can be used to support the translation and transcription processes that strengthen the memory trace.

### Glucose Modulates Memory

This framework makes a strong prediction: if epinephrine modulates memory strength through signaling the liver to secrete glucose, then one should be able to modulate the memory strength by directly increasing available glucose.

**Figure 13.12**
An arousing event activates the adrenal medulla to release epinephrine into the blood system where it binds to adrenergic receptors in the liver cell. This results in the liver secreting glucose into the blood where it enters the brain via the cerebral vasculature system.

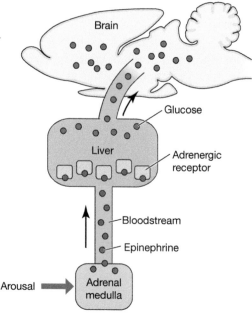

There are numerous reports that injecting glucose systemically immediately following a training experience can do this (Gold, 2005; Messier, 2004). Figure 13.13 provides a useful example. It compares the effects of systemic glucose injections with a systemic injection of epinephrine on animals trained on an inhibitory avoidance task. Note that (a) in both cases the effect was dose dependent with both low and high doses having minimal effects, and (b) consistent with the modulation framework, when the interval separating training and injection was 1 hour, the optimal dose had no effect—the effect was time dependent. There also is evidence that glucose infused directly into memory storage sites enhances memory function (Gold and Korol, 2012).

## Glucose and Aging

An interesting change happens when animals age (Figure 13.14A,B)—arousing events generate the release of epinephrine in old animals but this increase is not accompanied by an increase in the level of blood glucose (Mabry et al., 1995). Moreover, even though old animals often can acquire memories they forget more rapidly than younger animals (Gold, 2005). For example, when young rats acquire an inhibitory avoidance memory it remains stable for weeks, yet old rats lose the memory for this experience within several days.

(A)

(B)

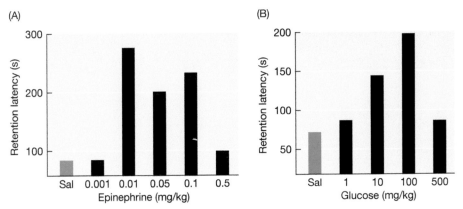

**Figure 13.13**
This figure illustrates that systemic injections of either epinephrine or glucose influence memory strength in a dose-dependent manner. (After Gold and Korol, 2012.) These data support the view that epinephrine modulates memory by binding to adrenergic receptors on the liver cells causing them to release glucose. Sal = saline.

Gold and his colleagues have advanced the hypothesis that the rapid forgetting seen in old animals is related to the failure of the liver to respond to epinephrine by secreting glucose. This hypothesis predicts that rapid forgetting by old animals can be prevented by a systemic injection of glucose. As predicted, injections of glucose reverse age-related rapid forgetting of memories established in several tasks. Figure 13.14C illustrates this outcome for rats trained on an inhibitory avoidance task. Note that old rats (24 to 25 months old) were severely impaired compared to young rats (3 to 4 months old) when the retention interval was 7 days. Remarkably, an infusion of glucose into the dorsal hippocampus following training completely reversed this impairment (Morris and Gold, 2013).

## Glucose and Transcription

Long-lasting memories depend in part on genes targeted by the transcription factor CREB (see Chapter 11). Moreover, old rats display impaired CREB activation in response to memory-inducing behavioral training (Countryman and Gold, 2007; Kudo et al., 2005). There is evidence that impaired CREB activation is related in part to age-related changes in the adrenal response to arousal. This point is illustrated in Figure 13.14D, which shows that a systemic injection of either epinephrine or glucose following training increased phosphorylated CREB in the dentate gyrus region of the dorsal hippocampus of young rats. However, only glucose increased levels of phosphorylated CREB

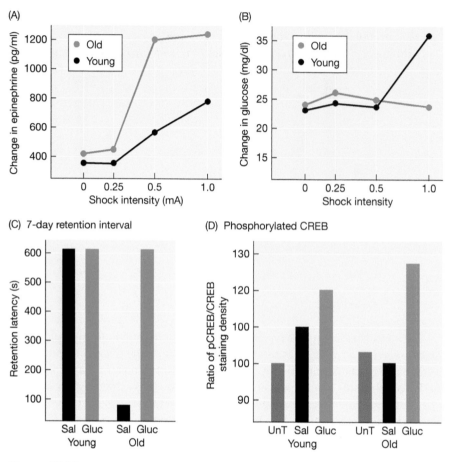

**Figure 13.14**
(A) In response to an arousing event (footshock), the adrenal gland releases epineph-rine in both young and old rats. (B) Nevertheless, the liver of only young rats secretes glucose. (After Mabry et al., 1995.) (C) A systemic injection of glucose prevents forgetting in old rats tested 7 days after inhibitory avoidance training. (D) Enduring memories depend on new genes targeted by the transcription factor CREB (see Chapter 11). (After Morris and Gold, 2013.) Avoidance training does not lead to CREB phosphorylation (pCREB) in old rats. However, if glucose is injected following training, phosphorylated CREB is detected. mA = milliamp; UnT = untrained; Sal = saline; Gluc = glucose; pg/ml = picograms per milliliter; mg/dl = milligrams per deciliter.

in old rats (Morris and Gold, 2013). Similar results were found when CREB activation was measured in the CA1 region of the dorsal hippocampus. This pattern is consistent with the view that enduring memories depend in part on the adrenal hormones and their targets—adrenergic receptors on the liver and vagal nerve—to support transcription and translation processes that produce the new protein needed to consolidate memories.

Gold and Korol (2012) have suggested another provocative conclusion. Given that glucose can reverse rapid forgetting in old rats, they propose that the underlying intracellular molecular machinery needed to consolidate memories may not be diminished. Instead, these translation and transcription processes require a contribution from the neuro-adrenal hormonal modulation system. It is the age-related deficit in the adrenal medulla response to "arousing events" that is the problem. As they put it, "… in some sense, even seemingly salient events are non-emotional for old rats and are not remembered well" (Gold and Korol, 2012, p. 6).

## Glucocorticoids: The Other Adrenal Hormones

Highly arousing behavioral experiences can also cause the release by the adrenal cortex of the hormone **corticosterone**. Corticosterone is also classified as a **glucocorticoid** because it is involved in the metabolism of glucose. In contrast to adrenaline, glucocorticoids can directly enter the brain.

Glucocorticoids can also modulate memory (McEwen and Sapolsky, 1995; Roozendaal et al., 2006), and there is evidence that their influence depends on the BLA. If the synthetic glucocorticoid dexamethasone is administered systemically after inhibitory avoidance training, retention performance is enhanced. However, if the basolateral nucleus is lesioned, this effect is eliminated. In contrast, similar destruction of the central nucleus has no effect on the ability of dexamethazone to enhance retention. If RU 28362, a glucocorticoid receptor agonist, is injected into the basolateral nucleus following inhibitory avoidance training, retention performance is enhanced. No enhancement occurs, however, if it is injected into the central nucleus.

Glucocorticoids modulate memory but their influence depends on norepineprine binding to adrenergic receptors in the BLA. To illustrate this point, consider the experiment by Quirarte et al. (1997). They trained rats on the inhibitory avoidance task with weak shock. As expected, rats that were injected systemically with dexamethazone showed enhanced retention performance. However, if propranolol was directly injected into the BLA, dexamethazone did not enhance retention (Figure 13.15). Thus, it appears that the amygdala's ability to modulate memory storage depends on a coordinated adrenal gland response to a behavioral experience. Experiences that raise circulating levels of the two adrenal hormones, epinephrine and glucocorticoids, can result in a stronger memory. There is evidence that glucocorticoids influence memory by enhancing norepinephrene's intiation of the cAMP–PKA signaling cascade (Roozandaal et al., 2006).

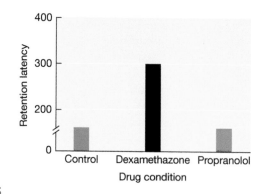

**Figure 13.15**
Dexamethazone is a synthetic glucocorticoid. When it is injected systemically following inhibitory avoidance training, it enhances retention. However, the effect of dexamethazone also depends on epinephrine being released in the amygdala, because when injected into the amygdala, propranolol prevents dexamethazone from enhancing retention. (After Quirarte et al., 1997.)

## Summary

The discovery of a memory modulation system and its principal hormonal and neural components is one of the important achievements of biologically driven memory research. This work supports the importance of distinguishing between neural systems that store memories and neuro-hormonal systems that modulate storage circuits. This discovery also brings a whole-organism integrative perspective into the biological basis of memory. Specifically, memory consolidation is not just the product of the brain; it reflects the integration of behavioral influences on the brain and the adrenal gland component of the endocrine system.

Epinephrine is the principle memory-modulating hormone. Arousing stimulation causes the adrenal medulla to secrete it into the blood. However, it is too large to cross the blood–brain barrier, so its effects on the brain depend on two intermediary pathways.

One intermediary is the vagal nerve, where it binds to adrenergic receptors and ultimately signals the locus coeruleus to release norepinephrine into the BLA and other regions of the brain. Norepinephrine binds to adrenergic G-protein-coupled receptors and initiates the cAMP–PKA signaling cascade. This results in BLA neurons releasing glutamate onto neurons in storage areas and likely enhances release of endoplasmic reticulum calcium to facilitate the translation of local proteins, such as Arc and CaMKII.

The second intermediary is glucose. Epinephrine binds to adrenergic receptors on liver cells causing them to secrete glucose into the blood and the cerebral vascular system brings it into the brain. This sequence provides the brain with energy to carry out the signaling cascades that activate transcription factors, such as CREB, to target memory genes (see Chapter 11) needed to produce a long-lasting memory. Old animals still mount an epinephrine response to arousing stimulation. However, this increase in epinephrine does not produce increased blood levels of glucose. The failure to mount a glucose response may be responsible for rapid forgetting by old animals. This is because systemic glucose injections following training enhance the level of phosphorylated CREB and prevent rapid forgetting.

Glucocorticoids can also modulate memory strength. This adrenal hormone crosses the blood–brain barrier and facilitates the action of norepinephrine, perhaps by augmenting its ability to engage the cAMP–PKA cascade.

Arousal usually signals something important has happened that should be remembered. To ensure this outcome, multiple pathways exist by which the adrenal gland can influence neurons that store memories of arousing events.

## References

Cahill, L. and Alkire, M. (2003). Epinephrine enhancement of human memory consolidation: interaction with arousal at encoding. *Neurobiology of Learning and Memory, 79*, 194–198.

Clark, K. B., Smith, D. C., Hassert, D. L., Browning, R. A., Naritoku, D. K., and Jensen, R. A. (1998). Posttraining electrical stimulation of vagal afferents with concomitant vagal efferent inactivation enhances memory storage processes in the rat. *Neurobiology of Learning and Memory, 70*, 364–373.

Countryman, R. A. and Gold, P. E. (2007). Rapid forgetting of social transmission of food preferences in aged rats: relationship to hippocampal CREB activation. *Learning and Memory, 14*, 350–358.

Dorr, A. E. and Debonnel, G. (2006). Effect of vagus nerve stimulation on serotonergic and noradrenergic transmission. *Journal of Pharmacology and Experimental Therapeutics, 318*, 890–898.

Gallagher, M., Kapp, B. S., Musty, R. E., and Driscoll, P. A. (1977). Memory formation: evidence for a specific neurochemical system in the amygdala. *Science, 198*, 423–435.

Gelinas, J. N. and Nguyen, P. V. (2005). Beta-adrenergic receptor activation facilitates induction of a protein synthesis-dependent late phase of long-term potentiation. *Journal of Neuroscience, 25*, 3294–3303.

Gold, P. E. (2005). Glucose and age-related changes in memory. *Neurobiology of Aging, 26*, 664.

Gold, P. E. and Korol, D. L. (2012). Making memories matter. *Frontiers in Integrative Neuroscience, 6*, Article 116.

Gold, P. E. and Van Buskirk, R. B. (1975). Facilitation of time-dependent memory processes with posttrial epinephrine injections. *Behavioral Biology, 13,* 145–153.

Hassert, D. L., Miyashita, T., and Williams, C. L. (2004). The effects of peripheral vagal nerve stimulation at a memory-modulating intensity on norepinephrine output in the basolateral amygdala. *Behavioral Neuroscience, 118,* 79–88.

Hatfield, T. and McGaugh, J. L. (1999). Norepinephrine infused into the basolateral amygdala posttraining enhances retention in a spatial water maze task. *Neurobiology of Learning and Memory, 71,* 232–239.

Holloway, C. M. and McIntyre, C. K. (2011). Post-training disruption of Arc protein expression in the anterior cingulate cortex impairs long-term memory for inhibitory avoidance training. *Neurobiology of Learning and Memory, 95,* 425–432.

Holloway-Erickson, C. M., McReynolds, J. R., and McIntyre, C. K. (2012). Memory-enhancing intra-basolateral amygdala infusions of clenbuterol increase Arc and CaM-KIIa protein expression in the rostral anterior cingulate cortex. *Frontiers in Behavioral Neuroscience, 6,* 17.

Hu, H., Real, E., Takamiya, K., Kang, M. G., LeDoux, J., Huganir, R. L, and Malinow, R. (2007). Emotion enhances learning via norepinephrine regulation of AMPA receptor trafficking. *Cell, 131,* 160–173.

Katsuki, H., Izumi, Y., and Zorumski, C. F. (1997). Noradrenergic regulation of synaptic plasticity in the hippocampal CA1 region. *Journal of Neurophysiology, 77,* 3013–3020.

King, S. O. and Williams, C. L. (2009). Novelty-induced arousal enhances memory for cued classical fear conditioning: interactions between peripheral adrenergic and brainstem glutamatergic systems. *Learning and Memory, 16,* 625–634.

Kudo, K., Wati, H., Qiao, C., Arita, J., and Kanba, S. (2005). Age-related disturbance of memory and CREB phosphorylation in CA1 area of hippocampus of rats. *Brain Research, 1054,* 30–37.

Lashley, K. S. (1917). The effects of strychnine and caffeine upon the rate of learning. *Psychobiology, 1,* 141–170.

Liang, K. C., Juler, R. G., and McGaugh, J. L. (1986). Modulating effects of posttraining epinephrine on memory: involvement of the amygdala noradrenergic system. *Brain Research, 368,* 125–133.

Mabry, T. R., Gold, P. E., and McCarty, R. (1995). Age-related changes in plasma catecholamine and glucose response of F-344 rats to a single footshock as used in inhibitory avoidance training. *Neurobiology of Learning and Memory, 64,* 146–155.

McEwen, B. S. and Sapolsky, R. M. (1995). Stress and cognitive function. *Current Opinion in Neurobiology, 5,* 205–216.

McGaugh, J. L. (1959). Some neurochemical factors in learning. Unpublished PhD thesis, University of California, Berkeley.

McGaugh, J. L. (2002). Memory consolidation and the amygdala, a systems perspective. *Trends in Neurosciences, 25,* 456–462.

McGaugh, J. L. (2003). *Memory and emotion.* New York: Columbia University Press.

McGaugh, J. L. (2004). The amygdala modulates the consolidation of memories of emotionally arousing experiences. *Annual Review of Neuroscience, 27*, 1–28.

McGaugh, J. L. and Petrinovich, L. (1959). The effect of strychnine sulfate on maze learning. *The American Journal of Psychology, 72*, 99–102.

McGaugh, J. L., Roozendaal, B., and Cahill, L. (2000). Modulation of memory storage by stress hormones and the amygdala complex. In M. S. Gazzaniga (Ed.), *The new cognitive neurosciences* (pp. 1981–1998). Cambridge, MA: MIT Press.

McIntyre, C. K., Hatfield, T., and McGaugh, J. L. (2002). Amygdala norepinephrine levels after training predict inhibitory avoidance retention performance in rats. *European Journal of Neuroscience, 16*, 1223–1226.

McIntyre, C. K., McGaugh, J. L., and Williams, C. L. (2012). Interacting brain systems modulate memory consolidation. *Neuroscience and Biobehavioral Reviews, 36*, 1750–1756.

McIntyre, C. K., Miyoshita, T., Setlow, B., Marjon, K. D., Steward, O., Guzowski, J. F., and McGaugh, J. L. (2005). Memory-influencing intra-basolateral amygdala drug infusions modulate expression of Arc protein in the hippocampus. *Proceedings of the National Academy of Sciences, 102*, 10718–10723.

McReynolds, J. R. and McIntyre, C. K. (2012). Emotional modulation of the synapse. *Reviews in the Neurosciences, 23*, 449–461.

Messier, C. (2004). Glucose improvement of memory: a review. *European Journal of Pharmacology, 490*, 33–57.

Miyashita, T. and Williams, C. L. (2006). Epinephrine administration increases neural impulses propagated along the vagus nerve: role of peripheral beta-adrenergic receptors. *Neurobiology of Learning and Memory, 85*, 116–124.

Morris, K. A. and Gold, P. E. (2013). Epinephrine and glucose modulate training-related CREB phosphorylation in old rats: relationships to age-related memory impairments. *Experimental Gerontology, 48*, 115–127.

Packard, M., Cahill, L., and McGaugh, J. L. (1994). Amygdala modulation of hippocampal-dependent and caudate nucleus-dependent memory processes. *Proceedings of the National Academy of Sciences, 91*, 8477–8481.

Packard, M. G. and Teather, L. A. (1998). Amygdala modulation of multiple memory systems: hippocampus and caudate-putamen. *Neurobiology of Learning and Memory, 69*, 163–200.

Parent, M. B. and McGaugh, J. L. (1994). Posttraining infusion of lidocaine into the amygdala basolateral complex impairs retention of inhibitory avoidance training. *Brain Research, 66*, 97–103.

Quirarte, G. L., Galvez, R., Roozendaal, B., and McGaugh, J. L. (1998). Norepinephrine release in the amygdala in response to footshock and opioid peptidergic drugs. *Brain Research, 808*, 134–140.

Quirarte, G. L., Roozendaal, B., and McGaugh, J. L. (1997). Glucocorticoid enhancement of memory storage involves noradrenergic activation in the basolateral amygdala. *Proceedings of the National Academy of Sciences, 94*, 14048–14053.

Roozendaal, B., Okuda, S., Van der Zee, E. A., and McGaugh, J. L. (2006). Glucocorticoid enhancement of memory requires arousal-induced noradrenergic activation in the basolateral amygdala. *Proceedings of the National Academy of Sciences, 103*, 6741–6746.

Sutherland, R. J. and McDonald, R. J. (1990). Hippocampus, amygdala, and memory deficits in rats. *Behavioural Brain Research, 12*, 57–79.

Williams, C. L. and McGaugh, J. L. (1993). Reversible lesions of the nucleus of the solitary tract attenuate the memory-modulating effects of posttraining epinephrine. *Behavioral Neuroscience, 6*, 955–962.

# 14 The Fate of Retrieved Memories

A persistent theme in memory research is that memory traces consolidate—
they become less vulnerable to disruption as they age. Much of the described
research has focused on identifying the cellular–molecular processes that
consolidate the memory trace. Memory traces are especially vulnerable to
disruption immediately following a learning experience. However, it has
become clear that the age of a memory trace is not the only determinant of
its vulnerability. Under some conditions, *retrieving or reactivating the memory
can return it to an active, labile state*. The goal of this chapter is to provide an
understanding of the empirical facts and theoretical concepts that are associated with this observation.

First, the basic findings are introduced. Two theoretical interpretations are
then described—**active trace theory** and **reconsolidation theory**. The discussion is then directed at two fundamental questions associated with reconsolidation theory: *how does retrieval return the trace to an unstable, labile*

*state and how is it restabilized?* The issue of how the memory trace is restabilized is discussed within the context of the concept of trace updating. Memory erasure as a potentially successful treatment for memory-based behavioral disorders is then discussed. The chapter ends by considering some of the boundary conditions of the effects of reactivating the memory trace.

## Reactivated Memory Disrupted by ECS

That retrieved memory traces are vulnerable to disruption first came to light about 45 years ago when Don Lewis and his colleagues (Misanin et al., 1968) reported that simply retrieving or reactivating a fear memory trace made it vulnerable to the disruptive effects of electroconvulsive shock (ECS).

In the Lewis study, a Pavlovian fear-conditioning procedure was used to establish the fear memory trace. Rats received a single pairing of a noise–conditioned stimulus (CS) and a shock–unconditioned stimulus (US). The next day, after the trace was "consolidated," some rats were brought to the training environment where the noise–CS was presented for 2 seconds. This experience was designed to retrieve or reactivate the fear memory trace. In order to determine if the reactivated trace was vulnerable to disruption, some of these rats also received ECS immediately after the reactivation experience. Other rats also received ECS the next day, but without the reactivation experience. Rats that received both the reactivation treatment and ECS were extremely impaired when given a full test the next day, that is, they showed no fear in the presence of the noise (Figure 14.1). ECS had disrupted a fear memory trace that had already had time to consolidate and attain long-term memory status.

## Active Trace Theory

As noted in Chapter 9, consolidation theory assumes that memory traces are vulnerable to disruption shortly after they are first established but, with time, the trace becomes stable and resistant to disrupting events. This relationship is generally true. However, based on the results of the work described above, Lewis (1979) suggested that the age of the memory trace at the time of the disrupting event might not be the only variable that determines its vulnerability.

Recall from previous chapters (for example, Chapter 9) that memory traces can be distinguished by their state of activation. Lewis proposed that this dimension might also be a critical determinant of the vulnerability of the trace to disruption. Memories in the active state are more vulnerable to disruption than memories in an inactive state. His theory is called active trace theory. The specific assumptions of this framework are as follows (Figure 14.2).

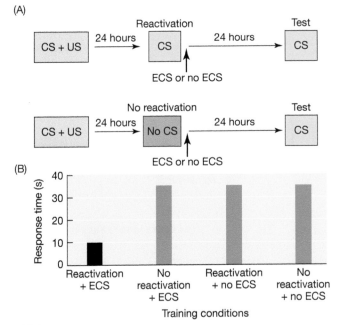

**Figure 14.1**
(A) A fear-conditioning experiment was used to study the vulnerability of a reactivated memory—a noise CS was paired with a shock US. In one condition, 24 hours after fear conditioning, the CS was presented to reactivate the fear memory. Some animals received electroconvulsive shock (ECS), while others did not. In the second condition, the fear memory was not reactivated, but animals received either ECS or no ECS. All animals were tested for fear of the CS. (B) The results of the experiment. Note that when the memory trace was reactivated by briefly presenting the CS, ECS disrupted the memory for the CS–shock experience. ECS had no effect when it was presented in the absence of shock.

- Memories can exist in either a short-term memory active state or long-term memory inactive state.
- There are two ways a memory trace can be put into the short-term active state:
  1. Novel experiences generate new active memory traces.
  2. Retrieving or reactivating existing long-term memory traces will return these traces to the short-term active state.
- Memories in the active state are vulnerable to disruption.
- Memory traces become inactive with time, and in the inactive state they are less vulnerable to disruption.

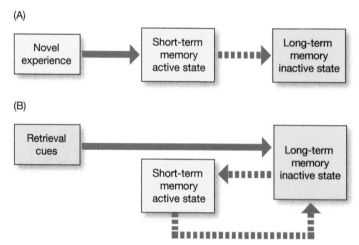

**Figure 14.2**
This figure illustrates the assumptions of active trace theory. Memories exist in either a short-term memory (STM) active state or a long-term memory (LTM) inactive state. (A) Novel experience can create an active STM trace that will decay into the inactive LTM state. (B) Retrieval cues can retrieve an inactive LTM trace and place it in the active state that then will decay into the inactive LTM state. Memories in the active state are more vulnerable to disruption than memories in the inactive state.

Lewis's results and theory were intriguing but also generated much controversy. Although some researchers replicated these results, others did not, and no one had any idea as to why this was the case. Thus, the idea that retrieved memories are placed in a state of vulnerability lay dormant for about 25 years. Two findings, however, brought the idea that reactivated memories are vulnerable to disruption out of hibernation and the second of these findings contributed to a new theoretical interpretation—reconsolidation theory.

Susan Sara

## Reconsolidation Theory

Susan Sara reported the first important result (Przybyslawski and Sara, 1997). Rats were first trained to solve a spatial learning task. The researchers discovered that if an NMDA antagonist was systemically injected following the reactivation of this memory trace, the rats were not able to perform the task the next day. They also reported that memory was disrupted only if the drug was given within 90 minutes of reactivating the memory. This suggested the intriguing possibility that reactivated memories might need to be reconsolidated.

Shortly thereafter, Karim Nader and his colleagues (Nader et al., 2000) published their novel findings and the fate of retrieved memories and the concept of reconsolidation entered center stage. Nader's experiments were similar to the Lewis experiment (Misanin et al., 1968) with two exceptions:

- The protein synthesis inhibitor anisomycin was injected into the BLA following the reactivation of a Pavlovian conditioned auditory-cue fear memory, instead of delivering ECS.

- The rats were tested twice. One test was designed to measure the effect of anisomcyin on short-term memory. The other test, at a longer retention interval, was designed to test anisomycin's effect on long-term memory.

Anisomycin had no effect on the short-term memory test but produced a large impairment on the long-term memory test (Figure 14.3).

The idea that active memory traces are vulnerable to disruption was not new. The reason Nader's result captured the interest of neurobiologists was that he proposed a bold new idea called reconsolidation theory to explain the result (Nader, 2003). Although it shared

Karim Nader

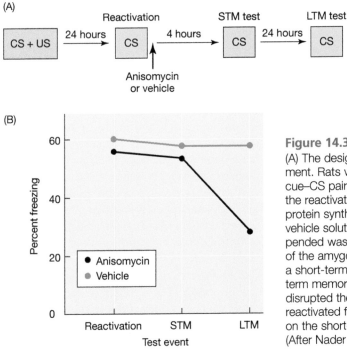

**Figure 14.3**
(A) The design of Nader et al.'s 2000 experiment. Rats were conditioned to an auditory-cue–CS paired with a shock–US. Following the reactivation of the fear memory, the protein synthesis inhibitor anisomycin or the vehicle solution in which the drug was suspended was injected into the lateral nucleus of the amygdala. Rats were then given either a short-term memory (STM) test or a long-term memory (LTM) test. (B) Anisomycin disrupted the long-term retention of the reactivated fear memory but had no effect on the short-term retention of the memory. (After Nader et al., 2000.)

(A)

(B)

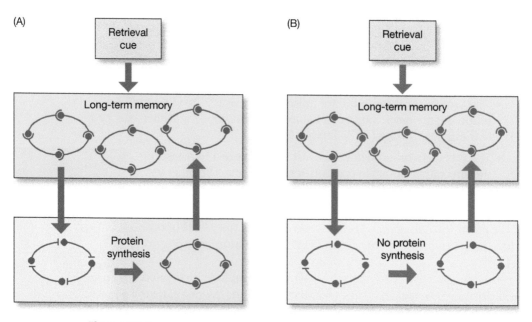

**Figure 14.4**

(A) A retrieval cue activates a well consolidated but inactive memory trace from long-term memory. The synaptic connections linking the neurons involved in the trace become unbound. However, retrieval also initiates protein synthesis and the memory trace is reconsolidated. Thus, when it returns to the inactive state it will be stable. (B) If protein synthesis is prevented, the memory trace will be weakened or lost when it returns to the inactive state.

Lewis's idea about the importance of the activation state of the memory, in other ways reconsolidation theory was quite different.

Nader's theory, which has two parts, is illustrated in Figure 14.4. First, he proposed that when a memory is retrieved *the synapses underlying the trace become unbound or weakened.* This means that retrieval itself can disrupt an established memory trace and thereby produce amnesia. This thought is disconcerting. It implies that the very act of retrieval can potentially cause the memory to be lost. The reason this does not happen is explained by his second assumption—that *retrieval also initiates another round of protein synthesis so that the trace is reconsolidated.* The new round of protein synthesis rescues the trace weakened by retrieval.

It is instructive to compare Nader's theory with active trace theory (Figure 14.5). The differences are subtle but important. The active trace theory account stipulates that when a memory trace has been retrieved into the active state, it is vulnerable to disruption by amnesic agents such as ECS or anisomycin; the agent is the cause of the amnesia. In contrast, reconsolidation theory

| | Active trace theory | Reconsolidation theory |
|---|---|---|
| Memory retrieval | Makes the trace vulnerable to amnestic agents | A. Initiates processes that degrade the trace<br><br>B. Initiates a new round of protein synthesis that saves the trace from degradation |
| Anisomycin | Causes amnesia when the memory trace is in an active state | Blocks protein synthesis needed to rebuild the trace. It does not cause amnesia; it reveals the amnesia produced by retrieval. |

**Figure 14.5**
A comparison of Lewis's active trace theory and Nader's reconsolidation theory. For each theory, the role played by memory retrieval and anisomycin is shown.

stipulates that the act of retrieval itself is the cause of the amnesia because it uncouples or destabilizes the synapses that contain the trace. Anisomycin itself does not disrupt the memory trace; it blocks the synthesis of the proteins needed to rebuild the trace. Note that, unless a protein synthesis inhibitor follows the retrieved memory, one would not know that the synapses holding the trace together had destabilized.

## Assessing Reconsolidation Theory

Although empirical support for reconsolidation theory has been somewhat inconsistent, there is now a large literature that supports it (Finnie and Nader, 2012). Reactivated memory traces are not just vulnerable to disruption by protein synthesis inhibitors; they can be influenced by a variety of pharmacological agents targeted at specific molecules that have been shown to be important in memory consolidation (Alberini et al., 2006; Dudai and Eisenberg, 2004; Tronson and Taylor, 2007). An experiment by Joseph LeDoux and his colleagues (Doyere et al., 2007) provides a useful illustration. To influence the reactivated memory, they injected a drug called U0126, which inhibits the activity of a kinase called MAPK, into the lateral nucleus of the amygdala of rats. This drug has previously been shown to influence the initial storage of an auditory-cue fear memory trace (Schafe et al., 2001).

Rats were conditioned to two quite different auditory-cue conditioned stimuli, CS1 and CS2, thus establishing two memories. During the reactivation phase, however, they presented only CS1. Prior to presenting CS1, U0126 was injected into the amygdala. They later tested the rats for fear of both CS1 and CS2. The important finding was that the U0126 disrupted the rats' fear

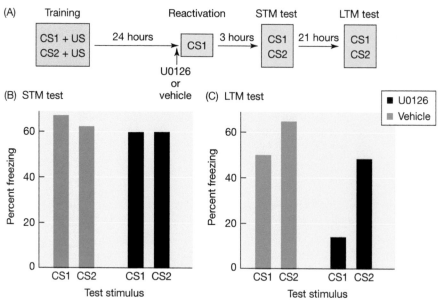

**Figure 14.6**
(A) In Doyere et al.'s experiment (2007) two different auditory stimuli, CS1 and CS2, were paired with a shock–US. However, only the fear memory associated with CS1 was reactivated. CS2 was not presented. (B) and (C) Infusing the MAPK inhibitor U0126 into the amygdala just prior to reactivating the fear memory associated with CS1 had no effect on the short-term memory (STM) test with CS1, but significantly reduced the fear response to CS1 on the long-term memory (LTM) test. Note that U0126 had no effect on the ability of CS2 to retrieve the fear response on either the STM or LTM test. This last outcome indicates that unless the fear memory is reactivated it is not vulnerable to disruption by U0126.

response only to CS1, the CS used to reactivate a memory. It did not disrupt the fear response to CS2, presumably because the memory trace associated with CS2 was not in the active state when U0126 was injected (Figure 14.6). Two points should be emphasized. First, even though the two memories were similar, only the reactivated memory was disrupted. So U0126 influenced only the neurons in that active state. Second, given the many side effects associated with anisomycin, it is important that other pharmacological agents can be shown to prevent reconsolidation.

## How Does Reactivation Destabilize the Trace?

Reconsolidation theory assumes that retrieving a memory will unbind or destabilize the synapses that support the memory. This is a novel and provocative assertion. If it is true then it should be possible to identify the cellular–molecular events that are responsible for trace destabilization. Some of the contributing events have been uncovered.

Trace destabilization depends on a reactivating stimulus increasing dendritic spine levels of calcium, either (a) by activating NMDA receptors, as is the case in the amygdala (Ben Mamou et al., 2006; Jarome et al., 2011), or (b) through voltage-dependent calcium channels (vdCCs), as is the case in the hippocampus (Suzuki et al., 2008). If NMDA receptors or vdCCs are antagonized prior to reactivation, the trace does not destabilize and anisomycin has no influence on the reactivated memory.

Increased calcium levels contribute to trace destabilization by their influence on the ubiquitin proteasome system (UPS, see Chapter 6). The activation of the UPS is associated with two effects:

- Key scaffolding proteins (for example, GKAP and Shank) are ubiquitinated—tagged for degradation.

- CaMKII is activated and participates in activating proteasomes and translocating them from the dendritic shaft to the spine.

Bong-Kiun Kaang and his colleagues were the first to implicate the UPS as important for trace destabilization (Kaang and Choi, 2012; Lee et al., 2008). They demonstrated that reactivation of a contextual fear memory ubiquitinates scaffolding proteins in the dorsal hippocampus. These conditions set the stage for active proteasomes to degrade these proteins. One of these, Shank, has been described as a master scaffolding protein that holds together other scaffolding proteins in the post-synaptic density (Ehlers, 2003). Thus, degrading this protein would result in a major disruption of the PSD. One potential consequence of this disturbance would be the loss of the anchoring scaffolding protein, such as PSD-95, that traps AMPA receptors in the PSD. In this case there would be a decrease in the

Bong-Kiun Kaang

surface levels of these receptors, thereby de-potentiating the synapse. Thus, unless new protein were generated, the reactivated memory trace would not restabilize and the memory would be weakened (Figure 14.7).

This hypothesis makes a strong prediction. If the proteasome system is inhibited, scaffolding proteins will not be degraded and therefore new protein will not be needed. Normally, if a protein synthesis inhibitor (anisomycin) is administered following reactivation, the memory will be weakened. Thus, this hypothesis can be evaluated by determining if inhibiting proteasome activity will prevent the memory loss normally produced by anisomycin. In support of this hypothesis, Kaang's group reported that inhibiting proteasome activity in the hippocampus prevents the loss of a reactivated contextual fear memory (Lee et al., 2008), and Helmstetter's group reported that inhibiting proteasome

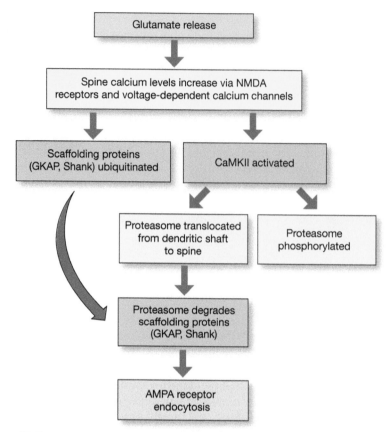

**Figure 14.7**
This figure illustrates key events that destabilize the synaptic basis of a memory trace. In response to glutamate released by neurons responding to the reactivating stimulus, calcium levels in the spine compartment are increased. This leads to ubiquitination of scaffolding proteins and the activation of CaMKII. CaMKII phosphorylates proteasomes and translocates them from the dendritic shaft to the spine where they degrade scaffolding proteins. The disturbance of the scaffolding complex could then lead to AMPA receptor endocytosis and de-potentiation of the synapse. Consequently, new protein is required to restabilize the trace. However, if NMDA receptors (in the hippocampus) or voltage-dependent calcium channels (in the BLA) are antagonized prior to reactivation, the trace will not destabilize. If the proteasome is inhibited, anisomycin will not affect the reactivated memory because new protein is not needed to restabilize the trace.

activity in the basolateral amygdala protects both reactivated contextual and auditory-cue fear memories from the effect of anisomycin (Jarome et al., 2011).

## Trace Restabilization and Trace Updating

Under normal circumstances reactivation will not produce memory loss. In fact, some believe that recalling a memory in some cases can strengthen it (Hardt et al., 2013). Thus, reactivation not only destabilizes the trace, it initiates processes that restabilize it (Nader, 2003). What processes restabilize the trace? One answer has been framed around the question, *do trace consolidation and reconsolidation depend on the same processes?* A general answer to this question is that many but not all of the same general processes that support consolidation, which were described in previous chapters, are involved in restabilizing the trace (Alberini et al., 2006; Dudai and Eisenberg, 2004).

A more interesting answer to this question, however, can be appreciated in the context of a position offered years ago by Norman "Skip" Spear (1973). He argued that the division between acquisition of a memory and memory retrieval is a distinction that may not be honored by the brain. Acquisition and retrieval are words used to describe experimental manipulations or phases of an experiment. However, from the standpoint of the subject experiencing a reactivation treatment, the retrieval episode is just another experience. It contains both old and potential new information, and the role of the brain is to assess this new content and integrate it with previously acquired information. So a reactivated trace is never just simply reconsolidated, it is modified to include information contained in the new experience.

This view has now been incorporated into the field to broaden the significance of Nader's (2003) original position (Dudai and Eisenberg, 2004; McKenzie and Eichenbaum, 2011). In this new framework, called **trace updating**, the functional significance of trace destabilization is to allow new information to be incorporated into existing memory ensembles (Dudai and Eisenberg, 2004). In this way the present is integrated with the past.

An implication of the trace-updating framework is that a destabilized trace can be bi-directionally modified—it can be weakened or strengthened. Research by Natalie Tronson and her colleagues (Tronson et al., 2006) supports this implication. They demonstrated that a fear memory trace could be strengthened by a drug called N6-benzoyladenosine-3′,5′-cyclic monophosphate (6-BNZ-cAMP), which activates PKA. They first used a low level of shock to establish a weak fear memory. They then injected 6-BNZ-cAMP into the BLA following presentations of only the CS. As shown in Figure

Natalie Tronson

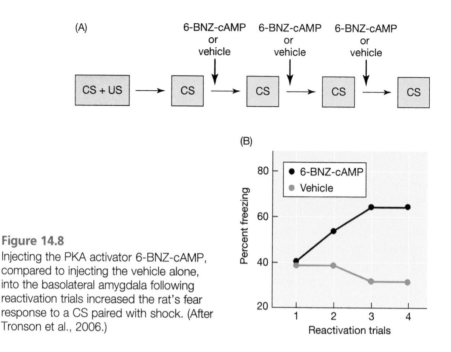

**Figure 14.8**
Injecting the PKA activator 6-BNZ-cAMP, compared to injecting the vehicle alone, into the basolateral amygdala following reactivation trials increased the rat's fear response to a CS paired with shock. (After Tronson et al., 2006.)

14.8, the fear response of rats with repeated CS-only presentations followed by the drug injection increased. Injecting the drug without reactivating the fear memory, however, had no effect. In contrast, when the PKA inhibitor Rp-cAMPS (Rp-Adenosine 3′,5′-cyclic monophosphorothioate) was injected into the BLA following reactivation of the fear memory, it impaired the subsequent retrieval of the memory. Thus, a retrieved memory trace can be weakened by interfering with biochemical processes that consolidate memories, but it can also be strengthened by enhancing these processes.

It is common knowledge that repetition of the same experience strengthens the memory trace. Jonathan Lee (2008) suggested another implication of the trace-updating framework—that in order to further strengthen an established memory, repetition must destabilize the trace. He evaluated this prediction by employing a slight variation on the standard reconsolidation experiment. The standard experiment consists of two sessions: (1) the memory acquisition trial (for example, context + shock) and (2) reactivation (context alone) followed by anisomycin. Note that the shock is omitted during the reactivation session. Lee's paradigm was identical except that he turned the reactivation session into a second "acquisition" session by also presenting the shock. He found that just as an injection of anisomcyin into the hippocampus prevented restabilization of a

Jonathan Lee

reactivated context fear memory, it also prevented additional strengthening of the memory. This effect of anisomycin, however, depended on the additional training event destabilizing the memory trace because an injection of the proteasome inhibitor βlactone prevented anisomycin from disrupting the processes that strengthen the memory.

## Memory Erasure: A Potential Therapy

Reactivated memories are vulnerable to disruption. This fact has encouraged researchers to pursue the possibility that drug treatments given after reactivation might be successful in eliminating memories that are the basis of serious behavioral disorders. This strategy has been pursued to develop potential treatments for two important clinical problems: (1) drug addiction relapse, and (2) debilitating fears such as those associated with post-traumatic stress disorder.

### *Preventing Drug Addiction Relapse*

One of the major problems associated with drug addiction is relapse (Figure 14.9). Even after drug addicts have gone through what appears to be successful treatment, they often relapse into the addictive cycle. Environmental cues associated with drugs are one important contributor to relapse. When a drug such as cocaine is taken, the environmental cues become associated with some properties of the drug. This is another example of Pavlovian conditioning. When these cues are encountered, they induce or create a craving or urge to take the drug (Figure 14.10). This state is well documented in people (Childress et al., 1999). In some ways it is similar to the urge one experiences when encountering a bag of potato chips or the sight of chocolate candy. However, the urge associated with drug-related cues is much more potent and difficult to resist.

Imagine that a person with a specific drug addiction has gone through treatment and is now off the drug. Unfortunately, when he or she later encounters cues that were

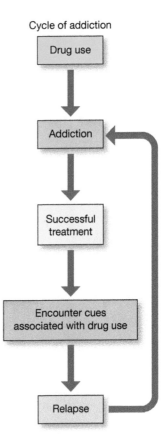

**Figure 14.9**
This figure illustrates the drug addiction–relapse cycle. Encountering cues associated with drug use can lead to relapse.

**Figure 14.10**
Cues associated with drug use induce a conditioned cocaine high, a craving for cocaine, and a wish to get high. The graph shows changes in the subjective state of recovering cocaine addicts after viewing a video showing simulated purchase, preparation, and smoking of crack cocaine. The subjects were patients in a treatment center and had not used cocaine for about 14 days. (After Childress et al., 1999.)

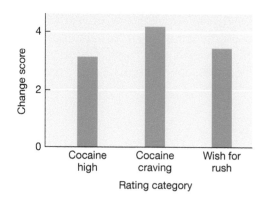

associated with the drug, the urge produced can be so powerful that relapse occurs and the individual reverts back to taking the drug. Given the power of these drug-related cues to evoke memories that produce relapse, it would be of enormous benefit to find treatment methods that could be used to attenuate or erase these memories. Recent studies with rodents suggest that this might eventually be possible.

Barry Everitt and his colleagues (Lee et al., 2005, 2006) have used the reactivation procedure to eliminate the ability of drug-related cues to produce relapse in rats that have learned to self-administer cocaine. The exact procedures for their experiments are complicated but basically entail training rats to learn a lever-press response that produces an infusion of cocaine (Figure 14.11A). This is the drug-seeking response. During this training the delivery of the cocaine is also paired with a Pavlovian CS, the presentation of a light. The light is thus associated with the drug. Theoretically, the light acquires the ability to evoke an urge to take the drug and its presence can lead to relapse. To demonstrate relapse, rats receive a session of training in which the response no longer produces the drug or the light. This results in the elimination of the drug-seeking response. If these rats then receive presentations of the light CS, they will relapse into drug-seeking behavior.

Barry Everitt

Everitt's group asked if the reactivation procedure could be used to eliminate the memory evoked by the CS and thus prevent relapse. To do this they presented rats with multiple presentations of the CS without the drug. They then infused an antisense into the BLA, which was designed to prevent translation of a gene called *Zif268*. This protein is expressed in the amygdala in response to presentations of the drug-associated CS. Thus, Everitt reasoned that it might be involved in the reconsolidation of the reactivated drug memory. Remarkably, preventing the expression of the *Zif268* protein completely

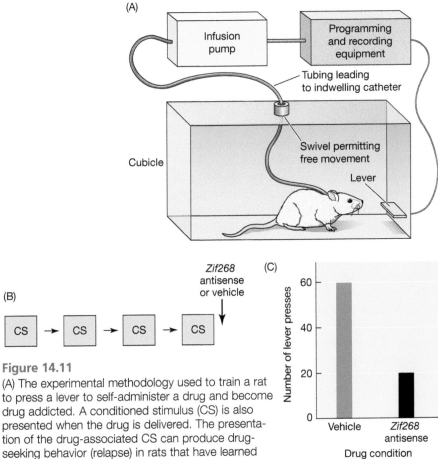

**Figure 14.11**
(A) The experimental methodology used to train a rat to press a lever to self-administer a drug and become drug addicted. A conditioned stimulus (CS) is also presented when the drug is delivered. The presentation of the drug-associated CS can produce drug-seeking behavior (relapse) in rats that have learned that lever pressing no longer produces the drug. (B) The vehicle or an antisense that blocks the translation of the gene *Zif268* is delivered after repeated CS presentations. (C) This graph shows that during the test for relapse the rats treated with *Zif268* antisense made fewer bar presses than rats who received the vehicle. This result suggests that *Zif268* antisense prevented the reconsolidation of the drug memory associated with the CS.

eliminated the ability of the CS to induce relapse. The rats behaved as if the light–drug memory had been erased (Figure 14.11B).

There are many reports from animal models that disrupting their reconsolidation can impair drug-related memories. Moreover, many of the signaling pathways involved in reconsolidation of these memories have been identified. However, as yet there has not been any strong evidence that the tools of the reconsolidation procedure have been translated into clinical treatment programs (Sorg, 2012).

*Eliminating Debilitating Fears*

Post-traumatic stress disorder is a severe anxiety disorder that can occur in a person who experiences one or more traumatic events. Although not conclusive, the evidence suggests that giving propranolol (the adrenergic receptor antagonist) during the post-trauma period may retard the development of this syndrome. Even if this treatment proves effective, it may not be applicable to people who have already developed the syndrome. Given the vulnerability of reactivated memories to disruption, there is some hope that it might be possible to develop therapies based on this methodology to treat people with existing debilitating fears.

The possible application of the reactivation procedure to help eliminate fear was explicitly recognized by Przybyslawski et al. (1999). They reported that the systemic administration of propranolol following the reactivation of an inhibitory avoidance memory greatly attenuated subsequent avoidance responding. Debiec and Nader (2004) also found that systemic injections of propranolol following the reactivation of the auditory-cue fear memory attenuated the rat's subsequent response to that cue.

Such experiments are far removed from clinical application, and unfortunately attempts at translating these tools to the clinical setting have been disappointing. In reviewing the current state of affairs, Roger Pitman (2011) concluded that "the translational gap to clinical application is huge (p. 1)" and described many of the difficulties that will have to be overcome if there ever will be clinical benefit from this work. So the promissory note is not yet fulfilled.

## Stepping Back: Boundary Conditions

The idea that the act of retrieving a memory destabilizes the trace has received great attention and received much experimental support. However, it is reasonable to ask, how general is this phenomenon? Does every retrieved memory destabilize and have to restabilize (for example, Biedenkapp and Rudy, 2004). If not, then what are the boundary conditions that determine when this process happens? Does the type of memory matter? For example, most experiments use training procedures that are aversive or highly arousing. Does this matter? Does the strength of the memory trace matter? Are weak memories more prone to destabilization than strong memories? Does the age of the memory matter (Inda et al., 2011)? Are more recently established memories more prone to destabilization than old memories? While researchers are engaged by these questions, current understanding is too limited to offer any complete answers to them (see Finnie and Nader, 2012, for a discussion of these and other related issues). These questions will continue to motivate researchers.

## Summary

Forty-five years ago, Don Lewis reported that reactivated memories might be vulnerable to disruption. He suggested that it is the state of the memory trace—active versus inactive—that makes it vulnerable to disruption. Interest in the fate of retrieved memory traces increased when Nader proposed the reconsolidation hypothesis—that retrieving a memory has two effects: (1) it unbinds the synapses that hold the trace, and (2) it initiates a new round of protein synthesis that will ensure that the memory trace is restabilized. Researchers have uncovered some cellular–molecular events that contribute to both destabilizing and restabilizing the memory trace. The functional significance of Nader's original framework has been broadened to incorporate the idea that trace destabilization provides the opportunity for trace updating. There is much interest in applying the tools of the reconsolidation framework to clinical domains but the verdict is still out on its utility.

## References

Alberini, C. M., Milekic, M. H., and Tronel, S. (2006). Mechanisms of memory stabilization and de-stabilization. *Cell Molecular Life Science, 63,* 999–1008.

Ben Mamou, C., Gamache, K., and Nader, K. (2006). NMDA receptors are critical for unleashing consolidated auditory fear memories. *Nature Neuroscience, 9* (10), 1237–1239.

Biedenkapp, J. C. and Rudy, J. W. (2004). Context memories and reactivation: constraints on the reconsolidation hypothesis. *Behavioral Neuroscience, 118,* 956–964.

Childress, A. R., Mozley, P. D., McElgin, W., Fitzgerald, J., Reivich, M., and O'Brien, C. P. (1999). Limbic activation during cue-induced cocaine craving. *American Journal of Psychiatry, 156,* 11–18.

Debiec, J. and Nader, K. (2004). Disruption of reconsolidation but not consolidation of auditory fear conditioning by noradrenergic blockade in the amygdala. *Neuroscience, 129,* 267–272.

Doyere, V., Debiec, J., Monfils, M. H., Schafe, G. E., and LeDoux, J. E. (2007). Synapse-specific reconsolidation of distinct fear memories in the lateral amygdala. *Nature Neuroscience, 10,* 414–416.

Dudai, Y. and Eisenberg, M. (2004). Rites of passage of the engram: reconsolidation and the lingering consolidation hypothesis. *Neuron, 44,* 93–100.

Ehlers, M. (2003). Ubiquitin and the deconstruction of synapses. *Science, 302,* 800–801.

Finnie, P. S. B. and Nader, K. (2012). The role of metaplasticity mechanisms in regulating memory stabilization. *Neuroscience and Biobehavioral Reviews, 36,* 1667–1707.

Hardt, O., Nader, K., and Nadel, L. (2013). Decay happens: the role of active forgetting in memory. *Trends in Cognitive Neuroscience, 17,* 111–120.

Inda, M. C., Muravieva, E. V., and Alberini, C. M. (2011). Memory retrieval and the passage of time: from reconsolidation and strengthening to memory extinction. *Journal of Neuroscience, 31*, 1635–1643.

Jarome, T. J., Werner, C. T., Kwapis, J. L., and Helmstetter, F. J. (2011). Activity dependent protein degradation is critical for the formation and stability of fear memories in the amygdala. *PLoS One, 6*: e24349.

Kaang, B-K. and Choi, J. H. (2012). Synaptic protein degradation in memory reorganization. *Advances in Experimental Medicine and Biology, 970*, 221–240.

Lee, J. L. (2008). Memory reconsolidation mediates the strengthening of memories by additional learning. *Nature Neuroscience, 11*, 1264–1266.

Lee, J. L., DiCiano, P., Thomas, K. L., and Everitt, B. J. (2005). Disrupting reconsolidation of drug memories reduces cocaine-seeking behavior. *Neuron, 47*, 795–801.

Lee, J. L., Milton, A. L., and Everitt, B. J. (2006). Cue-induced cocaine seeking and relapse are reduced by disruption of drug memory reconsolidation. *Journal of Neuroscience, 26*, 5881–5887.

Lee, S. H., Choi, J. H., Lee, N., Lee, H. R., Kim, J. I., Yu, N. K., Choi, S. L., Kim, H., and Kaang, B-K. (2008). Synaptic protein degradation underlies destabilization of retrieved fear memory. *Science, 319*, 1253–1256.

Lewis, D. J. (1979). Psychobiology of active and inactive memory. *Psychological Bulletin, 86*, 1054–1083.

McKenzie, S. and Eichenbaum, H. (2011). Consolidation and reconsolidation: two lives of memories? *Neuron, 71*, 224–233.

Misanin, J. R., Miller, R. R., and Lewis, D. J. (1968). Retrograde amnesia produced by electroconvulsive shock after reactivation of a consolidated memory trace. *Science, 160*, 554–558.

Nader, K. (2003). Memory traces unbound. *Trends in Neurosciences, 26*, 65–72.

Nader, K., Schafe, G. E., and LeDoux, J. E. (2000). Fear memories require protein synthesis in the amygdala for reconsolidation after retrieval. *Nature, 406*, 722–726.

Pitman, R. K. (2011). Will reconsolidation blockade offer a novel treatment for post-traumatic stress disorder? *Frontiers of Behavioral Neuroscience, 5*, 11.

Przybyslawski, J., Roullet, P., and Sara, S. J. (1999). Attenuation of emotional and non-emotional memories after their reactivation: role of beta adrenergic receptors. *Journal of Neuroscience, 19*, 6623–6238.

Przybyslawski, J. and Sara, S. J. (1997). Reconsolidation of memory after its reactivation. *Behavioural Brain Research, 84*, 241–246.

Schafe, G. E., Nader, K., Blair, H. T., and LeDoux, J. E. (2001). Memory consolidation of Pavlovian fear conditioning: a cellular and molecular perspective. *Trends in Neurosciences, 24*, 540–546.

Sorg, B. A. (2012). Reconsolidation of drug memories. *Neuroscience and Biobehavioral Reviews, 36*, 1400–1417.

Spear, N. E. (1973). Retrieval of memory in animals. *Psychological Review, 80*, 163–194.

Suzuki, A., Mukawa, T., Tsukagoshi, A., Frankland, P. W., and Kida, S. (2008). Activation of LVGCCs and CB1 receptors required for destabilization of reactivated contextual fear memories. *Learning and Memory, 15,* 426–433.

Tronson, N. C. and Taylor, J. R. (2007). Molecular mechanisms of memory reconsolidation. *Nature Reviews Neuroscience, 8,* 262–275.

Tronson, N. C., Wiseman, S. L., Olausson, P., and Taylor, J. R. (2006). Bidirectional behavioral plasticity of memory reconsolidation depends on amygdalar protein kinase A. *Nature Neuroscience, 2,* 161–169.

# PART 3
## Neural Systems and Memory

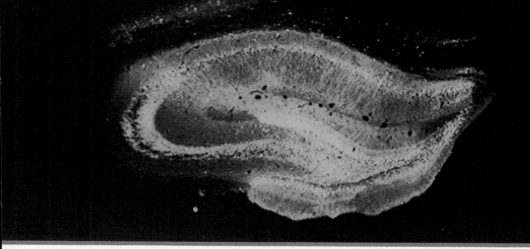

# 15 Memory Systems and the Hippocampus

We are our memories. Without a record of our experiences we would be disconnected from our past, have no recognition of our relatives and friends, possess no knowledge of the world, and would always be completely lost. We could not anticipate dangerous situations or locate the food and water we need to survive. We would be unable to acquire even the most rudimentary of skills, let alone learn to drive a car or become an expert violinist or tennis player. We could not be left alone.

The activities and functions that our memories support are remarkably varied and should make us ask, *how can the brain do all of this*? A part of the answer is that the brain contains specialized systems that are designed to store and utilize the different kinds of information contained in our experiences. Neurobiologists have achieved some basic understanding of how these systems are organized to support different types of memory.

The purpose of this chapter and the remaining ones is to introduce some of what is now known about these different systems. It begins with a quick overview of the multiple memory systems perspective, one of the important achievements of modern memory research (see Squire, 2004, for a historical overview).

## The Multiple Memory Systems Perspective

The content of our experience matters to the brain. It sorts content and assigns its storage to different regions of the brain. This idea is the essence of what is called the **multiple memory systems** perspective (McDonald and White, 1993; Squire, 2004; White and McDonald, 2002). Some examples will help to explain this concept.

### Example 1: Personal Facts and Emotions

Suppose you were in a minor automobile accident and no one was injured. As a consequence of that experience, you would very likely remember many of the details leading up to the accident—whom you were with, where it happened, who you thought was at fault, and so on. Now imagine that you were in a much more serious accident, you suffered facial lacerations and multiple fractures in one leg, and you were pinned in the car for some time. It was bad. This second case contains additional content. The experience was quite aversive and frightening. In addition to recording the details of the accident, your brain would record the aversive aspects of the experience in ways that might later alter your behavior. Not only would you be able to recall the cold facts of the experience, you might be afraid to drive or even get into an automobile.

The details that make up an episode and the impact of the experience are stored in different brain regions. Memory researchers have been aware of this possibility for a long time. For example, Édouard Claparède (1951), a French psychologist, reported on a test he performed on an amnesic patient with a brain pathology. He concealed a pin in his hand and then shook hands with the patient, who quickly withdrew her hand in pain. A few minutes later Claparède offered his hand to the patient again. The patient resisted shaking it. When asked why, the patient replied, "Doesn't one have a right to withdraw her hand?" Claparède then insisted on further explanation and the patient said, "Is there, perhaps, a pin hidden in your hand?" However, the patient could not give any reason why she had this suspicion.

Consider how you would react to such an experience. You also would be reluctant to shake hands, but you would be able to recall the content of the experience as an explanation of your behavior. Although Claparède's patient's brain pathology produced amnesia for the episode, it is reasonable to conclude that this pathology spared the system in the brain that was modified to produce a reluctance to shake hands. This example suggests that some aspect of the aversive content of the experience, as well as associations with the cues of the doctor, were stored outside of the region of the brain that supported recollection of the experience.

## Example 2: Personal Facts and Skills

We ride bikes, drive cars, play musical instruments, ride skateboards, and do many other things quite well. The level of accomplishment obtained by individuals such as concert violinists or professional skateboarders is truly amazing. Obviously, to achieve even a functional level of performance, such as needed to safely drive a car, requires an enormous amount of practice. Once a skill is acquired, it can be performed without having any sense of awareness. The many hours of practice have left an enduring impression in the brain that now supports the skill. In addition to acquiring a skill, however, we will also remember much about the practice sessions, where they occurred, who the instructors were, and how difficult it was initially to perform. Nevertheless, these aspects of our memory have absolutely nothing to do with our ability to perform the skill. We know this because people who are amnesic in the sense of having no recollection of their training episodes can still perform (Bayley et al., 2005). The inescapable conclusion is that the memory system that supports skillful behaviors is outside of the region of the brain that supports our ability to recollect the training episodes.

Such examples and brain research have led memory researchers to believe that: (1) a complete understanding of memory can only be achieved by recognizing that the content of experience is important; and (2) memories are segregated into different brain regions according to their content. The remainder of this chapter explores the episodic memory system, how memory researchers learned that episodic memory depends on a neural system that involves the hippocampus (Figure 15.1), and different models researchers have used to study this system. The story begins with patient H.M.

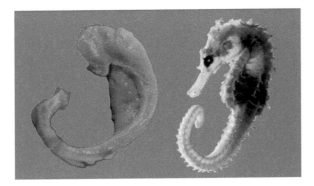

**Figure 15.1**

A hippocampus dissected from a human brain (left) and the tropical fish *hippocampus* or seahorse (right). The striking similarity in shape is undoubtedly why the Bolognese anatomist Giulio Cesare Aranzi named this brain region the hippocampus (Andersen et al., 2007). (Photo courtesy of Professor Laszio Seress, University of Pécs, Hungary.)

## The Case of Henry Molaison

Henry Molaison

The two previous examples made the point that brain insults can result in the loss of the ability to recall personal experiences, while sparing memories such as those that support emotional responses, skills, and habits. It was not until Brenda Milner reported her analysis of the anonymous amnesic, Henry Molaison (previously known only as H.M.), that memory researchers first gained insight into the regions of the brain that are responsible for the ability to remember experiences.

Henry Molaison is the most famous and important amnesic in the history of memory research. His personal tragedy revolutionized how we think about the relationship between memory and the brain. The seeds of Henry's tragedy were sown when, at the age of nine, he sustained a head injury that eventually led to epilepsy. Over the years his seizures became more frequent, and by the age of 27 they were so disturbing that he was no longer able to function. Because Henry's seizures were thought to originate in the temporal lobes, the decision was made to bilaterally remove these regions. This was the first time these regions had been bilaterally removed. The surgery was successful in reducing his epilepsy. Moreover, Henry's cognitive abilities were left intact; his IQ actually increased. Unfortunately, however, shortly after the surgery it was discovered that the surgery profoundly and permanently affected his memory.

Henry was brought to the attention of Brenda Milner, who then tested him in a variety of ways and described her results to the scientific community (Milner, 1970; Scoville and Milner, 1957). The essence of her analysis was that Henry had severe anterograde amnesia; he could not acquire some types of new memories. For example, he never recognized Milner even though they interacted many times. Soon after eating he could not remember what he ate or that he had eaten. His experiences registered initially and could be maintained for a short period of time. However, the memory vanished if he was distracted. Thus, although H.M.'s short-term memory was intact, his long-term memory was severely disturbed.

Although Henry had some preserved childhood memories, he had extensive retrograde amnesia that disconnected him with most of his personal past. Thus, even though other intellectual capacities remained intact, Henry could not acquire enduring new memories or remember a significant part of his past.

In spite of these severe memory impairments, formal tests revealed that some of his memory capacities were spared. For example, he was able to learn and remember the skill of mirror tracing

Brenda Milner

(A) The mirror-tracing task

**Figure 15.2**
(A) The mirror-tracing task.
(B) H.M.'s performance improved with training.

(B) Performance of H.M. on mirror-tracing task

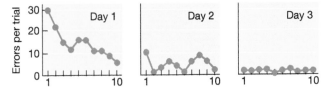

(Figure 15.2), which requires coordinating hand movement with an inverted image of the object being traced, and a rotary-pursuit task (Corkin, 1968), which requires acquiring a new motor skill. Remarkably, even though Henry's performance improved on these tasks, he never recalled the training experiences that established the skills.

Although Henry was severely amnesic, he had some understanding of his state. Milner (1970) reports that between tests he would suddenly look up and say rather anxiously: "Right now, I'm wondering. Have I done or said anything amiss? You see, at this moment everything looks clear to me, but what happened just before? That's what worries me. It's like waking from a dream; I just don't remember" (p. 37).

It is difficult to overestimate how important Henry's tragedy was for memory research. He wasn't the first patient to display amnesia for certain types of information. What was unique was that the location of the brain damage was known because the surgeon, William Scoville, had made a careful record of the surgery. This meant that for the first time researchers had a testable hypothesis about just what regions of the brain may be critical for memory. In addition, that Henry's intellectual capacities were intact meant that memory

functions could be separated from other cognitive abilities. That his anterograde and retrograde amnesia were restricted to certain kinds of content also
provided a foundation for the multiple memory systems view.

## The Episodic Memory System

Today many researchers believe that the removal of Henry's medial temporal
lobes disrupted what is called the **episodic memory system**. This is the system
that supports what most people mean when they use the term memory. It
extracts and stores the content from their experiences (episodes), which allows
them to answer questions such as: What did you have for lunch? Where did
you park your car? Who went with you to the movies? Thus, it supports the
ability to consciously recollect and report on facts and events that they experienced. They can declare that they have a memory. The episodic memory
system has other properties that are discussed in more detail in Chapter 16.

It is important to emphasize that Henry had some spared memory capacities. He could learn and retain the skills needed to perform the mirror-tracing
and rotary-pursuit tasks. These abilities and others are supported by memory
systems that depend on different regions of the brain. Some of these other
systems will be discussed in later chapters.

Henry's tragedy revealed that there are regions in the brain that are essential to the episodic memory system. At the time of surgery, Scoville estimated
that a large part of what is called the medial temporal lobe was bilaterally
removed, including much of the hippocampus, amygdala, and some of the
surrounding regions of the underlying neocortex (Figure 15.3). Modern neuroimaging techniques largely confirmed Scoville's estimates. However, it is
notable that more of the posterior part of the hippocampus was spared than
was originally estimated. Portions of the ventral perirhinal cortex were spared
and the parahippocampal cortex was largely intact (Corkin et al., 1997).

Given the extent of Henry's brain damage, it is difficult to know if one
region was more critical to the episodic memory system than any other. It is
interesting, however, that based on her analysis of patients with different com-
binations of brain damage, Milner (1970) speculated that the hippocampus
might have been a critical region of the medial temporal lobes that supported
the recall of the memories lost by Henry. Much research has been directed at
trying to define critical regions of the brain responsible for Henry's memory
impairment.

There are two ways that one can determine the critical brain regions that
support episodic memory. One is by using laboratory animals (rodents and
primates) to answer the question. The other is by studying patients that have

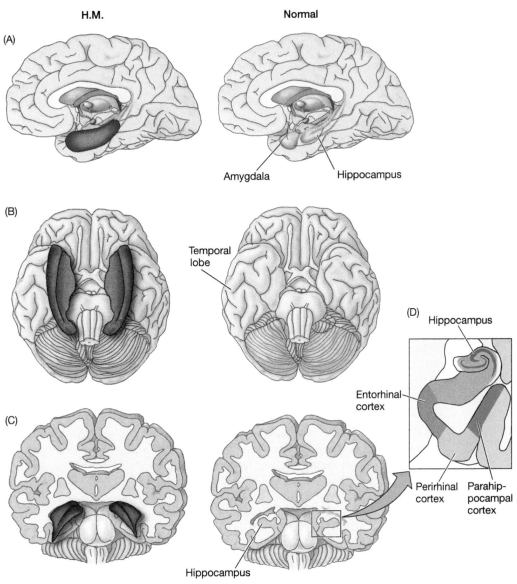

**Figure 15.3**
The tissue removed from H.M.'s brain. (A) This sagittal view of the brain shows that most of the amygdala and hippocampus were removed. (B) This view shows the extent to which underlying cortical tissue was removed. (After Scoville and Milner, 1957.) (C) This coronal section illustrates the combined loss of the cortical regions and hippocampus. (D) Another coronal view shows the cortical regions (entorhinal cortex, perirhinal cortex, parahippocampal cortex) and hippocampus in more detail.

selective damage to a particular medial temporal lobe structure or structures. Let's first consider the animal model strategy, including a memory testing procedure developed to determine what part of the brain supports episodic memory, before discussing humans with hippocampal damage.

## The Animal Model Strategy

The animal model strategy has the advantage that the researcher has some control over the location of the brain damage and can selectively target different regions. However, there is a fundamental problem with this approach that has never been completely solved. Specifically, the most important and easily demonstrated property of the episodic memory system is that it supports our ability to consciously recall our experiences. When I ask my wife what she had for lunch and she tells me she had a salad, unless she lied I can be confident that she consciously recalled the experience, and that her response depended on her episodic memory system. In contrast, my cat also might remember what it had for breakfast, but I have no way of knowing that it can consciously recollect this experience. Thus, researchers who use the animal model approach are faced with the problem of trying to convince themselves, and the rest of the scientific community, that the particular task they use measures episodic memory.

Milner's analysis of H.M. provides a related problem for animal models of episodic memory. H.M.'s primary impairment was relatively selective. He lost the ability to acquire memories that could be consciously recollected. However, some of his other memory capacities, such as his ability to improve on the rotary-pursuit task, were spared. Since we cannot ask animals to consciously recollect their daily events, it is likely that many of the tasks used to study memory in animals may not depend on the hippocampus because the memory-based performance can be supported by other neural systems that do not include the hippocampus. Given these problems, it is not surprising that it is difficult to develop a consensus on an animal model of episodic memory.

The primate brain is anatomically similar to our brain, so in the late 1970s Mortimer Mishkin (1978, 1982) decided to use primates to determine what brain regions contributed to Henry's memory loss. To do this he developed a memory testing procedure called **delayed nonmatching to sample (DNMS)**, which is illustrated in Figure 15.4. In the DNMS task each trial consists of two components. First, the monkey is shown a three-dimensional object. It is called the sample. Some time later he is presented with a choice between the sample object and a new object. This is called the choice component. If the monkey chooses the new object, it will find a reward such as a

Mortimer Mishkin

Sample  Test  Food found under the
nonmatching object

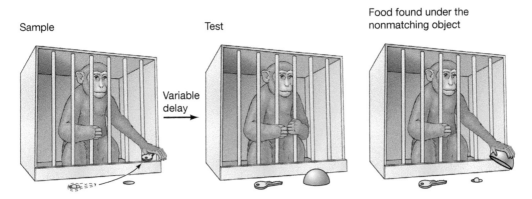

Variable
delay

**Figure 15.4**
The delayed nonmatching-to-sample task was invented to study episodic memory in
monkeys. The animal's task is to remember the object it sampled and to choose the
novel object on the choice trial.

grape or a peanut. The task is called nonmatching to sample because the correct object on the choice test does not match the sample. There are two important features of this task: (1) new objects are used on every trial; and (2) the
experimenter can vary the interval between the sample and the choice trial.

To make the correct choice the monkey must retain information about the
sampled object. It is the to-be-remembered episode. Implicit in the use of
the DNMS task is the assumption that when the monkey chooses the correct
object, it is telling the experimenter, "I remember seeing the old object at a
particular time and in this particular place." If this assumption is true, then
this task depends on the episodic memory system. If one believes that the
DNMS task exclusively measures episodic memory, then evaluating monkeys
with selective damage to medial temporal lobes should reveal which of these
regions were responsible for Henry's amnesia.

Mishkin initially used this task to determine if damage to the hippocampus
and/or amygdala caused Henry's amnesia. Viewed against Milner's hypothesis, the results of his experiments and others were somewhat surprising.
They revealed that damage to either the hippocampus or the amygdala had
very little effect on DNMS performance; however, damage to both regions
dramatically impaired performance. Moreover, monkeys with damage to both
of these regions were able to acquire motor skills (Squire, 1987). This outcome
initially encouraged the belief that it was the combined damage to both the
hippocampus and the amygdala that produced Henry's amnesia.

Larry Squire, however, pointed out that the surgical approaches used to
remove both the hippocampus and amygdala produced extensive damage
to the immediate surrounding cortical tissue compared to when only the

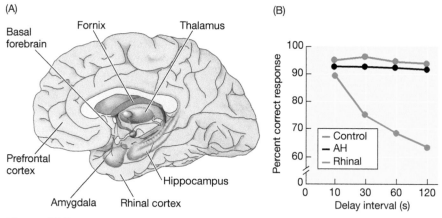

**Figure 15.5**
(A) A saggital view of the human brain. (B) The performance on the delayed non-matching-to-sample task. Primates with damage to both the amygdala and hippocampus (AH) performed normally. However, removal of the rhinal cortical regions profoundly disrupted performance. (After Meunier et al., 1993; Murray and Mishkin, 1998.)

Larry Squire

hippocampus was surgically removed (Squire, 1987). Subsequent research led to the conclusion that it was the damage to the rhinal cortex, not damage to either the amygdala or hippocampus, which drastically impaired performance on the DNMS task (Meunier et al., 1993; Murray and Mishkin, 1998; Zola-Morgan et al., 1989). An example of these results is presented in Figure 15.5. Thus, researchers agree that this medial temporal lobe region is critical for performance on the DNMS, and that neither the hippocampus nor the amygdala is critical.

### Studies of Patients with Selective Hippocampal Damage

The above discussion illustrates the difficulties one encounters using the DNMS animal model to define a neural circuit for episodic memory. We don't know when nonverbal animals are actually recollecting events from their past. Thus, ultimately conclusions about the critical contribution the hippocampus makes to the episodic memory system must be derived from people with brain damage limited to the hippocampus. A number of patients with relatively selective damage to the hippocampus have been identified. Although there is debate about the recognition memory capacity of these patients, no one doubts that they all are impaired in acquiring new episodic memories.

Steward Zola-Morgan et al. (1986) described patient R.B. The onset of R.B.'s amnesia was associated with complications of a second artery bypass surgery. Zola-Morgan and his colleagues tested R.B.'s memory and, at his death, conducted an extensive neuropathological evaluation of R.B.'s brain. Formal memory tests indicate that he had difficulty acquiring new information. For example, after a story was read to him, R.B. could recall only a small fraction of the material. He also could recall only a small percentage of words that were read to him twice. Informally R.B. reported that he had severe memory problems. He reported that if he had talked to his children on the phone he did not remember doing so the next day. Thus, R.B. had significant anterograde amnesia. However, formal tests found no evidence of retrograde amnesia, that is, loss of memory for events that occurred prior to the cardiac episode. There was some speculation based on informal observations that he may have had loss of memory for some events that occurred a few years prior to the cardiac episode.

Remarkably, the neuropathological assessment of R.B.'s brain indicated that the pathology was restricted to the CA1 region of the hippocampus (Figure 15.6). Bilaterally, there was a complete loss of neurons from the CA1 field. The CA1 field is a final stage whereby information processed by other regions is sent out via the subiculum and entorhinal cortex. Thus, although the damage was restricted, it was in a location that would be expected to significantly diminish the ability of the hippocampus to make its normal contribution to memory.

Cipolotti et al. (2001) described the case of V.C., who became profoundly amnesic at the age of 67, apparently after experiencing an epileptic seizure. Assessment of his brain damage by magnetic resonance imaging indicated that there was significant loss of volume over the entire rostral–caudal length of the hippocampus. However, critical surrounding cortical regions—the entorhinal and parahippocampus cortices—were normal, as were the adjacent

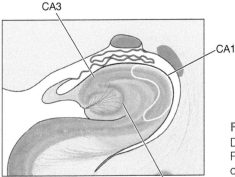

**Figure 15.6**
Damage to the hippocampus of patient R.B. was restricted to a massive loss of neurons in the CA1 field, outlined in white in the figure.

temporal lobes. Thus, V.C.'s damage was restricted primarily to the hippo-campus. Formal tests revealed that V.C. had profound anterograde amnesia. He was severely impaired on all measures of recall, such as the recall of a story and word associations. V.C. also had extensive retrograde amnesia.

Thus, studies of patients with much more selective damage to the hippo-campus support Brenda Milner's original conjecture that the hippocampus is critically involved in episodic memory.

## The DNMS Paradox Resolved

The results generated by the DNMS task—that monkeys with damage to the hippocampus are not impaired on this task—are both surprising and discon-certing as they imply that the hippocampus is not part of the episodic memory system. And that conclusion runs counter to Milner's hypothesis that it was damage to the hippocampus that was responsible for H.M.'s selective memory impairments.

Baxter and Murray (2001) reviewed all of the relevant studies and con-cluded that extensive damage to the hippocampus has a smaller effect on DNMS than does limited damage (but see Zola and Squire, 2001). Based on this review, one would have to conclude that either (a) the hippocampus is not part of the episodic memory system or (b) the DNMS task has a solution that does not depend on episodic memory. Given that it is now generally agreed that the hippocampus *is* a central component of the episodic memory system, the latter hypothesis is the more likely explanation and there are theoretical reasons for favoring it.

The DNMS task belongs to a category of tasks called **recognition memory tasks**. Such tasks require the subject to make a judgment about whether some-thing has previously occurred. Today many theorists believe that two differ-ent processes can support recognition. One type is called **familiarity** and the other is called **recollection** (Brown and Aggleton, 2001; Rugg and Yonelinas, 2003; Sutherland and Rudy, 1989). To appreciate this distinction you need only to reflect on how often you have recognized a person as familiar without being able to recall information about the place and time you met her. This would be an example of recognition without recall. It would be based on familiarity and not recollection. Recollection would also include the information about such things as where and when you met the person and her name, content that is supported by the episodic memory system, as described in the next chapter. Often you will get a sense of familiarity before you recollect the details of past encounters.

Contemporary theorists have proposed that recognition based on recollec-tion depends on the hippocampus, whereas recognition based on familiarity depends on surrounding cortices (Brown and Aggleton, 2001). If two processes can support recognition memory, it is possible to explain why extensive damage to the hippocampus can have little or no effect on DNMS performance. The monkeys in the DNMS task were using the familiarity process to make their correct choice (Sutherland and Rudy, 1989) and this does not depend on the episodic memory system that supports recollection.

## Summary

The content of experience matters to the brain. Different attributes are assigned to different regions of the brain for storage. The idea that the brain has multiple memory systems is now central to the neurobiology of memory.

The perspective that different brain regions support different memory systems gained support when Brenda Milner's analysis of patient H.M. revealed that the removal of the medial temporal lobes left him with no long-term episodic memory but did not influence his ability to learn complex motor tasks or perceptual motor adjustments. Milner proposed that it was the damage to the hippocampus that was critical to H.M.'s profound episodic memory impairment.

The delayed nonmatching-to-sample recognition memory task was invented in an attempt to develop an animal model aimed at determining which regions of the medial temporal lobes are critical for episodic memory. This research revealed that the hippocampus is not necessary for animals to perform this task but that the cortical areas surrounding the hippocampus are. However, studies of human patients with more selective damage to the hippocampus support Milner's hypothesis that the hippocampus is critical for episodic memory.

Most researchers believe that recognition is based on both a familiarity process that depends on the cortical areas surrounding the hippocampus and a recollection process that contains information about where and when the event happens, which depends on the hippocampus. Just how the hippocampus supports episodic memory is the topic of the next chapter.

## References

Andersen, P., Morris, R., Amaral, D., Bliss, T., and O'Keefe, J. (2007). Historical perspective: proposed functions, biological characteristics, and neurobiological models of the hippocampus. In P. Andersen, R. Morris, D. Amaral, T. Bliss, and J. O'Keefe (Eds.), *The hippocampus book* (pp. 9–36). New York: Oxford University Press.

Baxter, M. G. and Murray, E. A. (2001). Opposite relationship of hippocampal and rhinal cortex damage to delayed nonmatching-to-sample deficits in monkeys. *Hippocampus, 11,* 61–71.

Bayley, P. J., Frascino, J. C., and Squire, L. R. (2005). Robust habit learning in the absence of awareness and independent of the medial temporal lobe. *Nature, 436,* 550–553.

Brown, M. W. and Aggleton, J. P. (2001). Recognition memory: what are the roles of the perirhinal cortex and hippocampus? *Nature Reviews Neuroscience, 2,* 51–61.

Cipolotti, L., Shallice, T., Chan, D., Fox, N., Scahill, R., Harrison, G., Stevens, J., and Rudge, P. (2001). Long-term retrograde amnesia...the crucial role of the hippocampus. *Neuropsychologia, 39,* 151–172.

Claparède, É. (1951). Recognition and me-ness. In D. Rapaport (Ed.), *Organization and pathology of thought* (pp. 58–75). New York: Columbia University Press.

Corkin, S. (1968). Acquisition of a motor skill after bilateral medial temporal lobe excision. *Neuropsychologia, 6,* 255–265.

Corkin, S., Amaral, D. G., Gonzalez, R. G., Johnson, K. A., and Hyman, B. T. (1997). H.M.'s medial temporal lobe lesion: findings from magnetic resonance imaging. *Journal of Neuroscience, 17,* 3964–3979.

McDonald, R. J. and White, N. M. (1993). A triple dissociation of memory systems: hippocampus, amygdala, and dorsal striatum. *Behavioral Neuroscience, 107,* 3–22.

Meunier, M., Bachevalier, J., Mishkin, M., and Murray, E. A. (1993). Effects on visual recognition of combined and separate ablations of the entorhinal and perirhinal cortex in rhesus monkeys. *Journal of Neuroscience, 13,* 5418–5432.

Milner, B. (1970). Memory and the medial temporal lobe regions of the brain. In K. H. Pribram and D. E. Broadbent (Eds.), *Biology of memory* (pp. 29–50). New York: Academic Press.

Mishkin, M. (1978). Memory in monkeys severely impaired by combined but not by separate removal of amygdala and hippocampus. *Nature, 273,* 297–298.

Mishkin, M. (1982). A memory system in the monkey. *Philosophical Transactions of the Royal Society London, 298,* 83–95.

Murray, E. A. and Mishkin, M. (1998). Object recognition and location memory in monkeys with excitotoxic lesions of the amygdala and hippocampus. *Journal of Neuroscience, 18,* 6568–6582.

Rugg, M. D. and Yonelinas, A. P. (2003). Human recognition memory: a cognitive neuroscience perspective. *Trends in Cognitive Sciences, 7,* 313–319.

Scoville, W. B. and Milner, B. (1957). Loss of recent memory after bilateral hippocampal lesions. *Journal of Neurology, Neurosurgery, and Psychiatry, 20,* 11–12.

Squire, L. R. (1987). *Memory and brain.* New York: Oxford University Press.

Squire, L. R. (2004). Memory systems of the brain: a brief history and current perspective. *Neurobiology of Learning and Memory, 82,* 171–177.

Sutherland, R. J. and Rudy, J. W. (1989). Configural association theory: the role of the hippocampal formation in learning, memory, and amnesia. *Psychobiology*, *17*: 22, 129–144.

White, N. M. and McDonald, R. J. (2002). Multiple parallel memory systems in the brain of the rat. *Neurobiology of Learning and Memory*, *77*, 125–184.

Zola, S. M. and Squire, L. R. (2001) Relationship between magnitude of damage to the hippocampus and impaired recognition memory in monkeys. *Hippocampus*, *11*, 92–98.

Zola-Morgan, S., Squire, L. R., and Amaral, D. G. (1986). Human amnesia and the medial temporal region: enduring memory impairment following a bilateral lesion limited to field CA1 of the hippocampus. *Journal of Neuroscience*, *6*, 2950–2967.

Zola-Morgan, S., Squire, L. R., Amaral, D. G., and Suzuki, W. A. (1989). Lesions of perirhinal and parahippocampal cortex that spare the amygdala and hippocampal formation produce severe memory impairment. *Journal of Neuroscience*, *9*, 4355–4370.

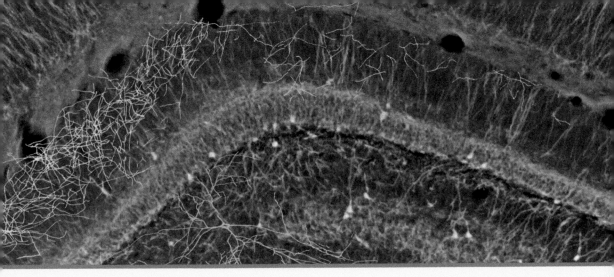

# 16 The Hippocampus Index and Episodic Memory

As learned in the previous chapter, the episodic memory system captures the content of our experiences in a form that permits us to recollect or replay them. When the hippocampus is significantly damaged, this capacity is lost and we become disconnected from our past. Thus, there is something special about the hippocampus and its connections with other brain regions that is fundamental to the episodic memory system. How do the hippocampus and its related cortical structures store the content of our personal experiences so that it can be recollected or recalled? The goal of this chapter is to answer this question, by describing:

- properties of the episodic memory system;
- the neural system in which the hippocampus is situated;
- the indexing theory of episodic memory; and
- current evidence supporting the indexing theory.

## Properties of Episodic Memory

Episodic memory has several important properties or attributes, including (1) its support of conscious recollection and storage of temporal–spatial contextual information for later retrieval, (2) its ability to automatically capture episodic and incidental information, and (3) its ability to acquire information about an event that occurs only once, yet protect the representations it stores from interfering with each other.

### Conscious Recollection and Contextual Information Storage

The episodic system is most often described as supporting memories that can be consciously recollected or recalled. The term **conscious recollection** has two meanings:

1. It means that you intentionally initiated a search of your memory. This meaning refers to the manner in which retrieval is initiated.

2. It also means that you have an awareness of remembering—a sense that a memory trace has been successfully activated. This meaning refers to a subjective feeling that is a product of the retrieval process (Schacter, 1989).

Our personal experience is consistent with the idea that we can be aware that we have retrieved a memory or had a remembering experience. It also is the case that we can intentionally initiate a memory search that leads to recalling a memory. However, this does not mean that memories retrieved from the episodic system have to evoke a state of conscious awareness to influence behavior. Nor does it mean that our episodic memory system can only be accessed if we intentionally initiate a search.

To appreciate this last point, we also can draw on personal experiences such as encountering a friend whom we haven't seen in a while or visiting an old neighborhood. Such experiences often initiate the recall of many events associated with the friend or neighborhood without any intention on our part to retrieve these memories. Moreover, it is likely that we became aware of having a remembering experience.

The subjective state of conscious awareness that can occur when we have successfully remembered some event may be associated with the content of the memory trace. A number of researchers agree that the feeling of remembering emerges when a retrieved memory trace contains information about the time, place, or context of the experience that established the memory (Nadel and Moscovitch, 1997; Squire and Kandel, 1999; Squire and Zola-Morgan, 1991). Being able to retrieve this contextual information enables a replay of the experience and allows us to declare that we remember. In describing the importance of contextual information for recollection, for example, Squire and Kandel (1999, p. 69) wrote, "Once the context is reconstructed, it may seem surprising how easy it is to recall the scene and what took place. In this way, one can become immersed in sustained recollection, sometimes accompanied by strong emotions and by a compelling sense of personal familiarity with what is remembered."

Obviously, information about the spatial and temporal context of the experience must be stored if conscious recollection depends on its retrieval. Thus, the episodic memory system must be critically involved in both the storage and retrieval of contextual information.

## Automatic Capture of Episodic and Incidental Information

Many theorists believe that the episodic memory system automatically captures information simply as a consequence of our exploring and experiencing the environment (Morris et al., 2003; O'Keefe and Nadel, 1978; O'Reilly and Rudy, 2001; Teyler and DiScenna, 1986; Teyler and Rudy, 2007). The term automatic is used to note that the information is captured without intention on our part to do so. You can prove this is true by recalling your experiences of the past several days. You will undoubtedly remember a surprising amount of information. Now ask yourself if you intentionally attempted to store any of this information. Your likely answer will be no.

To be sure, you may be able to co-opt this system by instructing yourself to remember a phone number or an address. However, the basic point is that the hippocampus does not need to be driven by our intentions or goals to capture information. It contributes to the episodic memory system by automatically capturing the information it receives as we attend to and explore the world. For this reason, some researchers also say that the episodic memory system captures incidental information. This means that it will capture information that is incidental to the task at hand. Thus, when you deliberately remember a phone number, it is unlikely that you intend to remember the episode of memorizing the number, but it is likely that you will. Or, if you are trying to learn a new tune on the piano, you do not instruct yourself to remember the practice session. Nevertheless, the episodic memory system likely captures a great deal of this incidental information so that you can later recall much about the practice session.

## Single Episode Capture with Protection from Interference

The term episodic memory means that the system captures information about single episodes of our lives. What constitutes the duration of an episode is vague. However, the gist of this idea is that the episodic memory system can acquire information about an event that occurs only once. It has been suggested that from the viewpoint of the episodic system, every episode of our lives is unique, even if it contains highly overlapping information (Nadel and Moscovitch, 1997). Thus, we can remember many different instances of practicing the piano or driving our car to the same parking lot.

If the episodic memory system is constantly capturing information about our daily events, then it must be able to store highly similar episodes, such as where you parked your car today versus where you parked it yesterday, so that these memories do not interfere with each other. Our success in keeping memories of similar events separate suggests that an important property of the episodic system is that the representations it stores are somehow protected from interference (O'Keefe and Nadel, 1978; O'Reilly and McClelland, 1994; O'Reilly and Rudy, 2001).

### Properties Summary

In summary, many researchers agree about the fundamental attributes of the episodic memory system. It automatically captures information about the single episodes of our lives. The memory trace includes information about the spatial and temporal context of the episode and it is when this contextual information is retrieved that we are consciously aware of the memory and can declare that we remembered some event. The next sections describe how the hippocampus contributes to these properties and supports memories.

## A Neural System that Supports Episodic Memory

The hippocampus can support episodic memories because (a) it is embedded in a neural system in which it interacts with other regions of the brain and (b) both its intrinsic organization and the properties of its synaptic connections are unique. The work of a number of neuroanatomists has led to an understanding of the connectivity of these regions of the brain (Amaral and Lavenex, 2007; Lavenex and Amaral, 2000; Van Hoesen and Pandya, 1975).

### The Hierarchy and the Loop

The neural system that supports episodic memory can be organized around two principles (Lavenex and Amaral, 2000) that are illustrated in Figure 16.1.

1. The organization is hierarchical. The level of integration or abstraction of information increases as it flows from the neocortex to the perirhinal and parahippocampal cortices to the entorhinal cortex and through the hippocampus.

2. The circuit is a loop. This means that information carried forward to the hippocampus also is then projected back to the sites lower in the hierarchy that initially brought the information to the hippocampus.

The flow of information to the medial temporal lobes begins when sensory information (for example, visual, auditory, somatosensory) arrives at different regions of the neocortex (called unimodel associative and polymodal associative areas). Information at this level is not well integrated. However, these regions project to what Lavenex and Amaral call the first level of integration—the perirhinal and parahippocampus cortices. Information from these regions projects forward to the second level of integration in the entorhinal cortex that projects to the highest level of integration—the hippocampus. At each stage the information becomes more compressed or abstract.

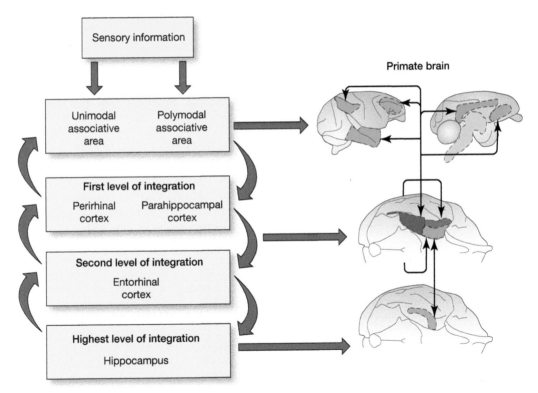

**Figure 16.1**
On the left is a schematic representation of the flow of information from the neocortical unimodal and polymodal associative areas to the medial temporal lobe regions. Information flows to the highest level of integration and then loops back to the neocortical areas. (After Lavenex and Amaral, 2000.) The location of these regions in the primate brain is shown on the right. (After Eichenbaum, 2000.)

**Figure 16.2**

This figure illustrates the flow of information into and out of the hippocampus, from and to the entorhinal cortex. The combination of hippocampal components and the subiculum is sometimes referred to as the hippocampal formation.

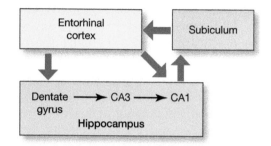

Information is processed through the hippocampus and then projects back to the entorhinal cortex. The entorhinal cortex also projects back to the perirhinal and parahippocampal cortices that in turn project back to the neocortical regions. Figure 16.2 provides a more complete representation of the flow of information into and out of the hippocampus. It shows that the entorhinal cortex projects into two regions of the hippocampus, the dentate gyrus and the CA1 region, and that information projects out of the hippocampus to the entorhinal cortex via a region called the **subiculum**. This combination of hippocampal components and the subiculum is sometimes called the **hippocampal formation**.

## The MTH System

Most researchers agree that the critical components of this hierarchical system are located in the medial temporal lobes. This system is sometimes referred to as the **medial temporal hippocampal (MTH) system**, consisting of the perirhinal, parahippocampal, and entorhinal cortices and the hippocampal formation (shown in Figure 16.2). This MTH system has the following functional implications.

1. Because the hippocampus sits at the top of a hierarchically organized system, it is in a position to receive convergent information from a wide range of cortical regions. In a sense, it sees what is going on in other regions of the brain.

2. The information is so highly processed by the time it reaches the hippocampus that it is described as amodal (Lavenex and Amaral, 2000). This means that hippocampal neurons do not know whether they are receiving auditory, visual, or somatosensory information.

3. The perirhinal, parahippocampal, and entorhinal cortices also have to be considered as part of the episodic memory system because without them the hippocampus receives no information. They are the last stage

of information processing before information enters the hippocampus. Thus, whether or not these regions can support other memory functions, such as familiarity-based recognition, they are critical to episodic memory.

Now consider a theory of just what the hippocampus contributes to episodic memory.

## The Indexing Theory of Episodic Memory

Any theoretical account of how the hippocampus supports episodic memory must be consistent with the anatomy and physiology of the system. Tim Teyler and Pascal DiScenna (1986) provided one such account and called it the **indexing theory of hippocampal memory** (see also Marr, 1971). This theory has been supported by a wealth of data (Teyler and Rudy, 2007) and its basic ideas are shared by a number of theorists (Marr, 1971; McNaughton, 1991; McNaughton and Morris, 1987; Morris et al., 2003; O'Reilly and Rudy, 2001; Squire, 1992).

Tim Teyler

Figure 16.3 provides a simple illustration of indexing theory. The theory assumes that the individual features that make up a particular episode establish a memory trace by activating patterns of neocortical activity, which then project to the hippocampus (Figure 16.3B). As a consequence, synapses in the hippocampus responding to the neocortical inputs are strengthened by mechanisms that support long-term potentiation (discussed in Chapters 2 through 6). The experience is represented simply as the set of strengthened synapses in the hippocampus that result from the input pattern, that is, there are no modifications among the neocortical activity patterns. Thus, the memory trace is a representation in the hippocampus of co-occurring patterns of activity in the neocortex.

The "indexing" nature of the memory trace can be illustrated in relationship to memory retrieval. Note in Figure 16.3C that a subset of the original neocortical pattern is received by the hippocampus. The projections from these input patterns activate the now connected neurons in the hippocampus representing the original experience. The activation of this representation then projects back to the neocortex to activate the pattern representing the entire experience (Figure 16.3D). It is this projection back to the neocortex that conveys the indexing property to the hippocampus representation. This process is called pattern completion and is described more fully below.

The indexing idea can be understood in relationship to a library. A library often contains thousands of books. This creates an obvious problem—how do you find the one you want? Librarians solved the retrieval problem by

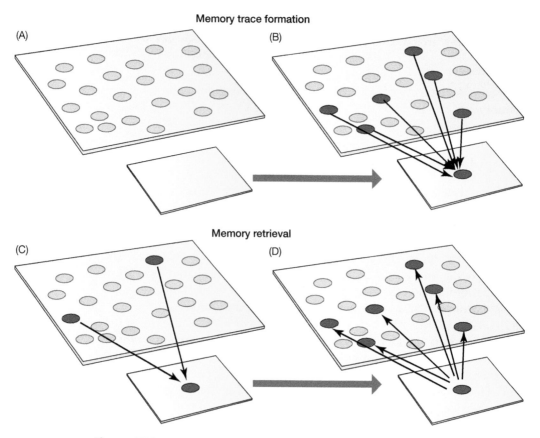

**Figure 16.3**
This figure illustrates the important ideas represented in the indexing theory of the hippocampus. (A) In memory trace formation, the top layer represents potential patterns of neocortical activity, while the bottom layer represents the hippocampus. (B) A set of neocortical patterns (purple dots) activated by a particular experience is projected to the hippocampus and activates a unique set of synapses. (C) In memory retrieval, a subset of the initial input pattern can activate the hippocampal representation. (D) When this occurs, output from the hippocampus projects back to the neocortex to activate the entire pattern. Thus, the hippocampus stores an index to neocortical patterns that can be used to retrieve the memory.

creating an indexing system that contains information about the location of the book. So you go to the index and find the book's address. Note that the content you are looking for is in the book. The index has no content; it just tells you where to find the book that contains the desired information. Likewise, the episodic memory indexing theory assumes the rich content of our experience is stored in neocortical regions of the brain and all that the hippocampus stores is information about how to retrieve the memories stored in the neocortex. It provides an index to the content represented in the neocortex.

## The Hippocampus Does Not Store Content

It is worth reiterating the basic character of the memory trace provided by this system. The content of the memory is contained in the unique patterns of activity in the neocortical regions of the brain activated by the experience. There is no memory content per se contained in the hippocampus. All that it contains is the information that a specific pattern of activity in different cortical regions has occurred. This pattern is represented by (a) strengthening the synaptic connections between the input from the neocortex and the neurons activated in the hippocampus and (b) strengthening connections among the neurons that were activated. The only way the full content of the memory experience can be replayed is by outputs from the hippocampus activating the cortical representations of the experience. Thus, the hippocampus simply represents the conjunction of co-occurring input patterns and provides a map to the relevant cortical sites that contain the content of our experiences.

In this context there are two important related concepts that need to be further discussed in relationship to indexing theory—**pattern completion** and **pattern separation**. Understanding these concepts is central to understanding how the index retrieves an episodic memory.

## Pattern Completion and Pattern Separation

When a subset or portion of the experience that originally established the memory trace is encountered, it can activate or replay the entire experience. The process by which this happens is called pattern completion. It is the most fundamental process provided by the index. This process is possible (a) because synapses on neurons in the hippocampus that represent the patterns of activity in the neocortex have been strengthened (this is the index) and (b) because neurons in the hippocampus project back to the same neocortical regions (for example, entorhinal cortex) that projected to it (shown previously in Figures 16.1 and 16.2). Note that this could not happen if there were no return projections back from the hippocampus to the neocortex.

As noted previously, one of the remarkable aspects of the episodic memory system is that it has the capacity to maintain distinct representations of similar, but separately occurring, episodes. Many theorists believe that this property of episodic memory derives from the architecture of the hippocampus and its relationship to the neocortex. The basic idea is that outputs from widespread patterns of activity in the neocortex will randomly converge onto and activate a much smaller set of neurons in the hippocampus (O'Reilly and

McClelland, 1994; O'Reilly and Rudy, 2001). Because the similar (but different) inputs are likely to converge onto different neurons in the hippocampus, the two similar patterns are likely to create different indices. Thus, the hippocampus is said to support a process called pattern separation that keeps representations of similar experiences segregated.

## Why Not Just Store the Memory in the Neocortex?

The way in which the memory trace is built by this indexing system might seem overly complex. Why should the brain need an elaborate hierarchical system in which neocortical regions project to the hippocampus and then loop back to the neocortex to store a memory? Why not just directly strengthen the connections between those patterns of activity in the neocortex? There are at least two reasons why a hierarchical system has evolved. The first has to do with the associative connectivity problem, while the second is related to the interference problem.

The associative connectivity problem relates to the potential connections among neurons in the different neocortical regions that support representations of experience. There may not be enough of these connections to support the rapid changes needed to associate patterns of activation distributed widely across the neocortex (Rolls and Treves, 1998). Thus, although there may be on the order of $10^{10}$ principal neurons in the cortex, they are not richly interconnected. This makes it difficult to strengthen associative connections among the patterns of activity produced by experience. Without these patterns being strongly connected, pattern completion (the activation of the entire pattern by a subset of the original experience) would be difficult.

In contrast, two regions in the hippocampus, the dentate gyrus and CA3, have high internal connectivity and modifiable synapses. In CA3, in particular, interconnectivity is so high that most of the pyramidal cells are connected within two to three synaptic steps (Rolls and Treves, 1998). Thus, unlike neocortex, the hippocampus is well designed to associate arbitrary input patterns. Moreover, these synapses are easily modified, and mechanisms of synaptic plasticity revealed by studies of LTP (discussed in Chapters 2 through 6) may very well support the changes in synaptic strength needed to maintain new associative connections.

The second reason why the hierarchical organization may be favored is related to the interference problem. Many of the episodes that make up our daily experiences occur in similar situations. For these individual episodes to be kept separate, they must be stored so that two similar episodes are not confused. Memory traces composed of directly connected patterns of neocortical activity may not be well suited to solve this problem. Consider what might

(A)

(B) Neocortex representation of the overlapping inputs

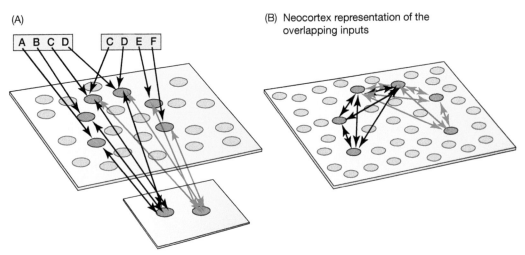

**Figure 16.4**
The hippocampus keeps memories of similar episodes separated. Two similar input patterns (ABCD and CDEF) activate their respective patterns of neocortical activity. Projections from these similar neocortical patterns converge onto different neurons in the hippocampus. The synaptic connections from the cortical projections to and among the hippocampus neurons are strengthened. Thus, the hippocampus provides a separate index for the two similar memories that keeps them separated. Presenting the AC combination selectively activates the ABCD pattern, and the CE combination activates the CDEF pattern. In contrast, the neocortex has difficulty keeping the memories for similar episodes separated. Because the patterns share common features (CD), they are interconnected and the memories for the different episodes lose their identity. Any combination of inputs (for example, AC, CE, or BD) activates the entire blended network.

happen if you have two related experiences such as lunch in the same place with two different friends. As described earlier, the hippocampus index supports pattern separation and thus would keep these two related but different experiences separate (illustrated in Figure 16.4A as ABCD and CDEF). In the neocortex, however, these two similar experiences would be integrated into a common representation. The key difference, shown in Figure 16.4B, is that in the neocortex any combination of inputs (AC, CE, or BD) would activate the integrated representation.

## Indexing Theory and Properties of Episodic Memory

Indexing theory was developed with the intent of explaining how the neural system in which the hippocampus is situated can support the fundamental features of episodic memory. The properties of episodic memory emerge quite naturally from this theory.

- Conscious recollection and awareness emerge when pattern completion processes activate a representation of the entire event, including the context in which it occurs, sufficiently to replay the memory.

- The automatic or incidental storage property emerges because the synapses that support the memory are automatically strengthened just by the fact that experience generates new patterns of neural activity in the neocortex that project into the hippocampus. Such a mechanism captures the contextual information in which experience occurs because it binds the cortical representations of the entire experience.

- The episodic nature of the memory trace is due to single experiences, each generating unique patterns of neural activity in the neocortex that are captured by the hippocampus index.

- Interference among similar memory traces is reduced because the hippocampus supports pattern separation.

## Evidence for the Indexing Theory

A wealth of evidence supports the indexing theory of episodic memory. In this section some of the literature that provides support for these ideas is presented. This evidence is intended to be illustrative rather than comprehensive. The experiments were chosen because they comment on some component of the theoretical ideas that have been presented. Two sources of the data include studies of amnesic people with damage to the hippocampus and studies of animals.

As described in Chapter 15, people with significant damage to the hippocampus are selectively impaired in their ability to consciously recall episodes of their personal experiences and events that occurred at specific times and places. Recall that H.M. improved his performance on motor and perceptual reorganization tasks, yet he had no recollection of ever participating in these tasks. Formal tests of other patients with much more selective damage to the hippocampus (such as patients R.B. and V.C.) also revealed that their recall of recent experiences was severely impaired (Cipolotti et al., 2001; Zola-Morgan et al., 1986).

Animals in the studies have been primarily rodents, with experimentally induced selective damage to the hippocampus. The next section explores the role of the hippocampus in episodic memory as evidenced through a sampling of these animal studies.

## Animal Studies

As previously noted, an advantage of studying memory in animals other than people is that the experimenter can precisely damage a particular region of the brain, including the hippocampus or its surrounding cortical regions. The disadvantage of this approach is that non-human animals cannot consciously recollect. Nevertheless, Howard Eichenbaum (2000) has made the point that the anatomical organization of the neural system that contains the hippocampus in primates and rodents is remarkably similar to that system in humans (illustrated previously in Figure 16.1). Thus, even though conscious recollection can be demonstrated only in people, given the anatomy of the rodent brain one should expect that it could support a rudimentary episodic memory system.

Indexing theory makes several claims about the role of the hippocampus in episodic memory that can be evaluated even in animals that cannot consciously recollect. These claims are that the hippocampus:

- is critical to forming context representations;
- is the basis for conscious awareness and recollection;
- automatically captures context (incidental) information;
- captures single episodes;
- supports cued recall through pattern completion; and
- keeps separate episodes distinct.

CONTEXT REPRESENTATIONS  A large number of studies with rodents support the idea that the hippocampus is critical to forming a representation of the context in which events are experienced. The **context preexposure paradigm** developed by Michael Fanselow (1990) provides a powerful tool to study context representations. It is based on a phenomenon called the **immediate shock effect**. If a rat is placed into a fear-conditioning chamber and shocked immediately (within 6 seconds), it will later show little or no fear of the conditioning chamber. However, if the rat is allowed to explore the conditioning chamber for a couple of minutes the day before it receives immediate shock, it will subsequently show substantial fear to that context (Figure 16.5). This result is believed to demonstrate that the rat acquired a representation of the context when it explored it during the preexposure phase. Thus, rats that were not preexposed to the shock–test context failed to show conditioned fear because they did not have time before the shock to acquire a representation of the context.

There are a number of reasons to believe that acquiring a representation depends on the hippocampus (Rudy et al., 2004). Studies have shown that: (1) rats with damage to the dorsal part of the hippocampus do not acquire

(A)

| Context preexposure | Immediate shock | Fear test |

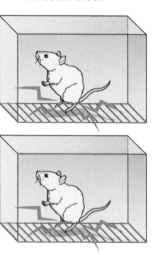
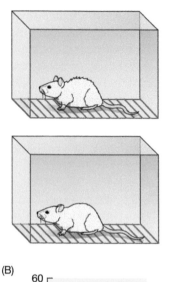

**Figure 16.5**
(A) The top of the figure illustrates the experimental design reveal-
ing that the rat acquires a representation of an explored context.
It takes advantage of the fact that rats that are simply placed
into a particular context and immediately shocked do not later
fear that context. However, if they are preexposed to that context the day before the immediate shock experience, they do
later show fear. (B) This graph shows that immediate shock itself
does produce fear of the context, but that context preexposure
markedly increases the fear produced by immediate shock.
This result, called the context preexposure effect, indicates that
the rat acquires a representation of the explored context. (After
Fanselow, 1990.)

(B)

Percent freezing (y-axis: 0, 20, 40, 60)

Immediate shock | Context preexposure + Immediate shock

a representation of an explored context (Rudy et al., 2002), and (2) injecting
the NMDA receptor antagonist D-APV into the dorsal hippocampus before
context preexposure impairs the acquisition of a representation of context
(Matus-Amat et al., 2007).

CONSCIOUS AWARENESS AND RECOLLECTION   Indexing theory assumes that
conscious recollection derives, in part, from the index representation that
binds components of the episode into a representation of the context. Thus,
encountering some component of the episode activates the index that in turn
projects back to the neocortex and activates the cortical representation of the

context. Strong activation of this representation might provide a basis for conscious awareness (see Eichenbaum et al., 2007, for a similar analysis).

Animals other than people cannot express their subjective feelings. However, it is possible to tell if they have the kind of representation just described. Studies of object recognition indicate that they do. For example, when given a choice between exploring a novel object and one previously experienced (a familiar object), rats spend more time exploring the novel object. Rats with damage to the hippocampus also explore a novel object more than a familiar one. However, what they apparently can't do is remember the context in which a particular object was experienced. This point is illustrated in Figure 16.6A. A normal rat is first allowed to explore the cube in context A and the cylinder in context B. In the test phase, the rat is presented with each object in

(A) Exploration

(B) Test

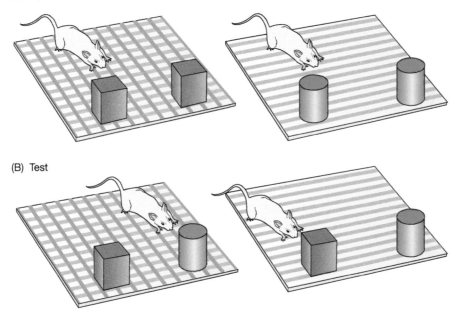

**Figure 16.6**
(A) Rats were allowed to explore two objects, a cube and a cylinder. Each object was explored in a different context. (B) The rats were then tested twice. Both objects were presented in each context. Control rats spent more time exploring the object that had not previously been experienced in the test context. In contrast, rats with damage to the hippocampus explored the objects equally. This means that control animals had a memory of the object and the context in which it occurred, but rats with damage to the hippocampus did not.

context A and in context B (see Figure 16.6B). A normal rat will explore the object presented in the different context as if it were novel. This means the representation of the object was bound together with features of the context in which it was explored. This kind of representation should require an index and be dependent on the hippocampus. In fact, rats with damage to the hippocampus treat explored objects as familiar, whether they are tested in their training context or the other context (Eacott and Norman, 2004; Mumby et al., 2002; see Eichenbaum et al., 2007 for a review).

AUTOMATIC INFORMATION CAPTURE   As noted earlier, the episodic memory system is always online, automatically capturing the events that make up our daily experiences. The studies just described make the case that this property also depends on the hippocampus. To appreciate this point, reconsider the context dependency of the object-recognition study illustrated in Figure 16.6. There are no explicit demands embedded in an object-recognition task. Nothing forces the animal to remember that the cube occurred in context A and the cylinder occurred in context B, any more than a normal person must remember where he or she had breakfast. However, this happens and it depends on an intact hippocampus.

Consider another example based on a different version of object-recognition memory. In this case the rat is allowed to explore two different objects that occupy different locations in a training arena. For example, object A might be in the corner of the arena and object B in the center. The normal rat stores a memory of the position of these objects because if the position of one of the objects is changed during the test, the rat will explore it as novel. Nothing forces the normal rat to remember the location of the objects (Figure 16.7). Rats with damage to the hippocampus, however, are not sensitive to the location of the objects changing (Eacott and Norman, 2004; Mumby et al., 2002). Thus, the hippocampus supports the processes that automatically capture this information.

SINGLE EPISODE CAPTURE   There is evidence that the hippocampus is part of the memory system that captures single episodes. For example, when the location of the hidden platform of the Morris water-escape task is altered on a daily basis, normal rats show dramatic improvement, even on the second trial and even if the inter-trial interval is 2 hours. In contrast, rats with damage to the hippocampus show no improvement. Moreover, an injection of the NMDA-receptor antagonist APV into the dorsal hippocampus prior to the first trial also dramatically impairs performance on the second trial (Steele and Morris, 1999). Morris's group also developed and used a landmark place-learning task (described in Chapter 9) to make the same point—that the

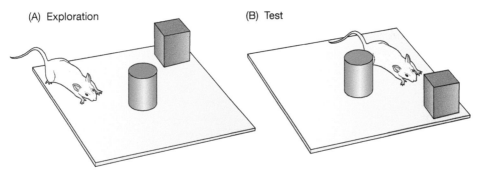

**Figure 16.7**
(A) Rats were allowed to explore an arena containing two objects. (B) In the test phase the rat was returned to the arena but the location of one of the objects was changed. Control rats explored the moved object much more than they explored the unmoved object. They responded to it as if it were novel. Rats with damage to the hippocampus explored the two objects equally. Thus, automatically capturing information about the location of the objects depended on the hippocampus.

hippocampus is part of the episodic memory system that captures information from a single experience (Bast et al., 2005; Day et al., 2003).

CUED RECALL THROUGH PATTERN COMPLETION   An important implication of indexing theory is that when a subset of the features that make up an episode activates the hippocampus, the index activates the entire pattern of neocortical activity generated by the episode. This implies that it should be possible to demonstrate cued recall of a memory in animals. There is good evidence that this occurs (Rudy et al., 2004; Rudy and O'Reilly, 2001).

A compelling example is based on the context preexposure–immediate shock paradigm. My colleagues and I (Rudy and O'Reilly, 2001; Rudy et al., 2002) used this paradigm to demonstrate that a memory of context can be retrieved and associated with shock. Our experiment is illustrated in Figure 16.8. During the preexposure session, rats were transported several times to a particular context (context A). The purpose was to establish a link between the transport (T) cage and a representation of context A. On the immediate shock day, however, the rats were transported to a novel and very different context (context B) and immediately shocked. The rats were later tested in either context A or context B.

Note that the indexing theory makes the unusual prediction that the rats should display fear when tested in context A but no fear in context B, where they were actually shocked. This prediction is unusual because the rats were never shocked in context A. This prediction is made because the transport

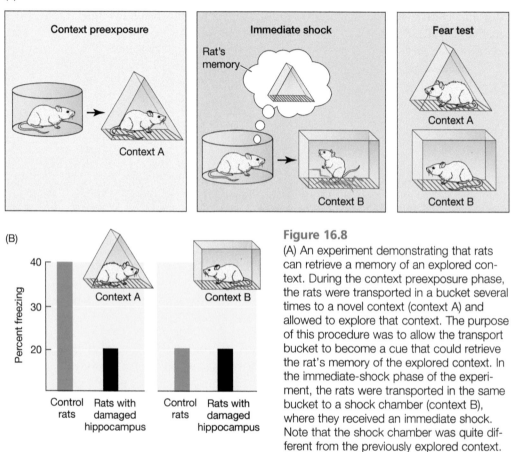

**Figure 16.8**

(A) An experiment demonstrating that rats can retrieve a memory of an explored context. During the context preexposure phase, the rats were transported in a bucket several times to a novel context (context A) and allowed to explore that context. The purpose of this procedure was to allow the transport bucket to become a cue that could retrieve the rat's memory of the explored context. In the immediate-shock phase of the experiment, the rats were transported in the same bucket to a shock chamber (context B), where they received an immediate shock. Note that the shock chamber was quite different from the previously explored context. The rats were then tested in either context A or context B. (B) The control rats displayed no fear in context B, where they were actually shocked, but displayed fear in context A, where they had been allowed to explore and had received no shock. This means that during the immediate-shock phase the control rats recalled the memory of context A (where they thought they were being transported to) and associated it with the shock. Rats with damage to the hippocampus, however, did not show fear to either context A or context B, which means they were not able to acquire or retrieve the memory representation of the preexposed context. (After Rudy et al., 2002.)

cue should complete the pattern of activity that represents context A, and this representation should be available for the animals to associate with the shock. They should not display fear when tested in context B, where they were shocked, because they had never experienced it before and they did not have the opportunity to construct a representation of that context before they were shocked.

As shown in Figure 16.8, this is exactly what was found. Moreover, damage to, or inactivation of, the dorsal hippocampus prevented this result (Matus-Amat et al., 2004; Rudy et al., 2002). Thus, these results indicate that rodents can acquire a representation of a context that can be activated by a subset of the features that make up the episode. In other words, pattern completion supports cued recall in animals other than people, and this depends on the hippocampus.

PATTERN SEPARATION   One of the important properties of the episodic memory system is that it keeps similar episodes somewhat distinct. As noted, an index in the hippocampus provides an advantage over a straight neocortical memory system. There is evidence that pattern separation is better when the hippocampus is intact. One source of such evidence is the study of what is called generalized **contextual fear conditioning**. In such studies, rats are shocked in one context (context A) and then tested in either that context or a similar but not identical context (context B). To the extent that they show fear to the similar context, they are said to generalize their fear to another context.

Imagine that you were in an automobile accident. You might display fear of being in the specific car involved in the accident and/or generalized fear to other, similar cars. Rats lacking a hippocampus display more generalized fear than normal rats (Antoniadis and McDonald, 2000; Frankland et al., 1998). This result suggests that the hippocampus provides processes that enable the rat to discriminate the context paired with shock from a similar one that was not paired with shock.

Gilbert and Kesner (2006) have provided another source of evidence that the hippocampus is necessary for pattern separation. They reported that rats with selective neurotoxic damage to the dentate gyrus could discriminate the location of two identical objects (a covered food well, for example) when the physical distance between them (their spatial separation) was great, but they performed poorly as the distance decreased. In contrast, normal rats were unaffected by the degree of spatial separation. Thus, the hippocampus was necessary for the rats to remember separate, similar spatial locations.

## Shining Light on the Index

Memory content for a behavioral experience is distributed widely across different brain regions. By creating a map to the co-occurring patterns of neuronal activity representing the experience, the hippocampus index provides an economical way to access the content. This view has a provocative implication. If one could identify specific neurons in the hippocampus that index a particular memory, and had the means to specifically activate these neurons, then *it would be possible to active the memory by activating just these neurons.*

Optogenetics (see Chapter 9) has made it possible to evaluate this assertion. To do this Tonegawa and his colleagues (Liu et al., 2011) used a viral
vector system to deliver *channelrhodopsin-2* (*ChR2*) to a small set of neurons
in the dentate gyrus. The gene was coupled with a promoter (the immediate
early gene, *c-fos*), and the entire construct was injected into mice genetically
engineered so that the experimenter could control when the promoter would
be expressed in response to neural activity. Specifically, so long as the mice
were maintained on a diet that contained doxycycline, a commonly used
antibiotic, synaptic activity would not activate the promoter and the *ChR2*
gene would not be expressed. However, removing doxycycline from the diet
allowed synaptic activity to activate the promoter and in turn the expression
of *ChR2* in the neurons containing the gene.

Under normal conditions the hippocampus supports contextual fear conditioning, so Liu et al. used this procedure to establish the memory. The day
before training, however, doxycycline was removed from the diet. Thus, when
the mice were conditioned, neurons in the dentate that were activated by the
contextual fear conditioning experience (context + shock) would express the
channels. After the conditioning session, doxycycline was again introduced
into the diet to prevent other neurons from expressing *ChR2*. Thus, by this
means the neurons that were part of the hippocampus index could be identified and, if activated, could retrieve the memory.

To determine if this was the case, Liu et al. took the conditioned mice
into a familiar context that had never been associated with shock and thus
would not evoke a fear memory. Then, through the fiber optics cable that had
been implanted in the dentate gyrus, they delivered blue light to specifically
activate the neurons expressing *ChR2*. Remarkably, the activation of these
channels resulted in the mice displaying the freezing response, and when the
light was turned off freezing terminated. This did not happen if *ChR2* was
expressed in mice that explored the context but were not shocked, or in mice
that had been shocked in the context but were on the doxycycline diet that
prevented expression of the *ChR2* (Figure 16.9). These results directly confirm
a major principle of indexing theory. Directly activating neurons that are part
of the index can retrieve the memory.

Optogenetics has also been used to support other implications of indexing
theory. Specifically, it should be possible to prevent contextual fear conditioning and its retrieval by infecting neurons in the hippocampus with channels
that inhibit their activation. By using light to inhibit these neurons during
acquisition it should be possible to prevent the acquisition of the contextual
fear memory, and by inhibiting these neurons during fear testing it should
be possible to prevent the retrieval of the contextual fear memory. Both of
these outcomes have been observed in mice in which the gene for inhibitory

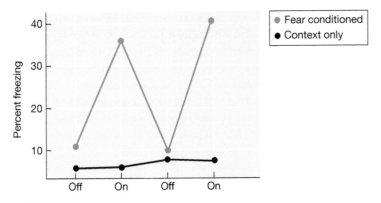

**Figure 16.9**
In this experiment, Liu et al. (2011) used optogenetic methods to test indexing theory. Hippocampal neurons in the dentate gyrus that were active during a contextual fear conditioning experience expressed *channelrhodopsin-2*. When these neurons were activated by a light, the mice displayed fear in a context where they had never been shocked. When the light was off the mice displayed no fear. Mice that were not conditioned displayed no fear whether the light was on or off.

channels (*eNpHR3*) was delivered to pyramidal cells in the CA1 output region of the hippocampus (Goshen et al., 2011).

## Summary

The episodic memory system supports our ability to consciously recollect the daily episodes of our lives. The hippocampus is a critical component of the neural system that supports the storage and retrieval of episodic memories. Information flows from the neocortical regions to the hippocampus and then returns to the neocortical projection sites. The indexing theory assumes that the content of experience is stored in the neocortex and that the hippocampus creates indices to memories for different episodes. It does this by binding the inputs it receives from different regions of the neocortex into a neural ensemble that represents the conjunction of their co-occurrence. Because the hippocampus projects back to the projecting areas, when this index is activated it can activate or replay the activity patterns that are the memory of the episode.

The hippocampus is said to support the process called pattern completion, whereby a subset of the original episode can activate the whole pattern. It also supports pattern separation by creating different indices for similar episodes and thus segregating them. The neocortex is not well suited to rapidly acquire memories for single episodes because potential associative connectivity across neocortical regions is low and patterns of neocortical activity produced by separate but similar experiences may become blended and thus lose their episodic nature. Studies with both people and rodents support this view of the role of the hippocampus in episodic memory.

Indexing theory predicts that if the specific neurons in the hippocampus that were active during memory acquisition could be identified, it would be possible to later retrieve that memory just by activating those neurons directly. The development of optogenetics has made it possible to verify this prediction by shining light on such identified neurons to activate the index and retrieve a contextual fear conditioning memory.

## References

Amaral, D. and Lavenex, P. (2007). Hippocampal anatomy. In P. Andersen, R. Morris, D. Amaral, T. Bliss, and J. O'Keefe (Eds.), *The hippocampus book* (pp. 37–114). New York: Oxford Press.

Antoniadis, E. A. and McDonald, R. J. (2000). Amygdala, hippocampus, and discrimination fear conditioning to context. *Behavioural Brain Research, 108*, 1–19.

Bast, T., da Silva, B. M., and Morris, R. G. (2005). Distinct contributions of hippocampal NMDA and AMPA receptors to encoding and retrieval of one-trial place memory. *Journal of Neuroscience, 25*, 5845–5856.

Cipolotti, L., Shallice, T., Chan, D., Fox, N., Scahill, R., Harrison, G. J., Stevens, J., and Rudge, P. (2001). Long-term retrograde amnesia: the crucial role of the hippocampus. *Neuropsychologia, 39*, 151–172.

Day, M. R., Langston, R., and Morris, R. G. (2003). Glutamate-receptor-mediated encoding and retrieval of paired-associate learning. *Nature, 424*, 205–209.

Eacott, M. J. and Norman, G. (2004). Integrated memory for object, place, and context in rats: a possible model of episodic-like memory? *Journal of Neuroscience, 24*, 1948–1953.

Eichenbaum, H. (2000). A cortical-hippocampal system for declarative memory. *Nature Reviews Neuroscience, 1*, 41–50.

Eichenbaum, H., Yonelinas, A. R., and Ranganath, C. (2007). The medial temporal lobe and recognition memory. *Annual Reviews of Neuroscience, 30*, 123–152.

Fanselow, M. S. (1990). Factors governing one-trial contextual conditioning. *Animal Learning and Behavior, 18*, 264–270.

Frankland, P. W., Cestari, V., Filipkowski, R. K., McDonald, R. J., and Silva, A. J. (1998). The dorsal hippocampus is essential for context discrimination but not for contextual conditioning. *Behavioral Neuroscience, 112*, 863–874.

Gilbert, P. E. and Kesner, R. P. (2006). The role of dorsal CA3 hippocampal subregion in spatial working memory and pattern separation. *Behavioural Brain Research, 169,* 142–149.

Goshen, I., Brodsky, M., Prakash, R., Wallace, J., Gradinaru, V., Ramakrishnan, C., and Deisseroth, K. (2011). Dynamics of retrieval strategies for remote memories. *Cell, 147,* 678–689.

Lavenex, P. and Amaral, D. G. (2000). Hippocampal–neocortical interaction: a hierarchy of associativity. *Hippocampus, 10,* 420–430.

Liu, X., Ramirez, S., Pang, P. T., Puryear, C. B., Govindarajan, A., Deisseroth, K., and Tonegawa, S. (2011). Optogenetic stimulation of a hippocampal engram activates fear memory recall. *Nature, 22,* 381–385.

Marr, D. (1971). Simple memory: a theory for archicortex. *Proceedings of the Royal Society of London B Biological Sciences, 262,* 23–81.

Matus-Amat, P., Higgins, E. A., Barrientos, R. M., and Rudy, J. W. (2004). The role of the dorsal hippocampus in the acquisition and retrieval of context memory representations. *Journal of Neuroscience, 24,* 2431–2439.

Matus-Amat, P., Higgins, E. A., Sprunger, D., Wright-Hardesty, K., and Rudy, J. W. (2007). The role of dorsal hippocampus and basolateral amygdala NMDA receptors in the acquisition and retrieval of context and context fear memories. *Behavioral Neuroscience, 121* (4), 721–731.

McNaughton, B. L. (1991). Associative pattern completion in hippocampal circuits: new evidence and new questions. *Brain Research Review, 16,* 193–220.

McNaughton, B. L. and Morris, R. G. M. (1987). Hippocampal synaptic enhancement and information storage within a distributed memory system. *Trends in Neurosciences, 10,* 408–415.

Morris, R. G., Moser, E. I., Riedel, G., Martin, S. J., Sandin, J., Day, M., and O'Carroll, C. (2003). Elements of a neurobiological theory of the hippocampus: the role of activity-dependent synaptic plasticity in memory. *Philosophical Transactions of the Royal Society of London B Biological Sciences, 358* (1432), 773–786.

Mumby, D. G., Gaskin, S., Glenn, M. J., Schramek, T. E., and Lehmann, H. (2002). Hippocampal damage and exploratory preferences in rats: memory for objects, places, and contexts. *Learning and Memory, 9,* 49–57.

Nadel, L. and Moscovitch, M. (1997). Memory consolidation, retrograde amnesia and the hippocampal complex. *Current Opinion in Neurobiology, 17,* 217–227.

O'Keefe, J. and Nadel, L. (1978). *The hippocampus as a cognitive map.* Oxford: Clarendon Press.

O'Reilly, R. C. and McClelland, J. L. (1994). Hippocampal conjunctive encoding, storage, and recall: avoiding a trade-off. *Hippocampus, 4,* 661–682.

O'Reilly, R. C. and Rudy, J. W. (2001). Conjunctive representations in learning and memory: principles of cortical and hippocampal function. *Psychological Review, 108,* 311–345.

Rolls, E. T. and Treves, A. (1998). *Neural networks and brain function*. Oxford: Oxford University Press.

Rudy, J. W., Barrientos, R. M., and O'Reilly, R. C. (2002). The hippocampal formation supports conditioning to memory of a context. *Behavioral Neuroscience, 116*, 530–538.

Rudy, J. W., Huff, N. C., and Matus-Amat, P. (2004). Understanding contextual fear conditioning: insights from a two process model. *Neuroscience Biobehavioral Review, 28*, 675–686.

Rudy, J. W. and O'Reilly, R. C. (2001). Conjunctive representations, the hippocampus, and contextual fear conditioning. *Cognitive Affective Behavioral Neuroscience, 1*, 66–82.

Schacter, D. L. (1989). On the relation between memory and consciousness: dissociable interactions and conscious experience. In H. L. Roediger, III, and F. I. M. Craik (Eds.), *Varieties of memory and consciousness: essays in honor of Endel Tulving* (pp. 355–389). Hillsdale, NJ: Erlbaum Associates.

Squire, L. R. (1992). Memory and the hippocampus: a synthesis from findings with rats, monkeys and humans. *Psychology Review, 99*, 195–231.

Squire, L. R. and Kandel, E. R. (1999). *Memory: from mind to molecules*. New York: W. H. Freeman and Company.

Squire, L. R. and Zola-Morgan, S. (1991). The medial temporal lobe memory system. *Science, 253*, 1380–1386.

Steele, R. J. and Morris, R. G. (1999). Delay-dependent impairment of a matching-to-place task with chronic and intrahippocampal infusion of the NMDA-antagonist D-AP5. *Hippocampus, 9*, 118–136.

Teyler, T. J. and DiScenna, P. (1986). The hippocampal memory indexing theory. *Behavioral Neuroscience, 100*, 147–152.

Teyler, T. J. and Rudy, J. W. (2007). The hippocampus indexing theory of episodic memory: updating the index. *Hippocampus, 17*, 1158–1169.

Van Hoesen, G. and Pandya, D. N. (1975). Some connections of the entorhinal (area 28) and perirhinal (area 35) cortices of the rhesus monkey. I. Temporal lobe afferents. *Brain Research, 95*, 1–24.

Zola-Morgan, S., Squire, L. R., and Amaral, D. G. (1986). Human amnesia and the medial temporal region: enduring memory impairment following a bilateral lesion limited to field CA1 of the hippocampus. *Journal of Neuroscience, 6*, 2950–2967.

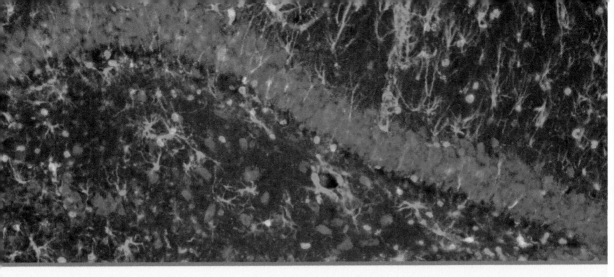

# 17 The MTH System: Episodic Memory, Semantic Memory, and Ribot's Law

Some memory researchers believe the episodic memory belongs to a broader, long-term memory category called declarative memory, which includes not only episodic memory but also **semantic memory**. Semantic memory is believed to support memory for facts and the ability to extract generalizations from multiple experiences. For example, past experiences allow us to answer questions like, is a violin a musical instrument or an automobile? We can also answer factual questions such as, what day was your mother born? Note that to answer these questions requires intentional retrieval and explicit recollection. Thus, semantic memory and episodic memory are similar in that we can intentionally retrieve information from them and in some sense declare we have the memory. The content of semantic memory, however, is not tied to the place or context where it was acquired. It is sometimes said to be context free. This means that we can know the facts about something without remembering when or where we learned them.

(A) Unitary view

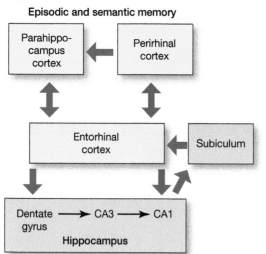

**Figure 17.1**
(A) The unitary view of the medial temporal hippocampal (MTH) system. Supporters of this view believe that the system is needed to support both episodic and semantic memory.
(B) The modular view. Supporters of this view believe that the entire system, including the hippocampal formation, is required for episodic memory but that semantic memory does not require the hippocampus.

(B) Modular view

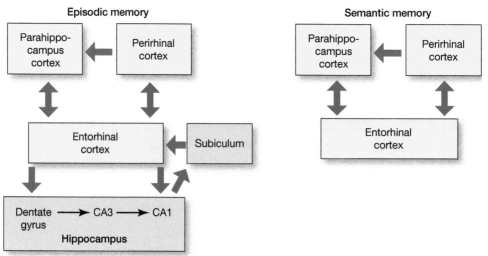

The inclusion of both episodic and semantic memory into a more general category—**declarative memory**—implies that they are supported by the same neural system. Indeed, some researchers (Manns, Hopkins, Reed et al., 2003; Squire and Zola, 1996, 1998; Squire and Zola-Morgan, 1991) have argued that the MTH (medial temporal hippocampal) system (which is composed of the parahippocampus cortex, perirhinal cortex, entorhinal cortex, hippocampus, and subiculum) provides support for both types of memory. This is called the

**unitary view** (Figure 17.1A). It suggests that damage to any component of this system will produce the same degree of impairment in tests of episodic and semantic memory.

Other researchers, however, believe that only episodic memory requires the entire MTH system. This is called the **modular view**. Researchers who support this view believe that (a) semantic memories can be acquired even when the hippocampus is selectively removed, and (b) while episodic and semantic memory may share some components of the MTH system, the overlap is not complete and episodic and semantic memory are not part of a single declarative memory system (Figure 17.1B). This position suggests that the MTH system has a modular organization—that is, components of the system are relatively dedicated to specific functions.

This chapter explores the implications of these views. First, some of the evidence that encouraged the modular view of episodic versus semantic memory is reviewed. The phenomenon of recognition memory (see Chapter 15) is revisited within the context of a modular MTH system. The remainder of the chapter revisits Ribot's Law (see Chapter 1) through the lens of contemporary theories—the standard model of systems consolidation and the multiple trace theory—and relating them to the MTH system.

## A Modular MTH System

The components of the MTH system are highly interconnected, so one might imagine that it would be difficult to assign particular functions to them. Nevertheless, several lines of research suggest that a modular view of the MTH system is useful. Two sources of evidence are considered. One comes from the discovery of individuals who grew up with a compromised hippocampus, while the other comes from studies of recognition memory.

### Growing Up without the Hippocampus

The modular view emerged when Faraneh Vargha-Khadem and her colleagues (Vargha-Khadem et al., 1997) reported the results for three patients with amnesia caused by relatively selective damage to the hippocampus sustained very early in life. Each of these patients developed pronounced memory impairments as a result of an anoxic–ischemic episode, that is, they experienced a reduction in oxygen supply (hypoxia) combined with reduced blood flow (ischemia) to the brain.

As revealed by quantitative magnetic resonance imaging, these patients had bilateral damage to approximately 50% of their hippocampus and very little damage to the surrounding cortices. The insult producing the pathology occurred at birth or when the patient was 4 or 9 years old. These children thus grew up without a functioning hippocampus.

These patients were 13, 16, and 19 years old when they received their first neuropsychological examination. The IQ of one of the patients was 109, which is well within the average range, whereas the IQs of the other two were in the low average range (82 and 86). Their memory for everyday experiences was so poor that none of them could be left alone for any extended period of time. Formal tests of their memory confirmed that they were profoundly amnesic.

Faraneh Vargha-Khadem

The surprising aspect of these patients is that even though they had no episodic memory, they all developed normal language and social skills. Moreover, they were all educated in mainstream schools. They learned to read and write and acquired new factual information at levels consistent with their verbal IQs. In fact, all three patients had fully normal scores on the vocabulary, information, and comprehension subtests of the Weschler Intelligence Scale. Given these findings, Vargha-Khadem and her colleagues concluded that there was a disproportionate sparing of semantic memory compared to episodic memory in these patients who suffered selective damage to their hippocampus early in life.

Endel Tulving

The strong implication of the Vargha-Khadem findings is that the MTH system is not a homogeneous system (Mishkin et al., 1997; Vargha-Khadem et al., 1997) and that semantic memory may be supported by components of the MTH system that remain after the hippocampus has been removed. This view is consistent with the position proposed by Endel Tulving, who was first to strongly argue for the distinction between episodic and semantic memory (Tulving, 1972). He argued that episodic memory should be considered as separate from declarative memory (Tulving and Markowitsch, 1998).

More recent reports have provided additional support for the modular view of the MTH system (Bindschaedler et al., 2010; Gadian et al., 2000). For example, Bindschaedler and his colleagues reported on patient V.J., who had severe atrophy of the hippocampus but otherwise had a normal perirhinal cortex. His hippocampus loss was believed to be the result of a neurological episode experienced a few hours after birth. When V.J. was 8 years old, his parents became concerned that he might have memory disturbances. This was confirmed and researchers have been testing him on a regular basis from that age to his teenage years. Based on this extensive testing, Bindschaedler and his colleagues concluded that V.J. had persistent impairments related to his episodic memory. Remarkably, at 8 years of age, his general world knowledge and understanding of the meaning of words was spared. Moreover, V.J.'s memory progression to teenage years was normal. Bindschaedler and his colleagues concluded that V.J.'s case adds support to the view that episodic and semantic memory are partially independent.

The organization of the MTH system may be modular but it should be appreciated that the absence of the hippocampus, which interacts with the other components of the MTH, will compromise acquisition of semantic information. For example, Holdstock et al. (2002) suggest that the hippocampal formation is critical for rapid acquisition of new semantic information, whereas semantic information via the adjacent cortices is acquired slowly over multiple trials.

## Recognition Memory and MTH Modularity

In Chapter 15 it was noted that Mishkin (1978) developed the delayed non-matching-to-sample task to determine the contribution of medial temporal brain regions to episodic memory. Research during his era, however, revealed that the hippocampus was not needed to recognize previously experienced objects. In discussing this outcome it was noted that this type of recognition memory task could be solved based on either a familiarity signal or by recollection-based processes. In the current context, the familiarity signal does not contain information about the context of the experience, whereas recollection-based recognition contains such information (see Sutherland and Rudy, 1989). Based on this analysis, damage to the hippocampus spared performance because the surrounding perirhinal cortex was able to support familiarity-based recognition.

If this conclusion is correct, then studies of recognition memory should provide additional support for a modular view of the MTH system. Additional evidence is provided by functional neuroimaging studies of both normal and brain-damaged patients. The general conclusion from this work is that recollection-based recognition is associated with the hippocampus, whereas familiarity is supported by perirhinal cortex (Aggleton et al., 2005; Vilberg and Rugg, 2007; Yonelinas et al., 2002). It is worth mentioning that V.J., who grew up without the hippocampus, displayed relatively spared recognition compared to recall and that "overall pattern of performance was consistent with the hypothesis that spared recognition was based on familiarity processes" (Bindschaedler et al., 2010, p. 941).

Research with rodents also supports the modular view. Rats with damage to the hippocampus recognize previously experienced objects. However, as described earlier in Figure 16.6, they cannot remember the context where an object was experienced (Mumby et al., 2002; Mumby et al., 2005). These results are consistent with the idea that the hippocampus is not required to support familiarity-based recognition but is required to place the recognized item into the surrounding context and thus provide an episodic quality to the memory.

Although there is strong support for the modular view, it is not universally accepted (see Manns, Hopkins, Reed et al., 2003; Manns, Hopkins, and Squire, 2003). Manns and his colleagues, for example, presented data from patients thought to have bilateral damage primarily to the hippocampal region and claimed that their ability to acquire factual knowledge was just as impaired as their memory for episodes. They suggested that the division of labor among the medial structures might not be absolute and that it may not be possible to map psychological categories like episodic and semantic memory precisely onto the hippocampal formation and its adjacent cortical regions because these regions are so interconnected. This is a difficult argument to reject, in part because when damage is inflicted on the hippocampus it is difficult to know the extent to which it spreads and causes damage to the surrounding cortices. Moreover, it is difficult to know exactly how to compare the extent to which semantic memory for facts is impaired relative to episodic memory.

## The MTH System and Ribot's Law

Episodic memories are supported by the medial temporal hippocampal system. What happens to these memories as they age? Should they stay or should they go? There is no simple answer to this question because in some cases the memory trace is likely lost, but in other cases the trace might endure or even be strengthened.

The episodic memory system is designed to automatically record the events of our daily lives. However, much of what is experienced is of no significance—such as what we had for breakfast, whom we encountered at the grocery store, or some conversation that we had about the weather. Recall of such events is decent for a day or so but it gets more difficult as more time passes. There is no great loss if such memories are forgotten because they are of no particular importance, and the case can be made that forgetting of such incidental episodes is the product of active cellular molecular events that de-potentiate synapses linking the neurons indexing these memories (Hardt et al., 2013; see Chapter 12).

Although it is likely that most everyday non-eventful memories established in the MTH system will be lost, Ribot's Law suggests that as memories age they become resistant to disruption (see Chapter 1). By itself this claim is not surprising because (a) the experience that produced the initial memory is more likely to be repeated and (b) older memories, compared to new memories, are more likely to have been recalled a few times. Both of these factors would increase the strength of the memory. However, in the modern era Ribot's Law has been nuanced to give an explicit role for the MTH system in protecting old memories from disruption.

This remainder of this section explores the debate surrounding theories of how the MTH system might contribute to Ribot's Law. First the standard model of systems consolidation is discussed, then the multiple trace theory is described. Evidence evaluating the theories is presented, including a large pool of data from both human and animal studies.

## The Standard Model of Systems Consolidation

David Marr (1971), a pioneer in the development of theory about the role of the hippocampus in memory, laid the groundwork for the line of thinking that gives an explicit role for the MTH system in protecting old memories from disruption. Relatively speaking, the neocortex is quite large and the hippocampal formation is quite small. So Marr suggested that although the hippocampus can rapidly acquire information, it serves only as a *temporary* memory store. Memories are permanently stored in the much larger neocortex. However, for a limited time period the hippocampus plays an important role in establishing the permanent neocortical memory trace. Once the memory trace in the neocortex is consolidated, the hippocampus is no longer needed to retrieve the memory. By temporary Marr meant something on the order of a few days.

When the memory impairments associated with H.M. were first reported it was believed that his retrograde amnesia was temporarily graded—meaning that it was intact except for the 2 to 3 years just prior to the surgical removal of his medial temporal lobe. Based largely on this observation, Larry Squire, Neal Cohen, and Lynn Nadel (1984) proposed that Ribot's Law could be related to the MTH system and thus brought Marr's ideas firmly into the modern literature.

Their position is now called the **standard model of systems consolidation**. They proposed that experience initially lays down a memory trace that depends, for both storage and retrieval, on interactions between the neocortical areas and the MTH system, described in Figure 17.2. There are two other critical assumptions associated with this position (Squire et al., 1984, p. 202).

First, the critical interaction between the MTH system and other cortical sites is required for only a limited time after learning. When a memory is originally formed, the MTH system maintains its coherence—it holds together the components of the trace that are distributed over various regions of the brain. Processes intrinsic to the neocortical storage sites are responsible for consolidating the memory in the brain regions outside of the MTH system. During this period the integrity of the MTH system is also necessary to retrieve

New memory trace

Old memory trace

Neocortex

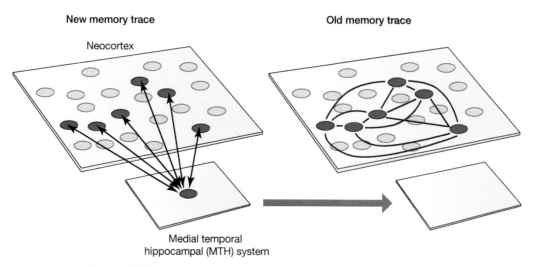

Medial temporal
hippocampal (MTH) system

**Figure 17.2**
A schematic representation of the standard model of systems consolidation. Initially the memory trace consists of weakly connected neocortical representations of the features (purple circles) of the experience held together by their temporary connections with the medial temporal hippocampal (MTH) system. New memories require the MTH system for retrieval. As the memory ages, intrinsic processes result in the consolidation or strengthening of the connections among the neocortical representations. Because of the strengthened connections the memory can now be retrieved without the hippocampus.

the memory. Once this process is sufficiently complete, however, the MTH system is no longer needed for retrieval of that memory. Squire and his colleagues never specified what constitutes a limited amount of time. However, based on their discussion of H.M. and other literature, it appears that they assumed consolidation requires about 3 years.

Second, the MTH system–neocortical interaction is needed only to consolidate declarative memory (episodic and semantic memories). It is not involved in what is sometimes called **procedural memory**—memories that support learned skills such as bike riding or skiing.

In summary, the standard model explains Ribot's Law by assuming that

- disruptive events primarily impact the MTH system;

- new memories require the hippocampus for ongoing systems consolidation and retrieval; and

- old memories are more resistant to disruption than new memories because they have been consolidated in the neocortex and liberated from the MTH system.

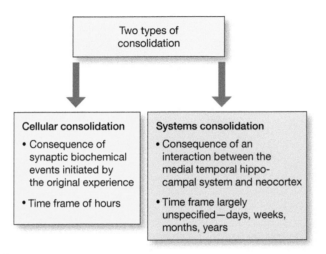

**Figure 17.3**
Two types of processes are thought to contribute to the consolidation of long-term stability of memories.

It should be noted that the concept of **systems consolidation** is quite different from the concept of **cellular consolidation**. Cellular consolidation refers to the biochemical and molecular events that take place immediately following the behavioral experience that initially forms the memory trace. Several hours may be required for these processes, which were discussed extensively in previous chapters, to consolidate the trace. Systems consolidation refers to changes in the strength of the memory trace brought about by interactions between brain regions (the MTH system and neocortex) that take place after the memory is initially established. Systems consolidation begins after the trace is initially stored and operates over a much longer time frame—days, months, or years (Figure 17.3).

Two other points about systems consolidation need to be considered. First, there is no mention of a role for recall or repetition with this framework. So experience lays down the trace and for months thereafter intrinsic processes operate to consolidate the memory in the cortex, while the hippocampus in some way maintains the coherence of the neural patterns in the cortex that represent the memory. Thus, in principle this intrinsic activity requires no additional input from experience (recall or repetition) to carry out its function. Second, the standard model assumes that this process consolidates declarative memories (both episodic and semantic). The previous discussion of the MTH led to the conclusion that semantic and episodic memories may not belong to the same broad category (declarative memory). This will prove to be important in considering an evaluation of the standard model.

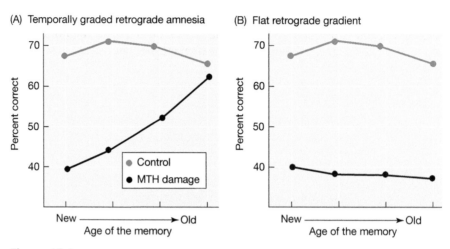

**Figure 17.4**

These graphs illustrate patterns of results that would either support or be evidence against the standard model of systems consolidation. (A) This pattern would support the model because it shows that damage to the hippocampus results in temporally graded retrograde amnesia. (B) This pattern would be evidence against the standard model because it shows that damage to the hippocampus produces a flat retrograde amnesia.

## Challenges to the Standard Model

The standard model makes only one critical prediction: damage to the hippocampal formation will spare old episodic and semantic memories, but new episodic and semantic memories will be lost. Experimental results that reveal that damage to the MTH system produces a **temporally graded retrograde amnesia** would support this theoretical model (Figure 17.4A). However, if damage to the MTH system produces a flat gradient (Figure 17.4B), then the theory would be wrong.

The primary data for evaluating the standard model come from case studies of individuals who are known to have damage to regions in the medial temporal lobes. For many years, H.M. was the only patient available with known bilateral damage to the medial temporal lobes. Over the years, however, a number of patients with damage to the MTH system have been identified and evaluated. When Lynn Nadel and Morris Moscovitch (1997) reviewed this literature, they reached a surprising conclusion: the evidence does not support the standard model. They concluded that when damage to the MTH system is complete there is no sparing of either new or remote episodic memories. Spared remote episodic memories are found only when damage to the MTH system is incomplete. Thus, they asserted that the MTH system continues to be critical to retrieval throughout the life of an episodic memory. Their conclusion regarding the fate of old semantic memories was less clear. They suggested that retrograde damage for general semantic memories is more variable but less severe.

The relevant literature reviewed by Nadel and Moscovitch is complex and controversial; not everyone agrees with their conclusion. For example, some researchers argue that the loss of remote memories reflects the fact that the brain injury extends beyond the MTH system into neocortical areas that would be the storage sites of remote memories (Bayley et al., 2003; Bayley et al., 2005; Reed and Squire, 1998). Thus, it is useful to consider two relevant case studies as well as to reconsider the case of H.M.

Lisa Cipolotti and her colleagues (2001) describe the case of V.C., who became profoundly amnesic at the age of 67. His performance on general intelligence tests and other measures of cognitive function, however, remained intact. Careful assessment of his brain indicated that there was significant loss of volume over the entire rostral–caudal length of the hippocampus. However, critical surrounding cortical regions—the entorhinal cortex and para-hippocampus—were normal, as were the adjacent temporal lobes. Thus, V.C.'s damage was believed to be restricted primarily to the hippocampus.

If the standard model is correct, then this patient should have displayed a temporally graded retrograde amnesia with remote memories spared. V.C.'s episodic memory was tested in a variety of ways. His retrograde amnesia was extensive and was equally evident for both old and new memories (Figure 17.5). Given that the researchers

Morris Moscovitch

Lynn Nadel

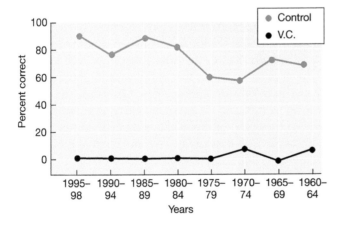

**Figure 17.5**
This figure illustrates V.C.'s flat retrograde amnesia for recall of famous public events. This memory test was conducted in 1998. Control subjects were chosen to match V.C.'s age and educational level.

correctly identified the extent of V.C.'s brain damage, then V.C.'s data should be considered as strong evidence *against* the standard model.

Larry Squire and his colleagues (Stefanacci et al., 2000) described the case of patient E.P. He became amnesic at the age of 70 when viral encephalitis destroyed the medial temporal lobes of his brain. E.P.'s temporal lobe damage was more severe than that of V.C. In addition to significant damage to the hippocampal formation, there was damage to the entorhinal and perirhinal cortices and the rostral parahippocampal cortex.

Like V.C., patient E.P.'s retrograde amnesia was also extensive. On tests of information about public events and famous faces, E.P. had no recall regardless of the age of the memory. He also had almost complete amnesia for autobiographical events that extended over the immediate 20-year period before the onset of the disease. The remarkable fact was that his memory for some personal childhood experiences was as good as age-matched controls. He also evidenced remarkable sparing of his spatial memory for the organization of his childhood neighborhood.

There is no simple explanation for why patient E.P., who had more damage to the medial lobes than patient V.C., displayed pockets of remote memory for adolescent and childhood personal experiences. However, even where there was some sparing of remote memories it was only for events that had been experienced more than 20 years prior to when his medial temporal lobes were damaged. So, unless one is willing to accept an unusual definition of what constitutes a temporary memory storage system, E.P.'s extraordinary memory for childhood and adolescent experiences offers no support for the idea that the MTH system is only temporarily needed for retrieval.

Suzanne Corkin (2002) has known and worked with H.M. since she was a graduate student in 1962. She and her colleagues (Steinvorth et al., 2005) more recently re-evaluated H.M. to determine the extent of his retrograde amnesia. They concluded that H.M.'s episodic memory was severely impaired and that there was no sparing of remote memories. Moreover, his semantic memory was very much in the range of control subjects matched for age, IQ, and level of education. It is interesting that H.M.'s episodic memory impairment was much more severe than was initially believed (Corkin, 1984; Milner et al., 1968). Corkin and her colleagues (Steinvorth et al., 2005) believe that the extent of H.M.'s retrograde amnesia was previously underestimated because the early evaluators did not fully appreciate how autobiographical episodic memories differ from semantic memories and thus did not pursue the magnitude of H.M.'s episodic memory impairment.

Based on the new clinical data a number of contemporary researchers believe that damage to the MTH system or perhaps even just to the hippocampal formation produces a profound retrograde

Suzanne Corkin

amnesia for both new and old episodic memories. If this is true, then the human clinical literature provides little or no support for the standard model of systems consolidation and its view that for the retrieval of episodic memories the MTH system is needed only for a limited time. If it were true that old semantic memories are spared, this would provide additional support for the modular view of the MTH system.

## Multiple Trace Theory

Faced with their conclusion that even remote episodic memories require the hippocampal formation for retrieval, Nadel and Moscovitch (1997) proposed a new theory called **multiple trace theory** (Figure 17.6) to explain why partial damage to the hippocampus could spare old remote episodic memories. They assume that:

- regardless of its age, an episodic memory always requires the hippocampus for retrieval;

- the initial episodic memory trace consists of the patterns of neocortical activity bound together by neurons in the hippocampal formation that serve as an index (as described in Chapter 16);

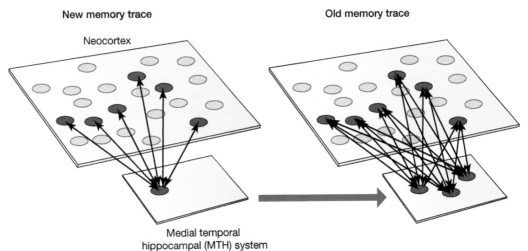

**Figure 17.6**

The assumptions of the multiple trace theory of systems consolidation. Old memories still depend on the hippocampus but are more resistant to disruption because they have had more opportunity to be reactivated than new memories, and each reactivation generates another index in the hippocampus. Because these copies are distributed, the memory can survive partial but not complete damage to the hippocampus and will be more resistant to other insults such as a brain concussion.

- each time the memory trace is reactivated, a new index is established to the original neocortical pattern of activity and to other, new patterns of activity that are present, which results in multiple traces that share information with the original trace; and

- older memories are reactivated more often than newer memories and thus have more copies or indices distributed throughout the hippocampus than do new memories.

It is important to note that Nadel and Moscovitch do not place a special burden on intrinsic processes to provide support for old episodic memories but instead emphasize reactivation processes. In the end, it is the redundancy of the trace that protects an old episodic memory from disruption. Some of the fidelity of the memory will be lost because the copies are not perfect, but the gist of the experience can still be recalled. Thus, old episodic memories would be more likely to survive some damage to the hippocampus and be more resistant to other disruptive events such as ECS therapy or a brain concussion.

## Other Evidence Relevant to the Debate

The primary evidence for evaluating theories of how the MTH system might contribute to Ribot's Law comes from people with damage to this system. However, the complexities associated with this literature make it unlikely that data from people with brain damage can resolve the fundamental theoretical debate between the standard model and the multiple trace theory of systems consolidation—whether or not remote memories become independent of the hippocampus. There are, however, other sources of evidence that are potentially relevant to this debate. One source comes from studies that image the brain while people are retrieving new and old episodic memories. Another source comes from studies in which the hippocampus of laboratory animals is damaged at different times following the acquisition of a new memory.

HUMAN BRAIN IMAGING   Modern researchers are now able to image levels of activity in the brain while a person is engaged in cognitive activities such as retrieving memories. The most widely used method is called **functional magnetic resonance imaging (fMRI)**, illustrated in Figure 17.7. In the context of systems consolidation, this methodology allows researchers to study patterns of brain activity produced when normal subjects are asked to retrieve newly acquired memories compared to when they are asked to retrieve old memories.

If retrieval of old memories becomes independent of the MTH system, as proposed by the standard model, then one would expect much less activity

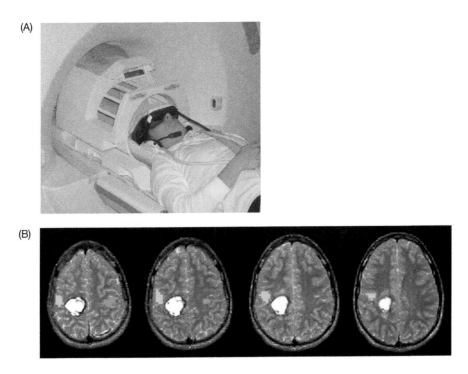

**Figure 17.7**
(A) In functional magnetic resonance imaging (fMRI) the participant's head is placed in the center of a large magnet. A radiofrequency antenna coil is placed around the head to excite and record the magnetic resonance signal of hydrogen atoms. Stimuli can be presented to the subject using virtual reality video goggles and stereo headphones. fMRI is based on the fact that hemoglobin in the iron-containing, oxygen-transport metalloprotein in the red blood cells slightly distorts the magnetic resonance properties of hydrogen nuclei in the vicinity and the amount of magnetic distortion changes, depending on whether the hemoglobin has oxygen bound to it. When a brain area is activated by a specific task, it begins to use more oxygen and within seconds the brain microvasculature responds by increasing the flow of oxygen-rich blood to the active area. These changes in the concentration of oxygen and blood flow lead to what is called a blood-oxygenation level-dependent (BOLD) signal—changes in the magnetic resonance signal. (B) fMRI activity during a hand-motion task. Left hand activity is shown in yellow and right hand activity is shown in green. (Photo and images from Purves et al., 2012.)

in the MTH system when the subject is asked to retrieve an old memory than when asked to retrieve a new memory. In contrast, the multiple trace theory predicts either no difference or that, if anything, more activity in the hippocampus will be observed when the subject is asked to retrieve old memories

**Figure 17.8**

This figure illustrates the predictions that the standard model (SM) and multiple trace theory (MTT) of systems consolidation make about activation in the medial temporal hippocampal (MTH) system. Multiple trace theory predicts that retrieval of both new and old memories should activate the MTH system. The standard model predicts that the retrieval of only new memories should activate the system.

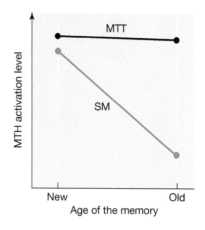

than when asked to retrieve new memories (Figure 17.8). This might be expected because the core memory trace of an old memory will have more copies represented in the hippocampus.

Several imaging studies have addressed the theoretical predictions of the standard model and multiple trace theory of systems consolidation. A study by Rekkas and Constable (2005) evaluated these predictions by asking the participants (21-year-old college students) questions designed to facilitate the retrieval of actual episodes from their past. For example, to probe their recall of remote memories they were asked questions such as: Can you recall the schoolyard of your elementary school? or Can you recall a specific high school English teacher? The mean age of the remote memories being queried was 8 years. Recall of remote memories was compared to recent memories established about 2.5 days before the experiment, when the participants were given a tour of the investigator's laboratory. To facilitate recall of the recent episodes, they were asked questions such as: Can you recall the male researcher who came into the interview room? or Can you recall being shown anything specific in the lab? During the period following such questions, images of the participants' brains were captured. Rekkas and Constable reported that retrieving remote memories produced significantly more activation of the hippocampus proper than retrieving the recently acquired memories. This result provides no support for the standard model but is consistent with multiple trace theory.

Steinvorth et al. (2006) used another methodology to determine if the retrieval of new and old memories differentially depends on the MTH system. They developed sentences individually tailored to each participant that asked about salient aspects of specific events that had occurred in their personal past, such as: "Last Thanksgiving, did Jonathan burn the turkey?" (a recent memory probe) or "At a birthday party, who spilled wine on your pants?" (a remote memory probe). They reported that the retrieval of recent and remote memories activated the same constellation of brain regions and that the MTH system was equally activated when either type of memory was retrieved. These data provide support for multiple trace theory but are inconsistent with the prediction of the standard model because the MTH system was equally activated whether new or old memories were being retrieved.

Frédéric Bernard and his colleagues (2004) used an entirely different memory probe—recognition of remote and recent famous faces—to address the issue. They found that recognition of recent and old famous faces equally activated the hippocampus. Again, this report provides no support for the standard model (but see Haist et al., 2001, for a somewhat similar study that claimed support for the standard model).

Based on this brief overview, fMRI studies appear to support multiple trace theory and provide almost no evidence for the standard model. However, as Cabeza and St. Jacques (2007) noted, there is an important caveat that applies to these studies that may limit their theoretical importance. Specifically, as we know, the indexing theory of the hippocampus (which is at the core of the multiple trace theory) assumes that the MTH system is capturing a continuous record of the patterns of neural activity in the neocortex. Researchers using imaging techniques to evaluate theories of systems consolidation assume that activity in the MTH system is produced by the retrieval cues activating the neurons in that region that represent the index. However, this may not be the case. Suppose, as the standard model assumes, that an old memory is retrieved directly from the neocortical sites. Once these sites are activated they will project to the MTH system to cause activation there. If this happens, then the activity in the MTH system will not reflect retrieval of the memory through activating the existing index but instead will reflect the retrieval experience laying down a new copy of the trace—generating a new index. In fact, multiple trace theory predicts this should happen. In summary, fMRI studies appear to support multiple trace theory. However, given the above caveat, one should be cautious in concluding that this support is unequivocal.

ANIMAL STUDIES   There are many problems associated with testing people who have damage to the medial temporal lobes produced by such occurrences as strokes or encephalitis. Two main problems are that (1) the brain damage extends beyond the regions of interest and (2) there is no way to completely control for the initial strength of the memory. For these reasons researchers have used laboratory animals, primarily rodents, to determine the contribution the hippocampus makes to new and old memories. This strategy has the obvious advantage that one can (a) provide animals with a known behavioral experience, (b) vary the exact time between the experience and the occurrence of the brain damage, and (c) vary the extent of the brain damage. One can also hold constant the length of time between when the brain is damaged and when the animals are tested.

Although there is some debate about the modularity of the MTH system, every one agrees that the *hippocampal component is critical for the initial acquisition and retrieval of episodic memories.* As noted, there is an inherent difficulty in studying episodic memory in rodents and nonhuman primates—for the simple reason that they cannot directly tell the experimenter about their past experiences. They cannot tell us what they had for lunch. Nevertheless, their hippocampal systems do support the acquisition of context representations, pattern completion, and pattern separation. So, contextual fear conditioning provides the most useful paradigm to investigate the role of the hippocampus in new and old memories.

Some initial reports suggested that limited damage to the hippocampus spares old contextual fear memories while disrupting retrieval of new memories (for example, Kim and Fanselow, 1992). However, more systematic explorations of this paradigm have revealed that both partial and complete damage to the hippocampus equally disrupt old and new contextual fear memories. For example, Robert Sutherland and his colleagues (Lehmann et al., 2007) have compared the effects of partial and complete lesions of the hippocampus on the rat's contextual fear memory. They damaged the hippocampus either 1 week, 3 months, or 6 months following the conditioning session. Partial damage to the hippocampus produced less amnesia than large lesions, but the age of the memory at the time of the lesion did not matter (Figure 17.9). These results obviously provide no support for the standard model. They also provide no support for multiple trace theory because remote memories were not spared in rats with partial damage to the hippocampus. More recently Broadbent and Clark (2013) explored a range of parameters, including the type of lesion, extent of the damage to the hippocampus, and number of conditioning trials. No matter what the condition, old contextual fear memories were not protected from disruption by hippocampal damage. They concluded that the preponderance of currently available evidence indicates that context fear memory remains hippocampus-dependent indefinitely.

Learning the spatial locations of the type required by the place-learning version of the Morris water-escape task requires that animals acquire what is sometimes called a cognitive map (O'Keefe and Nadel, 1978)—a representation that links together the various features of the environment into a coherent framework which can then be used to guide behavior. This representation is similar to that formed in a contextual-fear conditioning experiment. Moreover, animals with damage to the hippocampus cannot learn the location of a hidden platform. Thus, researchers have also asked if old memories for place location are protected from damage to the

Robert Sutherland

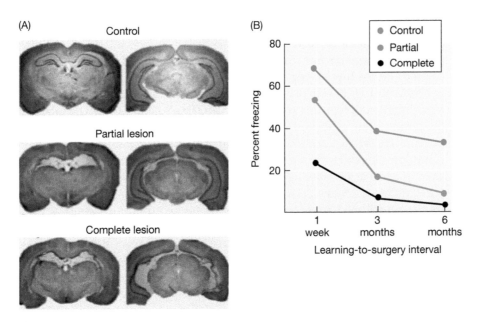

**Figure 17.9**
(A) These images illustrate the extent of the damage to the hippocampus. (Images courtesy of Robert Sutherland.) (B) These data show that over the 6-month retention interval, control rats showed evidence of forgetting. Note, however, that there was no evidence that the 3-month and 6-month-old memories were protected from damage to the hippocampus.

hippocampus. A variety of tasks have been used to address this question and in every case the answer is no—old memories are just as disrupted by damage to the hippocampus as new memories (Clark et al., 2005a,b; Martin et al., 2005; Sutherland et al., 2001).

The surgical removal of a brain region is often used to gain insight into the role of that structure in memory. However, interpretation of the data is complicated. For example, it is possible that a resulting impairment is due to unintended damage to other nearby regions. Optogenetics, however, provides a much more precise means of identifying the contribution of specific sets of neurons to a particular behavioral outcome and eliminates many issues that are associated with lesions or other methodologies (see Chapter 9). So it has been used to address the contribution of hippocampal neurons to the retrieval of new and old contextual fear memories.

To do this, Goshen et al. (2011) used a viral vector system to deliver *eNpHR3.1*, a gene for inhibitory channels, to CA1 neurons, the output region of the hippocampus. When activated by light, neurons expressing these channels are inhibited. To the researchers' surprise, inhibiting these neurons during the retrieval test equally impaired the expression of both new (1-day old) and old (4 to 12 weeks old) contextual fear memories. This experiment provides strong support for the idea that the contextual fear memory trace depends on the hippocampus for the life of the memory.

Goshen et al. (2011) provided an additional observation. In the initial experiments the neurons were inactivated only during the few minutes of the retrieval test. In a subsequent experiment, however, they inhibited these neurons for 30 minutes prior to and during the retrieval test. Under these conditions, the old memory was retrieved. This result indicates that it is possible to retrieve a contextual fear memory when a small set of CA1 neurons are inhibited. However, it is difficult to know what if any implications these results have for systems consolidation. This is because these researchers did not examine the effect of this long-lasting inhibition on retrieval of a new fear memory. So it is very possible this same treatment would also allow the retrieval of a new memory.

Although contextual fear memories normally depend on the hippocampus, it is clear that under some conditions a contextual fear memory can be established that does not depend on the hippocampus for retrieval. This happens when animals receive several sessions of context–shock pairing, distributed over several days. Under these conditions even new contextual fear memories survive post-training damage to the hippocampus (Lehmann et al., 2009; Wang et al., 2009). This finding reinforces an important point: the hippocampus is required to rapidly form episodic memories. However, other brain regions also can capture representations of experience when the experience is often repeated or recalled.

The hippocampal system learns rapidly but other systems learn more slowly. This principle has been recognized by several theorists (McClelland et al., 1995; O'Reilly and Rudy, 2001; Sherry and Schachter, 1987) and is sometimes called the **complementary memory systems** view. This view assumes that different memory systems evolved to serve different and sometimes incompatible functions. In this context, appropriate behavioral adaptations require one memory system that can rapidly acquire information about single episodes and another system that gradually collects information about repeated experience to build representations of stable features of the environment. The complementary memory systems framework provides a natural way of understanding how memories can become independent of the MTH.

## Ribot's Law Revisited: Summary

Theories of the MTH system assume that this region supports episodic memory by constructing a representation of the context in which events are stored. Animal models have provided overwhelming evidence for this assumption.

So based on the standard model of systems consolidation, one would predict that retrieval of old contextual memories should become independent of the hippocampus. Both lesion and optogenetic studies, however, indicate that old contextual fear memories are just as dependent on the hippocampus as new ones. Thus, this animal literature is consistent with the human literature, indicating that episodic memories always require the hippocampus. The hippocampus is required to retrieve new and old episodic memories. Nevertheless, neocortical regions can support memories for experiences that might also be captured by the hippocampal system. Such cortical representations may be the result of repeated experiences or repeated recall and can be retrieved without a functioning hippocampus, regardless of their age. This conclusion suggests that the age of a memory has limited value in explaining the resistance of a memory trace to disruption. Other variables such as repetition and frequency of reactivation or recall of the memory, which are more likely to be the case for old memories, are probably the important variables.

## Summary

This chapter explored the relationship between the medial temporal hippocampal neural system and episodic and semantic memories. Studies of patients with selective hippocampus pathology that developed at a young age suggest that episodic memories require the entire MTH system, but semantic memories can be acquired when the hippocampal formation is removed. Such findings support the idea that the organization of the MTH system is modular. The modular view is also supported by studies that show that recollection-based recognition memory requires the entire MTH system but familiarity-based recognition does not require the hippocampus.

This chapter also explored the contribution of the MTH system to the fate of old memories. A primary role of the MTH system is to provide support for episodic memories—the everyday events that make up our lives. Much of daily life is uneventful and need not be remembered for any appreciable period of time. In contrast to forgetting that occurs with time, Ribot proposed that memories become more resistant to disruption as they age. This standard model of systems consolidation proposed that the MTH system was fundamental to Ribot's Law. Old memories are resistant to disruption because they have become consolidated in the neocortical regions that are more immune to disrupting influences. This idea has proven controversial and unsupported by a large body of human clinical data and animal research focused on contextual fear conditioning and spatial learning. Memories can become independent of the MTH system, but their age per se may not be a major variable determining their resistance to disruption.

# References

Aggleton, J. P., Vann, S. D., Denby, C., Dix, S., Mayes, A. R., Roberts, N., and Yonelinas, A. P. (2005). Sparing of the familiarity component of recognition memory in a patient with hippocampal pathology. *Neuropsychologia, 43*, 1810–1843.

Bayley, P. J., Gold, J. J., Hopkins, R. O., and Squire, L. R. (2005). The neuroanatomy of remote memory. *Neuron, 46*, 799–810.

Bayley, P. J., Hopkins, R. O., and Squire, L. R. (2003). Successful recollection of remote autobiographical memories by amnesic patients with medial temporal lobe lesions. *Neuron, 38*, 135–144.

Bernard, F. A., Bullmore, E. T., Graham, K. S., Thompson, S. A., Hodges, J. R., and Fletcher, P. C. (2004). The hippocampal region is involved in successful recognition of both remote and recent famous faces. *NeuroImage, 22*, 1704–1714.

Bindschaedler, C., Peter-Favre, C., Maeder, P., Hirsbrunner, T., and Clarke, S. (2010). Growing up with bilateral hippocampal atrophy: from childhood to teenage. *Cortex, 47*, 931.

Broadbent, N. J. and Clark, R. E. (2013). Remote context fear conditioning remains hippocampus-dependent irrespective of training protocol, training–surgery interval, lesion size, and lesion method. *Neurobiology of Learning and Memory*. Available online at http://dx.doi.org/10.1016/j.nlm.2013.08.008.

Cabeza, R. and St. Jacques, P. (2007). Functional neuroimaging of autobiographical memory. *Trends in Cognitive Science, 11*, 219–227.

Cipolotti, L., Shallice, T., Chan, D., Fox, N., Scahill, R., Harrison, G., Stevens, J., and Rudge, P. (2001) Long-term retrograde amnesia: the crucial role of the hippocampus. *Neuropsychologia, 39*, 151–172.

Clark, R. E., Broadbent, N. J., and Squire L. R. (2005a). Hippocampus and remote spatial memory in rats. *Hippocampus, 15*, 260–272.

Clark, R. E., Broadbent, N. J, and Squire, L. R. (2005b). Impaired remote spatial memory after hippocampal lesions despite extensive training beginning early in life. *Hippocampus, 15*, 340–346.

Corkin, S. (1984). Lasting consequences of bilateral medial temporal lobectomy: clinical course and experimental findings in H.M. *Seminars in Neurology, 4*, 249–259.

Corkin, S. (2002). What's new with the amnesic patient H.M.? *Nature Reviews Neuroscience, 2*, 153–160.

Gadian, D. G., Aicardi, J., Watkins, K. E., Porter, D. A., Mishkin, M., and Vargha-Khadem, F. (2000). Developmental amnesia associated with early hypoxic-ischaemic injury. *Brain, 123*, 499–507.

Goshen, I., Brodsky, M., Prakash, R., Wallace, J., Gradinaru, V., Ramakrishnan, C., and Deisseroth, K. (2011). Dynamics of retrieval strategies for remote memories. *Cell, 147*, 678–689.

Haist, F., Gore, J. B., and Mao, H. (2001). Consolidation of human memory over decades revealed by functional magnetic resonance imaging. *Nature Neuroscience, 4*, 1139–1145.

Hardt, O., Nader, K., and Nadel, L. (2013). Decay happens: the role of active forgetting in memory. *Trends in Cognitive Neuroscience, 17*, 111–120.

Holdstock, J. S., Mayes, A. R., Isaac, C. L., Gong, Q., and Roberts, N. (2002). Differential involvement of the hippocampus and temporal lobes cortices in rapid and slow learning of new semantic information. *Neuropsychologia, 40*, 748–768.

Kim, J. J. and Fanselow, M. S. (1992). Modality-specific retrograde amnesia of fear. *Science, 256*, 675–677.

Lehmann, H., Lacanilao, S., and Sutherland, R. J. (2007). Complete or partial hippocampal damage produces equivalent retrograde amnesia for remote contextual fear memories. *European Journal of Neuroscience, 25*, 1278–1286.

Lehmann, H., Sparks, F. T., Spanswick, S. C., Hadikin, C., McDonald, R. J., and Sutherland, R. J. (2009). Making context memories independent of the hippocampus. *Learning and Memory, 16*, 417–420.

Manns, J. R., Hopkins, R. O., Reed, J. M., Kitchener, E. G., and Squire, L. R. (2003). Recognition memory and the human hippocampus. *Neuron, 37*, 171–180.

Manns, J. R., Hopkins, R. O., and Squire, L. R. (2003). Semantic memory and the human hippocampus. *Neuron, 38*, 127–133.

Marr, D. (1971). Simple memory: a theory for archicortex. *Philosophical Transactions of the Royal Society of London, Series B, 262*, 23–81.

Martin, S. J., de Hoz, L., and Morris, R. G. (2005). Retrograde amnesia: neither partial nor complete hippocampal lesions in rats result in preferential sparing of remote spatial memory, even after reminding. *Neuropsychologia, 43*, 609–624.

McClelland, J. L., McNaughton, B. L., and O'Reilly, R. C. (1995). Why there are complementary learning systems in the hippocampus and neocortex: insights from the successes and failures of connectionist models of learning and memory. *Psychological Review, 102*, 419–457.

Milner, B., Corkin, S., and Teuber, H. L. (1968). Further analysis of the hippocampal amnesic syndrome: 14-year follow-up study of H.M. *Neuropsychologia, 6*, 215–234.

Mishkin, M. (1978). Memory in monkeys severely impaired by combined but not by separate removal of amygdala and hippocampus. *Nature, 273*, 297–298.

Mishkin, M., Suzuki, W. A., Gadian, D. G., and Vargha-Khadem, F. (1997). Hierarchical organization of cognitive memory. *Philosophical Transactions of the Royal Society of London Series B, 352*, 1461–1467.

Mumby, D. G., Gaskin, S., Glenn, M. J., Schramek, T. E., and Lehmann, H. (2002). Hippocampal damage and exploratory preferences in rats: memory for objects, places, and contexts. *Learning and Memory, 9*, 49–57.

Mumby, D. G., Tremblay, A., Lecluse, V., and Lehmann, H. (2005). Hippocampal damage and anterograde object-recognition in rats after long retention intervals. *Hippocampus, 15*, 1050–1056.

Nadel, L. and Moscovitch, M. (1997). Memory consolidation, retrograde amnesia and the hippocampal complex. *Current Opinion in Neurobiology, 7*, 217–227.

O'Keefe, J. and Nadel, L. (1978). *The hippocampus as a cognitive map*. Oxford: Clarendon Press.

O'Reilly, R. C. and Rudy, J. W. (2001). Conjunctive representations in learning and memory: principles of cortical and hippocampal function. *Psychological Review, 108*, 311–345.

Purves, D., Augustine, G. J., Fitzpatrick, D., Hall, W. C., LaMantia, A. S., McNamara, J. O., and White, L. E. (2012). *Neuroscience, Fifth Edition*. Sunderland, MA: Sinauer Associates, Inc.

Reed , J. M. and Squire, L. R. (1998). Retrograde amnesia for facts and events: findings from four new cases. *Journal of Neuroscience, 18*, 3943–3954.

Rekkas, P. V. and Constable, R. T. (2005). Evidence that autobiographic memory retrieval does not become independent of the hippocampus: an fMRI study contrasting very recent with remote events. *Journal of Cognitive Neuroscience, 17*, 1950–1961.

Sherry, D. F. and Schacter, D. L. (1987). The evolution of multiple memory systems. *Psychological Review, 94*, 439–454.

Squire, L. R., Cohen, N. J., and Nadel, L. (1984). The medial temporal region and memory consolidation: a new hypothesis. In H. Weingartner and E. Parker (Eds.), *Memory consolidation* (pp. 185–210). Hillsdale, NJ: Erlbaum and Associates.

Squire, L. R. and Zola, S. M. (1996). Structure and function of declarative and non-declarative memory systems. *Proceedings of the National Academy of Sciences USA, 93*, 13515–13522.

Squire, L. R. and Zola, S. M. (1998). Episodic memory, semantic memory, and amnesia. *Hippocampus, 8*, 205–211.

Squire, L. R. and Zola-Morgan, S. (1991). The medial temporal lobe memory system. *Science, 253*, 1380–1386.

Stefanacci, L., Buffalo, E. A., Schmolck, H., and Squire, L. R. (2000). Profound amnesia after damage to the medial temporal lobe: a neuroanatomical and neuropsychological profile of patient E.P. *Journal of Neuroscience, 20*, 7024–7036.

Steinvorth, S., Corkin, S., and Halgren, E. (2006). Ecphory of autobiographical memories: an fMRI study of recent and remote memory retrieval. *NeuroImage, 30*, 285–298.

Steinvorth, S., Levine, B., and Corkin, S. (2005). Medial temporal lobe structures are needed to re-experience remote autobiographical memories: evidence from H.M. and W.R. *Neuropsychologia, 43*, 479–496.

Sutherland, R. J. and Rudy, J. W. (1989). Configural association theory: the role of the hippocampus in learning, memory, and amnesia. *Psychobiology, 17*, 129–144.

Sutherland, R. J., Weisend, M. P., Mumby, D., Astur, R. S., Hanlon, F. M., Koerner, A., Thomas, M. J., Wu, Y., Moses, S. N., and Cole, C. (2001). Retrograde amnesia after hippocampal damage: recent vs. remote memories in two tasks. *Hippocampus, 11*, 27–42.

Tulving, E. (1972). Episodic and semantic memory. In E. Tulving and W. Donaldson (Eds.), *Organization of memory*. New York: Academic Press.

Tulving, E. and Markowitsch, H. J. (1998). Episodic and declarative memory: role of the hippocampus. *Hippocampus, 8*, 198–204.

Vargha-Khadem, F., Gadian, D. G., Watkins, K. E., Connelly, A., Van Paesschen, W., and Mishkin, M. (1997). Differential effects of early hippocampal pathology on episodic and semantic memory. *Science*, *277*, 376–380.

Vilberg, K. L. and Rugg, M. D. (2007). Dissociation of the neural correlates of recognition memory according to familiarity, recollection, and amount of recollected information. *Neuropsychologia*, *45*, 2216–2225.

Wang, S. H., Teixeira, C. M., Wheeler, A. L., Frankland, P. W. (2009). The precision of remote context memories does not require the hippocampus. *Nature Neuroscience*, *12*, 253–255.

Yonelinas, A. P., Kroll, N. E. A., Quamme, J. R., Lazzara, M. M., Sauve, M. J., and Widaman, K. F. (2002). Effects of extensive temporal lobe damage or mild hypoxia on recollection and familiarity. *Nature Neuroscience*, *5*, 1236–1241.

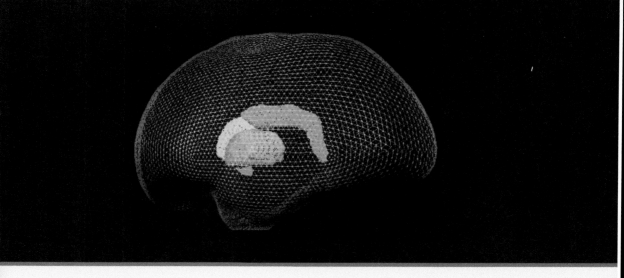

# 18 Actions, Habits, and the Cortico-Striatal System

Our brains are sensitive to the outcomes produced by our behaviors. Consequently, we can rapidly adjust our behaviors in response to a changing world and acquire complex behavioral skills. Psychologists have been concerned with how this happens for more than 100 years, and in the last 25 years neurobiologists have also weighed in on this topic. We now understand some of the basic psychological principles that govern the acquisition of new behaviors and how those principles might relate to systems in the brain. This chapter explores that complex relationship, first discussing the concept and two theories of instrumental behavior and then describing two categories of such behavior—**actions** and **habits**—and the cortico-striatal neural system of the brain that supports them.

To appreciate the basic problems addressed in this chapter, you might think back to when you initially learned to drive a car. In order to competently drive you had to learn and coordinate many complex behaviors, such as:

- Insert the ignition key
- Turn on the ignition key
- Release the handbrake
- Put the car in gear
- Put your foot on the accelerator
- Generate just the right amount of gas
- Adjust the steering wheel to maintain or change the trajectory
- Apply just the amount of pressure on the brake to stop

Remarkably, once these skills are learned, a competent driver can execute them in a seamless manner and at the same time carry on a conversation and sometimes drive for miles while unaware of even being on the road. However, this was certainly not the case when you were learning to drive. The initial execution of each of these behaviors was an intentional, goal-driven act that was motivated by your knowledge or expectancy that it would produce a particular outcome. Only with extensive practice did you acquire and integrate into a well-coordinated process the individual behaviors that comprise the collection of skills needed to drive a car. The initial crude actions you performed while learning to drive later became highly refined motor patterns, liberated from your intentions and conscious control. Driving then became a habit.

## The Concept of Instrumental Behavior

Most psychologists use the term instrumental learning or **instrumental behavior** when referring to the study of how behavior is modified by the outcome it produces. This term recognizes that our behaviors can be viewed as instruments that can change or modify our environments. For example, when you turn the ignition key, the engine starts.

The experimental study of instrumental learning emerged when, as a graduate student, E. L. Thorndike (1898) wanted to gain some insight into the "mind" of animals. He was unhappy with the speculation of his contemporaries about what kinds of representations of the world existed in the minds of dogs and cats and how these representations were acquired. This was because the speculation was made on the basis of anecdotal accounts of the behavior of animals and, when explaining behavior, psychologists of his era tended to anthropomorphize, that is, attribute to animals human characteristics. So, as described in Chapter 1, Thorndike developed a novel methodology, called the Thorndike puzzle box, to study how animals solve problems and represent the solution. This methodology was previously illustrated in Figure 1.10. A

(A) Learning curve

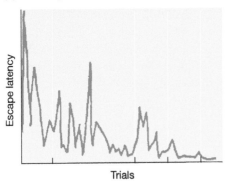

Trials

(B) Law of Effect

**Figure 18.1**

Thorndike contributed the puzzle box and learning curves to the study of instrumental learning. (A) These learning curves represented escape latency as a function of trials. (B) He also proposed a theory of instrumental learning known as the Law of Effect. Training experiences: When the animal is placed in the puzzle box, the stimulus situation (S) initiates many responses (R1, R2, R3, R4). The S–R connections linking S to wrong responses (R1, R2, R3) are followed by annoying consequences. The connection linking S to the correct response (R4, ring pull) is followed by a satisfying consequence (the door opens). Resulting changes: Over trials the incorrect S–R connections are weakened and the correct connection is strengthened, as represented by the red arrow.

cat, dog, or chicken was placed into the box and it had to learn a particular behavior to escape—for example, to pull the ring attached by a rope to the door.

The important feature of this methodology was that it arranged an explicit contingency between the animal's behavior and a change in the environment. Specifically, the opening of the escape door was contingent or dependent upon the animal generating a particular behavior—pulling the ring. If the specified response was not made, the door did not open.

More importantly, the animal's behavior was modified by the behavioral contingency Thorndike arranged. In attempting to escape from the box, the animal initially engaged in a wide range of behaviors that had no influence on its situation. However, it gradually learned the behavior that opened the door. Thorndike documented this change in behavior by presenting what may have been the first example of "learning curves." These learning curves represented escape latency as a function of trials (Figure 18.1). He found that escape latency gradually decreased as a function of those trials, indicating that the animal had learned to escape.

## Two Theories of Instrumental Behavior

Two general ideas about how outcomes change our behavior emerged quite early in the history of experimental psychology and continue to be influential. One idea, called the **Law of Effect**, originated with Thorndike. The second idea, called **cognitive expectancy theory**, is associated with Edward C. Tolman (1948, 1949).

### Thorndike's Law of Effect

The essence of Thorndike's theory is that outcomes produced by behavior ultimately adapt the animal to the situation by strengthening and weakening existing stimulus–response (S–R) connections. Outcomes that are rewarding strengthen S–R connections, while nonrewarding outcomes weaken connections. His Law of Effect, illustrated in Figure 18.1, is stated as follows: "If in the presence of a stimulus a response is followed by a satisfying state of affairs, the connection between the stimulus and the response will be strengthened. If the response is followed by an annoying state of affairs, the connection between the stimulus and response will be weakened."

Note that Thorndike described outcomes as resulting in either annoying or satisfying events. The term **reward** or **reinforcer** is often used to represent an outcome that strengthens stimulus–response connections and the term **nonreward** is used to designate an event that weakens such connections.

It is useful to highlight some of the implications of Thorndike's theory. A strengthened S–R connection can produce the appropriate response, but it contains no information about either the behavioral contingency (that is, that the outcome depended on the response) or the nature of the outcome (a reward or nonreward). More generally stated, the instrumental behavior itself should not be considered purposeful or goal directed. Thus, if you asked Thorndike's cat why it pulled the ring every time it was placed in the box, if it could answer it would say something like, "I don't know. It's very strange but when I am placed into the box I get an irresistible urge to pull the ring." A behavior supported by S–R connections is a habit, acquired through frequent repetition.

### Tolman's Cognitive Expectancy Theory

No one believes that Thorndike's theory provides a complete description of the processes that control our behavior or how we represent our past experiences. Tolman certainly did not accept this theory. He believed that instrumental behaviors are purposeful and organized around goals. He would say that

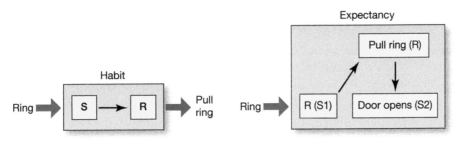

**Figure 18.2**
This figure provides a comparison of the S–R habit versus an expectancy representation of the cat's solution to the puzzle box (see Figure 1.10). Note, that the sight of the ring directly evokes a strengthened S–R connection to produce the pull-ring response. In contrast, according to expectancy theory, the sight of the ring activates the representation of the pull-ring response and the consequence it produces—the door opening. Activating the expectancy does not necessarily result in the response. Thus, the expectancy contains information about what would happen, but it does not force a response. This depends on the value of the outcome.

when the cat solves Thorndike's puzzle box it would learn the relationship between its behavior and the outcome that it produced. The cat acquired an expectancy about the relationship between its actions and the outcomes they produced. More generally speaking, Tolman believed that our brains detect and store information about relationships among all the events provided by a particular experience. An **expectancy** is a three-term association (S1–R–S2) that includes a representation of the stimulus situation (S1) that preceded the response, a representation of the response (R), and a representation of the outcome (S2) produced by the response. The expectancy concept is illustrated in Figure 18.2 in relation to Thorndike's S–R habit.

Edward C. Tolman

Tolman's cognitive expectancy–goal-directed theory of behavior placed a heavy emphasis on the value of the outcome produced by an instrumental behavior. The associations that make up an expectancy contain information about relationships between stimuli and relationships between behavior and stimulus outcomes. Whether or not you act, however, depends on the value of the outcome you expect the behavior to produce. So even though the cat "knows" how to escape from the box, it does not have to automatically initiate the escape response. It does so only if the outcome has value—if the cat has some motivation to escape. Similarly, you may know a friend's telephone number, but seeing a telephone does not always result in your dialing the number. You only do so when you want to speak to your friend, that is, when the outcome has value.

## Action and Habit Systems

Together, the theories of Thorndike and Tolman imply that there are two categories of instrumental behavior (Figure 18.3). Hereafter they will be called actions and habits. They differ on four dimensions.

- *Purpose.* The action system is goal directed and purposeful and motivated by an anticipated outcome. Habits are not goal directed or purposeful.

- *Sensitivity to outcomes.* The action system is sensitive to the response–reward contingencies. It rapidly detects outcomes associated with behavior and assesses the causal relationship—did the response actually produce the outcome? The habit system is not sensitive to response–reward contingencies.

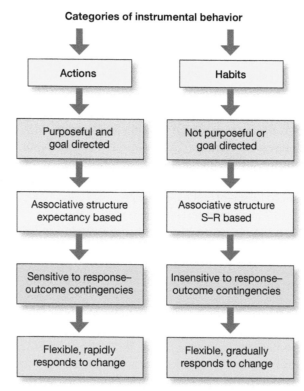

Categories of instrumental behavior

| Actions | Habits |
|---|---|
| Purposeful and goal directed | Not purposeful or goal directed |
| Associative structure expectancy based | Associative structure S–R based |
| Sensitive to response–outcome contingencies | Insensitive to response–outcome contingencies |
| Flexible, rapidly responds to change | Flexible, gradually responds to change |

**Figure 18.3**
Instrumental behaviors can be classified as either actions or habits.

- *Associative structure.* The action system acquires expectancies, whereas the habit system acquires stimulus–response associations.

- *Flexibility.* The action system is flexible and designed to rapidly respond to changes in response contingencies. The habit system response adapts more slowly to incremental changes and has to unlearn existing S–R associations and or slowly acquire new ones.

Under normal circumstances if you were watching a cat escape from the puzzle box or someone opened a door, you would have difficulty determining if the behavior was an action or a habit. However, researchers have used two strategies to determine if a particular instrumental behavior is supported by the action system or the habit system: the reward devaluation strategy and the discrimination reversal learning strategy.

The **reward devaluation** strategy is used to determine if the instrumental behavior is purposeful and goal directed. This strategy centers on changing the value of the outcome after the animal has solved the problem. The logic of the strategy, which has been used with both primates and rodents, is described as follows.

Since actions are purposeful and generated to produce a specific outcome, when the outcome has value, the animal should produce the appropriate response. But when the outcome has no value, the animal may not produce the response. In contrast, since habits are not goal directed, they should be produced regardless of the value of the outcome or reward. Thus, by changing the value of the reward–outcome after an instrumental response has been learned, one can determine if the response is an action or a habit. If the response is controlled by the action system, devaluing the outcome should reduce the likelihood that the response will occur. If it is a habit, then reward devaluation will not influence the behavior.

An example of the devaluation strategy is illustrated in Figure 18.4. A monkey is trained to solve two discriminations. In the first problem the reward is a grape. If the monkey chooses the pyramid it will find the grape, but it will receive nothing if it chooses the cylinder. In the second problem the reward is a peanut. If it chooses the cube it will find the peanut, but if it chooses the cone it will find nothing. Monkeys easily solve such problems. How can you tell whether the correct response is an action supported by an expectancy or a habit supported by an S–R connection? The answer is, *by changing the value of the reward.*

This can easily be done. After the problems have been solved the monkey receives a test in which the two correct stimuli from each discrimination problem—the pyramid (with the grape) and the cube (with the peanut)—are presented several times. Before the test, however, the monkey is satiated with

Training

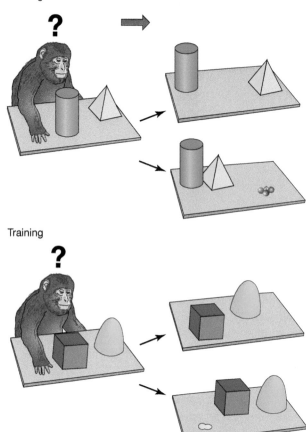

Training

**Figure 18.4**
The figure illustrates the satiation method for devaluing a reward. A monkey is trained to solve two discrimination problems. In the first problem the pyramid is the correct choice and the reward is a grape. In the second problem the correct choice is the cube and the reward is a peanut. After solving the two problems, the monkey is given a choice between the two correct objects (cube and pyramid). Before the test, however, the monkey is allowed to have either all the grapes or all the peanuts it wants, thus reducing the value of one of the outcomes. Typically, monkeys choose the object that contains the reward that it was not fed prior to the test. (After Baxter and Murray, 2002.)

Tests

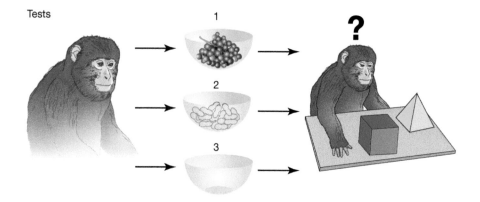

one of the rewards. It is allowed to eat either all the peanuts or all the grapes it wants. This treatment reduces the value of one of the rewards. No reward is given on the test. If the monkey's response is an action, it will choose the object associated with the reward that still has "value." However, if the monkey's choice is random this means that the choice response was a habit.

The action system is said to be more flexible than the habit system. This means that the action system is more sensitive to changes in the contingencies associated with behavior than the habit system and it can use new information to rapidly adapt to changes in the environment. For example, someone raised in the United States who visits England faces a potentially lethal situation. In the United States when a pedestrian prepares to cross a street the dominant response is to look to the left before crossing. This is because cars in the closest lane will be coming from the left. However, in England if you look left and then step into the street you have a good chance of being hit by a car because in England traffic in the inside lane is coming from the pedestrian's right. Thus, to survive in England, one has to rapidly adjust to the new response contingencies and learn to look to the right before crossing. The action system is thought to provide the basis for this rapid adjustment and to override the habit system, which is thought to respond to change by incrementally changing S–R connections.

The **discrimination reversal learning** strategy is commonly used to assess the flexibility of the system supporting the instrumental response. For example, after the monkey initially solves the cylinder (reward) versus pyramid (no reward) problem, the solution would be reversed and it would have to learn that the pyramid is now the correct choice. The idea behind this strategy is that the action system would facilitate learning these reversals but the habit system would interfere with reversal learning because it is slow to change.

## With Practice, Actions Become Habits

The devaluation methodology has provided evidence for the existence of both actions and habits. In addition, research with animals has revealed a dominance principle. With limited training instrumental behaviors are goal-directed actions, but with practice, instrumental behaviors tend to shift from actions to habits, meaning they become insensitive to reward devaluation.

This point is illustrated in Figure 18.5, which presents the results of an experiment in which rats were trained to press a lever to receive food. Thus, lever pressing was the instrumental response and food was the outcome–reward. In one condition the rats were given only a limited amount of lever-press training, while in the other they were given extended training. Prior to the test phase, the outcome–reward was devalued for one set of rats. During

(A)

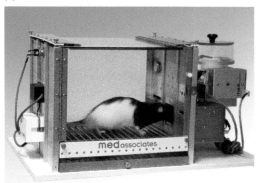

(B)

**Figure 18.5**
(A) A rat is collecting food produced by pressing a lever. In this experiment, in one condition the rats were given only a limited amount of lever-press training, while in the other they were given extended training. Prior to the test phase, the food reward was devalued for one set of rats. (B) Rats that had limited training were sensitive to the value of the reward, pressing the lever less than control rats. In this case, the lever press was considered an action. In contrast, rats that had experienced extended training were insensitive to the value of the reward, pressing the lever as often as the control rats. In this case the lever press was considered a habit. (After Adams and Dickinson, 1981.)

the test phase, food was no longer delivered in response to lever pressing. Rats that had limited training were sensitive to the value of the reward, making fewer lever-pressing responses than the control rats. In this case, the lever press was considered an action. In contrast, rats that had experienced extended training were insensitive to the value of the reward, pressing the lever as often as the control rats (Adams and Dickinson, 1981). In this case the lever press was considered a habit.

With repetition, an action can become a habit. However, one should not conclude that the expectancy representation of an action is replaced by an S–R representation of a habit. Instead, once established, the two representations co-exist. As the next section explains, what changes with practice is which representation controls behavior (Killcross and Coutureau, 2003).

## A Conceptual Model for Actions and Habits

Behavioral neuroscientists have begun to uncover regions in the brain that contribute to the support of actions and habits. The unfolding story is complex and incomplete, so to facilitate understanding of the concepts, a conceptual model is provided in Figure 18.6 to illustrate the general idea that instrumental behaviors can be generated by either an action system or a habit system.

In this simple model a stimulus–response–outcome experience is represented at two levels in the brain. The representations of the experience activated in level I are fed forward to level II. The processes operating in level

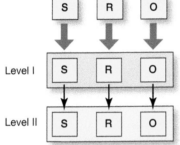
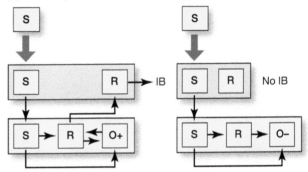
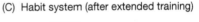
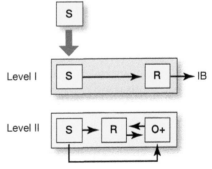

**Figure 18.6**
(A) An animal has an initial experience composed of a sequence of an antecedent stimulus (S), a response (R), and an outcome (O) produced by the response. This experience is represented in two levels of the brain, I and II. (B) With limited training, the representations in level II are associated with and can support an action. The diagram on the left shows that the action system generates an instrumental behavior (IB) if the outcome has value (+). In this case, when S occurs the level II associations are activated and the output of the action system projects back to the response representation in level I to generate the instrumental behavior. The diagram on the right illustrates the case when the outcome has been devalued (–). In this case the outcome representation does not strongly project onto the response representation in level II. Thus, the response representation in level I is not activated and the instrumental behavior is not produced. (C) With extended training, a habit is formed, that is, connections between the stimulus and response representations in level I become strong enough to support the generation of an instrumental behavior, without projections back from level II.

II are responsible for assembling these representations into a goal-directed action, but ultimately processes in level I that associate the stimulus representation and response representation produce habits. The action and habit systems both generate the instrumental behavior (IB) by activating the representation of the response in level I.

More specifically, the associations that support actions form in level II after limited training. They link (a) the stimulus representation to both the outcome representation and the response representation, (b) the response representation to the outcome representation, and (c) the outcome representation to the response representation. If the outcome representation has value (+), this association will contribute to activating the response representation in level II. If the response representation in level II is sufficiently activated, its output will project back to the response representation in level I and produce the instrumental behavior. However, if the outcome has no value (−), then the response representation in level II will not be sufficiently activated to stimulate the response representation in level I, and the instrumental behavior will not occur.

With extended training an S–R habit can emerge in level I (see Figure 18.6C). This happens because with repetition the action system repeatedly produces the same response in the presence of the antecedent stimulus, thereby creating the opportunity for it to be directly associated with a representation of the response. After extended training, both the action system and the habit system can produce the instrumental behavior, but the habit system tends to dominate.

## Action and Habit Systems Compete

Under normal circumstance the action and habit systems cooperate to allow us to adapt to our environment. The action system initially assembles the relevant task information to generate the correct instrumental response. Then, as the correct response is repeated it becomes controlled by the habit system. *But what happens when the response contingencies are changed?* For example, suppose a rat has learned to respond to two levers. However, pressing lever 1 is more likely to produce a reward than pressing lever 2. So the animal learns to press lever 1 more often than lever 2. After this pattern is established, the contingencies are reversed (using the discrimination reversal learning strategy described above), so that pressing lever 2 is more likely to produce a reward than pressing lever 1, and the animal now has to acquire this conflicting information and learn to respond more to lever 2 than lever 1.

The action system is designed to acquire the new information and provide a basis for a rapid shift to the lever that produces more rewards. However, the habit system is slow to adjust and its output may interfere with adjusting to the new contingencies. The animal must unlearn or suppress the old habit. This description suggests that information contained in the habit system will interfere with the rat learning to shift to the better lever. Wolfgang Pauli and his colleagues (Pauli et al., 2012) reasoned that if the action system were removed (by inactivating the region of the brain that supports the action system), rats would learn more slowly to make this adjustment. In contrast, if the habit system were removed (by inactivating the region of the brain that supports the habit system), rats would more rapidly learn to shift to the more favorable lever. (Note: these brain regions are described in great detail in the section below on the cortico-striatal system.) To test these predictions these regions were inactivated immediately prior to the test session when the response–reward contingencies reversed. The researchers' predictions were confirmed and the results of their experiment also support the hypothesis that the action and habit systems initially compete for control of instrumental behaviors when the requirements of a situation are reversed.

## Action Systems Are Vulnerable

Development of an instrumental response occurs in a temporally overlapping sequence in which the action system initially acquires the information needed to generate the response. However, once the appropriate response occurs reliably, the habit system takes over. These ideas now play a prominent role in guiding research in other areas (see Graybiel, 2008). One principle that has emerged is that the action system is more vulnerable to disruption than the habit system. For example, there is evidence that exposure to psycho-stimulants such as amphetamines can unduly favor control of instrumental behaviors by the habit system (Nelson and Killcross, 2006).

Jane Taylor and her colleagues (Gourly et al., 2013) report that an injection of cocaine following training prevents the consolidation of the memory supporting the action system's ability to store the memory of the response–reward contingency—the instrumental response of animals treated with cocaine was controlled by the habit system. Moreover, this group found that this happens because cocaine selectively interferes with actin reorganization in spines located on neurons in the region of the brain that supports the action system.

In another domain, it has been found that chronic stress dramatically alters components of the action system and this results in the habit system controlling instrumental behaviors (Dias-Ferreiri et al., 2009). Graybiel (2008) has discussed the implications of the action–habit analysis for a number of domains, such as obsessive–compulsive disorder and Tourette syndrome.

## A Cortico-Striatal System Supports Instrumental Behavior

The conceptual model for actions and habits described above is complex, but even so it is an oversimplification. The reality is that a large number of components of the brain make a contribution to the learning of instrumental behavior, and no one has yet provided a theory that shows how all the relevant components are integrated to produce such behavior. Nevertheless, important components of the neural system that supports the acquisition and production of instrumental behavior have been identified.

One important component of this system, located deep in the center of the brain, is the **basal ganglia**. This region of the brain consists of a number of subcortical nuclei including the caudate nucleus, putamen, globus pallidus, subthalamic nucleus, nucleus accumbens, and substantia nigra. Together, the caudate nucleus, putamen, and nucleus accumbens components of the basal ganglia form a region of the brain called the **striatum**.

The striatum is the basic input segment of the basal ganglia. It receives input from many cortical regions of the brain and projects out through the globus pallidus and substantia nigra to the thalamus and ultimately back to areas of the cortex from which it received input. Thus the striatum is at the center of what is sometimes called the **cortico-striatal system**. Because the striatum projects back to some of the cortical regions that project to it, the cortico-striatal system has the same sort of return-loop organization that characterizes the medial temporal hippocampal (MTH) system that supports episodic memory, discussed in Chapter 17. Note in particular that the striatum projects back to the motor cortex. This is important because motor cortices are critical for the generation of behaviors. Many researchers believe that the striatum is the key anatomical region for creating instrumental behaviors (Divac et al., 1967; Shiflett and Balleine, 2011; White and McDonald, 2002).

Raymond Kesner

An experiment by Raymond Kesner (Cook and Kesner, 1988) used a radial maze with eight arms to illustrate this point (Figure 18.7). Each rat was placed randomly into one of these arms and then released. Normally, when released the rat will move out into the arena and enter some distant arm. However, in what is called the **adjacent-arm task**, no matter which arm it was placed into to start a trial, the rat was only rewarded if its first choice upon release was to enter one of the two adjacent arms. Normal rats learned this task, but rats with damage to the striatum were quite impaired. Thus, these animals had difficulty learning what would appear to be the simple task of turning left or right.

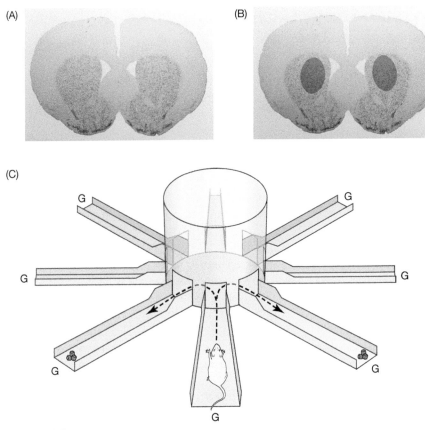

**Figure 18.7**
(A) This photomicrograph of a normal rat brain shows the cortex and striatum. (B) This photomicrograph illustrates the location of the experimentally induced lesion in the dorsal striatum. (C) An illustration of a rat in the eight-arm radial maze task. On each trial the rat is started randomly from one arm of the maze. In order to receive a reward the rat must leave the start arm and enter an adjacent arm. Rats with damage to the dorsal striatum are greatly impaired on this instrumental learning task. G = goal. (After Cook and Kesner, 1988.)

Figure 18.8 illustrates the rat's striatum and some of the cortical and other regions in the brain that it interacts with to produce instrumental behavior. This figure provides a framework for discussing some of the key components of the neural system that contribute to assembling and performing action patterns. It is useful to think of the cortico-striatal system as performing the functions of level II in the conceptual model of instrumental behavior described previously and illustrated in Figure 18.6.

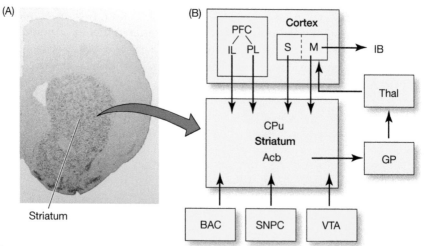

**Figure 18.8**
(A) The rodent striatum and surrounding cortex. (B) A highly schematic representation of the rat striatum and some of the important regions of the brain that project to it. Note that information processed by the striatum projects back to the motor (M) cortex via the thalamus (Thal). The striatum of the rat is composed of the caudate putamen (CPu) and the nucleus accumbens (Acb). S = sensory cortex; PFC = prefrontal cortex; PL = prelimbic cortex; IL = infralimbic cortex; BAC = basal amygdala complex; VTA = ventral tegmental area; SNPC = substantia nigra pars compacta; IB = instrumental behavior; GP = globus pallidus.

## Neural Support for Actions

Much of what is known about the contribution different regions of the brain make to support instrumental behavior comes from the combined use of neurobiological methods to influence the brain and devaluation techniques to determine if the instrumental response is an action or a habit. Researchers use lesions to permanently remove a particular component of the neural system and inactivation methods to temporarily but reversibly prevent a region from contributing to the behavioral outcome. In addition, drugs that influence synaptic plasticity, such as the NMDA receptor antagonist APV, are employed to determine if synapses in a particular region of the brain are modified by experience.

As noted earlier, actions are said to be goal directed and purposeful. Thus, the reward devaluation strategy is used to determine regions of the brain that are part of the action system. If a reward devaluation procedure reduces the production of the instrumental behavior, that behavior is said to be a goal-directed action. Consequently, if the function of a brain region is impaired and the reward devaluation procedure has no effect on instrumental responding (does not reduce responding), one might conclude that the brain region is part of the action system. In contrast, if the function of a brain region is impaired and the devaluation reduces instrumental responding, then one would conclude that this brain region is not part of the action system. Based on this logic, three brain regions have been linked to the action system: (1) the dorsomedial striatum, (2) the basolateral amygdala, and (3) the prelimbic prefrontal cortex.

DORSOMEDIAL STRIATUM   Bernard Balleine and his colleagues reported several findings that suggest that the **dorsomedial striatum (DMS)** plays an important role in goal-directed actions. In one study, they damaged this region of the brain either before or after training rats on a two-lever pressing task (Yin, Ostlund et al., 2005). Pressing each lever produced a different outcome: a food pellet or a sip of a sucrose solution. Prior to the test, they satiated the animals on one or the other of the rewards. During the test no reward was given. When satiated on food pellets, control rats were sensitive to the devaluation treatment and pressed the lever that in the past produced the sucrose. Rats with damage to the DMS, however, were not sensitive to the devaluation; they pressed the lever as much

Bernard Balleine

when the reward was devalued as they did when it was not, and they pressed each lever equally as often. These results (Figure 18.9) suggest that the control rats' behavior was produced by the action system and that the DMS is part of this system.

(A)

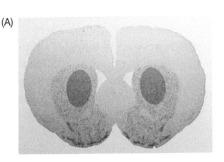

(B)

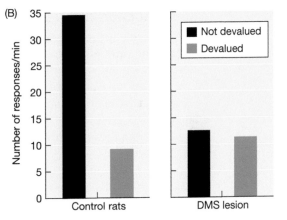

**Figure 18.9**
(A) This micrograph illustrates the location of damage to the dorsomedial striatum (DMS) in rats. In this experiment, the rats were trained to press two levers that each produced a different reward. Following training, one of the rewards was devalued. (B) During the test, when no rewards were delivered, control rats pressed the lever that was associated with the now devalued reward far less than they pressed the other lever. This result indicates that their instrumental behavior was controlled by the action system. In contrast, rats with damage to the DMS pressed the two levers equally often. This result suggests that the DMS is part of the neural system that supports actions.

A different set of experiments, in which the NMDA-receptor antagonist APV was injected into the DMS, resulted in similar findings, further supporting the idea that neurons in the DMS are important in action learning (Yin, Knowlton et al., 2005).

BASOLATERAL AMYGDALA   The production of an action depends on the value of the outcome it produces; however, outcomes have particular sensory qualities—steak does not taste like oatmeal and peanuts do not taste like raisins. When a particular food is experienced, a memory representation of the specific sensory features is established. Moreover, it appears that a particular value also is attached to this representation. So, for example, if a novel food is ingested, not only is a representation of its sensory properties acquired, an abstract value or rating of liking (+) or disliking (–) the food is also attached to the representation. Thus, if one were asked to retrieve a representation of an orange, not only is its color, shape, texture, and taste retrieved, so is a representation of its value.

Research with both primates and rodents has identified an important role for the amygdala, specifically the **basolateral amygdala**, in attaching value to outcomes (Balleine and Killcross, 2006). Animals with major damage to the amygdala can learn instrumental behaviors. However, these animals are not sensitive to changes in the value of an outcome. For example, monkeys with amygdala damage have no problem learning the visual object discriminations shown in Figure 18.4. However, they are completely insensitive to devaluation of the associated rewards (Malkova et al., 1997). Moreover, monkeys with amygdala damage can learn specific motor patterns when rewarded for making the appropriate response. For example, they can learn to move a lever to the right when the signal is a red light and they can learn to move the lever to the left when the signal is a blue light (Murray and Wise, 1996). Similar results have been obtained when researchers have examined the effect of amygdala damage on instrumental learning in rats (Balleine, 2005; Balleine et al., 2003). These study results support the idea that the amygdala contributes to learning the value of the outcome and thus plays an important role in the action system.

PRELIMBIC PREFRONTAL CORTEX   The action system rapidly captures information needed to assemble an instrumental response: sensory input, responses, outcomes, and value of the outcome. The dorsomedial striatum is likely involved in the integration of this information. However, for this to occur requires input from the **prelimbic prefrontal cortex**. The prelimbic region of the brain is important during the initial learning of the associations that support an action. However, once these associations are learned, this region is no longer critical. The evidence for these claims is that if this region is damaged before rats learn an instrumental response, they are insensitive to reward devaluation (Killcross and Coutureau, 2003; Ostlund and Balleine, 2005). So the instrumental response in this case would be called a habit. However, if the prelimbic region is damaged just after rats are allowed to learn the associations supporting the action, they remain sensitive to reward devaluation (Ostlund and Balleine, 2005). These results have two implications: (1) the prelimbic region is critical in the acquisition of the associations that support an action and (2) it is not the site in the brain where these associations are stored.

## Neural Support for Habits

As noted earlier, habits are not purposeful and, once established, they are insensitive to the value of the outcome that initially motivated the behavior. Many trials are required to engrain a habitual response and they are difficult to unlearn. Two brain regions are critical to the acquisition and maintenance of habits: (1) dorsolateral striatum and (2) infralimbic prefrontal cortex.

DORSOLATERAL STRIATUM   As previously illustrated in Figure 18.5, with limited training instrumental behavior is primarily supported by the action system—the behavior is sensitive to reward devaluation. However, with extensive training the behavior becomes a habit and is insensitive to reward devaluation. Thus, to determine if a particular brain region contributes to the acquisition or expression of a habit, animals receive extensive training before the reward devaluation treatment.

Henry Yin and his colleagues (Yin et al., 2004) used this strategy to reveal that the **dorsolateral striatum (DLS)** is critical to habit formation. They compared rats with lesions of the DLS to control rats that experienced the surgery but not the lesion. Following extensive training to produce a lever press, they devalued the sucrose reward and then tested the rats. No reward was given during this 5-minute test. As expected, the extensively trained rats in the control condition were not influenced by reward devaluation, indicating that the behavior was a habit. In contrast, damage to the DLS influenced reward devaluation—the rats' rate of responding was dramatically reduced. This indicates that in the absence of neurons in the DLS the behavior never became a habit.

INFRALIMBIC PREFRONTAL CORTEX   Just as the prelimbic region of the prefrontal cortex is critical to the action system, so the **infralimbic prefrontal cortex** is critical to the habit system. Killcross and Coutureau (2003) damaged this brain region prior to rats acquiring an instrumental response (bar pressing for food reward). Even after extensive training the behavior never became a habit. The devaluation procedure reduced responding in rats with damage to the infralimbic region. In addition, Coutureau and Killcross (2003) used a pharmacological treatment to temporarily inactivate infralimbic neurons in rats that had been extensively trained to demonstrate that the instrumental response should be supported by the habit system. However, the reward devaluation treatment greatly reduced responding during the test. More recently, Coutureau and Killcross's findings have been confirmed by using optogenetics (see Chapter 9) to control neurons in the infralimbic region (Smith et al., 2012). In this case, optogenetic methods were used to inhibit neurons in this region. Turning off these neurons almost instantaneously changed the control of the instrumental response from the habit system to the action system because these rats were sensitive to reward devaluation.

These results have three implications:

- The associations that support action-based behavior are still present even after the behavior becomes a habit. This implication follows because when the infralimbic function was impaired the rats became sensitive to the value of the reward.

- With extensive training, the infralimbic region exerts inhibitory control over the action system, taking it offline so that it does not influence behavior. This implication follows because depending upon the state of the neurons in the infralimbic region, a well trained instrumental response can be shown to be supported by either the action or habit system.

- When infralimbic neurons are turned off, the action system controls the response, but when these neurons are functioning, the habit system controls the response.

A comparison of the roles played by the prelimbic and infralimbic cortex is illustrated in Figure 18.10.

## The Striatum Stores Action and Habit Memories

While the DMS and DLS are part of the habit and action systems, Shiftlett and Balleine (2011) noted that it is not clear how these regions contribute to the acquisition and generation of the behavior. One possibility is that they are memory storage sites for the information that supports actions and habits. Alternatively, they may just help coordinate learning and memory storage that occurs in other brain regions.

Pauli et al. (2012) also addressed this issue. They reasoned that if the DMS and DLS actually store memories needed to support habits and actions, then it should be possible to erase this content by using the inhibitory peptide ZIP to disrupt the PKMζ function (see Chapter 7). They used the same reversal learning procedure described above to demonstrate that the action and habit

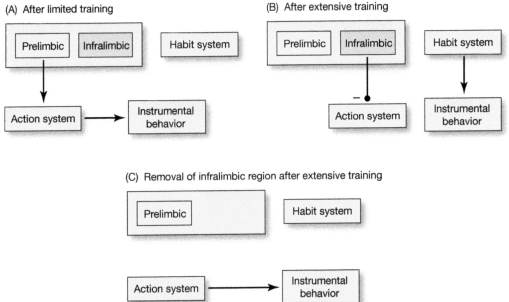

**Figure 18.10**
(A) After limited training, instrumental behavior is controlled by the action system. The prelimbic region is necessary early in training for building the action system that controls a particular instrumental behavior. Note at this stage that the habit system does not contribute to the generation of the instrumental behavior. (B) With extensive training, the prelimbic region is no longer necessary to generate an action. Moreover, the infralimbic region now suppresses the contribution of the action system, and instrumental behavior is produced by the habit system. (C) If the infralimbic region is removed after extensive training, the action system again assumes control over instrumental behavior. This means that after extensive training, associations that can produce instrumental behavior are present in both the action and habit systems.

systems compete. When ZIP was injected into the DMS the day before testing (theoretically erasing memory support for the action system), the rats rapidly learned to reverse their response choice. In contrast, when ZIP was injected into the DLS (theoretically erasing memory support for the habit system), rats were impaired in learning to reverse their response choices. Thus, erasing information in the habit system facilitated learning to reverse the discrimination, whereas erasing task information acquired by the action system retarded learning the reversal. These results are consistent with the idea that the DMS and DLS regions of the striatum are memory storage sites for the action and habit systems. Note, however, that these regions are unlikely to be the only storage sites for instrumental responses.

**Figure 18.11**
(A) This sagittal section of the rat brain illustrates the mesolimbic dopamine system. The dopamine neurons are located in the ventral tegmental area (VTA) and their fibers project into the nucleus accumbens of the striatum. (B) The dopamine theory of reinforcement. An outcome–reward has two functions: (1) It generates a representation (O), and (2) it activates dopamine neurons in the VTA that release dopamine into the striatum. This acts to strengthen synaptic connections between the representations of the stimulus (S) complex and the response (R) and perhaps between the representations of the response and the outcome.

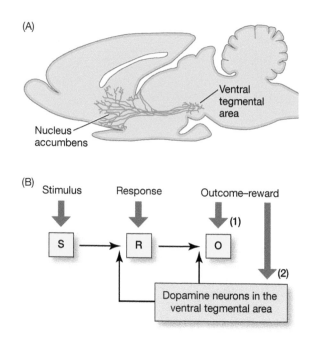

## The Neural Basis of Rewarding Outcomes

By definition, instrumental responses are behaviors that change the environment to produce rewards or reinforcers—rewards increase the likelihood that a behavior will be repeated and nonrewards decrease this likelihood. Two general ideas about how rewards influence behavior were also discussed earlier. One relates to Thorndike's argument that rewards strengthen associative connections. The other derives from Tolman's position that rewards provide incentive motivation for behavior. But what is the neural basis of rewards that enable them to serve these two functions?

Both of these ideas have been related to the influence rewards have on the release of the neurotransmitter, **dopamine**. This source of dopamine is provided by what is called the **mesolimbic dopamine system** (Berridge and Robinson, 1998). Dopamine in this system comes from neurons located in a region of the brain called the ventral tegmental area (VTA). In particular, the VTA responds to events often used to reinforce instrumental behavior and it has outputs that project into the striatum, specifically the nucleus accumbens (Figure 18.11A).

The **dopamine reinforcement hypothesis** relates dopamine to Thorndike's idea that rewards strengthen associative connections. In this case, it is easy to imagine that the outcome produced by behavior first turns on neurons in the VTA that then cause dopamine to be released into the striatum (the nucleus accumbens) and that this dopamine release strengthens the relevant synaptic

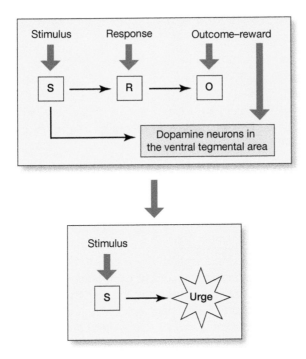

**Figure 18.12**
The incentive salience hypothesis assumes that the reward turns on dopamine neurons in the ventral tegmental area. In the normal sequence of events that establish instrumental behavior, the stimulus not only can associate with the response, it also can get associated with the incentive properties of the outcome. Subsequently, the stimulus complex itself can elicit strong urges or wants that lead the individual to seek out the reward. Berridge and Robinson (1998) have proposed that these urges play an important role in drug-addiction relapse. Even though an addict might go through drug withdrawal and be "clean," an encounter with stimuli associated with the drug experience can lead to relapse because they can produce irresistible urges to seek the drug.

connections supporting stimulus–response or response–outcome associative connections (Figure 18.11B).

Another hypothesis, called the **dopamine-incentive salience hypothesis,** links dopamine to the motivational significance of rewarding outcomes. It assumes that activation of the mesolimbic dopamine system by a rewarding outcome attaches motivational significance to stimuli associated with the outcome (Berridge, 2007). What this means is that the presence of a stimulus associated with a strongly rewarding outcome can evoke a strong urge for the outcome. The instrumental behavior occurs because it produces the outcome that satisfies the want (Figure 18.12).

Berridge and Robinson (1998) developed the dopamine-incentive salience hypothesis to provide an explanation for drug relapse (see Chapter 14). Their contention is that drug relapse occurs because addictive drugs strongly activate dopamine neurons, and neutral cues present at that time acquire the ability to produce the urge to take the drug. Thus the sight of a cigarette or the smell of cigarette smoke might evoke an intense urge to smoke a cigarette because these stimuli were associated with the activation of the dopamine system and acquired extreme incentive properties. These urges motivate the person to engage in instrumental behaviors that produce the outcome that reduces the urge.

## Summary

Instrumental behaviors change the environment—they produce outcomes—and their likelihood of reoccurring is modified by the nature of the outcome. Instrumental behaviors belong to two categories called actions and habits. Actions are purposeful and goal directed and supported by what are called expectancies. Actions are motivated by the expected outcomes they produce and the action system is flexible. Habits are not purposeful and thus are thought to be insensitive to the outcomes they produce. Instrumental behaviors begin as actions but with extensive repetition gradually become S–R habits. The reward devaluation strategy, which detects the animal's sensitivity to the goal, and the discrimination reversal strategy, which detects the flexibility of the two systems, can be employed to determine which system controls the instrumental response.

A cortico-striatal neural system linking a variety of cortical and midbrain regions is the system that integrates the elements of our experience—stimulus inputs, response inputs, and outcomes produced by the response—into actions and habits. The action system depends in part on three regions of the brain: the DMS, prelimbic prefrontal cortex, and the basolateral amygdala. The habit system depends on the DLS and infralimbic prefrontal cortex, which appears to suppress the action system. Both actions and habits likely depend on the mesolimbic dopamine system located in the ventral tegmental area of the brain. Neurons from this region project to the striatum and dopamine release may strengthen associative connections and serve as an incentive motivational signal.

## References

Adams, C. D. and Dickinson, A. (1981). Instrumental responding following reinforcer devaluation. *Quarterly Journal of Experimental Psychology, 33B*, 109–121.

Balleine, B. (2005). Neural bases of food-seeking: affect, arousal and reward in cortico-striatolimbic circuits. *Physiology and Behavior, 86,* 717–730.

Balleine, B. W. and Killcross, A. S. (2006). Parallel incentive processing: an integrated view of amygdala function. *Trends in Neurosciences, 29,* 272–279.

Balleine, B. W., Killcross, A. S., and Dickinson, A. (2003). The effect of lesions of the basolateral amygdala on instrumental conditioning. *Journal of Neuroscience, 23,* 666–678.

Baxter, M. G. and Murray, E. A. (2002). The amygdala and reward. *Nature Reviews Neuroscience, 3,* 563–573.

Berridge, K. C. (2007). The debate over dopamine's role in reward: the case for incentive salience. *Psychopharmacology, 191,* 391–431.

Berridge, K. C. and Robinson, T. E. (1998). What is the role of dopamine in reward: hedonic impact, reward learning, or incentive salience? *Brain Research Review, 28,* 309–369.

Cook, D. and Kesner, R. P. (1988). Caudate nucleus and memory for egocentric localization. *Behavioral Neural Biology, 49,* 332–343.

Coutureau, E. and Killcross, S. (2003). Inactivation of the infralimbic prefrontal cortex reinstates goal-directed responding in overtrained rats. *Behavioral Brain Research, 146,* 167–174.

Dias-Ferreira, E., Sousa. J. C., Melo, I., Morgado, P., Mesquita, A. R., João, J., Cerqueira, J. J., Costa, R. M., and Sousa, N. (2009). Chronic stress causes frontostriatal reorganization and affects decision-making. *Science, 325,* 621–625.

Divac, I., Rosvold, H. E., and Szwarcbart, M. K. (1967). Behavioral effects of selective ablation of the caudate nucleus. *Journal of Comparative and Physiological Psychology, 63,* 183–190.

Gourley, S. L., Olevska, A., Gordon, J., and Taylor, J. R. (2013). Cytoskeletal determinants of stimulus-response habits. *Journal of Neuroscience, 33,* 11811–11816.

Graybiel, A. M. (2008). Habits, rituals, and the evaluative brain. *Annual Review of Neuroscience, 31,* 359–387.

Killcross, S. and Coutureau, E. (2003). Coordination of actions and habits in the medial prefrontal cortex of rats. *Cerebral Cortex, 13,* 400–408.

Malkova, L. D., Gaffan, D., and Murray, E. (1997). Excitotoxic lesions of the amygdala fail to produce impairment in visual learning for auditory secondary reinforcement but interfere with reinforcer devaluation effects in rhesus monkeys. *Journal of Neuroscience, 17,* 6011–6020.

Murray, E. A. and Wise, S. P. (1996). Role of the hippocampus plus subjacent cortex but not amygdala in visuomotor conditional learning in rhesus monkeys. *Behavioral Neuroscience, 110,* 1261–1270.

Nelson, A. and Killcross, S. (2006). Amphetamine exposure enhances habit formation. *Journal of Neuroscience, 26,* 3805–3812.

Ostlund, S. B. and Balleine, B. W. (2005). Lesions of medial prefrontal cortex disrupt the acquisition but not the expression of goal-directed learning. *Journal of Neuroscience, 25,* 7763–7770.

Pauli, W. M., Clark, A. D., Guenther, H. J., O'Reilly, R. C., and Rudy, J. W. (2012). Inhibiting PKMζ reveals dorsal lateral and dorsal medial striatum store the different memories needed to support adaptive behavior. *Learning and Memory, 19,* 307–314.

Shiftlett, M. W. and Balleine, B. W. (2011). Molecular substrates of action control in cortico-striatal circuits. *Progress in Neurobiology, 95,* 1–13.

Smith, K. S., Virkud, A., Deisseroth, K., and Graybiel, A. M. (2012). Reversible online control of habitual behavior by optogenetic perturbation of medial prefrontal cortex. *Proceedings of the National Academy of Sciences USA, 109,* 18932–18937.

Thorndike, E. L. (1898). Animal Intelligence: an experimental study of associative processes in animals. *Psychological Monographs, 2,* Whole No. 8.

Tolman, E. C. (1948). Cognitive maps in rats and men. *Psychological Review, 55,* 189–208.

Tolman, E. C. (1949). There is more than one kind of learning. *Psychological Review, 56,* 144–155.

White, N. M. and McDonald, R. J. (2002). Multiple parallel memory systems in the brain of the rat. *Neurobiology of Learning and Memory, 77,* 125–84.

Yin, H. H., Knowlton, B. J., and Balleine, B. W. (2004). Lesions of dorsolateral striatum preserve outcome expectancy but disrupt habit formation in instrumental learning. *European Journal of Neuroscience, 19,* 181–189.

Yin, H. H., Knowlton, B. J., and Balleine, B. W. (2005). Blockade of NMDA receptors in the dorsomedial striatum prevents action–outcome learning in instrumental conditioning. *European Journal of Neuroscience, 22,* 505–512.

Yin, H. H., Ostlund, S. B., Knowlton, B. J., and Balleine, B. W. (2005). The role of the dorsomedial striatum in instrumental conditioning. *European Journal of Neuroscience, 22,* 513–523.

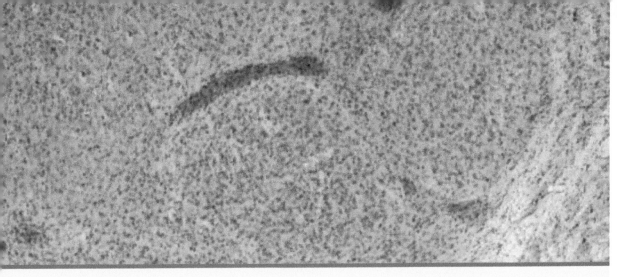

# 19 Learning about Danger: The Neurobiology of Fear Memories

All animals must solve fundamental problems associated with survival and reproduction. Thus, it should not come as a surprise that our evolutionary history has provided us with a brain that is designed to support what are called behavioral systems (Timberlake, 1994). A **behavioral system** is organized specifically to ensure that some particular need is met. There are specialized behavioral systems designed to support our reproductive and feeding-related activities and behavioral systems that allow us to avoid and escape dangerous situations.

According to the behavioral systems view, one major role of the processes that support learning and memory is to properly connect the behavioral infrastructure supported by a particular system to the ever-changing world in which we live. For example, we have the relevant behaviors for finding and ingesting food, but we have to learn the details about where the food is and what is fit to eat. We also have the relevant behaviors needed to avoid and escape from danger. But how do we know what is dangerous?

Some of this information is coded in our genes. However, in a dynamic world we have to adjust to changes in the environment. From a learning and memory perspective, the challenge is to understand how experience connects the neural systems that support our survival behaviors with the other features of our world that allow us to anticipate the occurrence of biologically significant events.

Understanding how learning and memory processes interface and tune our behavioral systems to this changing world is a large and complex endeavor because each of the several behavioral systems is specialized and has its own neural components. Rather than attempt a survey of all of these systems, this chapter focuses on just one—the so-called fear system. The importance of this system is obvious and much is known about its fundamental components. The chapter begins by describing the fear system and its neural basis, then considers how fears can be extinguished and concludes with a discussion of the neural basis of fear elimination.

Michael Fanselow

Caroline and Robert Blanchard

## The Fear System

The fear system evolved to allow us to escape from harmful events and to avoid them in the future. Robert Bolles (1970) developed the concept of species-specific defensive behaviors to describe the class of innate behaviors that are supported by the fear system. For example, the rat, a subject of hundreds of studies on the fear system, is equipped with several easily observable defensive behaviors, including freezing, flight, and fighting. Freezing is by far the most dominant of these behaviors. As previously noted, this response (in which the animal remains essentially motionless, except for breathing) is often used as a measure of fear conditioning. Freezing provides an innate strategy to avoid danger because a motionless animal is less likely to be spotted by a predator than one that is moving. Moreover, flight is not especially effective for rodents because relative to their predators they are very slow.

Michael Fanselow (1991) has argued that these defensive behaviors are organized around what he called a **predatory imminence gradient**, that is, when a potential predator is at a distance the rat will freeze, but as the predator moves within striking distance, the rat might attempt to flee the scene. If caught, it will engage in fighting in an attempt to escape. People respond to danger in much the same way. For example, Caroline and Robert Blanchard (1989), pioneers in research on defensive behaviors, have provided the following description of human defensive behavior:

If something unexpected occurs—a loud noise or sudden movement—people tend to respond immediately… stop what they are doing… orient toward the stimulus, and try to identify its potential for actual danger. This happens very quickly, in a reflex-like sequence in which action precedes any voluntary or consciously intentioned behavior. A poorly localizable or identifiable threat source, such as sound in the night, may elicit an active immobility so profound that the frightened person can hardly speak or even breathe, that is, freezing. However, if the danger source has been localized and an avenue for flight or concealment is plausible, the person will probably try to flee or hide…. Actual contact, particularly painful contact, with the threat source is also likely to elicit thrashing, biting, scratching and other potentially damaging activities by the terrified person.

In addition to activating these easily observed behaviors, a danger signal will engage our autonomic nervous system, causing changes in our internal physiology, including increased heart rate and blood pressure and the shunting of blood to the peripheral muscles to prepare for flight or fight. Danger signals also produce analgesia—insensitivity to pain—and can release adrenal gland hormones that support the flight–fight response and enhance memory (see Chapter 13). Some stimuli will innately activate the fear system. However, learning and memory processes provide the primary way to link stimuli to the neural systems that support fear behavior and allow us to anticipate danger and get out of harm's way. Figure 19.1 provides a schematic of the basic ideas of a defensive behavioral system.

Experience teaches us to identify dangerous situations. This happens because an experience with an aversive event will modify our response to the otherwise insignificant features of the environment that are also present.

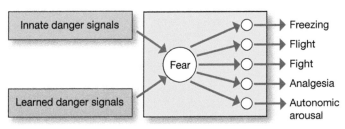

**Figure 19.1**
This figure illustrates a defensive behavioral system. This system organizes the expression of a variety of behaviors that have evolved to protect us from danger. It can be activated by innate danger signals, and experience allows this system to also be activated by learned danger signals.

Associative learning processes that support Pavlovian conditioning produce this outcome. The basic laboratory procedures used for creating conditioned fear were described in Chapter 9 (illustrated in Figure 9.8).

An aversive stimulus can establish fear to both the place–context where it occurred and the discrete phasic stimulus (a stimulus that has a distinct onset and termination) that preceded the shock. Fear as measured by defensive responses is easy to establish and increases with the intensity of the aversive event. Once established, memories for fear experience endure for a long time. Variations of this basic procedure in combination with methods for altering regions of the brain have been used to reveal much of what has been learned about the neural basis of learned fear.

## The Neural Basis of Fear

When confronted with signals of danger, animals can display several responses. As noted, they freeze, they flee, and they will fight when escape is not possible. They also display autonomic arousal. In this section, some of the major components of the neural circuitry that supports these fear responses are described. The system, illustrated in Figure 19.2, is organized to receive sensory information about the environment and to decide if fear behaviors should be generated.

**Midbrain subcortical nuclei** are responsible for generating fear behaviors. For example, neurons located in what is called the periaqueductal gray (PAG) produce freezing and analgesia, and other neurons in the lateral hypothalamus (LH) are responsible for the changes in autonomic responses (heart rate and blood pressure) produced by the sympathetic nervous system that prepare the body for action (Figure 19.2). Direct electrical stimulation of these brain regions can elicit fear behaviors, and damage to these regions impairs the expression of the behaviors (see Fanselow, 1991, and Kim and Jung, 2006, for reviews).

Midbrain nuclei provide the direct neural basis for specific defensive behaviors that make up the fear system. However, these regions are not directly linked to the sensory–perceptual systems by which the world is experienced. Instead, the sensory–perceptual systems interface with the midbrain nuclei by way of the amygdala (discussed previously in Chapter 13). The amygdala is an almond shaped structure composed of many nuclei and subdivisions. Three components of the amygdala are relevant to the fear system: (1) the basolateral amygdala (BLA), composed of the **lateral (LA)** and **basal (BA) nucleus**; (2) the **central amygdala (CE)**; and (3) **intercalated cells** (ITC-a and ITC-b in Figure 19.2), which release inhibitory neurotransmitters (GABA) onto their targets (Box 19.1).

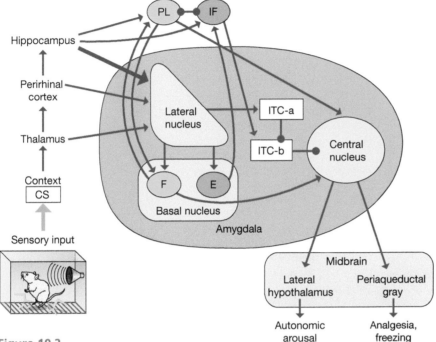

**Figure 19.2**
This figure illustrates the basic components of the fear system that can be modified by experience. The lateral nucleus receives sensory input from the sensory thalamus, perirhinal cortex, and hippocampus that provides information about the current state of the environment. The basal nucleus contains both fear and extinction neurons. Neurons in the central amygdala control midbrain structures that support the expression of fear behaviors. When neurons in the central amygdala depolarize they activate the midbrain nuclei to generate defensive behaviors. An ITC-b cluster normally inhibits central amygdala neurons. Arrows indicate excitatory connections, and round endings indicate inhibitory connections. PL = prelimbic; IF = infralimbic; F = fear; E = extinction.

The lateral nucleus provides the interface that links the content of a fear conditioning experience to other components of the amygdala. Joseph LeDoux (1994) has described two pathways that bring the content of the experience to the lateral nucleus, a **subcortical pathway** and a **cortical pathway** (Romanski and LeDoux, 1992). The subcortical pathway comes directly from the sensory thalamus, which is thought to provide a somewhat impoverished representation of the sensory experience. The cortical pathway carries information from the sensory thalamus to the neocortical regions of the brain including the perirhinal cortex and hippocampus, which also project to the lateral nucleus and provide a richer, more detailed

Joseph LeDoux

## BOX 19.1 Intercalated Cells Inhibit Fear

Denis Paré and his colleagues (Likhtik et al., 2008; Royer and Paré, 2002) identified clusters of intercalated cells (ITCs) located between the basolateral complex and the central amygdala. These neurons receive CS information from the basolateral amygdala and project to the central amygdala. When activated, these cells release the inhibitory neurotransmitter GABA and thus prevent their target neurons from depolarizing. In this way, they prevent neurons in the central amygdala from generating defensive behavior. ITC = Intercalated cells; BL = basolateral amygdala; LA = lateral amygdala; AB = accessory basal nucleus.

Denis Paré

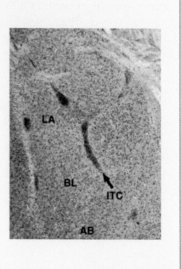

representation of the experience (Burwell et al., 2004). The lateral amygdala region projects to two regions—the basal nucleus and a cluster of intercalated cells (ITC-a)—that project to a second ITC cluster (ITC-b). The second cluster projects to neurons in the central amygdala and inhibits them.

Cyril Herry and his colleagues (Herry et al., 2008) discovered that the basal nucleus contains two types of neurons: (1) fear neurons that are active when fear behaviors are expressed and (2) extinction neurons that are active when fear has been extinguished (described later in this chapter). The fear neurons provide excitatory projections to the central nucleus and to neurons in the prelimbic region of the prefrontal cortex. Extinction neurons project to ITC-b cells.

The central amygdala can be thought of as the command center for initiating fear-related behaviors. It is an output region and projects to the midbrain regions that generate fear behaviors. Under normal, nonthreatening conditions, ITC-b cells inhibit central amygdala neurons. When these neurons are activated (depolarized), they activate neurons in the lateral hypothalamus and periaqueductal gray and generate fear behaviors. Thus, to generate fear behavior the neurons in the central amygdala must be depolarized.

Two regions of the prefrontal cortex (prelimbic and infralimbic) interact with the amygdala to modulate the fear response (Sotres-Bayon and Quirk, 2010). Neurons in the prelimbic region are

Cyril Herry

reciprocally connected to fear neurons in the basal nucleus. These reciprocal connections are designed to *amplify* the fear signal. Support for this function comes from the observation that activation of neurons in the lateral nucleus by a cue paired with shock lasts only a few 100 milliseconds, but prelimbic neurons show a sustained response for the duration of the CS (tens of seconds) that correlates with the duration of the fear response. In addition, inactivating PL neurons greatly reduces the expression of fear behaviors (Sotres-Bayon and Quirk, 2010). In contrast, the output from infralimbic neurons *inhibits* the fear response by activating ITC-b cells. They receive projections from the hippocampus and extinction neurons in the basal nucleus.

The fear system is complex. The main point, however, is that a conditioned fear response is produced because the fear circuit is reorganized (Figure 19.3). Synapses are strengthened that link the sensory content (context and CS) to neurons in the lateral amygdala and prelimbic cortex.

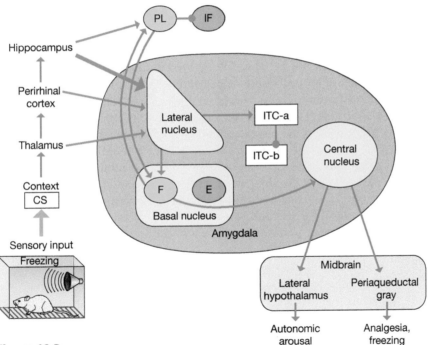

**Figure 19.3**
When an aversive event occurs, synapses are strengthened that link the sensory content (context and CS) to neurons in the lateral amygdala and prelimbic cortex. As a consequence, a re-encounter with these stimulus conditions will activate the fear circuit (in red). The inhibitory influence of ITC-b neurons on central neurons will be removed and excitatory drive provided by fear neurons and prelimbic cortex neurons will increase. PL = prelimbic; IF = infralimbic; F = fear; E = extinction.

Consequently, if these stimulus conditions are re-encountered the sensory input will excite neurons in the lateral nucleus and prelimbic cortex and this will result in (a) the removal of the ITC-b inhibitory block on central amygdala neurons and (b) the activation of fear neurons in the basal nucleus. Consequently, neurons in the central amygdala will be excited to generate fear behaviors (see Figure 19.3).

## Eliminating Dangerous Fears: Theories of Extinction

The fear system is designed to produce adaptive behaviors that keep us out of harm's way. However, the properties of this system that support rapid fear conditioning also can be maladaptive and lead to behavioral pathologies. Learned fears and anxieties such as panic attacks and **post-traumatic stress disorders** that result from intensive aversive experiences can be so debilitating that they greatly interfere with our ability to function normally. Consequently, the problem of how to eliminate learned fears is of great interest to basic researchers, clinical psychologists, and psychiatrists.

Researchers have focused on the Pavlovian conditioning methodology to study how to remove learned fears. Cues paired with aversive events acquire the ability to evoke a conditioned defensive response. In the language of Pavlovian conditioning, the cue paired with shock is called the conditioned stimulus (CS) and the aversive event is called the unconditioned stimulus (US). Since Pavlov's work, it has been known that a conditioned response (CR) can be eliminated. The procedure is called the method of extinction. With this procedure, after a conditioned response is established, the subject is presented the CS but the US is not presented. When the CS is repeatedly presented alone, it loses its ability to evoke the conditioned response. This outcome, the loss of the conditioned response, is called **extinction** (Figure 19.4). Note that the term extinction is used to describe *both a method and a fact*.

**Figure 19.4**
Paired presentations of the conditioned stimulus (CS) and unconditioned stimulus (US) produce acquisition. The CS acquires the ability to evoke the conditioned response (CR). If the CS is then presented alone, it will lose the ability to evoke the CR. This phenomenon is called extinction.

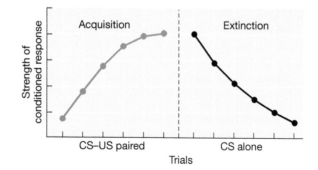

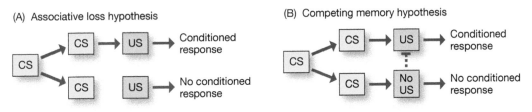

(A) Associative loss hypothesis

(B) Competing memory hypothesis

**Figure 19.5**
This figure illustrates two theories of extinction. The associative loss hypothesis assumes that extinction is due to a CS-alone presentation eliminating the original CS–US association. The competing memory hypothesis assumes that extinction produces a new association called a CS–noUS association. The original CS–US association that produced the CR remains intact. If the CS–noUS association occurs, it inhibits (–) the expression of the conditioned response.

Extinction is an empirical fact. Presenting the CS alone can eliminate the conditioned response. The theoretical question is, why does this method produce extinction? Two hypotheses have been proposed. One is called the **associative loss hypothesis**; the other is called the **competing memory hypothesis** (Figure 19.5). It is generally assumed that a CS paired with a US comes to evoke a conditioned response because it has become associated with the representation of the US. The associative loss hypothesis assumes that extinction is due to the CS-alone presentation eliminating or erasing the original CS–US association. However, the competing memory hypothesis assumes that the original CS–US association remains intact and instead a new association, called a **CS–noUS association**, is produced. If the CS activates the noUS pathway, expression of the conditioned response will be blocked or inhibited.

These two theories have different implications. The associative loss hypothesis implies that extinction should be *permanent* because the underlying association is erased. So, according to this theory, the CS must again be paired with the US in order to re-establish its ability to evoke a conditioned response. In contrast, the competing memory hypothesis allows that the conditioned response could recover without re-pairing of the CS and US because the original association is not lost—the CS just enters into a new association, the CS–noUS association.

Mark Bouton's research program has been critical to the contemporary view of extinction (Bouton, 1994; Bouton, 2002). The evidence indicates that extinction does not eliminate the underlying associative basis of the conditioned response. Instead, *extinction produces new learning*. Three observations support this conclusion (Figure 19.6).

- **Spontaneous recovery**. With the passage of time following extinction the CS recovers its ability to evoke the conditioned response. It does not have to be paired with the US again for the conditioned response to reappear.

Mark Bouton

- **Renewal effect.** In this case rats are given the CS–US pairings in one place or context, but extinction (CS-alone presentations) occurs in a different place. Even though extinction training eliminates the conditioned response, if the animal is returned to the original training environment, the CR recovers.

- **Reinstatement effect.** Just re-presenting the US in the training context can reinstate the ability of the CS to evoke a conditioned response. Note again that the CS does not have to be re-paired with the US.

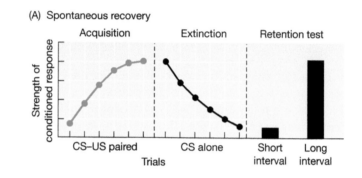

(A) Spontaneous recovery

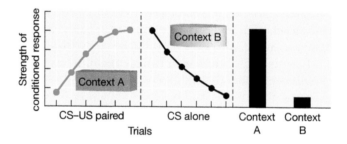

(B) Renewal effect

**Figure 19.6**
This figure illustrates three findings that indicate that extinction is not permanent. In each example the critical results are from the retention test where the CS is re-presented after extinction has taken place. (A) Spontaneous recovery can occur when there is a long retention interval between extinction and the test. (B) Renewal can occur when the context where extinction trials take place is different from the context in which training takes place, and the test occurs in the training context. (C) Reinstatement occurs if the US is re-presented without the CS. In all cases, recovery from extinction occurs even though the CS and US are never re-paired.

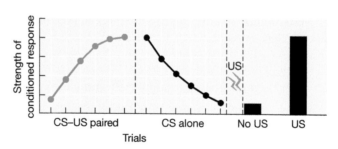

(C) Reinstatement effect

Note that in these examples the CS recovers the ability to evoke the CR even though it is not re-paired with the US. If presenting the CS alone erased the underlying CS–US association, this should not happen. Thus, these results support the competing memory hypothesis—that extinction does not erase the original CS–US association, rather the CS enters into a CS–noUS association.

## Neural Basis of Fear Extinction

Based on the results just discussed one would assume that at the completion of extinction, the CS is involved in two associations: the original CS–US association and the new CS–noUS association. The task for neurobiologists is to understand (a) how the neural circuitry supports a CS–noUS association and (b) what processes determine which association is expressed, the CS–US or the CS–noUS association—that is, why does the fear response recover?

### The CS–noUS Neural Circuit

The major outcome of extinction training is to reconfigure the fear circuit so that the CS activates intercalated clusters (described in Box 19.1) that inhibit neurons in the central amygdala. To accomplish this, extinction training strengthens synaptic connections linking the context and CS input to extinction neurons in the basal nucleus to ITCs and to neurons in the infralimbic prefrontal cortex that also projects to ITCs. Thus, when the CS is presented ITCs are activated and neurons in the central amygdala are inhibited (Maren, 2011; Pape and Paré, 2010; Sotres-Bayon and Quirk, 2010).

It is important to remember that extinction training does not erase the synaptic connections established during fear conditioning that excite central amygdala neurons to generate fear. Extinction results because new connections are strengthened that provide the inhibition needed to prevent those neurons from depolarizing and generating fear. Thus, the CS–noUS association can be thought of as *a reconfigured fear circuit that allows the extinguished CS to suppress the central amygdala*. Figure 19.7 provides a comparison of the circuit that is established by fear conditioning that generates fear (red lines) with the circuit that is established when fear is extinguished (black lines). Whether or not fear is renewed will be determined by which circuit dominates.

### Why Fear Renews: A Role for the Hippocampus

Fear acquisition training strengthens synapses that link the CS to fear neurons (CS–US association) and fear extinction training strengthen synapses that link the CS to extinction neurons (CS–noUS association). So how is the decision

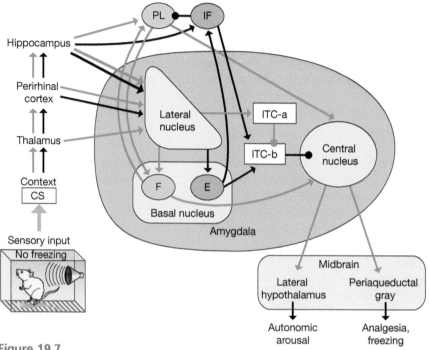

**Figure 19.7**
This figure illustrates how extinction training reconfigures the neural system to support extinction. The red arrows indicate how fear conditioning organizes the system to produce fear. The black arrows indicate how extinction training modifies the system to support no fear. The fundamental outcome produced by extinction training is to change synaptic connections that will increase inhibitory control over neurons in the central amygdala. This is accomplished by strengthening synapses linking the CS to extinction neurons in the basal region and to neurons in the infralimbic cortex. Both extinction and infralimbic cortex neurons project to ITCs that inhibit neurons in the central amygdala. The result is that the CS can now activate the new extinction circuit or the fear circuit and prevent neurons in the central amygdala from depolarizing and generating fear behaviors. Arrows indicate excitatory connections; round endings indicate inhibitory connections. PL = prelimbic; IF = infralimbic; F = fear; E = extinction.

made that determines whether the CS activates extinction neurons or fear neurons? Steve Maren and his colleagues (Corcoran and Maren, 2001; Ji and Maren, 2005, 2007) have revealed that the hippocampal system makes a critical contribution to this decision. Their fundamental behavioral observation is that extinction is context specific. Thus, if extinction occurs in context B, the CS will evoke no fear if the test occurs in context B. However, the CS will elicit the fear response if it is presented in new context C. This is the previously described renewal effect. From a psychological perspective one might say that the rat has learned that the CS signals the absence of shock only in context B.

The context specificity of extinction depends on the hippocampal system (Bouton et al., 2006). When the hippocampus is damaged or inactivated following extinction, context specificity is lost and rats do not display renewed fear (Corcoran and Maren, 2001; Ji and Maren, 2005, 2007). The context regulates expression of fear or extinction because the hippocampal system also projects on to extinction neurons, and during extinction training these synapses get strengthened. Thus, if the CS is presented in the extinction context the CS–noUS circuit will dominate and the fear response will not be generated. However, if the CS is presented in another context the renewal of fear will occur.

Steve Maren

## Extinction Learning Depends on NMDA Receptors

Extinction is the result of new learning. Thus, it is reasonable to ask if NMDA receptors are involved in strengthening the synaptic connection linking the sensory–perceptual content of experience to the neurons that support extinction. Several laboratories have reported that the injection of APV into the amygdala prior to CS-alone presentations significantly impairs the acquisition and retention of the learning that supports extinction (see Falls et al., 1992, and Myers and Davis, 2007, for a review). It also has been shown that the antagonist ifenprodil, which selectively blocks glutamate's access to the GluN2B subunit of the NMDA receptor, blocks the extinction of the fear response (Sotres-Bayon et al., 2007).

In addition to having glutamate binding sites, the NMDA receptor also has a glycine binding site (Figure 19.8). The glycine binding site is important because it contributes to the efficient opening of the NMDA receptor calcium channel. A number of researchers have asked if the glycine binding site makes a contribution to extinction. They used a partial agonist called **D-cycloserine** (**DCS**) that binds to the glycine site to enhance the opening of the NMDA receptor. This work revealed that if DCS is injected either before or immediately after extinction training, the next day the rodents display enhanced extinction (Ledgerwood et al., 2003; Walker et al., 2002; see Davis et al., 2006, for a review). Given that NMDA receptor antagonists can prevent extinction and the partial agonist DCS can facilitate extinction, it is reasonable to assume that synaptic changes that depend on NMDA receptors play a central role in the new learning that produces extinction.

The discovery that DCS facilitates extinction in the laboratory has encouraged researchers to pursue the possibility that DCS, in combination with behavioral theory, might have therapeutic value in eliminating learned fears

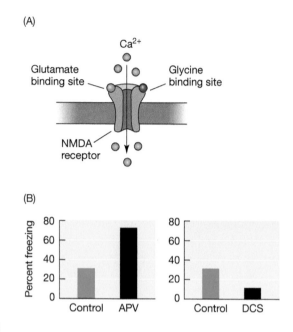

**Figure 19.8**
NMDA receptors have two binding sites, one for glutamate and one for glycine. APV antagonizes the glutamate binding site and interferes with extinction. D-cycloserine (DCS) is an agonist for the glycine site. When it is given before or after extinction training, it facilitates the processes that produce extinction. (See Davis et al., 2006, for a review.)

in people. Kerry Ressler and his colleagues (2004) have tested this hypothesis on people who suffer from acrophobia. People with acrophobia have a debilitating and irrational fear of heights. To test their hypothesis, Ressler's group used what is called **exposure therapy**. In this therapy, patients are forced to experience the stimulus situation that induces the fear response. It is used to treat a number of fear–anxiety disorders. Some participants received exposure therapy and in addition were required to take a pill containing DCS prior to exposure. Other participants received exposure therapy in combination with a placebo (a pill that contained no DCS). The patients had no knowledge of which pill they took. Several measures indicated a significant benefit to combining DCS with exposure therapy. When retested following the treatment, participants who had taken the DCS pill reported a decrease in discomfort produced by exposure. Their autonomic arousal decreased and they were more willing to expose themselves to heights. These benefits persisted for three months after the treatment. These are very promising results that will no doubt stimulate additional work to determine the generality of these effects (see Graham et al., 2011, for a discussion of pharmacological adjuncts to behavior therapies).

## New Insights: Extinction Can Erase Fear Memories

Rick Richardson

The fear circuit of adult animals is designed to preserve the synaptic changes that produce learned fears, even when the CS no longer signals danger. However, this is not the case for the infant rodent. Rick Richardson and his colleagues (Kim and Richardson, 2007a,b) discovered that following extinction training, infant rats (about 17 days old) do not display the major indicators that the original association (CS–US) is preserved—spontaneous recovery, renewal, and reinstatement (see also Carew and Rudy, 1991). These markers emerge when the rodents are about 21 days old, around the time they are weaned. Thus, there is a transition that takes place during the third week after birth when there is a shift from extinction erasing some aspect of the fear memory to extinction producing new learning.

This result could reflect developmental differences in components of the fear extinction circuit. For example, it is likely the hippocampal system, prefrontal cortex, and the inhibitory circuits that suppress fear are not fully functional. However, there are molecules in the extracellular matrix complex, called **perineuronal nets**, that have been directly linked to the different outcomes produced by extinction. Perineuronal nets surround neurons (especially inhibitory neurons) and have been discovered to be key developmental regulators of plasticity (Frischknecht and Gundelfiger, 2012). Studies of the development of the visual system, for example, indicate that early in development, when these nets are absent, synapses in the visual pathway are more easily modified than later in development when they are present (Pizzorousso et al., 2002).

Nadine Gogolla and her colleagues (Gogolla et al., 2009) have linked the development of these nets to the shift from when extinction training erases the fear memory to when it produces new learning (Figure 19.9). These nets are not present during the period early in development when extinction training erases the fear memory but are present later in development when extinction produces new learning.

Based on these observations, Gogolla and her colleagues hypothesized that by degrading the nets the processes supporting extinction could be returned to the early infant state when extinction erases the fear memory. Consistent with their hypothesis, injecting an enzyme that degrades the perineuronal net into the BLA *prior to fear conditioning* produced this result in adult rodents— following extinction training they did not display spontaneous recovery or

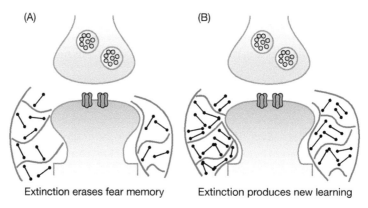

(A) Extinction erases fear memory    (B) Extinction produces new learning

**Figure 19.9**
(A) Early in development, perineuronal nets that surround spines are immature. During this period extinction training can erase the fear memory. (B) When these nets are mature, extinction training does not erase the fear memory and extinction is due to new learning. However, by degrading these nets the infant state can be reinstated and extinction training can again erase the fear memory.

renewal. However, injecting the enzyme *after conditioning* did produce this result—these mice displayed both spontaneous recovery and renewal. These results indicate that perineuronal nets support processes that protect the synapses strengthened by fear conditioning from erasure. A future task for neurobiologists will be identifying the properties of the perineuronal nets that produce erasure-resistant synapses.

## Extinction and Reconsolidation

Research guided by reconsolidation theory (see Chapter 14) has revealed that reactivating a memory trace creates a window of opportunity during which it is labile and can be either enhanced or degraded. This window may present researchers with another strategy to permanently eliminate memories that support debilitating fears. One specific idea is that extinction training can be more effective if it takes place while the fear memory is in this labile state. The underlying premise is that while the memory trace is labile it may be possible for the extinction procedure to overwrite or in some sense replace the content of the original fear memory with the new content—that the CS no longer is followed by shock.

There is support for this idea. Marie Monfils and her colleagues (Monfils et al., 2009) varied the interval between the reactivation treatment and extinction training. They reported that when extinction occurred within an hour of the reactivation treatment, the fear memory did not recover (as measured by the spontaneous recovery, renewal, or reinstatement). However, the fear memory did return if the interval was 6 hours or longer. A similar result has been obtained with humans that have had both fear training and fear extinction in the laboratory (Schiller et al., 2010).

Several other laboratories, however, have reported that extinction training administered shortly after the reactivation treatment *either reduces the effect of extinction training or has no effect* (Chan et al., 2010; Costanzi et al., 2011; Ishii et al., 2012; Morris et al., 2005; Stafford et al., 2013). The reasons for these conflicting outcomes are not yet clear. Given this range of outcomes, the appropriate conclusion at this time is that the reconsolidation window does provides an opportunity for extinction training to modify the existing fear memory, but the direction of the modification is uncertain. Future research will have to determine under what conditions these conflicting results occur.

## Summary

Our evolutionary history has provided us with neural systems designed to support behaviors that are organized to meet our most fundamental survival needs. These behavioral systems are finely tuned by our experiences. This chapter focused specifically on the fear system that supports defensive behaviors designed to allow us to anticipate danger and keep out of harm's way.

Animals continuously assess their environments for potential dangers. A set of species-specific defensive behaviors can be called out when danger lurks. Midbrain regions (lateral hypothalamus and periaqueductal gray) provide the proximal support for defensive behaviors. However, they are under the control of neurons in the basolateral and central amygdala separated by intercalated inhibitory neurons. Inputs from the thalamus, neocortex, prelimbic prefrontal cortex, and hippocampus converge onto neurons in the BLA to provide the various levels of detailed information about the environment that is present at the time an aversive event takes place. An aversive experience modifies the strength of these synaptic connections to fear neurons in the basal nucleus and neurons in the prelimbic region so that when elements of this experience are re-encountered they will drive the central amygdala to produce defensive behaviors.

The fear system generally produces adaptive behavior, but intensely aversive experiences can lead to excessive fears that become pathological and debilitating. One way to eliminate learned fears is to use Pavlovian procedures designed to produce extinction. Exposure to just the CS can greatly weaken its capacity to evoke fear. However, in adults extinction is the product of new learning (called a CS–noUS association) that links CS input to extinction neurons and to neurons in the infralimbic cortex. Extinction neurons in the basal nucleus and infralimbic prefrontal cortex neurons project to the ITCs, which can suppress the activity of neurons in the central amygdala. This system allows animals to learn to switch between fear and no fear states and thus to adapt rapidly to changes in their environment (Sotres-Bayona and Quirk, 2010).

Extinction training does not normally erase the fear memory. However, developmental research has identified components of the extracellular matrix—perineuronal nets—that prevent extinction training from erasing fear memories. These nets are absent during infancy stage when extinction training erases fear and they emerge at the stage when extinction produces new learning. Degrading the nets returns the adult animal to the infant stage.

## References

Blanchard, C. D. and Blanchard, R. J. (1989). Ethonoexperimental approaches to the biology of emotion. *Annual Review of Psychology, 39,* 43–68.

Bolles, R. C. (1970). Species specific defense reactions and avoidance learning. *Psychological Review, 79,* 32–48.

Bouton, M. E. (1994). Context, ambiguity, and classical conditioning. *Current Directions in Psychological Science, 3,* 49–53.

Bouton, M. E. (2002). Context, ambiguity, and unlearning sources of relapse after behavioral extinction. *Biological Psychiatry, 52,* 976–986.

Bouton, M. E., Westbrook, R. F., Corcoran, K. A., and Maren, S. (2006). Contextual and temporal modulation of extinction: behavioral and biological mechanisms. *Biological Psychiatry, 60,* 352–60.

Burwell, R. D., Bucci, D. J., Sanborn, M. R., and Jutras, M. J. (2004). Perirhinal and postrhinal contributions to remote memory for context. *Journal of Neuroscience, 24,* 11023–11028.

Carew, M. B. and Rudy, J. W. (1991). Multiple functions of context during conditioning: a developmental analysis. *Developmental Psychobiology, 21,* 191–209.

Chan, W. Y., Leung, H. T., Westbrook, R. F., and McNally, G. P. (2010). Effects of recent exposure to a conditioned stimulus on extinction of Pavlovian fear conditioning. *Learning and Memory, 17,* 512–521.

Corcoran, K. A. and Maren, S. (2001). Hippocampal inactivation disrupts contextual retrieval of fear memory after extinction. *Journal of Neuroscience, 2,* 1720–1726.

Costanzi, M., Cannas, S., Saraulli, D., Rossi-Arnaud, C., and Cestari, V. (2011). Extinction after retrieval: effects on the associative and nonassociative components of remote contextual fear memory. *Learning and Memory, 18,* 508–518.

Davis, M., Ressler, K., Rothbaum, B. O., and Richardson, R. (2006). Effects of D-cycloserine on extinction: translation from preclinical to clinical work. *Biological Psychiatry, 60,* 369–375.

Falls, W. A., Miserendino, M. J. D., and Davis, M. (1992). Extinction of fear-potentiated startle: blockade by infusion of an NMDA antagonist into the amygdala. *Journal of Neuroscience, 12,* 854–863.

Fanselow, M. S. (1991). The midbrain periaqueductal gray as coordinator of action in response to fear and anxiety. In A. Depaulis and R. Bandler (Eds.), *The midbrain peri-acqueductal gray matter* (pp. 151–171). New York: Plenum Press.

Frischknecht, R. and Gundelfiger, E. D. (2012). The brain's extracellular matrix and its role in synaptic plasticity. *Advances in Experimental Medicine and Biology, 970,* 153–171.

Gogolla, N., Caroni, P., Luthi, A., and Herry, C. (2009). Perineuronal nets protect fear memories from erasure. *Science, 325,* 1258–1261.

Graham B. M., Langton, J. M., and Richardson, R. (2011). Pharmacological enhancement of fear reduction: preclinical models. *British Journal of Pharmacology, 164,* 1230–1247.

Herry, C., Ciocchi, S., Senn, V., Demmou, L., Muller, C., and Luthi, A. (2008). Switching on and off fear by distinct neuronal circuits. *Nature, 454,* 600–606.

Ishii, D., Matsuzawa, D., Matsuda, S., Tomizawa, H., Sutoh, C, and Shimizu, E. (2012). No erasure effect of retrieval-extinction trial on fear memory in the hippocampus-independent and dependent paradigms. *Neuroscience Letters, 523,* 76–81.

Ji, J. and Maren, S. (2005). Electrolytic lesions of the dorsal hippocampus disrupt renewal of conditional fear after extinction. *Learning and Memory, 12,* 270–276.

Ji, J. and Maren S. (2007). Hippocampal involvement in contextual modulation of fear extinction. *Hippocampus, 17,* 749–758.

Kim, J. H. and Richardson, R. (2007a). A developmental dissociation of context and GABA effects on extinguished fear in rats. *Behavioral Neuroscience, 121,* 131–139.

Kim, J. H. and Richardson, R. (2007b). A developmental dissociation in reinstatement of an extinguished fear response in rats. *Neurobiology of Learning and Memory, 88,* 48–57.

Kim, J. J. and Jung, M. W. (2006). Neural circuits and mechanisms involved in Pavlovian fear conditioning: a critical review. *Neuroscience and Biobehavioral Review, 30,* 188–202.

Ledgerwood, L., Richardson, R., and Cranney, J. (2003). D-cycloserine facilitates extinction of conditioned fear as assessed by freezing in rats. *Behavioral Neuroscience, 117,* 341–349.

LeDoux, J. E. (1994). Emotion, memory and the brain. *Scientific American, 270,* 50–57.

Likhtik, E., Popa, D., Apergis-Schoute, J., Fidacaro, G. A., and Paré, D. (2008). Amygdala intercalated neurons are required for expression of fear extinction. *Nature, 454,* 642–645.

Maren, S. (2011). Seeking a spotless mind: extinction, deconsolidation and erasure of fear memory. *Neuron, 70,* 830–845.

Monfils, M. H., Cowansage, K. K., Klann, E., and LeDoux, J. E. (2009). Extinction-reconsolidation boundaries: key to persistent attenuation of fear memories. *Science, 324,* 951–955.

Morris, R. W., Furlong, T. M., and Westbrook, R. F. (2005). Recent exposure to a dangerous context impairs extinction and reinstates lost fear reactions. *Journal of Experimental Psychology, Animal Behavior Process, 31*, 40–55.

Myers, K. M. and Davis, M. (2007). Mechanisms of fear extinction. *Molecular Psychiatry, 12*, 120–150.

Pape, H. C. and Paré, D. (2010). Plastic synaptic networks of the amygdala for the acquisition, expression, and extinction of conditioned fear. *Physiological Review, 90*, 419–463.

Pizzorusso, T., Medini, P., Berardi, N., Chierzi, S., Fawcett, J. W., and Maffei, L. (2002). Reactivation of ocular dominance plasticity in the adult visual cortex. *Science, 298*, 1248–1251.

Ressler, K. J., Rothbaum, B. O., Tannenbaum, L., Anderson, P., Graap, K., Zimand, E., Hodges, L., and Davis, M. (2004). Cognitive enhancers as adjuncts to psychotherapy: use of D-cycloserine in phobic individuals to facilitate extinction of fear. *Archives of General Psychiatry, 61*, 1136–1144.

Romanski, L. M. and LeDoux, J. E. (1992). Equipotentiality of thalamo-amygdala and thalamo-cortico-amygdala circuits in auditory fear conditioning. *Journal of Neuroscience, 12*, 4501–4509.

Royer, S. and Paré, D. (2002). Bidirectional synaptic plasticity in intercalated amygdala neurons and the extinction of conditioned fear responses. *Neuroscience, 115*, 455–462.

Schiller, D., Monfils, M. H., Raio, C. M., Johnson, D. C., Ledoux, J. E., and Phelps, E. A. (2010). Preventing the return of fear in humans using reconsolidation update mechanisms. *Nature, 463*, 49–53.

Sotres-Bayon, F., Bush, D. E., and LeDoux, J. E. (2007). Acquisition of fear extinction requires activation of NR2B-containing NMDA receptors in the lateral amygdala. *Neuropsychopharmacology, 32*, 1929–1940.

Sotres-Bayon, F. and Quirk, G. J. (2010) Prefrontal control of fear: more than just extinction. *Current Opinion in Neurobiology, 20*, 231–235.

Stafford, J. M., Maughan, D. K., Ilioi, E. C., and Lattal, M. K. (2013). Exposure to a fearful context during periods of memory plasticity impairs extinction via hyperactivation of frontal-amygdalar circuits. *Learning and Memory, 20*, 156–163.

Timberlake, W. (1994). Behavioral systems, associationism, and Pavlovian conditioning. *Psychonomic Bulletin and Review, 1*, 405–420.

Walker, D. L., Ressler, K. J., Lu, K. T., and Davis, M. (2002). Facilitation of conditioned fear extinction by systemic administration or intra-amygdala infusions of D-cycloserine as assessed with fear-potentiated startle. *Journal of Neuroscience, 22*, 2343–2351.

# Photo Credits

*The Author would like to thank the following researchers for generously providing the images that appear at the beginning of each chapter.*

Chapter 1    Courtesy of Dr. Joseph C. Biedenkapp, University of Colorado

Chapter 2    Courtesy of Dr. Robert J. Sutherland and Neal Melvin, University of Lethbridge

Chapter 3    Image by Tamily Weissman in the laboratory of Jeff Lichtman. Mouse produced by Feng et al. 2000 (Imaging neuronal subsets in transgenic mice expressing multiple spectral variants of GFP, *Neuron*, 28, 41–51), with Judy Tollett.

Chapter 4    Courtesy of Dr. Robert D. Blitzer, Mount Sinai Medical School

Chapter 5    Courtesy of Dr. Gary J. Bassell, Emory University School of Medicine

Chapter 6    Courtesy of Dr. Robert J. Sutherland and Neal Melvin, University of Lethbridge

Chapter 7    Image by Tamily Weissman in the laboratory of Jeff Lichtman. Mouse produced by Feng et al. 2000 (Imaging neuronal subsets in transgenic mice expressing multiple spectral variants of GFP, *Neuron*, 28, 41–51), with Judy Tollett.

Chapter 8   Courtesy of Dr. Neal J. Waxham, University of Texas Medical School, Austin

Chapter 9   Courtesy of Dr. Patricia H. Reggio, University of North Carolina, Greensboro

Chapter 10  Courtesy of Dr. Robert D. Blitzer, Mount Sinai Medical School

Chapter 11  Courtesy of Jean Livet, Josh Sanes, and Jeff Lichtman, 2007, Harvard University

Chapter 12  Courtesy of Dr. Gyorgy Buzsáki, New York University

Chapter 13  © Sashkinw/istockphoto.com

Chapter 14  Courtesy of Dr. Gary J. Bassell, Emory University School of Medicine

Chapter 15  Courtesy of Dr. Michael Babcock, Montana State University

Chapter 16  Courtesy of Dr. Gyorgy Buzsáki, New York University

Chapter 17  Courtesy of Dr. Sondra T. Bland, University of Colorado

Chapter 18  Courtesy of Dr. Carol A. Seger, Colorado State University

Chapter 19  Courtesy of Dr. Denis A. Paré, Rutgers University

# Glossary

## A

**actin**  A cytoskeleton protein filament that exists in two states: globular actin (G-actin) and filament actin (F-actin).

**actin-depolymerization factor/cofilin**  A protein that depolymerizes F-actin; also called cofilin.

**action**  A category of instrumental behavior believed to be supported by expectancies and thought to be goal directed and purposeful.

**action potentials**  The electrical signal conducted along axons by which information is conveyed from one neuron to another in the nervous system.

**active decay theory**  The idea that over time molecular processes actively degrade the synaptic basis of unused memory traces.

**active trace theory**  A theory that suggests that both the age of a memory trace and its state of activation at the time of a disrupting event are determinants of the vulnerability of the trace to disruption.

**adjacent-arm task**  A version of the radial arm maze in which a rodent is released from one arm and rewarded for choosing to enter one of the two adjacent arms.

**adrenal gland**  An endocrine gland, located above the kidney, composed of two parts: the adrenal medulla (which secretes epinephrine) and the adrenal cortex (which secretes glucocorticoids).

**adrenaline**  A hormone secreted by the adrenal gland, often as a result of an arousing stimulus; also called epinephrine (EPI).

**adrenergic receptors**  Receptors that bind to adrenergics, that is, drugs that mimic the effects of epinephrine.

**after images**  Briefly lasting sensations; the first of three traces in William James's theory of memory.

**agonist**  A substance that binds to a specific receptor and triggers a response in the cell. It mimics the action of an endogenous ligand (such as a hormone or neurotransmitter) that binds to the same receptor.

**AMPA receptor**   An ionotropic glutamate receptor that is selective for Na⁺. AMPA receptors are major contributors to whether or not the sending neuron will depolarize the receiving neuron.

**AMPA receptor trafficking**   The movement of AMPA receptors into and out of the plasma membrane.

**ampakines**   A class of drugs that may enhance cognitive function. Ampakines cross the blood–brain barrier and bind to a site on the AMPA receptor.

**amygdala**   A collection of midbrain nuclei, some of which are involved in supporting fear conditioning and in modulating memory storage in other regions of the brain.

**annulus crossings**   A measure of place learning in the Morris water-escape task based on how many times during the probe trial the animal actually crosses the exact place where the platform was located during training compared to how many times it crosses the equivalent area in the other quadrants.

**antagonist**   A drug that opposes or inhibits the effects of a particular neurotransmitter on the postsynaptic cell.

**anterograde amnesia**   The loss of memory for events that occur after a brain insult or experimental treatment.

**antisense**   Antisense oligonucleotide is a synthesized strand of nucleic acid that will bind to mRNA and prevent its translation.

**Arc (activity-regulated, cytoskeleton-associated protein)**   An immediate early gene that is rapidly transcribed in the hippocampus when rats explore novel environments; also known as Arg3.1.

**associative loss hypothesis**   A hypothesis that assumes extinction is due to the CS–alone presentation eliminating the original CS–US association.

**autophosphorylation**   A special property of CaMKII that enables its active subunits to phosphorylate each other.

**axon**   The long fiber of a neuron that extends from the soma and conducts electrical signals away from the cell body.

**B**

**basal ganglia**   A region of the midbrain composed of the striatum (caudate nucleus and putamen), globus pallidus, subthalamic nucleus, nucleus accumbens, and substantia nigra.

**basal nucleus (BA)**   A nucleus of the amygdala that is thought to be an important part of the neural basis of fear; also referred to as the basal amygdala. The BA is a component of the BLA (basolateral amygdala).

**basolateral amygdala (BLA)**   A region of the amygdala that includes the basal and lateral nuclei. It is critically involved in memory modulation and storing fear memories and plays an important role in attaching value to outcomes.

**BDNF (brain-derived neurotrophic factor)**   A secreted protein that contributes to the consolidation of LTP and memory.

**BDNF–TrkB receptor pathway**   A signaling cascade that activates mTOR and local protein synthesis.

**behavioral system**   A system that is organized specifically to ensure that some particular need is met. For example, there are behavioral systems designed to support our reproductive and feeding-related activities and behavioral systems that allow us to avoid and escape dangerous situations.

**bioenergenics**   The flow of energy in cells.

**brain-derived neurotrophic factor**   See *BDNF*.

## C

**CA1**   A subregion of the hippocampus that receives input from the CA3 region via Schaffer collateral fibers and projects to the entorhinal cortex via the subiculum. It also receives input from the entorhinal cortex.

**CA3**   A subregion of the hippocampus that receives input from the dentate gyrus via mossy fibers and projects to the CA1 region via Schaffer collateral fibers.

**calcium ion (Ca$^{2+}$)**   A second messenger that activates other messenger proteins.

**calcium-induced calcium release (CICR)** The release of calcium from the endoplasmic reticulum; thought to occur when extracellular calcium enters the dendritic spine through an NMDA receptor and binds to ryanodine receptors.

**calmodulin**   A calcium-binding protein that can regulate a number of protein targets.

**calpains**   Proteins that belong to a class of enzymes called proteases that can degrade proteins.

**calpain–spectrin pathway**   A signaling pathway activated by calcium that degrades spectrin protein and results in disassembling actin networks.

**CaMKII (calcium-calmodulin-dependent protein kinase II)**   A kinase protein that, once activated by calmodulin, is able to phosphorylate other proteins in the cell.

**cAMP (cyclic adenosine monophosphate)** A second messenger activated in target cells in response to synaptic or hormonal stimulation.

**cannula**   A small needle used to inject chemical solutions into precise regions of the brain to damage neurons.

**catalytic domain**   A domain of a kinase that performs the phosphorylation reaction.

**ceiling effect**   A measurement problem that occurs when the value of the performance measure approaches its highest possible level and thus cannot be further increased by some other treatment.

**cellular consolidation**   The biochemical and molecular processes that take place immediately following the behavioral experience and initially stabilize the memory trace. This type of consolidation is thought to take several hours to complete.

**central nucleus (CE)**   A nucleus of the amygdala that is thought to be an important part of the neural basis of fear; also referred to as the central amygdala.

**cofilin**   See *actin-depolymerization factor*.

**cofilin pathway**   A signaling pathway that regulates actin polymerization.

**cognitive expectancy theory**   A theory proposed by Edward C. Tolman that assumes that learning produces representations of behaviors and their resulting outcomes.

**competing memory hypothesis**   A hypothesis that assumes extinction produces a new association called a CS–noUS association, while the original CS–US association that produced the CR remains intact.

**complementary memory systems view**   This view assumes that different memory systems evolved to serve different and sometimes incompatible functions.

**conditional knockout methodology**   A genetic engineering method used to knock out a particular gene in a very well specified region of the brain and to do this at different times in development.

**conscious recollection**   The intentional initiation of a memory with an awareness of remembering; a subjective feeling that is a product of the retrieval process.

**consolidation**   A stage of memory formation in which information in short-term memory is transferred to long-term memory.

**constitutive trafficking**   The routine movement of AMPA receptors in and out of dendritic spines.

**context preexposure paradigm**   A procedure used to study how rodents acquire a memory of an explored context.

**contextual fear conditioning**   Fear that is produced to the context or place in which the shock US is presented.

**cortical pathway**   A pathway that carries information from the sensory thalamus to the neocortical regions of the brain where a richer, more detailed representation of the experience is constructed.

**cortico-striatal system**   A brain system composed of the striatum and its afferent and efferent connections.

**corticosterone**   An adrenal hormone that can modulate memory storage; also classified as a glucocorticoid because it is involved in the metabolism of glucose.

**CREB (cAMP-responsive element binding) protein**   A transcription factor that is implicated in both synaptic plasticity and behavioral memory; a kind of molecular memory switch that in the *on* state initiates the production of memory-making messenger ribonucleic acid (mRNA).

**CS–noUS association**   A new association generated when the CS (conditioned stimulus) is no longer presented with the US (unconditioned stimulus). This idea forms the basis of the competing memory theory in extinction studies.

**cyclic adenosine monophosphate**   See *cAMP*.

**cytosol**   The internal fluid of the neuron.

**D**

**D-cycloserine (DCS)**   A drug that is a partial agonist and that binds to the glycine site of the NMDA receptor to enhance its opening.

**de novo protein synthesis hypothesis**   The hypothesis that the consolidation of the memory trace requires the to-be-remembered experience to initiate the synthesis of new proteins.

**declarative memory**   A category of memory that includes both episodic and semantic memory.

**delayed nonmatching to sample (DNMS)**   A memory testing procedure used to study recognition memory in primates.

**dendrites**   Branched projections of a neuron that receive synaptic input from the presynaptic terminal.

**dentate gyrus**   A subregion of the hippocampus that receives input from the entorhinal cortex via the perforant path and projects via mossy fibers to the CA3 region.

**depolarization**   The displacement of a cell's membrane potential toward a less negative value.

**discrimination reversal learning**   A strategy used to assess the flexibility of the system supporting the instrumental response and thus determine if it is an action or a habit.

**dopamine**   A neurotransmitter, related to norepinephrine and epinephrine, that belongs to a group called catecholamines.

**dopamine-incentive salience hypothesis**   The theory that the activation of the mesolimbic dopamine system by a rewarding outcome attaches motivational significance to stimuli associated with that outcome.

**dopamine reinforcement hypothesis**   The theory that the neurotransmitter dopamine is the primary candidate for strengthening the property of outcomes that influence instrumental behavior.

**dorsolateral striatum (DLS)**   A region of the striatum that is critical to the acquisition and maintenance of habits.

**dorsomedial striatum (DMS)**   A region of the striatum that supports goal-directed actions.

**E**

**electroconvulsive shock (ECS)**   A treatment for psychiatric disorders in which seizures are induced with electricity for therapeutic effect; also known as electroconvulsive therapy (ECT).

**electrode**   A fine wire used to deliver electric current to the brain.

**endocytotic zone**   A region that contains complex molecules designed to capture proteins such as AMPA receptors leaving the PSD and to repackage them in endosomes for recycling to the membrane.

**endoplasmic reticulum (ER)**   An organelle that is part of the endomembrane system and one of the elements of translation machinery. The ER extends continuously throughout the neuron and works with the plasma membrane to regulate many neuronal processes. It is also a calcium store and it can release calcium when ligands bind to receptors located on its surface.

**endosomes**   Membrane systems involved in the transport of molecules within the cell, they receive cell membrane molecules and sort them for either degradation or recycling back into the cell membrane.

**engram**   See *memory trace*.

**epinephrine (EPI)**   A hormone produced by the adrenal gland that modulates memory storage; also called adrenaline.

**episodic memory system**   The memory system that extracts and stores the content of personal experiences.

**ERK (extracellular-regulated kinase)**   A kinase that participates in many aspects of synaptic plasticity; see also *ERK–MAPK*.

**ERK–MAPK**   One of several possible signaling pathways or cascades, initiated by neurotrophic factors, that can converge to phosphorylate CREB protein and induce the transcription of plasticity-related mRNAs.

**escape latency**   The time between when a training trial starts and when the subject completes the trial.

**excitatory postsynaptic potential (EPSP)**   Depolarization of the postsynaptic membrane potential by the action of a synaptically released neurotransmitter.

**excitatory synapses**   Synapses that typically contain receptors that respond to glutamate and contribute to the depolarization of the neuron by allowing sodium ions to enter the neuron.

**expectancy**   A three-term association (S1–R–S2) that includes a representation of the stimulus situation (S1) that preceded the response, a representation of the response (R), and a representation of the outcome (S2) produced by the response.

**exposure therapy**   A therapy in which patients are forced to experience the stimulus situation that induces their fear response; used to treat a number of fear–anxiety disorders.

**extinction**   In a Pavlovian experiment, the elimination of a conditioned response (CR), achieved by presenting the conditioned stimulus (CS) without the unconditioned stimulus (US).

**extracellular matrix (ECM)**   A matrix composed of molecules synthesized and secreted by neurons and glial cells that forms a bridge between the pre and postsynaptic neurons. The molecules it contains interact with the neurons to influence their function.

## F

**filament actin (F-actin)**   A two-stranded helical polymer composed of globular actin.

**familiarity**   A process that can support recognition memory without recollection of the time or place of the experience.

**fear conditioning**   A form of learning in which fear comes to be associated with a previously neutral stimulus.

**fEPSP**   See *field potential*.

**fiber volley**   A measure of action potentials arriving at dendrites in the region of the recording site of an LTP (long-term potentiation) experiment.

**field potential (field extracellular excitatory postsynaptic potential)**   A measurement of the change in the ion composition of extracellular fluid as positive ions flow away from the extracellular recording and into the surrounding neurons. Also called fEPSP or field EPSP, it is the dependent variable in a long-term potentiation (LTP) experiment.

**first messenger**   A molecule that carries information from one neuron to another neuron.

**floor effect**   A measurement problem that occurs when the value of the performance measure is so low that it cannot be further reduced by some other treatment.

**freezing**   An innate defensive response of rodents in which they become immobile or still. Freezing has survival advantages because a moving animal is more likely to be detected by a predator than a still one.

**functional magnetic resonance imaging (fMRI)**   A method for imaging regional activity in the brain while the participant is engaged in cognitive activity.

## G

**G proteins (guanosine nucleotide-binding proteins)**   Second messenger proteins in the plasma membrane that are activated by glutamate binding to metabotropic glutamate receptors.

**globular actin (G-actin)**   Subunits of actin that serve as monomer building blocks and that assemble into F-actin.

**gene superconductance**   A genomic signaling cascade that causes an overproduction of mRNAs.

**genetic engineering**   A collection of methods used by scientists to alter the DNA of living organisms and thereby alter specific genes.

**genomic signaling**   Processes initiated by synaptic activity that lead to the production of new proteins through transcription and translation.

**gill withdrawal reflex**   A defensive behavior displayed by *Aplysia californica* when its skin is stimulated.

**glucocorticoids**   A class of hormones involved in the metabolism of glucose. In contrast to adrenaline, glucocorticoids can directly enter the brain.

**glutamate**   An excitatory amino acid neurotransmitter that is the primary neurotransmitter in the induction of long-term potentiation.

**GTPases**   Small proteins that regulate other biochemical processes. Most prominent among the regulatory GTPases are the G proteins.

## H

**habit**   A category of instrumental behavior believed to be the product of strengthening S–R connections and believed not to be goal directed or purposeful.

**habituation**   A term that represents the finding that the magnitude of the response to an eliciting stimulus decreases with repeated stimulation.

**hippocampal formation**   A region of the brain composed of the dentate gyrus (a subregion of the hippocampus), the hippocampus proper (CA1–CA3 fields), and the subiculum.

**hippocampus**   A region of the brain composed of the hippocampus proper (CA1–CA3 fields) and the dentate gyrus subregion. The hippocampus is believed to make a critical contribution to episodic memory.

**hyperpolarization**   The displacement of a cell's membrane potential toward a more negative value.

# I

**immediate shock effect**   The display of no fear to a context after rodents have been shocked without being allowed to first explore that context.

**in vitro preparation**   A method of performing an experiment in a controlled environment outside of a living organism. For example, a slice of hippocampus tissue is often used to conduct long-term potentiation (LTP) experiments.

**indexing theory of hippocampal memory**   A theory that assumes that the hippocampus stores an index to cortical patterns of neural activity that were generated by an episode.

**inducing stimulus**   The low-intensity, high-frequency stimulus used to induce LTP.

**infralimbic prefrontal cortex**   A cortical region that is believed to suppress the action system and thus to play an important role in selecting which system—the action or habit system—controls instrumental behavior.

**inhibitory avoidance conditioning**   A behavioral methodology used to train rodents to avoid where they previously experienced an aversive event.

**inhibitory domain**   A domain of a kinase protein that keeps the kinase in an inactive state.

**instrumental behavior (instrumental responses)**   Behavior that can change or modify the environment. Instrumental behaviors can be modified by the consequences they produce.

**instrumental learning**   Learning that a reward or reinforcer is contingent on the occurrence of a particular behavior.

**insulin growth factor-II (IGF-2)**   A protein that belongs to a system that is important for normal somatic growth and development, tissue repair, and regeneration.

**integrin receptors (integrins)**   Receptors that respond to molecules in the extracellular space or matrix and to intercellular signals such as calcium. They are classified as cell adhesion molecules.

**intercalated cells**   Clusters of cells in the amygdala that produce inhibitory output that, when fed forward to the central amygdala, can reduce the output of the neurons that generate defensive behavior.

**interference theory of forgetting**   A theory that attributes forgetting to additional experiences overwriting or producing new memories that interfere with the retrieval of a preexisting memory.

**inter-trial interval (ITI)**   The amount of time between separate trials in learning studies, typically measured from the start of one trial to the start of the next trial.

**ion**   An atom or a group of atoms that has acquired a net electric charge by gaining or losing one or more electrons.

**ionotropic receptors**   Receptors composed of several subunits that come together in the cell membrane to form a potential channel or pore which, when open, allows ions such as $Na^+$ or $Ca^{2+}$ to enter; also called ion-gated channels or ligand-gated ion channels.

**IP3 (inositol triphosphate)**   A second messenger that is synthesized when glutamate binds to the metabotropic glutamate receptor 1 (mGluR1).

**IP3R (inositol triphosphate receptor)**   A receptor that binds to the second messenger IP3, located on the endoplasmic reticulum in the dendritic compartment near the spines.

**K**

**kinase**   An enzyme that, once activated, catalyzes the transfer of a phosphate group from a donor to an acceptor.

**L**

**lateral nucleus (LA)**   A nucleus of the amygdala that is thought to be an important part of the neural basis of fear; also referred to as the lateral amygdala. The LA is a component of the BLA (basolateral amygdala).

**Law of Effect**   A theory of learning proposed by E. L. Thorndike that assumes that reinforcing events strengthen or weaken stimulus–response connections.

**learning–performance distinction**   A principle that recognizes that performance is influenced by a number of processes in addition to those of learning and memory.

**ligand**   Any chemical compound that binds to a specific site on a receptor.

**LIMK**   A kinase that phosphorylates the actin-depolymerization factor/cofilin site.

**local protein synthesis**   The translation of existing mRNA into protein that occurs in the dendrites.

**locus coeruleus**   A small region of the brain that contains only about 3,000 neurons, yet projects broadly and provides nearly all the norepinephrine to the cortex, limbic system, thalamus, and hypothalamus.

**long-lasting LTP (L-LTP)**   An enduring form of long-term potentiation thought to require the synthesis of new proteins.

**long-term depression**   A term used to represent the case in which synaptic activity weakens the strength of synaptic connections.

**long-term habituation**   A long-lasting form of habituation that is produced by many sessions of repeated stimulation.

**long-term memory trace**   A relatively enduring memory trace that is resistant to disruption.

**long-term potentiation (LTP)**   A persistent strengthening of synapses produced by low-frequency, intense electrical stimulation.

**M**

**MAPK (mitogen-activated protein kinase)**   A kinase that participates in many aspects of synaptic plasticity; see also *ERK–MAPK*.

**medial temporal hippocampal (MTH) system**   The region of the brain composed of the perirhinal, parahippocampal, and entorhinal cortices and the hippocampal formation.

**membrane potential**   The difference in the electrical charge inside the neuron's cell body compared to the charge outside the cell body.

**memory consolidation**   A process that stabilizes the memory and renders it resistant to disruption.

**memory modulation framework**   A theory that assumes that experience activates both the neurons that store the memory and other modulating neural–hormonal events that can influence the neurons that store the memory.

**memory modulators** The hormonal and other neural systems that are not part of the storage system but can nonetheless influence the synapses that store the memory.

**memory proper** See *secondary memory*.

**memory trace** A sustained neural representation of a behavioral experience; also called an engram.

**mesolimbic dopamine system** A small number of neurons located in a region of the brain called the ventral tegmental area (VTA) that provide dopamine to other regions of the brain.

**messenger ribonucleic acid (mRNA)** A molecule of RNA that carries a chemical blueprint for a protein product.

**metabotropic receptor** A G-protein receptor that stimulates or inhibits intracellular biochemical reactions. In contrast to ionotropic receptors, metabotropic receptors do not form an ion channel pore; rather, they are indirectly linked with ion channels on the plasma membrane of the cell through signal transduction mechanisms.

**mGluR1 (metabotropic glutamate receptor 1)** A subtype of metabotropic receptor located in the plasma membrane near dendritic spines.

**midbrain subcortical nuclei** Nuclei in the midbrain region that provide the direct neural basis for specific defensive behaviors that make up the fear system.

**modular view** The theory that only episodic memory depends on the entire medial temporal hippocampal system and that semantic memory does not require the hippocampus to contribute.

**mossy fibers** Axons that connect the dentate gyrus to the CA3 region of the hippocampus.

**mTOR** The mammalian target of rapamycin. This protein complex regulates many intracellular processes including local protein synthesis.

**mTOR–TOP pathway** A signaling pathway activated by BDNF that results in the local translation of proteins.

**multiple memory systems** A theory that different kinds of information are acquired and stored in different parts of the brain.

**multiple trace theory** A theory of systems consolidation that assumes that the medial temporal hippocampal system is always required to retrieve episodic memories but that semantic memories can become independent of this system.

**myosin IIb** A motor protein that can shear filament actin into segments.

## N

**NTS** See *solitary tract nucleus*.

**neural cadherins (N-cadherins)** Calcium-dependent cell adhesion molecules; strands of proteins held together by $Ca^{2+}$ ions. Cadherins can exist as either monomers or cis-stranded dimers.

**neurobiology of learning and memory** A scientific field that seeks to understand how the brain stores and retrieves information about our experiences.

**neuron doctrine** The idea that the brain is made up of discrete cells, called neurons or nerve cells, that are the elemental signal units of the brain.

**neurotransmitter** A substance released by synaptic terminals for the purpose of transmitting information from one neuron to another.

**neurotrophic factors** Molecules that promote survival of neural tissues and play a critical role in neural development and differentiation. Neurotrophic factors bind to Trk receptors.

**NMDA receptor** An ionotropic glutamate receptor selective for the agonist NMDA that plays a critical role in the induction of long-term potentiation (LTP).

**nonreward**   A term used to represent an outcome produced by an instrumental behavior that decreases the strength of that behavior.

**nonsense syllables**   Meaningless non-words created by placing a vowel between two consonants, for example, *nuh*, *vag*, or *boc*.

**norepinephrine (NE)**   An adrenergic neurotransmitter.

## O

**opsins**   Genes that code for proteins that in response to light can regulate the flow of ions across the membrane.

**optogenetics**   A methodology that combines genetic engineering with optics, the branch of physics that studies the properties of light, to provide a way to control the activity of individual neurons.

## P

**path length**   A measure of place learning in the Morris water-escape task; the distance a rodent swims before finding the hidden platform.

**pattern completion**   A process assumed to be supported by the hippocampus by which a subset or portion of an experience that originally established a memory trace can activate or replay the entire experience.

**pattern separation**   A process assumed to be supported by the hippocampus that enables very similar experiences to be segregated in memory.

**perforant path**   Fibers that connect the entorhinal cortex to the dentate gyrus.

**perineural nets**   Molecules in the extracellular matrix complex that surround neurons. These molecules prevent the erasure of fear memories by extinction.

**perirhinal cortex**   A cortical region adjacent to the hippocampus that is critically involved in object-recognition memory.

**phosphatases**   A class of enzymes whose function is to dephosphorylate proteins.

**phosphorylation**   The chemical addition of a phosphate group (phosphate and oxygen) to a protein or another compound that causes it to become active.

**PKA (protein kinase A)**   A kinase that is activated by the second messenger, cyclic adenosine monophosphate protein (cAMP), that participates in the process of exocytosis.

**PKC (protein kinase C)**   A kinase activated by calcium that participates in the process of exocytosis.

**PKMζ**   A kinase that lacks an inhibitory domain and is thought to play a critical role in the maintenance of LTP and memory.

**place-learning task**   A version of the Morris water-escape task in which a rat is required to find a platform hidden below the surface of the water; also called the hidden-platform task.

**plasticity**   The property of the brain that allows it to be modified by experience.

**plasticity products (PPs)**   Another name for mRNAs and proteins that are thought to be critical to the production of long-lasting changes in synaptic strength.

**polymer**   A chemical compound that is made of small molecules that are arranged in a simple repeating structure to form a larger molecule.

**polymerization**   The process of combining many smaller molecules (monomers) into a large organic module called a polymer.

**polyubiquitin chain**   A chain of unbiquitin molecules that tag a protein for degradation.

**postsynaptic dendrite**   The component of a neuron specialized for transmitter reception.

**postsynaptic density (PSD)**   A region at the tip of the dendritic spine that is the site of neurotransmitter receptors.

**postsynaptic depolarization**   The flow of positive ions into the postsynaptic neuron.

**postsynaptic potential**   A brief electrical event that is generated in the postsynaptic neuron when the synapse is activated.

**post-translation processes**   The processes that chemically modify a protein after its translation.

**post-traumatic stress disorder (PTSD)**   A syndrome in which individuals with this diagnosis have unusually vivid recall of the traumatic events they experienced, accompanied by severe emotional responses.

**predatory imminence gradient**   A measure of fear response in rodents that is dependent on the distance of a predator, that is, when a potential predator is at a distance a rat will freeze, but when the predator moves within striking distance, a rat might attempt to flee.

**prelimbic prefrontal cortex**   A region of the medial prefrontal cortex believed to be needed to acquire an action. However, once the associations that support an action are learned, this region is believed to no longer be critical.

**presynaptic terminal**   The component of a neuron that is specialized to release the transmitter.

**primary memory**   The persisting representation of an experience that forms part of a stream of consciousness; the second of three traces in William James's theory of memory.

**probe trial**   The stage in the Morris water-escape task in which the platform is removed to assess a rodent's memory of the platform location.

**procedural memory**   A category of memory that supports the performance of actions and skills.

**proteases**   A class of enzymes that can degrade proteins.

**protein synthesis**   The assembly of protein molecules from messenger ribonucleic acid (mRNA); also called translation.

## Q

**quadrant search time**   A measure of place learning in the Morris water-escape task. A rodent that has stored a memory of the location of the platform will spend more of its search time in the training quadrant than it will in the other quadrants.

## R

**Rac-PAK cascade**   A signaling cascade that contributes to the reorganization and crosslinking of actin filaments.

**recognition memory tasks**   Procedures used to study processes that support the ability to identify previously experienced objects.

**recollection**   A retrieval process that produces information about the time and place of an experience.

**reconsolidation theory**   A theory that assumes that the retrieval of a memory itself can disrupt an established memory trace but that the retrieval also initiates another round of protein synthesis so that the trace is "reconsolidated."

**reference memory**   Memory for the arms of the radial maze that consistently contain the reward.

**reinforcer** or **reward**   Terms used interchangeably to represent an outcome produced by an instrumental behavior that increases the strength of that behavior.

**reinstatement effect** One of several ways to recover an extinguished conditioned response (CR), in which simply re-presenting the unconditioned stimulus (US) in the training context can reinstate the ability of the conditioned stimulus (CS) to evoke the CR.

**renewal effect** One of several ways to recover an extinguished conditioned response (CR), achieved by changing the context for extinction but later returning an animal to the training context to recover the CR.

**resting membrane potential** The membrane potential or membrane voltage (about –70 mV) maintained by a neuron when it is not generating action potentials.

**retention interval** The time between the training experience that establishes the memory and the test used to retrieve the memory.

**retrieval failure** Amnesia that is the result of an inability to retrieve an existing memory.

**retrograde amnesia** The loss of memory for events that occurred prior to a brain insult or experimental treatment.

**reward** or **reinforcer** Terms used interchangeably to represent an outcome produced by an instrumental behavior that increases the strength of that behavior.

**reward devaluation** A method used to determine if an instrumental behavior is an action or a habit.

**Rho-Rock cascade** A signaling cascade that leads to the phosphorylation of cofilin and actin polymerization.

**ribosomes** Dense globular structures that take raw material in the form of amino acids and manufacture proteins using the blueprint provided by the mRNA.

**ryanodine receptors (RyRs)** Calcium-binding receptors located on the endoplasmic reticulum that extend into dendritic spines.

**S**

**Schaffer collateral fibers** Fibers that connect CA3 to CA1 pyramidal cells in the hippocampus.

**second messenger** A molecule that relays the signal received by receptors located in the plasma membrane (such as NMDA and AMPA receptors) to target molecules in the cells.

**secondary memory** The record of experiences that have receded from the stream of consciousness but can be later retrieved or recollected; the third of three traces in William James's theory of memory; also called memory proper.

**semantic memory** A category of memory that is believed to support memory for facts and the ability to extract generalizations across experiences.

**sensitization** An enhanced reflex response to a reflex-producing stimulus.

**short-lasting LTP (S-LTP)** Long-term potentiation with a limited duration, supported by post-translation processes.

**short-term habituation** A form of habituation that does not endure.

**short-term memory trace** A relatively short-lasting trace that is vulnerable to disruption.

**simple system approach** A strategy used to reduce the complexity of studying the neural basis of memory by studying an animal with the simplest nervous system that can support a modifiable behavior.

**solitary tract nucleus (NTS)** A brain stem region that receives information from the vagal nerve; also referred to as the NTS (derived from the Latin *nucleus tractus solitarius*).

**soma-to-nucleus signaling** A genomic signaling process that occurs when $Ca^{2+}$ enters the soma through voltage-dependent calcium channels opening as a result of action potentials.

**spatial learning**   Learning that requires the animal to use the spatial position of cues to locate a goal object.

**spectrins**   Proteins that crosslink and stabilize actin filaments.

**spontaneous recovery**   The recovery of a habituated response that occurs "spontaneously," with the passage of time.

**standard model of systems consolidation**   A theory that assumes that as episodic and semantic memories age they no longer require the medial temporal hippocampal system for retrieval.

**stereotaxic surgery**   A surgery that uses a coordinate system to locate specific targets inside the brain to enable some procedure to be carried out on them (for example, a lesion, injection, or cannula implantation).

**storage failure**   Amnesia that is the result of a failure to store the memory.

**striatum**   A subregion of the basal ganglia, composed of the caudate nucleus, putamen, and nucleus accumbens; the basic input segment of the basal ganglia.

**subcortical pathway**   A pathway that carries information from the sensory thalamus to the lateral nucleus of the amygdala (LA). It is thought to carry a somewhat impoverished representation of the sensory experience.

**subiculum**   The output component of the hippocampal formation.

**synapse**   The point of contact between the presynaptic sending neuron and the post-synaptic receiving neuron.

**synapse-to-nucleus signaling**   A genomic signaling process that begins at the synapse and results in transcription.

**synaptic cleft**   The space that separates the presynaptic terminal and the postsynaptic dendrite.

**synaptic plasticity hypothesis**   The hypothesis that the strength of synaptic connections—the ease with which an action potential in one cell excites (or inhibits) its target cell—is not fixed but is plastic and modifiable.

**synaptic strength**   A concept used to represent the ease with which a presynaptic neuron can excite the postsynaptic neuron.

**synaptic tag and capture hypothesis**   A theory that assumes that an LTP-inducing stimulus changes a dendritic spine so that it can capture plasticity products generated by strongly stimulated synapses. It does this through biologically marking (tagging) a synapse in the spine.

**synaptic vesicles**   Spherical membrane-bound organelles in presynaptic terminals that store neurotransmitters.

**systems consolidation**   A theory that assumes that a change in the strength of the memory trace is brought about by interactions between brain regions (the medial temporal hippocampal system and neocortex). Systems consolidation is assumed to take place over a long period of time, after the memory is initially established.

**T**

**TARP**   A transmembrane AMPA regulatory protein that co-assembles with AMPA receptors and contributes to trapping them in the postsynaptic density.

**temporally graded retrograde amnesia**
Amnesia that is more pronounced for recently experienced events than for more remotely experienced events.

**test stimulus**   The stimulus used to establish a baseline in an LTP experiment. It is also the stimulus used to determine that LTP has been established.

**theta-burst stimulation (TBS)**   A different stimulus protocol for inducing long-term potentiation and the forms of LTP it induces, modeled after an increased rate of pyramidal neuronal firing that occurs when a rodent is exploring a novel environment.

**TOP (terminal oligopyrimidine tract)** A class of mRNAs located in the dendritic spine that encode for proteins such as ribosomal proteins and elongation factors that are part of the translation machinery.

**transcription** The process of converting genetic material from DNA to messenger RNA (mRNA). The resulting mRNA is called a transcript.

**trace updating** The incorporation of new information into existing memory ensembles.

**transcription factors** Proteins that interact with DNA to produce mRNA.

**transcription repressor proteins** Proteins that inhibit transcription.

**translation** The process by which mRNA is converted to protein; also called protein synthesis.

**translation machinery** The molecules that participate in translating mRNA into protein.

**translator repressor proteins** Proteins that inhibit the translation of mRNA into protein.

**Trk receptors** A class of plasma membrane receptors in the tyrosine kinase family that bind to neurotrophic factors.

**TrkB receptors** A subset of tyrosine kinase receptors that have catalytic properties when activated.

**U**

**ubiquitin proteasome system (UPS)** A system composed of ubiquitin and proteasome molecules that cooperate to degrade proteins.

**ubiquitination** A process that creates a ubiquitin chain.

**unitary view** The theory that both semantic and episodic memory depend on the entire medial temporal hippocampal system.

**V**

**vagus** or **vagal nerve** Cranial nerve X, arising from the medulla and innervating the viscera of the thoracic and abdominal cavities, that carries information about the body into the brain.

**viral vector system** A new technique for delivering a gene to a particular region of the brain that involves genetically modifying a virus to carry the gene of interest.

**visible-platform task** A version of the Morris water-escape task in which a rat is required to find a platform that is visible above the surface of the water.

**voltage-dependent calcium channel (vdcc)** A membrane protein that forms a pore, which is permeable to calcium gated by depolarization of the membrane.

**W**

**working memory** The memory system that maintains and manipulates information to solve a particular problem or achieve a particular goal.

**Z**

**ZIP (zeta inhibitory peptide)** A peptide that can serve as an inhibitory unit for PKMζ.

# Author Index

Page numbers in *italics* indicate a full citation.

# Subject Index

Page numbers in *italics* indicate that the information will be found in figures or tables.